FOLLOWING THEIR WESTWARD STAR

An Oral History, Photos and Paintings
of Arizona's Verde Valley
and Sedona's Red Rock Country

F. RUTH JORDAN
In collaboration with
BECKY TOGNONI BOUDWAY

Featuring paintings by Helen Jordan

Foreword by Marshall Trimble

Cover and Maps by Don Ellis

All rights reserved.
Copyright © 2005 by F. Ruth Jordan
Second Printing 2006
Printed in the United States of America

Moore Graphics
11200 W. Michigan Ave., Youngtown, AZ 85363

In Memory

of all

Pioneers, Miners, Native Americans, and Soldiers

who participated in the Changing West

of the

Verde Valley and Sedona Red Rock Country

TABLE OF CONTENTS

Acknowledgements i

Foreword iii

Introduction v

Biography of the Artist vii

Chapter 1 Migrating West 1

Chapter 2 Providence and Parson Bristow 5

Chapter 3 At the Break of the Western Wave 23

Chapter 4 Match from Maine for Annie Bristow 33

Chapter 5 Wild Abundance 49

Chapter 6 Cattlemen's Country-Ranching and School Teaching 59

Helen the Artist - Examples of Her Work 77

Chapter 7 Congregations Above the Valley; Miners Gather on Cleopatra Hill .. 85

Chapter 8 Hayseed Justice 99

Chapter 9 Farming and Fruit Trees in Sedona 107

Chapter 10 Wheeling the Water 129

Chapter 11 Conclusion; Winter Ride Down Memory Lane 139

Chapter 12 Epilogue 147

Bibliography 151

Maps

Route of Parson Bristow's Wagon Train .... 12&13

Towns of the Verde Valley & Red Rock Country 20

Geographical Sites 73

Acknowledgments

It is with deep gratitude that I acknowledge all of the generous people who have helped with this project: **Margaret Luranda Bristow Stoever** and her sister **Helen Bristow Schmidt** for the handwritten document of Parson Bristow plus many Bristow family pictures**; Charles** and **Elnora Jordan** for loaning numerous pictures of the Jordan family and ranches**; Walter Jordan, Jr. and Anne Jordan Jackson** (my siblings) for sharing pictures from our childhood; **Jordan Jackson** (my nephew) for loaning the picture of Walter and his big catfish; A very special thanks to **Helen Coleman**, for her hospitality and sharing of Helen Jordan's paintings; **Margie Lambo, Jack Coleman, Eleanor Clark, Dick** and **Hazel Schieferstein. Vera Peck, Rev. Kenneth Kliever, Rev. Richard Anderson** and his wife **Becky, Maisy Houck, Dorothy Shaffer, Jacqueline Ruth Jackson** (my niece), and my sons and daughter-in-law, **Kevin** and **Darla Jackson,** and **Leland Jackson** who all graciously allowed photographs of Helen Jordan's paintings; **Mary Smith Wyatt** for her contribution of Dutch Oven Cooking; **Esther Henderson** for information and the story of A Christmas Eve On a Cattle Ranch….; **Ken Bristow** for photos of the "early days" and maps of the Bristow journey; and **Patricia Ceballos** and **Paula Hokanson**, granddaughters of Sedona and T. C. Schnebly, for insights into and information about their grandparents.

To my grandchildren, **Amelia Jackson, Anthony Jackson,** and **Gini Jackson**, a huge thanks for their patience in assisting with my computer skills, and to **Anthony** for formatting and creating the final copy. My husband **Lee Van Epps** deserves extra gratitude for his assistance with scanning pictures, and for his support in all of the trips for research and hours of writing. Also to my sons **Kevin** and **Leland Jackson** for reading and re-reading various drafts, photographing some of the paintings and advising. Nieces **Sally Jackson**, who shared information from her term paper, and **Jacqueline Ruth Jackson,** and **Debbie Roberts** for encouragement. To **John Van Epps**, our son, for assisting in promotion and in assisting with the websites. Any errors or omissions are unintentional.

To **Don Ellis** for wonderful advice and artwork.

Appreciation to **Victoria Clark** who gave valuable assistance in understanding the various methods of publishing.

A special thanks to **Bob** and **Jean Starling** who spent hours in editing, correcting and offering suggestions.

I am extremely grateful to long time friend, **Marshall Trimble**, for his willingness to write the foreword. Thanks Marshall!!

And to **Becky Boudway**, for her major role as collaborator, research assistant, photographer of Helen's paintings and transcriber of tape recordings. Thank you Becky for all of this plus your moral and motivational support.

Again, to all of you, many thanks!

F. Ruth Jordan (Jackson/Van Epps)

Foreword FOLLOWING THEIR WESTWARD STAR

Motion pictures, television and coffee table- books have made Sedona, Oak Creek Canyon, and the red rock country with its towering red sandstone cliffs, buttes and spires known throughout the world. And, there's much more. The Verde Valley offers tourists a wide variety of activities including Old Fort Verde State Park, the Verde Canyon Scenic Railroad, which winds its way along the Verde River past the Sycamore Canyon Wilderness Area. The town of Jerome, nestled on the slopes of cone-shaped Cleopatra Hill, was at one time a billion-dollar copper camp. When the mines closed in 1953 the population dwindled to a few residents. Today, the erstwhile ghost town thrives again with tourists. For centuries the prehistoric Sinagua Indians lived at Tuzigoot and Montezuma's Castle, along the banks of the Verde River and Beaver Creek. Geologists and geographers regard the valley as the one of the states best natural laboratories. All of these have made the area a mecca for arts, crafts, sports, photography and nature lovers. Yet, very little is known about the early pioneers who came here to settle during the latter half of the 19th century.

Like many parts of Arizona, the history of these settlers is little more than a footnote in the mainstream of the state's history. History books by their very nature have to focus on the major events that brought us from "there to here," and often times the richest part of history, the stories of the everyday working people, the people who farmed the land, built the schools, churches and raised families do not attract the attention of history writers. For example, when one thinks of Tombstone, the so-called "Gunfight at OK Corral," always comes to mind. One never thinks of the hundreds of hard rock miners who went down in the bowels of the earth each day to dig out the rich silver ore. Tombstone was really about mining but that doesn't sell as well as exciting tales of gunfighters and shoot outs. It's that way with Sedona and the surrounding area. Tourists are awed by the spectacular scenery, along with the myriad of shops that sell everything from New Age to Native American art. But few have any idea of what it was like before the world discovered Sedona.

One only has to watch one of those old western movies to see how the area has changed in the last fifty years. Houses and shops sit where Hollywood cowboys and Indians rode in films like "Broken Arrow," "The 3:10 to Yuma," and "Johnny Guitar."

The first time I saw Oak Creek Canyon was in the spring of 1951. I was raised in Ash Fork, just a few miles from the canyon as the crow flies, but a long way by highway. One had to travel east on Route 66 to Flagstaff, then south on US 89A down through Oak Creek Canyon. There was no I-17 back then. Ash Fork Schools always held their annual spring picnic at Indian Gardens. Water was scarce in Ash Fork. There were no wells and all the water was hauled in daily by train from Chino Valley, so despite the frigid water in early May, we spent most of the day swimming in the creek. After a short time our feet and hands had turned blue but even that didn't deter us.

The little village of Sedona at the mouth of Oak Creek Canyon must have looked like paradise to those early settlers, who were drawn there by the abundance of fresh water, mild climate, abundance of wildlife and game.

Ruth Jordan was born and raised in Sedona. Sedona Schnebly, for whom the town is named, was their closest neighbor, and took care of Ruth when she was a little girl. Ruth descends from the earliest settlers in the area and it's from them and through their eyes and words she weaves the stories of what life was in this beautiful country before it became a mecca for tourists, nature lovers, artists, photographers and crystal gazers.

She writes lovingly of her father, Walter Jordan, a storyteller, and her Aunt Helen Jordan, an artist. My favorite chapter was the last one, "Winter Ride Down Memory Lane" when Walter, then in his mid-80s, reminisces with his daughter Ruth on a drive from Sedona, down to Bridgeport, Cottonwood, Clarkdale and on to Rattlesnake Hill where he was born. His memories provide a wonderful roadside history of the heart of Arizona. There are a number of other storytellers, including my old friend, Jesse Goddard, taking turns spinning and weaving their tales of life in the Verde Valley they remembered so well. It makes the reader wish he was sitting around a camp fire on the banks of Oak Creek while each tells their story.

Without books like "Following Their Westward Star" much of Arizona's rich and colorful history would be lost forever with the passing of these pioneers and settlers.

Marshall Trimble
Official Arizona State Historian
October 21,2004

Introduction
FOLLOWING THEIR WESTWARD STAR

"Say, did I ever tell ya about…"and another wonderful storytelling time had begun. My father, Walter Jordan, an Arizona native, was one of those marvelous individuals who could "spin tales" one right after the other keeping the listeners spellbound. Even though many had been heard before, we all thrilled at hearing them again and again. Each was told with great animation, gesture, vivid description and voice inflection causing characters to spring to life. The listener could easily picture the settings and circumstances while being absorbed into the scenario, feeling an actual part of the happenings. We children were guilty on numerous occasions of prolonging bedtime by injecting, "Daddy tell us the one about…" He thoroughly enjoyed the telling of the stories and I can still hear his chuckle at the amusing parts. My desire to share and preserve some of these exciting memories of the early days in Arizona territory triggered the tape recording of many of his and other's stories.

Walter Jordan 1932

In 1912 at the age of ten my mother, Ruth Woolf Jordan, arrived in Arizona, the same year that the territory became a state. Growing up in Tempe provided the opportunity for her to attend Tempe Normal School, currently Arizona State University. Her dreams of owning a horse and teaching in a one room school took her north to Beaver Creek where she boarded at the Soda Springs Guest Ranch, a working cattle ranch. Here her longings became reality. Her stories bring poignancy to the many tasks early school teachers performed as well as personalizing life at a dude/cattle ranch. After she and Walter were married July 20th 1930, she took an active role in their farm in Sedona.

Ruth Woolf, Tempe 1920s

Walter's & Ruth's Wedding
5:00 am July 20th, 1930
Submitted by Larry Anderson

Aunt Helen Jordan, who was married to Walter's brother George, added another dimension as she helped sculpture my life through her variety of art mediums…water color, oil, pastel, charcoal, and sculpture. She also envisioned a history of Sedona and the Verde Valley, focusing on her memories as a part of the Jordan family. During the last year of her life she shared that desire with me. Thus began the idea of a history interspersed with pictures of some of her paintings, for her art in its own way tells much about the era and area.

In 1992, Becky Tognoni Boudway, author of the western mining history, *Treasure in the Dust*, was commissioned to begin transcribing the audio recordings that I, as an historical tour guide and lecturer had taped. Many of these recordings with Daddy and the sons and daughters of a number of other Arizona pioneers were taped while driving the countryside of Verde Valley, Sedona and the Mogollon Rim. In all oral histories there are as many different versions of one "happening" as there are storytellers. Following a brief history of Central Arizona, these memories have been mingled with published stories and the unpublished journal of my great-grandfather, Parson Bristow, plus the wonderful art of Aunt Helen, Uncle George's photography, and "old time" photos.

These are stories of those men and women who dared to travel west into hostile and unknown territory. They were people of spirit and determination who triumphed over hardship and tragedy, giving the west a reputation of strength, bravery, independence and persistence. They took a gamble that life in the new locale would be better, so they left all behind and started *Following Their Westward Star*.

Biography of the Artist

Helen Coleman Jordan

1905 – 1993

Helen Coleman circa 1906

Helen Coleman Jordan came to the Verde Valley of Central Arizona from Oklahoma in 1923. Her family would move on to California, where her father died, and then on again to Oregon to find work. Helen stayed in Arizona as a bride in 1928, marrying George Jordan, the Eastern educated grandson of the first Baptist preacher in Arizona. With her paintings and journals, she became one of the Verde Valley's historians. On large, glass photographic slides, George, too, made his record. They were daily surrounded by the "vast and unexpected" and its purpose became theirs: to capture places "designed for the soul - those ultimate places where things common become shadows and fail, and the divine part in us, which adores and desires, breathes its own air."[1]

Helen's parents, Mary and Arthur Coleman 1920s

They made their home in "Palakwapi," which in the Hopi language is "place of the red rocks." As Helen noted, "It was a picturesque stone house with 18" thick walls. No one had occupied the house for some time, and it was surrounded by weeds. Screens were missing and the floors splintery. The plastered walls were the color of Sedona mud, but it was a beginning."

Coleman Children: Gene, Vera, Helen, Juanita, Circa 1909

Built from hand-cut, native red rock in about 1912, this neglected abode where Helen set up housekeeping was the work of an itinerant Mexican builder known by his floor plans in the shape of a cross. Helen wrote, "We did very well for a few years before the Depression. We painted the walls of the house with calcimine and planted a large garden. We now had electricity from a hydro electric plant and running water in the house from the creek until George dug the well and put in the pipeline."

Oak Creek flood waters, capable of surprising fury, had driven away the inhabitants of antiquity as well as some of the homesteaders of this new era, but George and his brother Walter, whose stories are collected in *Following Their Westward Star*, built on high ground and routed the water emerging from Oak Creek Canyon to irrigate fruit orchards where the tiny settlement of Sedona had taken root. They would conquer the water with ditches, water wheel, hydro-electric plant, pumps and reservoirs. For a season, Helen stepped over the pieces of the water wheel as it was slowly assembled on the floor of her red rock home.

George & Helen Jordan married January 7, 1928

Original, red rock, cross-shaped house 1928

Helen wrote in an article for *Those Early Days*: "George bought a second-hand Hudson touring car, and converted it into a truck after installing an International truck rear end. It served for years, and as things wore out, they were replaced with other parts, until it had a Chevrolet truck cab, a Lincoln Zephyr motor, and extra gears of various sorts; we couldn't afford a new truck. ...To market the fruit and vegetables, it was necessary to travel very narrow dirt roads. The old Schnebly Road to Flagstaff was unsurfaced, so there was lots of dust in summer and mud up to the fenders when it stormed. ...In order to get to Flagstaff by the time the stores opened, he would leave long before daylight, taking along spare parts in case of a breakdown."[2]

Helen also commented, "Neighbors visited one another unannounced [in those days] since the only telephone was at the ranger station. We had school entertainments (dances) and musical programs and plays, and we had Sunday school - all of them in the school building." For the general merriment of any who would listen, George invented musical instruments: the "shovelin," a shovel painted black with the handle shortened and strung; the "cigarboxlin," a cigar box transformed as with the shovel both being played as a violin, and a "dishpandolin." Helen accompanied George on the piano and overcame her shyness to chirp her harmony. A favorite of George's was singing for church and community dinners while strumming his dishpandolin:

Mary ate some pork and beans

and Mary ate some ham.

Mary ate some jelly rolls

and Mary ate some jam.

Mary ate some sauerkraut

and Mary drank some beer

and she wondered why she felt

so very, very queer. (Author unknown)

Members of the audience would squeal in de-

George's homemade instruments: left to right Shovel-lin, cigarbox-lin, and dishpan-dolin

light, or disgust, as George positioned his dishpandolin to catch gluttonous Mary's imaginary spew, while continuing the second verse: "Up'll come the pork and beans, etc."

Helen confined her paintings and drawings to the margins of her school books as a girl, and to the furniture and cabinets of her home as a wife. In the late 1940s an artist friend from Phoenix, where Helen had gone to business college before marrying, persuaded

Drawing on school book margin

her to move her artistry to canvas. With her niece, Ruthie (author) in tow, Helen climbed to an overlook of Ruthie's parents' (Ruth and Walter Jordan) farm. There Helen Coleman Jordan began her formal career as a painter - in deep greens the orchards, in rusty shades of red the surrounding mountains. Helen's paintings outline the ghosts of forgotten settlers, like the iris still blooming in rows along the foundations of their obliterated homesteads. Her work embodies the energy and wonder of early Arizona both reasonable and noble, a spirit shared by George's older brother Walter in the pages of this book (see center for examples of paintings).

Artists who visited Helen were astonished at her ability to complete a painting while producing the daily meals and all the kitchen "goodies" needed for church and community functions. Simultaneously she also performed the innumerable duties of a farm wife plus taking intermittent turns at the easel with her paint brushes. Neighbors would laugh seeing Helen cooking beans with a paint brush clamped between her teeth. Frequently in her kitchen she gathered the children of the community, the Sunday school and 4-H clubs for learning activities, fun, games and food. Helen's diaries served as her accounting ledgers in the fruit store and detailed her busy life, including her progress with her painting and her excitement when the first painting sold for $40.00 on September 30, 1950, approximately three years after she embarked on this creative activity. Later, when she traveled widely after George's death, the diaries reveal her penchant for the game of Scrabble, her insatiable desire for knowledge of other people and cultures, her constant appraisal of all situations that could be included in her art forms, (often taking photographs to be used as guides when returning to her studio), and her consummate admiration for good hospitality.

During the years 1946 through 1953, the internationally known Dadaist painter and sculptor, Max Ernst and his painter paramour, Dorothea Tanning, worked in Sedona. Ernst found a kindred spirit in the home of George and Helen Jordan. In 1948, Ernst, who came to represent the will to invent among his contemporary European artists, created his Capricorn Sculpture. An interesting parallel can be drawn between his and George's desire to invent, as George was continually creating things, such as his variety of musical instruments, and the first Sedona water system. The sculpture could be compared to Jordan fruits

George's packing house, late 1940s

for both were a symbol of well-being for Sedona, a Capricorn. A recording in Helen Jordan's journal that year showed the impact of their fruit: "People came from everywhere to buy our fruit, so we built the market building along the highway."

Into both George's packing house and Ernst's art studio would go windows hauled by George from one of the mine buildings in Jerome in the mountains across the Verde Valley. Of building the packing house, again in her diary Helen wrote: "On the lower floor we had a large cold storage plant, and a shop for repairing farm machinery. [Upstairs was] a large apple grader and packing facility for apples. We had parties there, and our annual 4th of July lawn picnic could take refuge there [in a] sudden shower."

The windows of Helen's home framed intimate details of magnificence; she chuckled with George about the King and His Three Wives, monoliths which overlook Walter and Ruth's first home, because they were certain that Ruth would only allow Walter one wife. It was Walter who dubbed the tree on the king's breast his boutonniere. Rendered by Helen's brush, Courthouse Rock (now called Cathedral Rock) looked like the king's crumbling castle. In those days Helen never thought of herself as an artist. If Wendell Berry the farmer and philosopher-poet had known her, he would have said, "She lived in her subject. Her subject was her place in the world, and she lived in her place."[3]

At great personal sacrifice George and Helen Jordan had helped to end the pattern of settlement and abandonment in the Red Rock Country. Helen's diaries are filled with her deep concern over George's severe arthritis and trepidation at George's long hours in the damp and cold, protecting his crops from threatening storms or maintaining the water system which he faithfully regulated. He worked so often into the wee hours of the night that he put headlights on his tractor. When pain was so great he was unable to mount the bulldozer, he had someone lift him aboard. There he stayed many long hours digging water line trenches, not wanting to bother anyone to help him down and back up.

Her journals also testify to her struggle to paint: "March 21, 1956 - Just as I got my paints spread out preparatory to doing some work, Mrs. H. came to ask me to place some paintings in her shop. Then Georgia came to practice her song and the day was gone with no painting done. Kept hoping someone would come along wanting to go to Phoenix with George, but no one did. He resents my going just to help him drive, but I plan to go each time no one else does. [Due to his health she didn't want him making the trip alone]. March 23 - Guess I'll never get time to paint again!"

George and Helen never had any children of their own but they were parents to a community, even donating the land on which the Wayside Chapel on the old main street of Sedona still stands.

They lived in their red rock cross shaped home for 31 years until George retired from farming in 1958. They chose a spot for the home they designed on a hill above their old abode. In 1961, their packing house would become the home of Canyon Kiva Arts Center, the brainchild of Egyptian artist and teacher Nassan Gobran. Despite Gobran's wishes in the early 1970's, the red rock house, the old cross, was torn down to make room for a parking lot. The old fruit store served, appropriately, for a period as an art supply store, and still stands at the entrance to the old packing house, now the Sedona Art Center. These are enduring reminders of a time when traffic, tour buses and timeshare condominiums did not crowd the landscape. The mountains now look down on a grass-filled depression beside a Sedona road, a quiet collection of watershed sediments, the mysteriously level field already subdivided, the dot-to-dot remains of a concrete ditch above the bank of Oak Creek, the homogenous rubble on the side of the canyon where George and Walter dynamited, the red rock bunker beside a pull-off in the scenic road where pumps once rhythmically labored and where pipes at one time carried nourishing water.

Wayside Chapel under construction, circa 1946

Wayside Chapel "Built in the cleft of the rock," circa 1954

Standing as a sentinel on Water Tank Hill, the towering water tank of the Sedona water system proclaims George's legacy as it overlooks these remnants of the Jordan brother's farms and reservoirs.

George and Helen may be only footnotes in "wild west" histories of Sedona, but their spirit is still at work in the majestic walls of rock which Nassan Gobran said rose around him in Sedona like a divine Kiva — a place of sacramental learning. In Helen's words, the parking lot which paved over the footings of her red rock home was "much needed." She had no sense of self-importance stating: "I don't verbalize about art. The process of producing a painting is to me most satisfying. I never thought of myself as an artist. Yes. I paint...Everyone who ever lived in Sedona began a painting at some time or other."

George died in 1964 in a Phoenix hospital from complications of his rheumatoid arthritis. By 1978, Helen had built a small bungalow home and studio with red rock vistas around the hill from the home she and George had built. "Always one day a week is set aside for painting, but I keep busy like everyone else in Sedona with my garden, my music, my house, my church and my community. I do think living here has had a lot to do with my continuing to paint."

Her passion for her art would become as all-inclusive of media as of subject matter — hundreds of portraits, still lifes, florals, and, above all, landscapes — in oil, watercolor, ink, pastels, charcoal, and a masterly combination of media with which she broke through the illusions of daily duty and sense. Speaking of her work, she said, "It shows me I've progressed. I'm never really completely finished with my work, especially landscapes. [She continually dabbed at paintings already hanging on the walls of her home.] By having them around, it gives me an awareness of what I could have done."

Art critics in the *Red Rock News* called her versatility "amazing and wondrous"; her colors "the freshest in the show." For Helen each painting was like her first. She never ceased learning. She studied widely and diversely: portraiture with Ramon Froman in Cloudcroft, New Mexico; watercolor with Tony Van Hasselt and Dick Phillips; art classes in the summer with Harry Wood, head of the Arizona State University Art Department; and numerous workshops conducted by teaching artists of her day.

In her studio she welcomed students, and each week a number of artists would gather to paint and eat potluck. She became the artist with the longest continual residence in Sedona. When her family gathered around her for her 80th birthday, it was in the Wayside Chapel's fellowship hall - Jordan Hall. In 1993 when she died, Helen's portfolios and her Phoenix apartment were overflowing with her work, but after she left Sedona, she never painted again. In the year before Helen died, she envisioned with her niece, F. Ruth Jordan (Jackson/Van Epps), a history of Sedona and the Verde Valley.

In 1992, Becky Tognoni Boudway was commissioned to begin work transcribing the audio recordings that F. Ruth Jordan had made chiefly of her father, Walter Jordan, an Arizona native and lively storyteller. His stories are mingled with author Jordan's considerable command of Arizona history as a tour guide and lecturer; with the knowledge she collected on audio tape riding the countryside with a number of other pioneers; and with published stories by emigrants, most notably the 1933 publication *Pioneer Stories of the Verde Valley of Arizona* as told by themselves and compiled by the Book Committee, a committee of three including two aunts of Walter and George Jordan — Mrs. John Bristow and Mrs. D.W. Wingfield. All would be brought together in the book which Helen Jordan and F. Ruth Jordan conceived. Other collections of stories are sprinkled liberally with the writings of members of the Jordan family, including Helen's, but no one had unified the stories. No one yet had written *Following Their Westward Star*.

FOOTNOTES

(1) Belloc, Hilaire. "The Inn of the Mageride." Hills and the Sea. Marlboro, Vermont: The Marlboro P, 1966. N. pag.

(2) Jordan, Helen E. Early Sedona Fruit Growers. Those Early Days. Comp. Sedona Westerners' Book Committee. Cottonwood, Arizona: Verde Independent , 1968. 217.

(3) Berry, Wendell. What Are People For?. New York, New York: North Point P, 1990. 6-7.

(1) Bishop Jr., James. The Ancient Ones. Experience Sedona Legends & Legacies. Comp. Kate Ruland-Thorne. Sedona: Thorne Enterprises, 1989. 4.

Appendix Introduction

You are invited to my open studio art show and sale at 530 SUNSET DRIVE

10 AM - 5 PM

Please come!

Helen Jordan

282-7079

Sept 6-7

Invitation for open studio circa 1981

HELEN'S LEGACY

Today we honor a lady who was loved by all,
Her life truly was guided by an inner call.
We each pause to say in our own personal way,
"Helen, we appreciate you more every day."
With your brush you created great pictures with paint,
And as our Sunday School teacher, we all thought you were a Saint.
You taught lots of kids self-respect and pride,
And through 4-H, we learned life is no free ride!
From you I learned to sew and to bake,
Incredible what a person can make.
Measles and whooping cough you treated with tender loving care.
Oh yes, you even put pigtails in my hair.
You opened your home to many a friend
For picnics, parties and good times we thought would never end.
Ah yes, you shared your music talent too
In choir, the organ, or piano you always did whatever there was to do.
Spring, summer, winter and fall
You truly were an inspiration to us all.
Your spirit and love will continue to guide us
As we follow your path of a deep faith and trust.

Tribute by F. Ruth Jordan (Van Epps) given at Helen's memorial service Sept. 28, 1993

Chapter One
MIGRATING WEST

Apparently mankind was created with a desire for freedom and an innate Huckleberry Finn type of curiosity, longing to discover what is around the next bend, over the distant hill, behind the snow covered mountain or across the wide ocean. This spirit of adventure coupled with a desire to improve their economic conditions and gain freedom of thought, expression and religion, led many to set sail and endure a gruelling six-months journey westward across the treacherous Atlantic. Glad to get their feet on solid ground, folks settled along the coastal waters only to soon be confronted with harsh weather, Indian attacks and ravishing diseases. Gradually as more emigrants arrived on the shores of the "New World," settlements became towns, and towns became cities causing some to feel the need for more "elbow" room. At first only a few began the exodus of this easternmost area to the inland open country, but too soon many more were joining them. Again, folks felt crowded, and started moving on over the Appalachian Mountains to greater expanses of unclaimed land. Waves of people ventured by horseback, wagons and even rafts to locate their own little haven. The first group being mainly mountain men and fur trappers followed by settlers, adventurers, and fortune seekers. The Westward Movement had begun!

Following the physical, emotional, and economic devastation of the Civil War there arose a desperate need to find a way to make living more bearable and to rebuild a semblance of life formerly known. Awareness was building that somewhere, way out west, there was a land filled with promise and opportunity. A land of majestic mountains, magnificent canyons, and valleys lush with vegetation, tantalizing the imaginations of people clear across the continent. A land of dreams and hopes beckoning to all who were willing to "pull up stakes," leave home and loved ones behind and begin the trek of *Following Their Westward Star*. Interest increased as the homefolks received more and more letters describing a river valley with an abundance of water and grass growing "as high as the bellies of the cattle." Thus for many of this western wave of settlers the destination became the "Verdant Verde Valley" in Arizona territory. This strange sounding name, Arizona, was being heard more and more frequently in eastern communities, with folks wondering what a name like that could possibly mean, or where had it originated. For years students were taught the derivation given by James Mc Clintock, an historian; Arida, meaning "dry" and Zona meaning "zone," thus Arizona. Another version, is that the state's title came from an Aztec word "Arizuena," meaning "silver bearing." Isaac Smith attributes it to a third source, "Aleh-zon," the Native American word of the Tono O'Odham tribe (formerly Papago) meaning "Young Spring." Each of these described at least one facet of the territory. However, the most accepted explanation is that given by Will C. Barnes in <u>Arizona Place Names</u>: "The original name was that of a station of the Garca Mission called 'Arizonac.' The 'District of Arizonac' was a section of Sonora (Mexico) occupied in part by present day Pima County. In 1751 the Spaniards dropped the 'c' thus adapting the Indian (Papago) word to Spanish phonetics."[1]

Verde Rive limestone cliffs and Indian ruins, early 1900s

The Verde Valley stopping place could be likened to a beach, or a break in the wave, just as it had been in the southern migrations of, at first the Sinaguans, and then the Yavapais and the Tonto Apaches. The latter groups were still in residence when the wave of refugees, settlers, and adventurers from the disheartened eastern half of the nation began.

The verdent area, located in the Central Mountain Region of Arizona, and the canyons which form its watershed are at a geographic demarcation between the highlands of the state, known as the Colorado Plateau and with the Basin and Range Province to the south. Scar tissue in this weakened area of the earth's skin, the break line between the two blocks of terrain, took a variety of forms. First, the water from the ledge of the Colorado Plateau, falling over the volcanic cliffs of canyons like Oak Creek, formed a large lake depositing rich silt in the Verde Valley. In a second geologic era of uplift, the mountains blocking the water's southern exit broke at Box Canyon. This escape route for the water, which seasonally cascades from canyon walls above the Valley, became the Verde River. The old lake bed became the fertile farm land so successfully cultivated by the Prehistoric Sinaguans, the nomadic Apache and Yavapai, and then pioneer families like Parson Bristow's and Will Jordan's.

At this break between northern and southern Arizona, known as the Mogollon Rim, the Verde Valley became a display case of both geology and civilization. Volcanic shapes at geologic pressure points, the volcanic "pop-ups" given names like Queen Victoria, foreshadowed the drama of human affairs in the garden, which is the Verde Valley.

This drama came onto the valley stage with act I approximately 1100 AD, with the last curtain call for this link in the human chain coming around 1400 AD. These folks were a branch of those who had settled further north around the San Francisco Peaks. Finally being recognized by archaeologists as a subculture of the Anasazi, they were named Singaua. The Spanish word Sinagua, or "sin" and "agua," which translates to a people "without water," was chosen indicating the lack of water around the high mountains. As the Sinaguans migrated southward their civilization flourished in the uplifted ledges and mesas of limestone and sandstone laid down by the prehistoric water body. Here on high banks above the valley's flood plain, as well as on suitable rises in the terrain, many pueblo-style dwellings and community centers were constructed. Montezuma Castle, (named for the famous Aztec leader of Mexico, although he never was near this area), is a five-story "apartment" building. Due to the wide variety of items found here during excavations, it is believed to have been a major trade center. (See center for painting of Montezuma Castle)

Submitted by Charles Jordan
Montezuma Castle, early 1900s

Jesse Goddard, an old-timer dedicated to preserving an accurate history of the locale, indicates numerous other clusters of dwellings south of Montezuma Castle and the present town of Camp Verde. While pointing to the southwest into the Hackberry Mountains, Jesse talks of one of the many ruins he had explored. "On top o' that little butte, that whole thing was an enormous buildin' up there. People dug an' dug up there. Ya can't take a step without steppin' on pottery, but it's not good stuff. That ruin is a 'barrel o' th' same order' as Montezuma Castle, 'bout three stories high. I bet there was a lot more Indians lived there than there was at th' Castle!"

House Mountain (see map page 86), somewhat centrally located in the valley, has a hump resembling a house perched high on a ridge which was used for looking at the stars. As the seasons changed so did the position of the stars, and the house formation became a celestial marker or compass and calendar. It was also a natural communication center as a major portion of the Verde Valley was visible from its top. Almost all Indian apartment houses of any size could see House Mountain, thus making it the logical spot for signal fires, linking the various groups and dwellings together. From its vantage point, archaeologists were able to find some of the ruins, which had gone unnoticed.

About the time the hunting and gathering Sinaguans were moving south, it is believed the Hohokam, farmers of the Salt River Valley, (around the present city of Phoenix), traveled north. They established their homes in pit houses along Beaver Creek, a tributary to the Verde River. Irrigation ditches were constructed and water from the spring-fed creek was diverted to fields of maize, beans, squash and cotton. Apparently there was a blending of cultures here as evidenced by the advanced farming techniques of the Hohokam and by the replacement of the pit houses with Sinaguan-type structures, i.e. Montezuma Castle. A mystery remains as to why and where these folks went. One plausible theory is that they broke into smaller family units, scattering over a large area, possibly due to drought or having overused the land. There is also the belief that many of the current tribes of Arizona are direct descendants of these ancient ones - the Hopi from Anasazi and Sinaguans, the Pima from the Hohokams, etc. We can only be sure that the cultures as known prior to 1400 AD, had disappeared and yet there were inhabitants in this area when the Spanish began exploring in 1540. With the disappearance of the prehistoric folks, act I of the human drama closed and the stage was set for act II with the entrance of varied players.

Somewhere in these intervening, enigmatic years of 1400-1540 the Apaches, an Athabascan linguistic people migrated south from Canada. These folks, who were the more warlike relatives of the Navajo, split into their own segment and continued to travel further south. Their nomadic ways took them into central and southern parts of Arizona, New Mexico, and even into Old Mexico. Their name Apache is possibly a corruption of an old Zuni word meaning "enemy", or a combination of the Yuman words "apa" (man) and "ahwa" (war, battle fight). They definitely were "fighting men" and enemies to many. Their lives were centered around their warriors, depending on successful forays and plunder for survival. The total tribe was divided into several bands that at times fought against each other, as their hierarchy of loyalty was first to family, then to clan, followed by band/group and lastly, but rarely, to tribe.

As the Apaches were gradually infiltrating from the north, other migrations were in progress from the south and the east, as a result of Columbus' historic discovery. In 1528, Narvaez with 600 men set sail from Spain for the Florida coast. In the Gulf of Mexico a vicious storm wrecked their ship, leaving only a few alive. The final four survivors were picked-up by Indians and thus began their long and arduous journey back to civilization. While being traded from tribe to tribe, they were slowly moving westward. (Perhaps they could be called the first to be "Following Their Westward Star.") Always eager to learn more about this unusual territory, they felt a special interest in the stories regarding large cities to the north. Not realizing that theirs' and the natives' idea of large was quite different, the mental image they carried was rather grandiose. Eight eventful years later they were discovered by a group of their countrymen who were on a slave hunting expedition from western Mexico. They were taken directly to Mendoza, the Viceroy of New Spain, thus completing the trek of the first white men to enter what was later called Arizona Territory. Upon hearing their tales Mendoza felt fame and wealth were within his grasp and decided to reconnoiter the area before sending a large expedition. In 1539 one of the four of the shipwrecked party, Esteban a Moorish slave, was conscripted to serve as scout accompanying a friar named Marcos de Niza. Though Esteban was killed, possibly by Zuni Indians, de Niza returned to Mexico City and his exaggerated descriptions of the wealth triggered near pandemonium. Their imaginations fuelled by numerous stories of great riches, the "light eyes" had arrived in the New World with high expectations of getting wealthy quickly, and these tales only increased the fervor of all who heard. Among these were the Spanish Conquistadors, the best trained soldiers and warriors in the "Old World." Most of them were the younger sons of Spanish aristocracy who, under the laws of primogeniture, would receive none of the family wealth. The inheritance passed only to the oldest son, leaving the younger brothers to find their fortunes elsewhere. So it was, under the strict gaze of one of these dashing noblemen soldiers, Francisco Vasquez de Coronado, a large expedition was organized. This disparate bunch of soldiers, padres, slaves, and women traveled northeastward passing near the current town of Bisbee but completely missed the large silver deposits close by. After failing to recognize the minerals "in them thar hills" and deciding against going to California, Coronado had unwittingly by-passed his greatest opportunity for wealth. Nearly three years later he faced the reality of his failed mission and returned to Mexico disgraced. Little did he know he had claimed for Spain all of the American southwest. He was also with the first group of white men to gaze upon the Grand Canyon. Arizona territory, as yet, was not necessarily a destination in itself, but rather a route to reach the fabled seven cities of Cibola. (These were supposedly complete cities made of gold, but apparently were villages made of micaceous clay which reflected the sun's rays, causing them to look like gold.) A new era had begun and Arizona was soon to feel like "the middle of a sandwich" with the diverse branches of humanity converging from several directions.

Forty years after Coronado returned to Mexico, a party led by Antonio de Espejo journeyed up the Rio Grande searching for three padres and a legendary lake of gold. After separating from most of the party, Espejo and four companions continued westward to the area around the Verde Valley, being the first anglos to cross its stage. Here he was, in his own words, "in search of some rich mines there of which they told me. I found them and with my own hands I extracted ore from them, said by those who know, to be very rich and to contain much silver. The region where these mines are is for the most part mountainous, as is the road leading to them…"[2]

In the early 1600s Juan de Onate, colonizer of the Rio Grande Valley, took a small expedition and left New Mexico traveling to the west in search of a route to the "South Sea". (It is interesting to note that again, AZ was explored from east to west as if there was a magnetic force pulling the white men in that direction.). Onate's journey, when concluded, had taken them a greater distance through Arizona than any previous anglo visitors and revealed more of the territory's mineral wealth than had ever been reported. As a result many argonauts would follow to explore and claim the land, leaving numerous signs of their diggings for Americans to find two hundred-fifty years later. In 1607 when Onate returned to Mexico the era of "God, Gold, and Glory" terminated and the "3Gs" were replaced by the "3 Ms," Missions, Mexicans, and Mountain Men.

Throughout the remainder of the 17th century and the major portion of the 18th, Padres were attempting to Christianize the "heathen" in the southern portion of this hostile land. In the early part of the 19th century, revolution around Mexico City was spreading and the Spanish government was sent packing. A new nation was born calling itself Mexico. Again, there was very little impact on Central Arizona until years later.

Simultaneously, and to the north, men who lived alone in the mountains, trapped furs, and sold these at their annual rendezvous were becoming known as Mountain Men. These "free wanderers," although having adapted well to the wilds, knew what the survival of the fittest meant. Hostile Indians, hunger, thirst, accidents, storms, illness, and vicious animals, especially the grizzly bear, all added to the danger and the possibility of a shortened life span. To combat these factors the mountain man developed unique and unconventional ways of increasing his chances of being alive at the next rendezvous. A fire with little smoke was harder for the "enemy" to see, thus the use of buffalo chips or dried aspen wood. Fringes on homemade buckskin clothing helped the water to run off rather than soaking in when the weather was wet. Also after eating with his hands he could add more waterproofing by using his clothes as a napkin for wiping off the grease. Even with these precautions, there were times of very wet weather he would need to remove his clothes to protect them from shrinking. Some commented that it was good that the "old geazers hide didn't shrink!" Another trick-of-the-trade was hardening the leather shirt to serve as a kind or armor, increasing his possibilities of surviving an Indian arrow. The remainder of his wardrobe included moccasins, a skin cap and buffalo robe. Around his neck was a very essential item, the small leather "possibles" bag. It held personal things like, bullet mold, bullet pouch, pipe, etc. and some have said, healing herbs. His powder horn hung from his shoulder and around his waist was a hunting knife, pistol, and hatchet. His rifle was often carried in a scabbard fastened to his saddle and his traps would usually be in the bundle on the pack animal.

It seems that this group was the only part of the "3Ms" that possibly had an impact on the "stage" of the Verde Valley. Although there are some references to fur trapping on the Upper Verde, the major extent of the Mountain Man influence was through the establishment of trails and pathways. A number of these developed into wagon roads which heard the creak of many a prairie schooner swaying slowly westward, often being lead by a Mountain Man, who then was known as a "wagon master."

Apparently nothing could prevent the folks of these wagon trains from following the promise of something better to the West. Huston Horn refers to this desire as "an emotional urge… an itch in the brain, a restlessness in the feet…"[3] always leading towards the prairies and tall mountains just beyond the setting sun. Coming to the "New World" the movement has been from East to West. Henry David Thoreau sensed a great insight while walking in the woods of New England. "'Eastward,' he said, 'I go only by force but Westward I go free… the prevailing tendency of my countrymen.'"[4] The same sentiment was expressed by a pioneer woman:

> "When God made man,
> He seemed to think it best
> To make him in the East
> And let him travel west."[5]

As these immigrants moved gradually westward toward center stage of the Verde Valley, they brought act III to life as they continued "Following Their Westward Star" to the "wild and woolly" Arizona Territory.

FOOTNOTES

(1) Barnes, Will, Revised and Enlarged by Byrd H. Granger, <u>Arizona Place Names</u>, The Falconer Publishing Co., c. 1983, Pg. XV

(2) Wyllys, Rufus K., <u>Arizona, The History of a Frontier State</u>, Hobson and Herr, Phoenix, AZ, 1950, Pg. 34

(3) Horn, Huston, <u>The Pioneers</u>, Time Life Books, Edited by Hedley Donovan, Time Inc., 1974, Pg. 24

(4) Ibid

(5) Ibid

Chapter Two
PROVIDENCE AND PARSON BRISTOW

Prologue

In 1875, Parson James Clawson Bristow, his family and Missouri neighbors headed westward to find a better home for their families. They hoped to leave behind the poverty, strife, disease and death in the years of and surrounding the Civil War. Even after the Confederacy's surrender, for another twenty years, guerilla soldiers plundered the Missouri countryside. And before the war, when the U.S. Supreme Court ruled in 1857 that Missouri slave Dred Scott was only property, antislavery convictions of settlers in neighboring Kansas led to many killings. Peace was not an expectation, and the state's name may have been pronounced "misery" by more than a few.

America's bloody regeneration found many ready soldiers from this territory, known as "The Mother of the West." French fur traders in the region of Missouri fought on the side of the Patriots in the American Revolution by engaging the Red Coats in an extension of British hostilities with France. In 1846, Missouri soldiers stood ready to fight in the war with Mexico to protect their Mexican trade route, and relevant, in particular, to Parson Bristow's story, the war with Mexico added Arizona to United States territory.

During the Civil War, the Confederacy would map and divide the Southwest along an east-west parallel, a "blood meridian" of violence against native populations. The Union subdivided its own claim to the gold and silver wealth of the Southwest along the current boundary line between Arizona and New Mexico. After only one Civil War skirmish in Arizona, the matter was settled, and in 1863, Lieutenant Colonel J. Francisco Chaves and his troop of New Mexico Cavalry Volunteers escorted the Union's first territorial governor to Prescott, Arizona, near Fort Whipple. It was a two-day journey beyond the vast, verdant, mountain valley that the Mexicans called the Verde or green valley, Parson Bristow's destination.

"A beautiful sunset is her smile; the blue sky is the blue of her mantle, the rainbow is formed by the tears that she sheds for sinners," sang the Mexican cowboys, inspired by their faith and the horizons radiating around them. Parson Bristow most likely also

Submitted by Margaret Bristow Stoever

Parson Bristow in his later years with daughters Martha "Teedie" Ralston & Mary Evangelina Human

shed tears for his flock; however, he would specialize in shedding light from his King James Version. Under an old cottonwood tree in the Verde Valley, he would regularly hold the Good Book up to heaven at a spot which would be commemorated for the first Baptist sermon preached in the territory of Arizona.

There in the Middle Verde, at the age of 74 years, Parson Bristow recorded his life story, and many of those who traveled with him in the wave of emigrants westward left their stories with children and grandchildren and ultimately with the Verde Valley Pioneers Association. Here, we mix their voices with Parson Bristow's in an attempt to transform his solo into an opera of refugees, who eventually united a nation of States across North America.

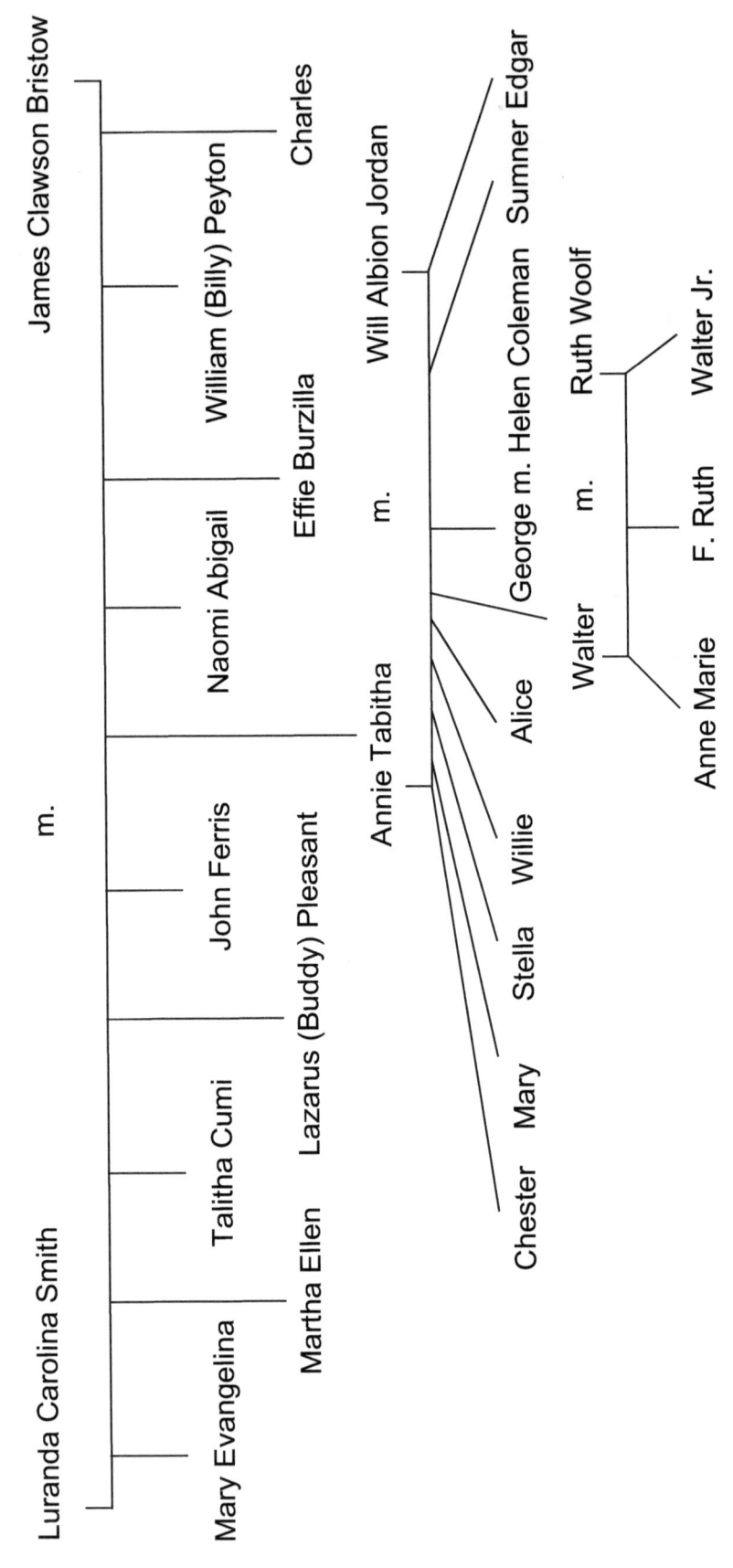

Family Tree of main characters in book.

Chapter 2 - *PROVIDENCE AND PARSON BRISTOW*

The Bristow Children
Family of Luranda and James Bristow
    Mary Evangelina Bristow - 1857-1919
    Married — James W. Human
    [Parents of storyteller, Dora Human]
    Martha Ellen Bristow [Aunt Teedie] - 1859-1937
    Married — John Will Ralston
    Talitha Cumi Bristow [Aunt Cumi] - 1861-1922
    Married — David Erastus Hawkins
    Lazarus Pleasant Bristow - 1864-1926
    Married — Lily Jones
    John Ferris Bristow - 1866-1934
    Married — Calista Woods
    [Parents of storyteller Allen Bristow]
    Annie Tabitha Bristow — 1869-1957,
    Married — Will Jordan
    [Parents of storyteller Stella Jordan and grandparents of F. Ruth Jordan a.k.a. Ruth or Ruthie]
    Naomi Abigail Bristow — 1871-1872
    Effie Burzilla Bristow [Aunt Effie] - 1873-1958
    Married — James Wingfield
    Rev. William Peyton Bristow — 1876-1934
    [Born in Arizona]
    Married — Florence Frances Miller
    Charles Owen Bristow — 1878-1921
    [Born in Arizona]

THE STORYTELLERS OF THIS CHAPTER
Story Tellers from Parson Bristow's Family
(In narrative order)

Parson James C. Bristow — Baptist evangelist who, at the age of 45 years, left Missouri with his family to pioneer in Arizona. The Parson fathered eleven children (including a little son of premature birth). Of two married daughters, one, Mary Human, made the trip with her husband; the other, Martha, followed two years later with her husband. One child born in 1871 died in 1872; one, Effie, made the trip at the age of two; and two would be born after the family settled in the Verde Valley. So his pregnant wife Luranda's brood consisted of five when they left Missouri: daughter Cumi, age 14; son Pleas, age 11; John, age 9; Annie, age 6; and baby Effie.

Stella Jordan — Born in the Verde Valley to the Parson's daughter Annie and Will Jordan. She was college educated in Tempe, Arizona, and took pride in photographing and writing about her Verde Valley heritage. She never married and, while teaching school, lived for most of her life with her parents in their Bridgeport home along the Verde. Stella was one of those sensitive, talented and willful souls whose ideas and desired lifestyle often vexed her family. Eventually it became necessary for her to have treatment unavailable in this rural community, so Stella for a time was a patient at the state mental hospital in Phoenix. With the development of Thorazine she became well enough to return to her beloved valley, living with her sister Alice.

Allen Bristow — Born in the Verde Valley to the Parson's son John and Calista Woods, a schoolteacher in Camp Verde. Ranch work forced Allen to miss school, but he finished high school in California in 1919 with the help of his Aunt Teedie [Parson Bristow's daughter Martha] and her husband John Will Ralston who was employed with the railroad. After a long career with a southern California rail company, Allen retired with his wife to Sedona, Arizona, where he was active at the Wayside Chapel and The Sedona Westerner's Club. A motorcycle enthusiast, he rode the countryside his cowboy father had worked on horseback.

F. Ruth Jordan [a.k.a. Ruth, Ruthie] — The daughter of Walter and Ruth Jordan was born and raised in Sedona, Arizona. Parson Bristow's daughter Annie was her grandmother. The stories of her father, Walter, inspired the creation of this book, and many of her own contributions come from transcripts of the tours and historical lectures she has given of the Verde Valley and Sedona. From 1957 to 1965, she and her husband, the Rev. Larry Jackson, served as Baptist missionaries on the Navajo and Hopi Indian reservations, making their home in Keams Canyon, Arizona until Larry's health broke and they were forced to retire in Phoenix, Arizona.

Annie Bristow Jordan — Daughter of the Parson and wife of Will Albion Jordan made a reputation for herself as the wild child of Parson Bristow's family, and later as the sternest Baptist wife of the region. As a girl and young woman she was also known as "the belle of the Verde Valley". The family she raised with Will Jordan, a farmer's son from Maine, is the branch of the Bristow family tree on which the chapter's of this history will climb.

Martha — aka Mrs. John Will Ralston or Aunt Teedie, only child of Parson Bristow to stay behind in Missouri. She and her husband arrived in the Verde Valley in 1877. They would move on to California, but their ties with her family remained strong.

Dora Human — aka Mrs. A.G. 'Dutch' Dickinson, daughter of Jim Human and Parson Bristow's daughter Mary. Dutch Dickinson's family, like Dora's, were among the settlers from Missouri in 1875.

Storytellers Not Related to Parson Bristow
Descendants of the 1875 group from Missouri
Martha Priscilla Burford — Daughter of one of

the leaders of this small band of settlers, P.W. Burford. Three years after arriving in the Verde Valley, she would marry Charles Dickinson, who was a young man of twenty-two in the party from Missouri.

Rowena Van Deren — Daughter of Charles Dickinson and Martha Priscilla Burford. The Van Deren family, which she married into, was much like the Bristows in size and a major family tree in the Middle Verde pioneer orchard.

Tack Gaddis — Like Charles Dickinson and Martha Priscilla Burford, Tack was a youngster in the 1875 group. His family reunited with relatives already established in the Valley, Mr. and Mrs. Wales Arnold, who ran the way-station and mail stop near Fort Verde. Tack and Annie Bristow's future husband, Will Jordan, would clear brush together on the banks of the Verde River after Will arrived from Maine in 1880, but that's Chapter Four.

So, come now, imagine yourself with others gathered 'round a campfire, the fiddling and singing have stopped and the storytelling time begins with each participant adding an expanded perspective, all blending into one song of how they all began "Following Their Westward Star."

Parson James Clawson Bristow: I was born in Indiana in the year of 1835 in Bedford County, but my first recollections are from my father's old home in Kentucky. In my memory with my father, we climbed Great Poplar Mountain. We begin at Grandma's house, and less than ten steps away is a fine spring with a house built over it and a large mulberry tree standing by the door. The apple orchard and the apple tree that I often climbed are beyond. We cross an old sage field to arrive at the foot of the mountain where my father boosts me onto a horse, which he leads up the trail. On the top of the mountain there is a little log cabin. Father's second wife and another woman are there at Medicine Springs for their health.

Submitted by Ken Bristow
James Clawson Bristow, circa 1890

The mountain is flat on top - solid rock a few hundred yards across with high cliffs on most sides. I walk out on a narrow ridge to Huckleberry Peak, where I gather berries until time to start back. We look down on the old ranch and upon the great scene where the youthful wonders of my father were displayed. Over there in the graveyard lie the bones of Grandpa and Uncle Ben, who were killed by a falling tree. And there on my right is a large sugar orchard. Between it and the house is a field of poplar trees with leaves that make the same music as the cottonwoods along the Verde River. I remember lying down on my back one day in that poplar field. I looked west and wondered what was far away. I did not know then, but I understand it now.

I was ten years old when we moved to southwest Missouri. When I was about fourteen, I left Father and his new family and went to live with Aunt Lina, my sister, and her husband. After a few years we moved to the foot of Iron Ore Knob.

Stella Jordan: Grandpa Bristow was the youngest of five children. His mother died when he was three years old, leaving him in the care of his oldest sister, Evangelina or Aunt Lina. The family moved to Kentucky, then to Missouri. His Christian character was molded under the influence of his father, a Hard-Shell Baptist. At the age of eighteen, my grandfather would be licensed to preach and would deliver his first sermon at the Mt. Enon Church in Cedar County, Missouri.

Submitted by Ken Bristow
J.C. Bristow in Missouri, circa 1870

Near Aunt Lina lived the Pleasant Smith family, and among the children was Luranda Carolina, who had been born in Kentucky in 1837. The friendship between the young preacher and Luranda led to their marriage in 1857.[1]

Parson Bristow: We moved into a house west of Aunt Lina where Mary and Martha were born. There many wonders were displayed when bushwhackers thought that around my neck they would lay a rope. I talked them out of it.

When the war broke out, I was living in another house where my third daughter, Cumi [pronounced Q-my] was born in 1861. I owned land, nine yoke of work oxen, and eight head of horses. Uncle Tom Smith was running my two ox teams hauling lead from the mine at Granby to the railroad. As he went out with his last load, he met soldiers coming south and had to throw the lead-ore out and return, as all business was off. During the war, I was moved out on the railroad to join the soldiers in Illinois and was gone about a year. In the fall of 1864, I moved back. [It is surmised that Parson Bristow served as a Chaplain.]

Leaving Missouri for Arizona came about in this way: there was a man by the name of Charlie Buster who left that country [Missouri] a few years before we did. He wandered out west and finally dropped into the Salt River Valley from where he wrote a letter back and gave a glowing account of it. Burford, a neighbor of mine, saw the letter, and as he was well acquainted with Buster, it set him on fire to go. So we made up our mind to go with him.

This was the first time that I ever heard of Arizona. I was not very anxious to go, but it seemed like the hand of Providence was pushing me out. There was not much time to prepare for the trip, and for a while it looked as if I would not make it. I traded my ranch to a man for about twenty cows and three young fillies. I still possessed two yoke of oxen. [Apparently while he was away in the army, his farm had declined, loosing his horses and most of his oxen.]

Allen Bristow: My father, John Bristow [fifth child of Parson Bristow and Luranda], was born in Missouri in 1866. His family had come down t' Humansville from Joplin, Missouri, t' see if they could get jobs there or do a little bit better. Instead o' that, they had a terrible time — nearly starved. They had, I think, scarlet fever or typhoid. Some o' them died. Grandma Bristow, [who we of the next generation called Bammie], and all o' them were sick with it, except my father. He remembered roaming around there alone while all th' rest were sick; just a little bitty kid, hungry and dirty. One o' Grandma's sisters took him in and cared for him. While they were there, a man that was in the Army at Camp Verde, Arizona told them about a beautiful, green mountain valley [Verde Valley], where th' grass grew up t' th' horses' bellies and where streams were flowing all over th' place. They didn't have much t' lose, so they made up their minds that they would go there.[2]

Parson Bristow: I, here, give a sketch of the character or make-up of those we started out with. The reason that I put all this down is so the reader may see what a novel set we were.

P.W. Burford was a man that when he made up his mind to do anything, it would be hard to turn him away from doing it. He was a man who had a strong passion to get rich, and he believed, from what Charlie Buster said, that if he could get into the Salt River Valley [where the city of Phoenix is located] he would be in heaven on earth. As it is so hot there, he would have come nearer the truth if he had turned his expectations the opposite direction from Heaven. He found this out when he got to the Salt River Valley, and he turned and went to Oregon.

There were some things in the make-up of Burford that I admired. He had three children, was a solid Baptist and belonged to the same church that I did before the war. He had worn the blue, and I could depend on him.

Burford's daughter [Martha Priscilla Dickinson]: In the year of 1875, my father hitched up Ben and Baldy, left our dear old home in Missouri, and started for Arizona to make our fortune in the West. With us was [Parson] James Bristow, a man who had a good head. If he had been educated, he would have made a good president. He claimed to have a Hope. He, also, had worn the blue in the time of war.[3]

Parson Bristow: The next to decide to come was *Brother Lett*, a strong Baptist and member of the same church I was. He was a Republican, but I do not know whether he had ever worn the blue or not. He was a good man, but he was so close in his dealing that, to use Uncle Dick Smith's expression, "he would skin a flea for his hide and tallow." He had no children of his own, but he had two orphan children.

Jim Davidson decided to come. If I may speak from the grave, the name "coward" has been edited from my pronouncements as penance for having forgotten, on occasion, my Savior's entreaty: "Judge not lest ye be judged." I will go so far as to say that as Davidson grew up, he took the big head and thought himself of some importance; however, he never could make that impression upon anyone else. He had worn the blue in time of the war. His religion was that when he was sick or there was trouble in the family he would believe in the Bible; but when that passed off, he was an infidel or something worse. (Well, I must forbear for reasons already stated.) He had some children.

Uncle Sam Dickinson fell in line too. I had never seen him but once before. Uncle Sam in those days was much of a man and no coward either, as will be seen further along. Uncle Sam had some religious notions that he had gathered from the Methodists. He told me that he joined the Methodists, but he said that he saw the preacher do things that he would not do, and so he was off. I do not know whether he ever wore the blue or not.

Mike Gaddis was the next. Mike was as long and slim as a pole. His fore-teeth were long and stuck nearly straight out. He looked ferocious and scary. Mike was a rebel in time of the war, but since then he had calmed down and was just a common Democrat. Mike had some religion too. He was a Presbyterian. But Mike was weak in theology. Mike heard me speak in a sermon on baptism here in the Verde Valley, but I used some Plaines [expressions peculiar to the plains states], so much so that Mike spoke out and said that what Webster said in his dictionary satisfied him. Poor goose! He was easily satisfied, for Webster only gave what was called baptism, not the spirit of it. I have always thought that if it had not been for Webster's dictionary, Mike would have taken the water. I was so anxious for that, I almost wished Webster had never written a word. Poor Mike! Webster's dictionary will cause him and thousands of others to go up before the Judge of the Earth having never been baptized.

[Webster defines baptism as "the ceremony of sacrament of admitting a person into Christianity or a specific Christian church by dipping him in water or sprinkling water on him, as a symbol of washing away sin". The key word in the definition may be "sprinkling" and Mike Gaddis may not have been objecting to the parson's manner of speech, but defending his infant baptism or "sprinkling" as sufficient despite Baptist dogma of emersion or "dipping."]

I almost forgot *Jim Human*, being the husband of my oldest daughter Mary. Jim was a strong Republican. Jim does not know a letter of the Book. If he had been educated, he would have made a good judge of the court. The reader can see from this that I believe in education. Jim had some religion, but he kept it a secret until a few years ago when he came out and was baptized.

I would not say that this picture of our group was complete without saying something about the little dog that made the trip with us. He was a remarkable dog. He came into our possession just a little while before we started and looked to be an old dog, but he lived many years after. He would be called a bench-leg feist, but in his manner there was no feist about him. I never knew him to run after anything and never saw him jump or quicken his pace like a feist will. Sometimes he would bark but not often; he was too lazy for that.

He was a dark brown color, had short legs — not over one foot high — and was very fat. His head was like the head of a bulldog; his eyes far apart, and the point of his ears dropped down. In one thing he was entirely wanting. To emphasize this I would say that if all the dogs among the living or the dead were to raise up and say that they had seen dogs with a shorter tail than he had, they would all be liars, for such a thing could not possibly be. His tail looked as if it had been bobbed, and for that reason we called him Bob.

Bob would not ride in the wagon, but he never fagged. The greatest detective in the world could not find any change in his appearance. If Bob ever did any good or evil, I never knew it. He was a great favorite with my son John. Bob died at a good old age, about 15 years. John and some of the other children buried him in the lane that went from our place down to the river.

The reader may now know how novel a looking set we were - Brother Mike with his long teeth, and there was Jim Davidson's wife with the longest nose of any woman that ever sniffed air. When the buzzards would fly over us, they would eye us and shy away. If the Indians had come upon us they would never have thought of their scalping knives — only of getting away as quick as possible. With this set, I ventured out on the eternal plains of the great West, a thing that some others had done and never seen the timber any more. For a man to talk about crossing the plains those days was to talk bigger than going to the North Pole.

Submitted by Margaret Bristow Stoever

Luranda Carolina Smith Bristow (Bammie), circa 1900

[Parson Bristow, through omission gives great validation to the lowly status of the female gender during this era. Greater space was given to describing dog Bob, than to all of the women put together, including his own wife, Luranda. According to others, she was a very gentle and kind person, proficient in the numerous and often physically strenuous chores required of pioneer women. From his journal, however, it appears that she never drove the team and wagon. Allen Bristow remembers his grandmother taking care of him as a small child and sewing for them, without the convenience of a sewing machine. This task must have required a great deal of patience.] He continues "…so nice, motherly and everything. I remember her that. When we lived with her, she took care of Woody so well, [a younger brother, who had been a "blue baby," and had many physical and mental problems]. She helped my folks and all that and of course ran the house. It was no easy job for a person in that time."[4] Daughter, Annie, also, tells of her cooking skills, developed using Dutch ovens over an open fireplace, and commented that "her hands were never idle." Years later, family members talking of her illness and death in 1904 seemed to believe she had colon cancer. Again, Allen shares his memories: "As I understood it she contracted cancer and she went over and Aunt Teedie Ralston [the second child of the Parson] was taking care of her. They, (my folks), went over t' Aunt Teedie's and Uncle Jim's place, right there where Cherry Creek comes into the Verde, and they went in t' see her. She was in bed and in very bad shape and they tried t' sit her up and she could hardly talk. I was just a little kid peekin' through

Bammie in front of her home with George, circa 1903

the door and I was sorta shocked about it. I know that it was just shortly after that she died and we buried her in the Middle Verde cemetery."[5] She was a remarkable woman, that all of the great-grand children would loved to have known.

Parson Bristow: We did not all live in the same settlement, and there was a point selected for us to meet. We all pulled out on the tenth day of May and met the next day - nine wagons - at Humansville, Missouri.

[Every wagon train had to have a leader who established some semblance of organization. We know very little of how tasks were divided among those with whom Parson Bristow traveled other than that Burford was named leader. However, we do know that many of the larger groups were often led by a mountain man, who then was known as a wagon master. His was the experienced voice on which all in the wagon train relied for finding the proper "trails," water holes, techniques for fording rivers and crossing mountains, and for quick decisions followed by right action in emergencies. Knowing the responsibility of getting the people to their destination safely and timely, many leaders wanted to prepare all in the group to be proficient in a wide variety of circumstances. A single mishap of one person or wagon could spell tragedy for the whole group, thus in today's vernacular "a training program was put in place." As a result the wagon master found himself wearing many hats…teacher/trainer, advisor, arbitrator, overseer, and at critical times absolute authoritarian.

It was imperative that some organization was established and one can surmise that the responsibility of supervising the jobs of caring for the horses, rounding up the cattle, gathering firewood, or anything which involved the group was given to those selected by the new "commander." The newly appointed "division" leaders then could choose others to help with their assigned tasks. Next, the strength of the wagons and teams was assessed and suggestions of improvements were made. Also the tools and spare parts for making repairs were evaluated for breakdowns were inevitable and each family had to be prepared to take care of their own problems. The purchasing of supplies for enroute, as well as needed items to establish themselves upon arrival, required advice from the leader, followed by thoughtful selection by individuals. Tools for cutting trees, sawing logs, clearing the land and planting fields were another necessity. Already monumental decisions of which household items to take and which to leave behind had been made. Practically every woman who headed west had to leave at least one of her "treasures," which she desperately wanted to bring. A major concern of the wagon master was the total weight in the wagons and how it was distributed. The settlers had a tendency to overload and many times were told to find a way to lighten the contents. Imagine the extreme disappointment of a lady when she would learn that another favorite item had to be removed. After lessening the weight and shifting things around, the leader was called to do a final inspection.

Many of these leader/guides, seasoned in Indian habits and warfare, were worried by the lack of marksmanship exhibited by a number of the immigrants. The farmers, in some instances were much more proficient with the hoe and shovel than with their guns. Given the type of weapons available, it is difficult to believe that more than just a few women could lift a rifle, let alone hold it steady enough to actually hit their target. Thus in some of the groups, target practice for men, women and older boys was required. The older girls were taught to load the weapons, and all were instructed in how to set up camp, quickly prepare to defend themselves and to survive an Indian attack.

The women and older girls who did not know how to handle a team and wagon were asked to learn, while all practiced to become more skillful in forming the traditional circle when stopping and in "falling in line" at departure times. As survival was the "name of the game," all including toddlers to grandparents, were expected to follow directions responsibly and quickly.

Granted not all hitting the westward trail were given this much instruction, but all had to make at least some of these preparations. Within a few days of their initial gathering, the outriders were given their orders and the heads of the households were told their designated place in line. The call from the wagon master to "move 'em out" was given and as the bawling of the cattle furnished an accompaniment to the creaking wagons whose canvas tops undulated in rhythm along the dusty road, the arduous journey had begun.]

Parson Bristow: We got 60 miles out to Fort Scott, *Tom Smith* and *Pleas* came up. I did not know that they were coming. Tom Smith was one of Luranda's older brothers. He lived with his wife and five children at a place within two or three miles of the old farm of Luranda's folks until the war broke out. He enlisted in the army and remained until the war was over. I cannot give the name of the regiment in which he served. Shortly after the war his wife lost her mind and was sent to the asylum. She was not there long before she died. She was a Christian. Tom lived for 20 years a Christian and exerted a Christian influence that was not questioned by any. But after he arrived in Arizona, he went off into the world and remained there for almost 20 years before he died [c.1893] in my Verde Valley home. *Pleas* was married to Tom's oldest daughter. [Although Pleas' surname was Bristow, he was of no known blood relation to Parson Bristow.]

Soon after Fort Scott, we came upon *Jim Hawkins*. He had been across the plains in an early day to California and was returning to the West with near 100 cows and some horses. I had the next largest number of cows to Hawkins. [Hawkins would take one of the Dickinson girls to be his wife and father two children. The oldest was only three when Jim Hawkins and his wife met their death in the Verde Valley.]

Minnie Hawkins-Smith, Hawkins' daughter: The Hawkins family began farming in the upper end of the valley on the banks of Pecks Lake. My parents, James and May Hawkins passed away when I was only one year old. My brother Charley was only three. My grandparents, Sammie and Nancy Jane Dickinson, raised me.[6]

Parson Bristow: So we rolled on. Before we got entirely away from timber, I remember that one morning Brother Lett and I woke up and found ourselves preparing yokes to hitch in cows to strengthen our teams. We would hitch up a cow by the side of an ox. Over this my conscience complained, but we had to do something. It was not long until nearly all of us were working cows. We would work a cow until her poor neck would get sore, and then we would put in a fresh one. So we changed until we had worked nearly every cow.

Burford's daughter [Martha Priscilla Diskinson]: My father drove our milk cows with their calves. The calves got all the milk in the daytime, but at night we tied them up so we always got all the morning's milk. My mother strained the milk into a great big churn that was kept in the front of the wagon. The motion of the wagon churned the milk, and we had butter all the time, which was fine. I remember Grandmother Dickinson had been telling her four boys that when she had time, she would give them all a whipping. My mother passed by the Dickinson tent one day and hearing a terrible racket inside, she looked in to ask, "What is the matter?" Grandma replied, "I told the boys when I had time, I was going to give them a whippin' an' today I have time!"[7]

F. Ruth Jordan: My grandmother [Annie] was six when her family left Missouri. It was springtime, and the rivers were at flood stage. She was frightened when the muddy water would flow up through some of the planks in the wagon floor. To keep her feet clean and dry, she would climb up on top of a dresser where she perched repeatedly during the early journey.

Parson Bristow: I don't want to forget, here, that the women made a quilt for me, each one working their family's name on a square with needle and thread. This was the greatest honor ever conferred on me up to that time.

So onward we came, passing in sight of Wichita and through Hutchison, Kansas. Before we got out of the settlement, we stopped for dinner. There was a house near, and to our surprise we found that Eaf Gufey lived there, although he was away at the time. It was Eaf who rode with me on that fateful night 18 years ago when Squire George said the words that forever kept me from being a bachelor.

During the 18 years since, he had wandered west, deceived a poor widow, married her, and got her farm. Eaf was a good fellow, but the homeliest being that ever moved or nearly so. At his place we traded a filly for two oxen. One was an old stag named Jeff, after Jefferson Davis. The younger steer was named Tom and had not been worked much. Now we had three yoke of oxen, and the cows and my conscience had a

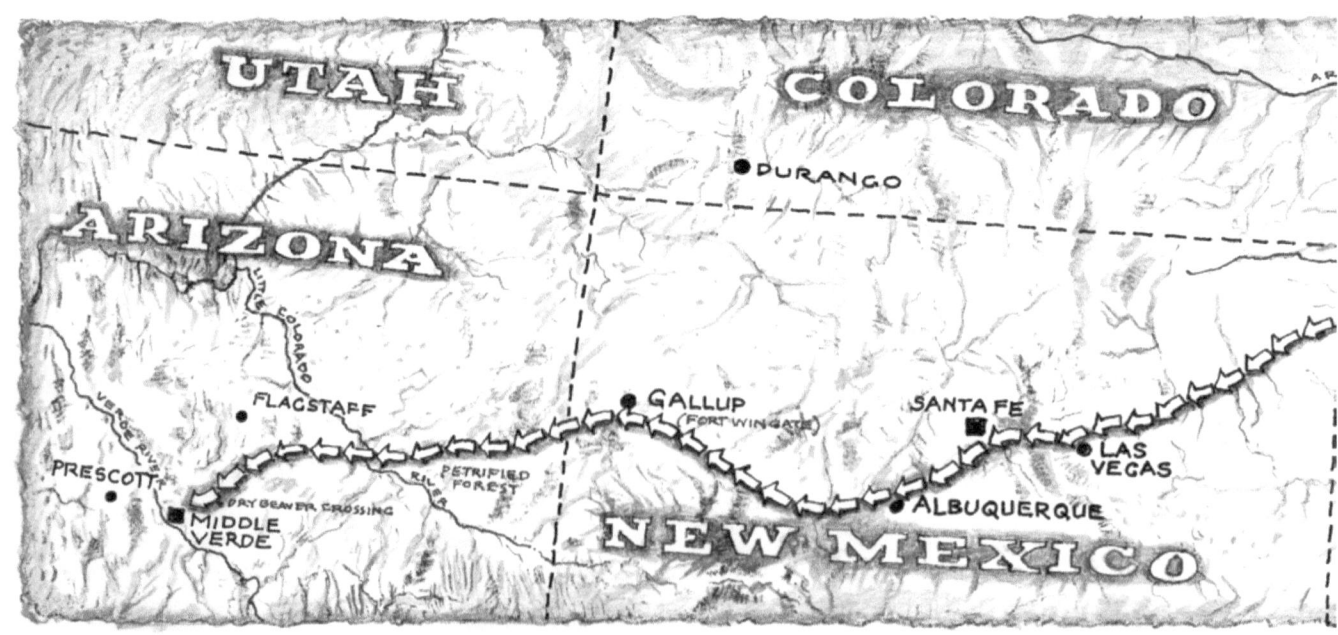

good long rest, but the trouble came up again later on.

Just before we got out of the settlement, I traded a two year old heifer for a gun, as I had none. I must say here that it was the best gun that I ever saw.

There was a young man living in this border settlement who claimed to have already been far out on the plains, and he wanted to travel out with us as far as he had been, so Burford took him in. His name was John Claxton, and he travelled out with us a long ways. I always believed that John was a horse thief and was afraid that we would lose some of our horses, so before he left, I managed to trade him two fillies for his horse.

When we reached the big Arkansas Bend, we had a little Indian scare. We had stopped a day to rest and to let the women rest. Claxton and Morris Smith [cousin to Mrs. Bristow] rode to the foothills to see if they could see any sign of Indians. When they came back in the evening, they reported that they had a battle with some Indians. Though I never believed a word of it, we corralled the wagons and kept guard that night. Nothing came of it.

Next day, Burford, whom we chose as captain [wagon master], had John and Morris ride along the foothills and watch out for Indians, but they never saw any. John travelled with us several days after this. For a few days before he left us, he would ride out alone and come in at night alone. One day he went out and never returned. The Indians may have gotten him.

It was not far before we lost sight of all timber. We would see, now and then, a pile of buffalo bones. After the Indians were corralled by the government troops, men rushed out and killed the buffalo for their hides which they hauled to the railroad and shipped to St. Louis. There was never such a slaughter of dumb brutes, none in all the annals of history - thousands of them slain by the deadly guns that were used in the Civil War. The gun that I got from one of these men would have brought a buffalo down from more than a quarter of a mile away.

We had entered upon the plains in earnest. [We may surmise here that the wagon train left the course of the Arkansas River and its tributaries and began south.] All hills disappeared. The fowls of the air were no more. No animals could be seen, not so much as a rabbit. No insect, not even a grasshopper. All directions looked the same, and the eye became weary. Many a time I would look down at the ground and refuse to look off farther than our train. We would search the horizon for an object or any small break in its flatness. Then we would head for it and look no more for some time. So it was day in and day out, week in and week out. Not a cloud to be seen. I cannot command the language to picture the scene - the sun pouring her merciless rays down on us.

I could not help thinking of poor Hagar, Abraham's wife [in the book of Genesis]. It has always been hard for me to believe that Abraham served Hagar right. He had married her in good faith, and in so doing he promised her that he would stand by her through winter and summer, heat and cold, day and night; that he would stand by her as long as there was a button on his shirt. Just because Sarah got a little mad at Hagar, he sends her and his one dear son off in the desert with no water. We were into it, like Hagar, and too far away to turn back. I will say here that I never had any desire to do so.

Martha Priscilla Burford: One night in Kansas there came up an awful storm, the cattle broke away from the guards and got in a grain field and destroyed

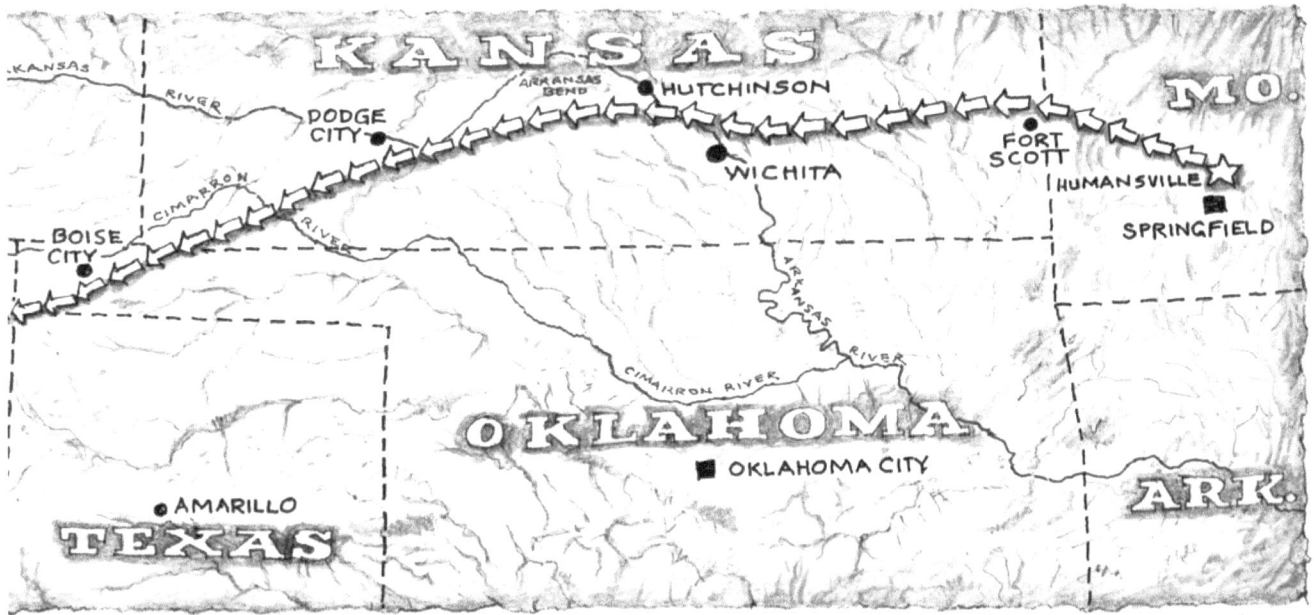

Route of Parson Bristow's Wagon Tain

lots of grain. The men had to pay $40 damage. Sometimes the women could not do any washing on account of not being able to find a place where there was plenty of feed and water for our stock. We also learned to wear our clothes un-ironed. For meat we had buffalo and buffalo calf meat to eat.[8]

Tack Gaddis: We came by way of Dodge City, Kansas, and struck what is now the Santa Fe Railroad. We followed it to Granada, Kansas, at the Arkansas River. That was the end of the track.[9]

Parson Bristow: So we pulled through Kansas - a stretch of six hundred miles. Then we crossed the state line into panhandle country. I do not know how long it took us to cross it, but when we got across it, the eye now found rest to see a giant peak high above all surrounding mountains. Here the imagination would stagger, and the mind would wonder how the mountain got its majestic form. Geologists say that the earth was once upheaved; and as it settled back, it wrinkled like a blanket. Such a theory is not satisfying to me, but we must go on.

Not long after this welcome sight, war broke out among us. We had camped for dinner, and Jim Davidson said something that riled some of the party. Uncle Sam Dickinson stepped up to him and said, 'Thirty years ago no man would have run over me in such a manner.'

At that Mike Gaddis jumped upon his wagon tongue and shouted, 'Dorcas, Dorcas, hand me my shotgun! Hand me my shotgun, Dorcas!'

Before Mike could get his shotgun, Jim Davidson (and here I forbear once more) backed out, and Uncle Sam's fury ran down. If Dorcas had been quicker, there is no telling how many of us would never have seen Arizona.

Everything calmed down, and we moved on as before, driving ourselves as hard as we could go. We wanted to see what we would find in New Mexico - the land of darkness. The Gospel had never been preached [as a Baptist would do it] in any part of New Mexico. For which I shall not blame the Catholics from Eternity's vantage point. The Catholics had ruled the people for many years and taught them that it would be right to steal, if they would give part of what they stole to the church.

Here we came to two roads that we had been advised would lead us to where we wanted to go, but we were told to take the southern route. Hawkins would not do it. Hawkins seemed to have some knowledge of the country. He had a brother who had travelled with a drove of cattle from Texas to Prescott, and I suppose that he got some knowledge of the route from him. Uncle Sam could not turn Hawkins from the course that he had lined out to go, so our party went separate ways. Jim Human and I went with Hawkins.

We moved on among a treacherous set of Mexicans. Within about two miles of Las Vegas, we camped for the night. The Mexicans stole three head of our horses, two from Hawkins and the last horse I had. Now we had but few horses to ride and drive the cows.

[Gruesome evidence of the violence in this corner of New Mexico is to be found in the account of the journey two years later by Parson Bristow's daughter, Martha, and her husband.]

Mrs. Martha [Bristow] Ralston [aka Aunt Teedie]: My husband and I stayed behind in Missouri when my father left with the others. We followed in 1877, and when we first entered New Mexico Territory, we made camp by a stream, the Cimarron, I think. When we led the mules down to drink, they snorted and refused. Looking for the cause, we found a man's bloody clothing in the water. Farther back, there was a deserted shack, and between that and the stream, we found the partly buried body of a murdered man. One foot and part of the head were out of the ground. We threw a lot more dirt over the poor fellow and went on to another camp.[10]

Parson Bristow: Surely and slowly we pulled for Albuquerque. We reached a little town where we sold old Jeff for eight dollars. His feet gave out, so we had to put one cow in Jeff's place in the yoke. At Albuquerque, we crossed the Rio Grande River. The river was up, and it was dangerous. I have forgotten how many trips it took the little boat to set us across. It seemed a miracle.

Annie: When we crossed the Rio Grande, the wagons were driven on the ferry boat, and the loose cattle swam across the river. I remember seeing my Uncle Tommy Smith swimming across after them through the ugly, muddy water.[11]

F. Ruth Jordan: My Dad would tell a story about one of the boys being swept out of his saddle as he crossed the river with the livestock and having to grab the tail of his horse to keep himself from being washed away.

Parson Bristow: Next, we aimed for Fort Wingate [east of Gallup, New Mexico]. On a high foothill in our path, we looked down and the ground was covered with sea shells. Had the ocean covered this land long ago? Was the ocean over all New Mexico and Arizona? If this were the case, wouldn't there be sea shells in many places? The questions that can not be answered are numerous. Later we would cross the Petrified Forest, one of Arizona's great wonders, and the questions without answers would come to me again. How is it that we would see trees lying there one hundred feet long that had turned to rock, but no standing timber was in sight? [Over 100 years later

Navajo couple, circa 1958

Ruth was leading a bus group of tourists through this area when suddenly one person demanded her money back because there were no standing trees, thus it could not be a forest!]

Near Fort Wingate, the Navajo Indian farmers seemed wealthy. The Indians numbered in the thousands, and they had large herds of stock. At Fort Wingate, our grub was running short. As the government had ordered rations to be given to emigrants that were moving into the territory, we drew some rations and stayed over night. The next morning we started for the Little Colorado River, a journey of about two hundred miles. [Little did he realize there was another group called Hopi, living approximately 75 miles northwest. Here about 80 years later his great granddaughter, F. Ruth and her husband Larry Jackson, followed in his footsteps as missionaries bringing his beloved Baptist teachings to the Navajos and Hopis.] (See center for paintings of Navajos and Hopis)

Noon of the first day out, we stopped at a spring. Here my pen reels to picture the scene. There were several Indians who rode up, some on burros and some on ponies. Some were naked. One Indian sitting naked on a burro fell off when the burro moved a little. The mother [Parson Bristow's wife Luranda] was looking at him and a queer feeling passed over her. That night or the next night she gave an untimely birth to a little brother, whom we buried just beneath the sod of that lonely country. [It appears here that, in spite of his Christian faith, Parson Bristow connected some superstitious belief to his wife's miscarriage and her seeing one of the Indians fall from the burro.]

As we passed down the hill from the Petrified Forest, I was walking beside the team with the mother in the wagon, sick. The cows were lowing, the mule braying, and the dogs howling for water. While under this scene, a lonely cloud settled down on my feelings that I shall never forget. We came down into the gulch and found some water. It was as red as blood, and the stock could not drink it. They had been without water for two days and nights. Night overtook us when we were about 15 miles of the river. The Hawkinses wanted to drive to the river that night, but I told them that I could go no further for the mother was sick. They talked very strongly of going on. I told them I would not go any further, so they decided not to leave me. If it had not been that Erastus Hawkins was stuck on Cumi, I believe that Hawkins would have left us.

F. Ruth Jordan: Priority of water went to the horses and to animals that were pulling the wagons. My grandmother, Annie, remembered being so thirsty that her mother picked the fruit of the prickly pear cactus to get some liquid for her children. When the family arrived in the Verde Valley, Annie could not wait to pick the pretty red fruit for herself. With a mouthful of tiny cactus needles, she realized how thoroughly her mother had cleaned the juicy bulbs.

Parson Bristow: The next day we reached the Little Colorado River. Here was a log house and one lone man. I think that the Mormons were preparing to build a settlement, though it might have been built by the government. We had but little chance to get information. The mailman was carrying the mail from Camp Verde to Fort Wingate, but we did not see him but a few times.

After crossing the Little Colorado River, we soon struck the foothills of the Mogollon Mountains. These foothills run up gradually to the steep break into the Verde Valley. On one of these long sloping foothills we camped in a spot that time could not erase from my memory. The mother was so much better that the lonely cloud lifted up, vanished away, and was forever gone during the balance of the way.

[Meanwhile, the members of the original party who had taken the southern route seemed to have had an easier time of their journey to the Verde Valley. Not until a few days before the descent into the valley does Parson Bristow's account of the way Hawkins took him coincide at Pine Springs with the path of the Burford-Dickinson-Gaddis Group.]

Tack Gaddis: The only Indians we saw were in western New Mexico or eastern Arizona. I don't know what tribe they were, but they were friendly. We came by way of St. Johns on the Little Colorado River which was just a little Mexican town. We travelled on down the river to where Holbrook is located now and beyond to Sunset Crossing, just a few miles above where the town of Winslow now stands. My folks and the Lett family stayed at this place a few days to allow their stock to rest. We were joined there by another wagon train from Arkansas. Our journey continued on through Sunset Pass and on up by Pine Springs, a station for the men carrying mail on horseback.[12]

Parson Bristow: At a place called the Indian Dam, an Indian came running down off the hill towards the team. My green steer, Tom from Eaf Gufey, got scared and ran away with the team nearly turning the wagon over a steep bank. I was hotter than the Kansas plains when the sun was shining no mercy upon man nor beast. If I had been a reach of that Indian, I would have given him a rap with my whip, but I had my hands full at the time controlling the team. If I could come across that Indian, I would settle with him yet for his ill-mannerly act.

Onward we came to Bartley's Tank where we

stayed the night before moving on to Pine Springs. Here we found a little log house built for the mail carrier to stop over night. Onward we came, and on the fourteenth day of August, we reached Stoneman's Lake. The water is down one or two hundred feet below the surface [in a volcanic crater and the only natural lake in Arizona], and abounds with fish. When we reached the lake [once known as Chaves Lake], we found Mr. Foster from Oregon. He had located on the lake, and built a little log cabin. I well remember going out about 100 yards from camp and killing a deer, the first game that was killed on the whole trip, that I can remember. Here we were having a good time.

The next noted place we came to was Rattle Snake Tank, where we stayed over night. We now had to pass through nine miles of cedar as thick as it could grow. In the road were fearful boulders as big as a half bushel and so thick that the team could hardly find room to set their feet. Here, I well remember a cow we called Old Bide. The wagon running over these boulders would violently jerk the team this way and that, until I got to feeling so sorry for Old Bide that my conscience lashed me with terrible severity. But I could only promise the old creature that when I got through I would not work her anymore. I kept that promise.

F. Ruth Jordan: My Dad would tell how they left Rattlesnake Tank in the morning, and Aunt Cumi was driving the lead wagon when out from behind the oak bushes jumped a couple of Indians, naked to the waist and all smeared with red paint. Cumi was so frightened she nearly overturned the wagon. The party of emigrants circled the wagons and prepared for an attack. All day they waited, but nothing more happened. Thinking back on it, Daddy figured maybe they were out from one of the forts hunting wild game.

Parson Bristow: Aiming for Dry Beaver Creek in the Verde Valley, we started down the mountain with cut cedar trees chained to the hind end of our wagons so as to come down easy. We stopped over night at Dry Beaver and next

Beaver Head Point where wagon road came down

morning switched across to Wet Beaver. There we found Wales Arnold and stayed all night.

F. Ruth Jordan: My father was fond of pointing out that the old road his Grandpa Bristow came down was still visible, if you look up on the side of the mountain off Beaver Head Point. When travelling south on highway 179 from Sedona, after passing through Village of Oak Creek and crossing Woods Canyon bridge, you can see that old mail route into Beaver Head. (See center for painting of Sycamore trees at Beaver Head)

Allen Bristow: You can see th' road goin' up over th' mountainside. They had t' make their own roads in places an' often tied cedar logs t' th' backs o' th' wagons t' help slow them on th' long downhill inclines. At times they even let their wagons down over some o' th' steepest hills, [more like cliffs] with ropes. They came int' th' valley at Beaver Head, which later became a stage stop. There was an historical marker there on Dry Beaver Creek north of where the Interstate crosses. [Unfortunately, in recent years the spot has been vandalized and the marker is no longer there.] That was one o' Helen's favorite places t' paint. She loved th' big sycamores an' that pond o' water around th' spring.

Grandpa Bristow followed th' Dry Beaver south t' where th' road crosses an' forks. One way went t' Camp Verde an' th' other t' Montezuma's Well. His bunch stopped at Montezuma's Well an' stayed until they looked around t' get situated. Wales Arnold had a kind o' way-station there. Ya could get some supplies an' little things. O'course it was business, but Wales an' his family helped people a whole lot.[13]

Tack Gaddis: We camped one night there [at Beaver Head]. The next day we went on to where McGuireville now stands. We got there on August 28th, 1875. My folks and the Lett family moved down to the Verde. Uncle Wales and Auntie Arnold owned what was later known as the Horseshoe Ranch on Beaver Creek. The Arnolds kept the mail station. It was a division point for the mail carried west on horseback to Prescott. My brother Will got a job herding the saddle horses that belonged to the mail line. In the summer of 1876, a new stage station was built at Beaver Head.[14]

Parson Bristow: Wales Arnold was a full-blooded Englishman and was one of the earliest settlers. From the looks of the ranch, he had lived there several years. He told about the Indians having driven off several head of large mules right before his eyes. [Around 1864, Wales Arnold was with a command of soldiers on their way through Arizona to Mexico. After his honorable discharge in Yuma, Arizona, he returned to Fort Lincoln, later named Camp Verde, to live.]

Across from Wales' place on Beaver Creek, Bill Schroeder had established himself. Bill said that he did not believe that there was any God. So the fool sayeth in his own heart that there is no God, but God is merciful to the thankful and to the unthankful. He sends his rain upon the just and upon the unjust. And day and night, and summer and winter, and heat and cold shall not cease as long as the earth abideth.

In a few days after we camped where the old adobe was afterwards built, Cumi and Rastus Hawkins went up to Prescott and were married. Then the Hawkinses moved up to Peck's Lake, (near present day Clarkdale), leaving me and Brother Lett alone.

Rowena Van Deren: My mother's parents, Preston W. Burford and Elizabeth Ann (Hornbeck) Burford landed at McGuireville on Dry Beaver Creek and built a cabin under the walnut trees there. Some of the rock wall and cave where grandmother put her milk and supplies are still there.[15]

Annie: My father had traded our home in Missouri for the cattle he brought. These were turned loose on the flats near the river with the other settlers' stock, and the children of the various families herded them during the day, driving them to their homes at night.

My mother sold butter and milk at the post [Camp Verde]. As soon as ditches could be dug from the river, grain and vegetables flourished in the rich soil. Corn was the principal grain. Wheat bread was a treat. Sometimes, as a change, we got a few loaves of baker's bread at the post. My mother did all the cooking over the fireplace in dutch ovens and iron pots, and how I used to love to watch her. Think of it now, it seems to me those patient hands were never idle.[16]

Allen Bristow: It was pretty hard scrabblin' around in those days, puttin' up livin' quarters, cuttin' that tall grass with a big hoe an' a scythe t' trade at th' fort where th' cut grass was hay for th' horses. I know one thing: Grandma made pants for my father and Uncle Buddie (Lazarus Pleasant Bristow) out of a canvas cover they had on the wagon. Yeah, she sewed them up. She didn't have a sewin' machine an' had to sew them by hand. My father called them 'shotgun pants,' and he hated them.[17]

Tack Gaddis: Father rented a part of what was later known as the Mahan Ranch on Beaver Creek in 1876, and raised a good garden, lots of watermelons. He would go to the post [Camp Verde] and sell or trade them to the soldiers for anything they had to spare that we could use. He also raised a good crop of corn and had a few head of cattle. In those days, there were no fences, so nothing could be turned loose. It was my job to herd the cattle for about four years. The Indian scouts at Camp Verde would sometimes come around and scare the life out of me. It was great sport for them.[18]

Parson Bristow: The Hance brothers [John and George] had the contract to furnish the post with hay, so I took a sub-contract from them to cut hay in the hayfield with hoes at nine dollars a ton. We moved to the Wilbur place in order to be near the work, but it was many years after that it was called the Wilbur Ranch. Jim and I cut $100 worth of hay. There were a good many Mexicans cutting hay at the same time.

Old Cottonwood Tree

A man with some cattle took up the old ranch on which I first lived. He set up some cottonwood pickets and threw on some willow brush and some dirt on the brush. That cabin was about twelve feet square. I bought him out, giving him fifteen dollars for it in the last of September, 1875. The price of flour at this time rose from $9 to $15 a 100, [pounds] but that did not last long. Bacon was forty cents a pound. I built a chimney to the house and wintered in it, and was living there when I preached at the tree.

Allen Bristow: I think it was th' first Sunday in October under th' old cottonwood tree down there at Middle Verde that Grandpa preached the first sermon.[19]

Stella Jordan: Seats were made by sawing cottonwood limbs into blocks and standing the blocks on end. The text for this first sermon was Romans 14:12 - 'So then every one of us shall give an account of himself unto God.' Among those present at this first meeting were George Hance, Mrs. Marjorie Back, Mrs. Eliza Davidson, two cowboys, and several soldiers from the post.[20]

Dora Human: My parents, James and Mary [Bristow] Human [Parson Bristow's oldest child] arrived in the Verde Valley in August of 1875. Their first child, a girl, Jane was born October 27, 1875. Their second child, a boy, died at birth in 1876. This was the first death among the early settlers. My grandfather [Parson Bristow] looked for a place to start a burial ground. They picked a place where flood waters would never cover, and it became known as Middle Verde Cemetery. In 1954, when my parents were buried there, it had nearly 200 graves.[21]

Rowena Van Deren: There was a baby born to my mother's parents [Burfords], and it died soon after birth. Mother's brother carried the little coffin on horseback and had to swim Dry Beaver to take the little body to Middle Verde Cemetery for burial. It was the second grave there, the other being a baby also.[22]

Parson Bristow: In the spring of that first year, I moved to the cottonwoods and paid the rent on the land by clearing it. We planted corn - thirteen tons of corn and got three cents a pound for it. In the fall after we had gathered and shelled the corn, I moved back to the little house and wintered there. I took 15 sacks of corn with two yoke of cattle over to the mill and had it ground into meal. Then I felt like I was back in the old country as I was eating corn bread again.

While I was out at the mill, I bought a horse from Bill Allen, who now lives on Cherry Creek. I gave him a thousand pounds of corn for that horse. Then I traded a yoke of cattle to Rile Casner for a mare. This was before I had hauled the crop down. Then I hauled the balance of the corn down with the two horses and have never worked oxen since.

On the ninth day of December, 1876, I picked up my shovel and walked up the river a little above where the old Congor Mill was built and commenced a ditch with the view to water the ranch and while I was up there the men on the O.K. Ditch [another irrigation ditch near-by] were dragging logs into the river to build a dam.

Tack Gaddis: There were six men in the O.K. Ditch Company: Mitch Birch, James Davidson, a man by the name of Hughes, Sam Dickinson, Press Burford and M.K. Gaddis. The ditch was completed to the first three ranches at Middle Verde, and they divided their land for that year with the three lower ranches. The next winter in 1877 and 1878, the ditch was completed.[23]

Parson Bristow: They had worked all summer and fall and had built their ditch. After I had worked a month or more on my ditch, Jim Human fell in with me, and on the seventeenth day of May, we got the water through to the ranch. I planted some corn and potatoes.

Allen Bristow: When John Will Ralston and Aunt Teedie (Martha Bristow) came out from Missouri in 1877, they took Grandpa Bristow's place on the west side of the river, and settled there. Grandpa farmed the east side. It was a better farm, and I think he had put in a ditch.[24]

Parson Bristow: When I look over all my past ditching, I only wish I had never worked on a ditch. If it were to do over, I never would work on a ditch. I believe that it would have gone better with me if I had preached more and ditched less. But alas, these days have gone and made their report in Eternity, and no tear nor sigh nor lamentation nor groan can bring them back. They are as unerasable as if numbered with the years before the flood.

Annie Bristow: We children were always delighted when Rev. Windes came over from Prescott. [Here he had founded the Lone Star Baptist Church in 1879] He was always jolly and told many jokes. He and my father would sit far into the night in friendly argument over the Scriptures. Rev. Windes finally changed my father from a "hardshell" to a "missionary" Baptist, and this belief he kept to the end.[25]

[Although the American Baptist Church was opposed to the rigid, "hardshell" Baptist sect, church history has it that Parson Bristow was commissioned by the American Baptist Home Missionary Society before he left from Missouri in 1875. Rev. Romulus Adolphus Windes was equally on fire to bring the Baptist brand of Christianity to Arizona. He bought a milk wagon after his graduation from the Baptist Seminary in Chicago, and converted it for travel to Arizona, where he and his wife founded the first Baptist churches. Like Parson Bristow, he had begun his preaching in the South while still in his teens.]

Allen Bristow: Grandpa Bristow preached at the Big Tree quite a bit. He was a circuit preacher and travelled to preach at Middle Verde and at Cottonwood and other places. There was quite a little story in the Baptist newspaper about him riding his old mare over to Prescott for some kind of convention.[26]

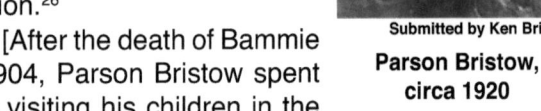

Submitted by Ken Bristow

Parson Bristow, circa 1920

[After the death of Bammie in 1904, Parson Bristow spent time visiting his children in the area, including Annie, Will and family. Near the end of his life Allen tells us that "Grandpa went to live with Aunt Agnes and Uncle Buddie, [his son Lazarus] who took care of him there until he passed away." It would seem that faith and his chewing tobacco were his comfort.]

Stella Jordan: His last sermon was preached at the 'Old Tree' on October 3, 1920, his text being Timothy I, 3:16 – "And evidently great is the mystery of Godliness, which was manifested in the flesh, was justified in the spirit, appeared unto angels, hath been preached unto the Gentiles, is believed in the world, is taken up in glory." Shortly after he answered the call, passing on at the age of almost 86 years, his son William Peyton Bristow [born during the family's first year in the Verde Valley] followed in his father's footsteps as a Baptist minister.[27]

[James C. Bristow died Saturday morning at sunrise January 29, 1921 at his home on Middle Verde. He was buried in the Middle Verde Cemetery. His granddaughter, Margaret Stoever, quotes from a local newspaper, "Mr. Bristow was as honest in his life as a citizen as he was convinced in his religious views. As a citizen no more honest, honorable man could be found. Verde Valley attended the funeral. Over 300 were present. Schools up and down the valley were closed, and flags were half masted."[28]]

F. Ruth Jordan: Bristow fervency deeply affected my family's life. My sister Ann and I would marry the oldest sons of Rev. Perry Jackson who, in the 1940's, founded, with his wife Dorothy, the mission church for Yavapai and Apaches at the site of my Great Grandfather's sermons. Over the years the American Baptists of Arizona commemorated the historical original sermon on the first Sunday of October. Folks from all over the state journeyed to the little limestone church to enjoy food, fellowship, and worship at the "Old Tree Meeting."

Larry Jackson and I both graduated from the University of Redlands where I remember opening my chapel hymnal to find that Great Grandpa Bristow's son - William Peyton Bristow had authored the University's hymn, "All Hail, U. of R."

The author of the following song was awarded the prize One Hundred Dollars, offered by a friend of the University to that student who would write the best college song of four stanzas to be set to the tune "Fair Harvard."

All hail "U. of R.!" of thy glories we sing,
  Of thy beauty and infinite worth;
With thy blue, sunny skies and thy mountains sublime,
  We proclaim thee the fairest of earth.
Like a rare, sparkling gem in its setting of gold,
  Midst the hills and the orange groves fair,
Thou dost stand in thy grandeur, the symbol of truth;
  None other with thee can compare.

By faith thou wast founded, sustained through the years,
  When thy burdens were heavy to bear;
By faith thou hast triumphed o'er doubts and o'er fears,
  And thy vict'ries the world may now share.
On eternal foundations thy buildings are reared,
  And no storm-cloud need cause thee alarm;
Upheld by the hand of Omnipotent Power,
  No foe can endanger or harm.

To thy halls have been welcomed the youth of the land,
  Whatsoever their fortunes might be;
And no bars against race, against color or creed,
  Have unjustly been raised up by thee.
But to all who have come seeking wisdom and truth,
  Thou hast been both a friend and a guide;
And the heart of thy teaching is faith, hope, and love,
  For these are the things that abide.

To the cherished ideals that gave thee thy birth,
  Thou wilt always be faithful and true;
And thy children who go to the ends of the earth,
  With thy teaching will others imbue.
May thy strength ever be as the strength of thy hills,
  And thy light as the light of the sun;
For thy God-given task ever beckons thee on
  To the heights that are yet to be won.[29]

  W.P. Bristow, '22

William Peyton Bristow was born in the first year of his parents' residence in the Verde Valley. He grew up helping his family on their ranch there and most likely gazed to the north regularly to the red cliffs at the mouth of Oak Creek - the inspiring red lands of Sedona, back-dropped by the snowy specters of Arizona's grandest extinct volcanoes. Such a childhood seems suited to the creating of hymns.

This "novel set" of travelers had Followed Their Westward Star believing they had been guided to this special locale, just as centuries ago a star had led sojourners, stopping to shine over the village of Bethlehem. Here in the Verde Valley their journey ended and they started farming, built homes, raised families and passed on to whatever rewards eternity had for them. Thus the stage of Central Arizona closed the curtain of Act III.

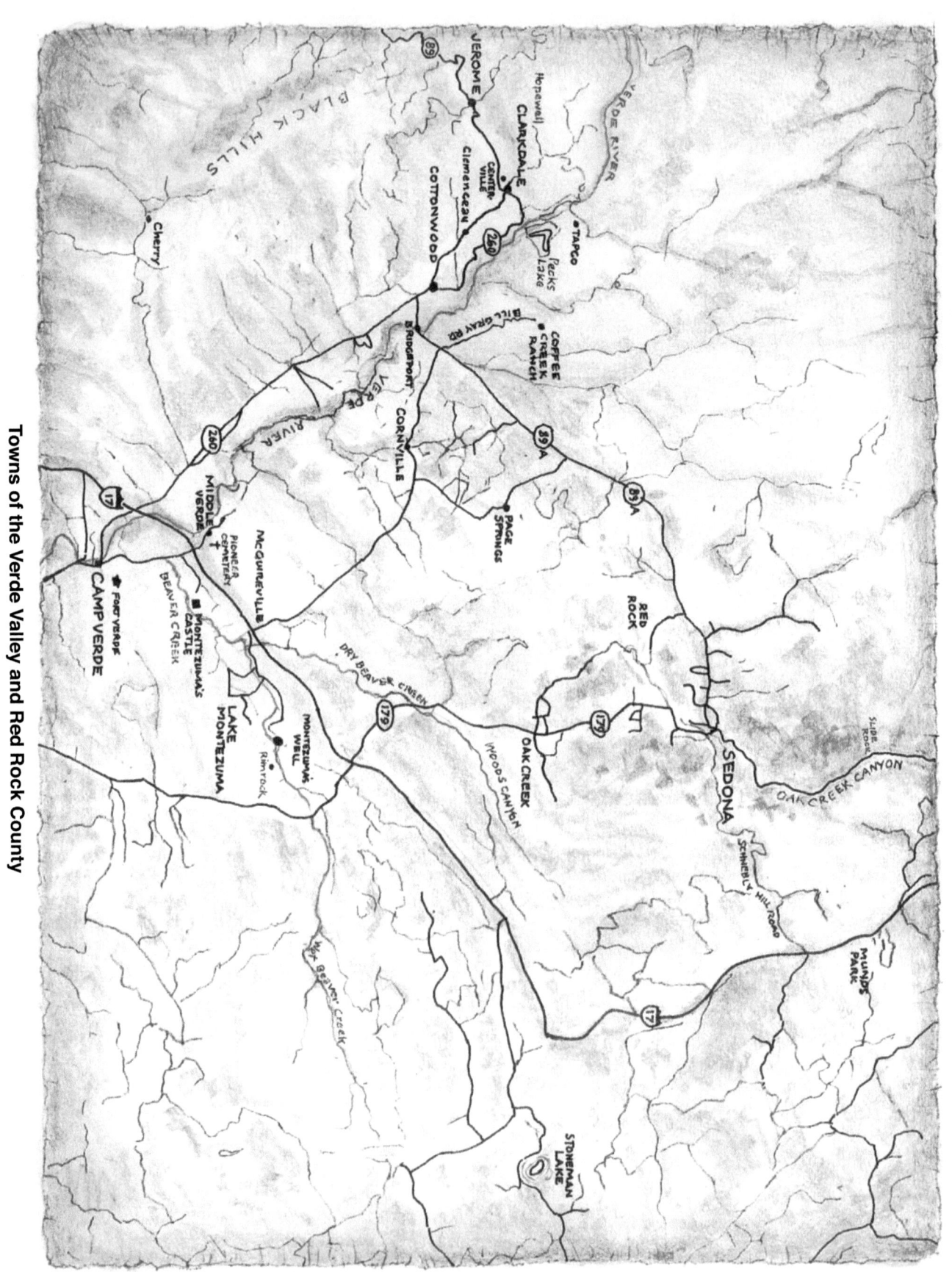

Towns of the Verde Valley and Red Rock County

FOOTNOTES

(1) Jordan, Stella M. Pioneer Stories of Arizona's Verde Valley. Comp. Mrs. John Bristow, Mrs. E.W. Monroe, and Mrs. D.W. Wingfield. Camp Verde: The Verde Valley Pioneers Association, 1933. 58.

(2) Bristow, Allen. Personal interview. 4 Feb. 1982.

(3) Burford-Dickinson, Mrs. Charles. Crossing the Plains in '75. Pioneer Stories of Arizona's Verde Valley. Comp. Mrs. John Bristow, Mrs. E.W. Monroe, and Mrs.   D.W. Wingfield. Camp Verde: The Verde Valley Pioneers Association, 1933. 22.

(4) Bristow, Allen. Personal interview. 4 Feb. 1982.

(5) Bristow, Allen. Personal interview. 4 Feb. 1982.

(6) Hawkins-Smith, Minnie. Samuel Loy and His Neighbors of 1877. Pioneer Stories of Arizona's Verde Valley. Comp. Mrs. John Bristow, Mrs. E.W. Monroe, and Mrs. D.W. Wingfield. Camp Verde: The Verde Valley Pioneers Association, 1933. 66-191.

(7) Burford-Dickinson, Mrs. Charles. Crossing the Plains in '75. Pioneer Stories of Arizona's Verde Valley. Comp. Mrs. John Bristow, Mrs. E.W. Monroe, and Mrs.   D.W. Wingfield. Camp Verde: The Verde Valley Pioneers Association, 1933. 22.

(8) Ibid

(9) Gladdis, Tack. Pioneer Stories of Arizona's Verde Valley. Comp. Mrs. John Bristow, Mrs. E.W. Monroe, and Mrs. D.W. Wingfield. Camp Verde: The Verde Valley Pioneers Association, 1954. 127.

(10) Bristow-Ralston, Mrs. Martha. Crossing the Plains from Missouri to Arizona. Pioneer Stories of Arizona's Verde Valley. Comp. Mrs. John Bristow, Mrs. E.W. Monroe, and Mrs. D.W. Smith. Camp Verde: The Verde Valley Pioneers Association, 1933. 46.

(11) Bristow-Jordan, Mrs. W.A.. Looking Down Memory's Lane. Pioneer Stories of Arizona's Verde Valley. Comp. Mrs. John Bristow, Mrs. E.W. Monroe, and Mrs. D.W. Wingfield. Camp Verde: The Verde Valley Pioneers Association, 1933. 63.

(12) Gaddis, Tack. Pioneer Stories of Arizona's Verde Valley. Comp. Mrs. John Bristow, Mrs. E.W. Monroe, and Mrs. D.W. Wingfield. Camp Verde: The Verde Valley Pioneers Association, 1954. 127.

(13) Bristow, Allen, excerpts from tapes made 2-4-82

(14) Gaddis, Tack. Pioneer Stories of Arizona's Verde Valley. Comp. Mrs. John Bristow, Mrs. E.W. Monroe, and Mrs. D.W. Wingfield. Camp Verde: The Verde Valley Pioneers Association, 1954. 127.

(15) VanDeren, Rowen. Pioneer Stories of Arizona's Verde Valley. Comp. Mrs. John Bristow, Mrs. E.W. Monroe, and Mrs. D.W. Wingfield. Camp Verde: The Verde Valley Pioneers Association, 1954. 125.

(16) Bristow-Jordan, Mrs. W.A.. Looking Down Memory's Lane. Pioneer Stories of Arizona's Verde Valley. Comp. Mrs. John Bristow, Mrs. E.W. Monroe, and Mrs. D.W. Wingfield. Camp Verde: The Verde Valley Pioneers Association, 1933. 63.

(17) Bristow, Allen. From Trail Dust to Jet Trials. Those Early Days. Comp. The Book Committee of Sedona Westerners. Cottonwood, Arizona: Verde Independent , 1968. 178.

(18) Gladdis, Tack. Pioneer Stories of Arizona's Verde Valley. Comp. Mrs. John Bristow, Mrs. E.W. Monroe, and Mrs. D.W. Wingfield. Camp Verde: The Verde Valley Pioneers Association, 1954. 127.

(19) Bristow, Allen. From Trail Dust to Jet Trials. Those Early Days. Comp. The Book Committee of Sedona

Westerners. Cottonwood, Arizona: Verde Independent , 1968. 178.

(20) Jordan, Stella M. Pioneer Stories of Arizona's Verde Valley. Comp. Mrs. John Bristow, Mrs. E.W. Monroe, and Mrs. D.W. Wingfield. Camp Verde: The Verde Valley Pioneers Association, 1933. 58.

(21) Human-Dickinson, Dora. Among the Early Settlers. Pioneer Stories of Arizona's Verde Valley. Comp. Mrs. John Bristow, Mrs. E.W. Monroe, and Mrs. D.W. Wingfield. Camp Verde: The Verde Valley Pioneers Association, 1933. N. pag.

(22) VanDeren, Rowen. Pioneer Stories of Arizona's Verde Valley. Comp. Mrs. John Bristow, Mrs. E.W. Monroe, and Mrs. D.W. Wingfield. Camp Verde: The Verde Valley Pioneers Association, 1954. 125.

(23) Gladdis, Tack. Pioneer Stories of Arizona's Verde Valley. Comp. Mrs. John Bristow, Mrs. E.W. Monroe, and Mrs. D.W. Wingfield. Camp Verde: The Verde Valley Pioneers Association, 1954. 127.

(24a) Bristow, Allen. Personal interview. 4 Feb. 1982.

(24b) Bristow, Allen. From Trail Dust to Jet Trials. Those Early Days. Comp. The Book Committee of Sedona Westerners. Cottonwood, Arizona: Verde Independent , 1968. 178.

(25) Bristow-Jordan, Mrs. W.A.. Looking Down Memory's Lane. Pioneer Stories of Arizona's Verde Valley. Comp. Mrs. John Bristow, Mrs. E.W. Monroe, and Mrs. D.W. Wingfield. Camp Verde: The Verde Valley Pioneers Association, 1933. 63.

(26) Bristow, Allen. Personal interview. 4 Feb. 1982.

(27) Jordan, Stella M. Pioneer Stories of Arizona's Verde Valley. Comp. Mrs. John Bristow, Mrs. E.W. Monroe, and Mrs. D.W. Wingfield. Camp Verde: The Verde Valley Pioneers Association, 1933. 58-59.

(28) Stoever, Margaret. Letter to the author. 15 Aug. 1996.

(29) "All Hail U. of R.." By William Peyton Bristow. 1922.

Courtesy of daughter of W. P. Bristow, Margaret Stoever, Riverside, CA 1997

Chapter Three

AT THE BREAK OF THE WESTERN WAVE

In addition to Walter Jordan's tales which are the core of this chapter, we also draw on the stories from Annie Jordan's nephew, Allen Bristow, and from stories collected on a trip, circa 1982, taken with Jesse Goddard, president of the Verde Valley Pioneer's Association in 1954 when the society published Pioneer Stories of Arizona's Verde Valley. Goddard's father, Bill Godard, "first came to the Verde Valley from Pueblo, Colorado about 1890. He eventually returned to Pueblo, and married in 1892."[1] A few years later he came back to the Verde Valley with his wife, Jesse's mother. All the contributors of this chapter were born in the Verde Valley. You might say they are the new natives, with the exception of Smylie, the Apache scout, whose tale has been lifted from the pages of Pioneer Stories of Arizona's Verde Valley.

As the Verde Valley became a "break in the wave" of the western migration, the settlers found Yavapai and Apache people residing in a nomadic type of existence. The old timers often referred to them as Mohave Apache and Tonto Apache and some even agreed with Walter that "There's three different tribes, Yavapai, Apache-Mohave an' Tonto. That's the way I understand it. They's all cousins or closely related but they's not o' th' renegade bands that Geronimo's an' Cochise's followers were. Th' Verde Valley Apaches were more like th' White Mountain Apaches that're cousins t' th' Cochise an' Geronimo tribes. Ole Geronimo's group was really renegades an' not really accepted b' most o' th' Arizona Apaches."

Jesse Goddard recollected differently, "Darned if I ever heard of a Yavapai Indian until I was 30 years old. They was always Apaches an' Tontos."

Jesse Goddard along General Crook Trail circa 1985

Speaking of Apaches and Geronimo, many stories have been passed along only verbally, becoming a part of our oral history. One of these goes that every time Geronimo got cold or hungry he would give himself up, surrender, get back into captivity, acquire some more clothing and food. Then when he was ready, he would break out and take off again. He always headed for Mexico where, of course, none of the U. S. Army could follow. Cartoonists even depicted Geronimo on the south side of the border looking back at soldiers and thumbing his nose!!

The Yavapai, mistakenly called Mohave Apache, are actually of similar ancestral background and language group as the Mohave, (located in northwestern AZ), but totally unrelated to the Apache. Although both groups were hunters and gatherers the Yavapai were better farmers. There even had been a small population living in Oak Creek Canyon and farming a little clearing which still bears the name, Indian Gardens. From here they fled the newcomers, leaving behind their garden. Although they grew some of their food, both groups led nomadic lives depending on "nature" and their surroundings for survival. In 1875, about the time of Parson Bristow's arrival, the Yavapai were moved from the Prescott area to a reservation at Camp Verde, which was under the watchful eyes of the soldiers at the nearby fort.

From the collection of Milton V. Lee

Geronimo (R) Natche (L) mid 1870s just after capture at Ford Bowie

On the eastside of the Verde the government had established a military compound known as Fort Lincoln, then called Fort Verde when moved to the westside and further south. Today it bears the third and final name, Camp Verde. To this army outpost several officials were sent by President Grant to promote a peace policy. It was hoped that a way could be found to solve peacefully the problem of land rights in the Verde Valley, through negotiations, not arms, and by replacing the corrupt Indian agents with reservations operated by Protestant churches.

From the collection of Milton V. Lee

Apache pole gambling game mid 1870s

In 1869 General Stoneman, (Stoneman Lake bears his name) commander of the Department of Arizona, added to these peaceful attempts by beginning schools for the Indians. Walter believes because of this training program, Will Jordan, (Walt's dad), was able, several years later, to hire English speaking Apaches who understood how he farmed. For a while the Indians were given the opportunity to come to the reservations voluntarily and work for the farmers. Although a number came to, or were placed on the reservations, many left and joined uncaptured renegade bands.

Despite the good intentions of the government, the settlers got along with the Indians no better than the various groups got along with each other. The Apache wanted their land back and the newcomers had no intention of cooperating. The natives continued guerilla warfare and raids, and the settlers continued to harass until the U.S. military resolved to end the conflict by removing the Indians. To accomplish this task General Stoneman was replaced by General Crook, although peaceful settlement was still being attempted.

After arriving in 1871, General Crook spent the remainder of the peaceful experimentation time astride his mule, visiting most of the reservations, learning the topography, and continuing to study the Apache's habits and techniques, later using what he learned to subdue and corral them. He waited until wintertime when they would have to be moving more for food and their fires would disclose their location. As the pursued could go where horses could not, the cavalrymen were told to "park" their horses and to follow on foot when necessary. Imagine the grumbling of cavalry personnel upon becoming regular army foot soldiers! They were also ordered to destroy any caches of food they found, thus increasing the "economic warfare" strategy. Walter told of a dramatic surrender, which was a direct result of these attacks on the winter food supply. "When one ole brave brought 'is bunch t' th' fort 'e was s' weak 'e just lay down on th' ground, usin' a sagebrush bush fer a pillow. 'E was overheard mumblin' t' a scout, 'We're hungry. We're sick. We're finished'. So that's how all o' 'em in that bunch came t' b' captives!" In addition, General Crook used the ongoing feud between the Yavapai and the Apache, as well as that between different Apache bands, to his advantage by hiring ones from opposite groups to spy on the others and serve as scouts. The enticement of army pay and other privileges was an additional factor in persuading many to change sides, developing a semblance of loyalty to the army. According to Lieutenant John G. Bourke, these scouts were invaluable. "It grew increasingly apparent that the success of the troops depended on the scouts. Without the scouts, the troops couldn't find the enemy; with the scouts they

From the collection of Milton V. Lee

Apache Scout and family, mid 1870s

rarely missed. It was as simple as that." He added, "The longer we knew the scouts the better we liked them."[2]. Supposedly when a powerful, tough old chief, Charleypun (pronounced Charley Pan), arrived at Fort Verde to surrender he confirmed the value of the scouts by telling Crook something to the effect of, "We could have fought the soldiers and won but could not fight each other at the same time!" According to Rose Hawk, author of Tuzigoot National Monument, he declared "We are not afraid of the Americans alone, but we cannot fight you and our own people together!"[3]

Many times the military unit would pause for the night, thinking they had a group surrounded, only to awaken in the morning to find, like the silent night wind, their prey was gone leaving no trace. Such was the situation where one of the few battles near Sedona was fought in Soldier Basin. The evening following the battle, all seemed under control with the enemy having no escape route. However, the next morning, to the army's great dismay, all of the Apaches had slipped through the underbrush, over Brin's Mesa to the northwest, into Dry Creek and vanished. Old rifle shells and uniform buttons can still be found at the battle site. (The dry wash draining from the area and dividing Sedona from West Sedona is called Soldiers Wash in memory of the battle.) This illustrates well the stealth and cunning of these warriors, showing how, when pursued "the band would split up like a covey of quail only to rendezvous at another point miles away."[4]

The combined tactics employed by General Crook worked in moving the Indian Wars of the Verde Valley toward a close. Crook believed that the main hope for the survival of these nomadic people was to settle down and become farmers. This became the goal in establishing the reservations at Middle Verde and Camp Verde, so irrigation ditches were dug and the Indians began tending crops. According to some, they seemed to be happy here. Crook promised to treat them fairly if they would promise to live peacefully. His plan apparently was working until the spring of 1875 when he was unfortunately transferred out of Arizona and his successor had a much different viewpoint. Crook was so angered, when even the faithful scouts were taken captive and sent to faraway reservations, that he attempted to persuade Washington officials to change their policies. His pleas fell on deaf ears, as no change was made. It is said that he then visited some of the scouts in captivity letting them know he still would honor his agreements, but he had been overruled. The tribal leaders believed him for he had always kept his promises, and for this they respected and trusted him. Belief in his credibility was shown several years later when news of his death reached the Apache at San Carlos, they wept. The greatest tribute was given to him by Red Cloud of the Sioux saying "He, at least, never lied to us."[5] Charles M. Robinson III, an expert on military affairs in the American West, wrote a biography of Crook, entitled "General Crook and the Western Frontier". (Published by University of Oklahoma Press, Norman, OK, 2001) Robinson is quoted in Wild West Magazine, "As an Indian fighter, Crook gained fame. As a humanitarian, he achieved greatness."[6] Political pressure and Washington's desire to put all Apache bands, plus the Yavapais, on the same land, eventually caused the move to San Carlos.

Although a number of years later the government had a "change of heart" and bought several farms in Middle Verde, establishing a place for both tribes to live jointly, to which the folks who chose could return. Only one major problem, it was for both Apaches and Yavapais. However, these folks were not friends and many problems arose. Even as late as the 1950s and 1960s, the two groups were still having their feuds, particularly at the time of electing a joint tribal council, etc. During those years there would be knifings and even a murder was mentioned. Each division wanted to have total control and their own distinct leadership.

One of the stories originating from the era of relocation involves the naming of the highest part of the mountains southwest of Camp Verde, Squaw Peak. Using a vivid imagination one can see the profile of a young woman lying down with her hair flowing back up the mountain to the west. It is said that when the last of the Apaches were being rounded-up to be taken to San Carlos, a young woman took her small son up on the mountain to hide. When found, she refused to go with the soldiers, putting up quite a fight. The ending to this struggle takes three directions depending upon who is telling it. One: The soldiers killed both her and her son and buried them on the mountain; two: She killed herself and her son by jumping over the cliff; and three: (which seems the most likely), eventually the soldiers brought both of them down to the fort at Camp Verde. There they joined the group for "The Long Walk," to the eastern edge of the territory. In any event, the mountain resembles the profile of a maiden lying down and is called Squaw Peak.

Naming the mountains may have been easier for the people of the wave from the eastern United States than distinguishing between the native peoples and calling them by the names they had chosen for themselves. (All mountains and geographic areas of importance referred to in the text are found on the map on page 86.) The settlers often gave the mountains, canyons etc., their own names or that of a person who settled near-by, for example: Lee Mountain, Munds Mountain and Munds Park, Wilson Mountain, Casner Canyon, Schnebly Hill. Sometimes the mountains were given the name of prevalent wildlife such as Bee Mountain and Porcupine Mountain; also names came from imagined likenesses, i.e., Bell Rock, or stories, as with Squaw Peak in the Verde Valley, which is by no means the only one on western horizons so named for the imagined reclining female form. (Although the word "Squa" was originally attributed to the Massachusetts Indians in the mid-1600s, meaning "young woman", in later years it acquired a vulgar connotation. Indian tribes have, in recent times petitioned unsuccessfully to change these appellations of the landscape.)

Dell Quail, an old Apache man, epitomized the exact opposite of our stereotype of ferocious Apaches. In his peaceful, soft-spoken manner, he recounted some memories of the move to San Carlos. When it was decided to move all Indians from the Verde Valley to San Carlos, no exceptions were made. He stated that those who were too old, too sick, or just plain refused to go, "were given poison by the white 'medicine man.'"[7] However, what most likely was happening was that the army personnel were trying to help those with malaria. Due to the swampy conditions of the Valley in those years, malaria was a big problem for all, including Anglos. The only known treatment at that time was quinine, which apparently caused severe allergic reactions among some of the Indians. Being unaware of this, instead of helping, the cavalry doctors were unwittingly intensifying the illness and in many instances causing death.

The trail from the Verde Valley to San Carlos, over which the Indians were marched, was a part of the military road that General Crook was instrumental in getting built. It stretched across the Arizona territory connecting the forts east and west. This greatly aided in the campaigns against the Apaches and in keeping the peace. Many who came after were grateful, as it made travel much easier through some mighty rough terrain, including mountains,

General Crook marker and Jesse

rivers and canyons. This, some have said, was Crooks' greatest legacy to Arizona. Today the highway going from Camp Verde to Payson, state route 260, follows along a portion of the old military road and is called General Crook Road. Traveling this highway Jesse commented that he thought it had mainly been used for "pack outfits." Pointing to some little metal "b's" fastened to trees, as well as large "B's" emblazoned on other trunks, he stated, "See that? There's another one right there. That shows where this road crosses over the old road. Ya' betcha', it goes back and forth lots o' times. Looka' there! That's even a piece o' the old road ya' can see! Oh, it was a rough bugger!"

Although supposedly all Indians were on the reservations, peace was not assured because numerous ones kept bolting and stirring up trouble. Such was the situation when Parson Bristow's group arrived. From his mother's stories, Walter recalls, "Our government 'ad a company o' soldiers out there at Camp Verde when m' mother first arrived. She was six years old. They was protectin' all th' farmers all through th' Valley. It was some o' them soldiers an' Indians that come t' that Cottonwood tree t' hear Grandpa preach 'is first sermon in October after they'd gotten t' Middle Verde. They'd been havin' s' many massacres with them wild Apaches, an' they was still catchin' 'em when m' mother landed there. They'd catch 'em an' take 'em over t' Fort Whipple an' tame 'em down. Why, Mama says when she was small they 'ad t' sit on th' porch an' watch fer Indians, or hobos, or bad guys. [In other words, anyone they didn't know]. If anyone came near, they'd run, a'yellin', 'Mama! Mama! Mama!' She, (my grandmother Bammie), would git th' kids inside, bar them doors with tables an' chairs an' wait on th' front porch with 'er big kettle o' boilin' water. She al'ays had one ready. She'd give a warnin' fer 'em t' stop. Some o' 'em were smart an' left, not gittin' any closer. If they didn't say who they was an' kept a comin', she slung that ole pot o' scaldin' water all over 'em! Mama says that after one such incident, [no one knows who the recipient of the treatment was], all persons o' ill intent made a wide berth 'round Bammie Bristow's cabin! Yes sir, they did! Oh say, did ya' know that m' mother Annie adopted th' same thing when livin' in 'er own home on Upper Verde?" As so often happened when Walter would finish telling a story he ducked his head, gave it a shake and with a chuckle would begin the next tale. "Oh well, That's a yarn fer 'nother day."

Parson Bristow was away a lot of the time caring for another homestead about 30 miles north at Upper Verde, later known as Clarkdale. His wife and children were alone at the Middle Verde home and she knew she needed to protect the family. She didn't want to learn to shoot a gun so instead she devised the boiling water method.

The last battle between the Apache and the U.S. Military would not be fought until July 17, 1882, — the Battle of Big Dry Wash. Jesse Goddard relates this historical event. "Th' trouble first started with th' Battle o' Big Dry Wash with a medicine man an' th' religious practice o' ghost dancin' over at Cibecu on th' San Carlos Reservation. Th' medicine man [Nakaidoklini, educated at a Christian school in Santa Fe] was kind o' a god. Ya' know he was a'gonna get rid o' all th' white people an' bring back all th' Indians that were ever killed an' have th' buffalo back an' all th' game an' ever'thing. 'E had them Indians all crazy, so th' soldiers arrested 'im. This stirred up th' Apaches an' even most o' th' scouts turned against th' soldiers. (See center for painting of crown dancers)

"That was in August o' 1881, an' then in 1882, well there was a bunch that broke off, 54 renegades — White Mountain Apaches. They kidnapped a few squaws, took horses, ammunition, an' ever'thing they wanted an' went up north pretty close t' Globe int' a minin' camp up there. Them miners'd been tipped off, an' they put their women an' children in an old mine shaft there, an' they were all set t' fight. Th' renegades were so darn mad they killed a group o' three men at those ranches there an' burned the places. All the soldiers from Fort Apache, Fort Thomas an' Fort Whipple got after 'em an' tracked their path o' destruction up on th' Mogollon Rim until they come to General Springs [named for General Crook]. Here them Apaches could look back up in th' canyon where th' soldiers were comin' through. [At this spot the cavalry leaders decided to try to trick their enemy.] Them Apaches thought th' cavalry had all white horses, an' they could see them white horses a'comin', but they couldn't see th' bays an' th' blacks in th' thick growth, so they thought that's all that was after 'em. They counted them white horses, an' they knew how many, an' they thought they could lay a trap fer that many. But instead, th' soldiers managed t' encircle th' Apache position. I think, like th' Indians do, that if it'd been some o' them old guys like Victorio, or Cochise, or Geronimo, they would'a known all that was behind them white horses. They'd 'ave gotten up on top o' th' mountain an' scattered like a bunch o' waves. The Battle o' Big Dry Wash never would 'ave happened."[8]

Stopping to look at a marker, "As ya' can tell they got this here marker in th' wrong place. Maybe it is put where them soldiers camped. Darn it, th' battle took place all th' way cross that big canyon!" As he points across to the proper location, we get a glimpse of Jesse's determination to have the history recorded correctly, and a misplaced marker offended his sense of accuracy.

Monument at the Battle of Big Dry Wash

The Marker reads:

"The Battle of the Big Dry Wash. July 17, 1882.
Just below are rock nests hastily built by a group of Apaches who had left the San Carlos Apache Reservation and hoped to ambush the pursuing troops of the United States Cavalry. Al Seiber's scouts discovered the trap, which enabled the soldiers to engage a frontal attack while flanking parties encircled the Apache position and attacked from the rear. A bitter four hour fight ensued which was halted by darkness and a heavy storm of hail and rain during which surviving Indians escaped by slipping through the soldiers' line back to the reservation."

On the back side of the monument all of the names of the cavalrymen and scouts who fought in the battle are listed. The only ones named to have been killed were Joseph McLernen of the cavalry and Private Pete of the scouts. Jesse suggests that perhaps Pete was one of the very few scouts to attempt to desert and join family members on the Apache side. "Maybe Pete saw his Dad an' brother in there so he throwed his gun down, an' took off. When Al Sieber told him to stop, he didn't so Sieber killed him."[9] One might wonder if possibly he was killed in the line of duty.

Besides the two who lost their lives several were wounded. Jesse continues, "Well, now there was a guy b' th' name o' Morgan. He was th' head o' a bunch o' troops an' he got wounded. It's funny, there was a bullet hit his arm, hit a rib an' went around an' lodged in his back. They thought he was shot though th' lungs so he wouldn't live, but that bullet went right on around him. It didn't go through him at all! That rib sent it in a different direction an' he lived t' get over it.

"But that ain't all. Well now, I'll tell ya th' crueler one. They'd left a guard over there [at the battle site]. Next mornin' that guy heard a moanin' and carryin' on so they had a group start t' go see what th' heck it was. Suddenly someone was a' shootin' at 'em, shot at 'em three times, so they just backed off. Pretty soon they rushed that place an' it was a real shock. It was a Indian gal about nineteen years old that had a six month old baby an' a old Indian woman. She fought 'em like th' dickens, that young'un did, even with a bad leg wound. Used a knife 'cause she was out o' ammunition, but they got her on a stretcher an' brought her over here. [Indicating the area that seemed to have been the main camp spot]. They was so busy helpin' their own soldiers they left her be. A big storm come up rainin' so hard with ice an' things that her an' that baby was drenched in ice cold water. Them Army guys couldn't get t' her that day — too busy, I guess — so then the next day they cut her leg off above her knee. Just cut that leg off without any kind o' pain killer, or nothin' whatsoever. Well not only that, there's two stories. I'll tell you about it. One, they fixed a crude saddle outfit an' put her on a mule an' give'r her baby, an' that ole squaw led 'em an' went t' Fort Apache. [Over 100 miles by today's roads.] Took 'em 'bout a week t' get there with the leg cut off an' that baby. Another story, they took her t' Camp Verde. Danged, if I don't believe that the three o' 'em went t' Fort Apache 'cause a guy said he'd seen 'er there two months after that a' goin' around with a crude crutch."[10]

As the battle ended the Indians made a hasty retreat and apparently some folks took it upon themselves to be heroes. Jesse got a real kick out of relaying this next portion of history: "I'll explain t' ya' what happened there. There was a bunch o' guys frum Globe 'at called theirselves th' Globe Rangers. They was a'gonna show them soldiers up, [for letting some escape] so they took off after them Indians, a'trailin' 'em. They took along lots o' good whiskey too! An' about that second night out they camped at an ole' place, an' either 'ad their horses hobbled out, or in the corral. About daylight next mornin' th' Indians shot a few shots int' th' camp an' then took off with them guys' horses. So them hot shot rangers 'ad t' walk back t' Globe. I imagine that they wasn't so smart when they found out that they was afoot, by God!"[11] [Here Jesse paused for a good laugh.] (See center for colored picture of Ruth Jordan and Jesse Goddard)

Still chuckling, he continued by shifting thoughts to tell of an experience some of the soldiers had while on the road back to their fort. (Probably Fort Whipple.) "One thing them soldiers found when they come t' a place that'd burnt, was a charred body. Somebody'd died, burnt up. So they give that body a decent burial. They named the remains, 'Christopher'. I guess so's they could put a marker. About that time the ol' man who'd lived there came back. Laughin' so hard he barely could talk he said he'd had two cabins an' th' Indians'd burnt both o' 'em. Earlier that ol' man'd killed a bear an' put it in one o' them cabins an' that was what those soldiers gave a decent burial! That bear, named Christopher!!" Jesse slapped his thigh in amusement and continued laughing. He concluded, "I imagine that's how Christopher Creek got its name."[12]

After returning to Fort Verde the loyalty of the scouts was demonstrated, as Jesse describes it: "They claim that there was so many o' them soldiers, that th' Indians was pretty near all wounded b'fore they got away, but one thing that was funny. There was an ol' Indian, one o' their scouts, right after this fight, not long after they got back t' Fort Apache, discovered five o' them Indians had got away from 'em an' 'ad went back t' th' mountains. He went an' told th' officers, 'Let's go git 'em an' kill 'em.' That's how loyal they was t' th' army when they took a job. Th' only time some o' 'em ever turned on the soldiers was at Cibeque when the medicine man 'ad 'em all stirred up. Most really stayed on th' soldiers' side. Why some even won medals. That Smiley from my memory in later years at Camp Verde had medals all over him."[13]

Occasionally small groups of Indians would create great trauma among the new inhabitants. Walter relates one of these hair-raising tales as told by his father Will Jordan: "My Dad could sure tell some wild stories an' oh boy! This is one 'e loved t' tell, an' this is th' way it went:

"B'fore m' mother an' father were married, Dad was livin' on Upper Verde. He an' a young man [approximately sixteen years old] named Tack Gaddis were down grubbin' out th' willows. [Tack had come west with Parson Bristow's group]. Across th' river was an open flat, an' Tack always had his eyes open fer wild Indians. Oh my! What a big scare these two had! While Tack an' Dad were workin' one day Tack suddenly got real excited an' half whispered, 'Looka there, Mr. Jordan! There's nine Indians over there. Look at 'em runnin' all over that flat. They're on horses. Look at them feathers in their heads! They even got rifles!'

"'Well, let's make a run fer th' cabin,' Dad ordered.

"Now, th' cabin was up on Rattlesnake Hill, where I was born an' raised an' quite a ways away. Tack says, 'Oh, no. I'm goin' t' hide out in th' brush.'

"Dad rushed t' the cabin an' was still loadin' shells with buck shot when th' whole string o' 'em, rode up t' 'is open door. They rode up right in front o' that door, nine o' 'em, but this first one, why, there was just blood all over 'im. It just frightened Dad nearly t' death. 'E thought 'e was a goner fer sure, but right over his door, 'e 'ad 'is old six-shooter there fer a emergency. The only way ya' could cock it was if ya' threw it down real hard an' brought it up right quick, then ya' could fire one shot b'fore ya ad t' throw it down again. [Walt demonstrates the action.] 'E figured, 'Well, I'll git th' leader b'fore 'e gits me.' Dad grabbed that gun off'a th' sill an' had it ready t' fire in a second's time, but that ole' Indian was faster. Dad saw him come up with 'is hand, an' b'tween two fingers 'e held out somethin' white an' hollered,

"'Don't shoot! Don't shoot!'

"He just kept sayin' that - 'Don't shoot!'"

"Dad walked out there scared half t' death. 'E still 'ad 'is gun on 'im, an' that Indian said ag'in, 'Don't shoot!' an' handed Dad th' slip o' paper. Dad saw it was a pass t' go deer huntin' frum th' government in Prescott. Dad said, 'What ya' got that blood all over ya' fer?'

"'Me kill'um big buck.'"

"The leader pointed out a nice little flat north o' th' cabin in th' mesquite an' said 'Want'um camp.'"

"'Alright, go ahead.' What else ya' goin' say t' nine armed Apaches?

"They went 'round back with their pack animals an' they pulled off all this stuff an' set up camp not far frum th' cabin. 'E let 'em camp there. Then th' borrowin' got started. First visit t' th' cabin, 'Want'um salt', second trip 'Want'um fryin' pan', an' last time 'Want'um lard.' Dad couldn't figger 'em out. 'What in th' world are they a'tryin' t' do t' me?'

"After dark Tack Gaddis come in frum 'is hidin' place. 'E was scared half t' death o' them Indians. Oh, ever'body was when they heard o' an Indian break out. Father said t' Tack, 'Well now Tack, I'll tell ya what I'm a'gonna do. I'm a'gonna put on m' rubber boots an' climb outta that back win'der an' go down over th' hill as fast as I cin about a mile an' a half t' our neighbors. I'm a'gonna wake 'em up t' see if they know anythin' about them Indians. I'm not too well satisfied. Ya' stay here an' don't ya' light a match er a light o' any kind 'cause they'll see ya' movin' through them chinks in th' logs.

From the collection of Milton V. Lee

Geronimo just prior to his death in 1909

Ya' stay here in th' dark. With a light, they could pick ya' off any second.'

"S' Dad put on 'is rubber boots an' 'e climbed outta th' winder on th' opposite side o' th' Indian camp. 'E went, 'e thought, real quiet like. When 'e got t' th' neighbor's about one o'clock in th' mornin', th' man's wife heard th' word Indians, an' th' only thing that would'a made 'er scream louder was if she'd heard th' name 'Geronimo.'" Here Walt paused while he had a good chuckle.

"'Calm down! Calm down! Will thinks there might b' no trouble.'

"'Do ya know anythin' about them nine Indians?'

"'Well, let's go wake Jack Duff up.'

"An' they did. Th' place where Jack Duff'd seen that bunch o' Indians that day is still called Duff's Mesa.

"'Yes, I think I saw them very Indians out there, an' they was chasin' all 'round, an' I'll tell ya' what they're a'doin'. Apaches're crazy about th' mockin'birds, an' when th' young mockin'bird gits off'a th' nest fer 'is first time, 'e ain't very strong. They can only fly a little distance at a time. Them Apaches were chasin' mockin'birds. When they catch 'em, they put 'em in cages, an' they love t' hear 'em sing. Yes, I think that's th' very bunch o' Indians, an' your description o' th' pass all fits in. I'd say they've been released frum th' fort on good behavior, just like th' pass said, an' it's likely ya' don't have t' worry about 'em.'

"S' Dad went back home. When 'e got there, Tack Gaddis was sittin' at th' table with th' lamp, an old kerosene lamp, lit. Dad really bawled 'im out, 'My goodness alive!! Don't ya know they could'a picked ya off any second!'

"'Mr. Jordan, I warn't gonna stay here alone in th' dark.'

"S', it went on that night – nothin' happened. Next mornin', th' leader brought Dad a quarter o' venison an' 'is fryin' pan. They 'ad their pack horses all ready t' head out. Th' leader thanked 'im fer allowin' 'em t' stay overnight, an' Dad's heart went back down int' th' right place. When th' leader turned t' walk away, 'e said, 'Hear'um ya' go out last night.'

"Them Indians warn't nobody's fools. They 'ad a guard on that night. There'r other stories like that. One time Tom Hawkins, then a half-grown kid, was ridin' th' Hawkins' race horse, accordin' t' others, 'Charlie' an' carryin' a basket o' eggs t' market at th' minin' camp [Jerome] goin' on th' Peck's Lake Trail. 'E was scared stiff b' a blood-smeared Apache leader, but th' bunch passed 'im with a few friendly 'Hows.' When 'e thought it was safe, 'e set down that basket o' eggs, an' put old Charlie t' 'is best speed. Back over that trail 'e went just a'flyin'. 'E got home an' told 'is brother Emery that there were a band o' warriors comin'. B'fore an Indian was in sight, Emery grabbed a gun an' threw it acrost th' front fence all ready t' fire away, but th' Indians waved a paper, (like my Dad's story,) an' shouted, 'Don't shoot! Don't shoot!'"

Many admired the endurance and stamina of the Indians. Will recalled one of his trips up Copper Canyon, the route of I-17 west of Camp Verde which was constructed nearly 75 years later. He was on his way to Fort Whipple with a wagon load of produce when a couple of "braves" came running down the road. He stopped and through a few words with many hand gestures he surmised that they wanted to know if he had any chewing tobacco. He reached under the wagon seat producing a plug of the brown stuff. Each of the three took a big junk and indicated that they were going to Fort Apache to visit. Walt quotes his Dad as saying, "Boy them fellers sure could cover th' territory. When they'd set of a jig-joggin' they'd cover up t' sixty miles a day."

Submitted by Charles Jordan
Apache wickie up, mother and children

Will Jordan hired from both tribes of Indians in the valley, but he could not put them in the same field to work together without disruptions. At one time he had six of the men working, two Tonto Apaches, and four Yavapais. Three of these gentlemen had been educated while on the San Carlos Reservation, which was a real benefit in communicating. They had also learned some farming techniques, possibly under General Crook's program. These skills were also helpful to Will.

Although they camped on opposite sides of the river, their feuding led to tragedy, like the story of Justin Head.

Walter remembers, "That was when I was a boy over there, an' I've heard m' Uncle John Bristow tell th' story many a time. Th' Tonto Apaches an' th' Mohave, [Yavapais], were enemies an' they kept their wigwams, [wickieups, made like a brush arbor with skins or fabric thrown over the top], about a half a mile apart. When they'd git liquored up a little on Tiswin or Chudapie, hell was a poppin'. They'd make th' Chudapie outta juniper berries, I think, an' th' Tiswin outta th' Spanish currants like th' ones growin' right out there in our front yard, standin' right out there. [Pointing out to bushes in the front yard at his home in Sedona] They have little white or red berries.

"Justin Head was a Tonto Apache, an' George Beauty was Apache Mohave, [Yavapai], an' they both worked fer Dad. Justin Head 'ad a beautiful wife, an' George Beauty got stuck on 'er. She got t' goin' with George Beauty, an' Justin Head went on th' war path. 'E shot George Beauty through th' elbow an' all th' rest o' them Indians hid out. Then Beauty went down in th' valley, an' 'e stopped at Cottonwood t' get all th' Apache Mohaves 'e could t' help 'im. 'E killed a Tonto, one named Frog, b'fore 'e led th' rest o' th' bunch after Justin Head.

"My Uncle John Bristow 'ad cattle in that wild country down in there [south of Cottonwood] an' he saw 'em tryin' t' kill Justin. Uncle John was on 'is horse when 'e heard a shot fired, so 'e got t' lookin' with that Black Beauty Telescope that 'e carried with 'im, an' 'e witnessed that shootout. They were a'firin' at Justin Head, an' it was a long range off. Head was watchin' 'em, an' 'he saw th' smokes o' th' guns, 'e'd fall t' try t' fool 'em. They finally captured 'im, an' they put 'im in the penitentiary at Florence where 'e died o' consumption. [Tuberculosis] My, but that was terrible. 'E was wonderful — a highly educated Indian, talked English as well as any o' us. Pete Ocotillo was th' only other Indian I knew who could speak English that good."

Stella, an older sister of Walter's, loved photography and would practice "picture taking" on everybody. One day she chased an Indian woman around the house three times trying to take her picture. In exasperation she asked Chester, her oldest brother, to help her. The idea was Chester would pretend to have a camera and chase the woman from one direction and Stella would wait around a corner and snap the picture as the "racers" passed by. This didn't prove to be terribly successful either. One day Stella asked Pete Ocotillo, "Why in the world do you people hate to have your picture taken?"

"Oh, we're dark, we look bad," Pete replied.

"No you won't, not in the picture. You'll look white!"

Walt picks up the story: "My sister knew how t' develop pictures, so finally she got Pete an' his wife an' Lily t' come over, that's their daughter, t' have their pictures taken. Lily was a beautiful young girl. One o' th' most beautiful Indian girls I ever saw. They come over an' Stella took them pictures an' developed 'em. Oh, my, when she showed 'em how they looked, they took them pictures over t' that tribe o' Indians an' passed 'em around. All that whole bunch come t' our place an' Stella 'ad more pictures t' take than she could take care o'.

"But before all o' this, George gotta hold o' a picture taken o' Jim Mockin'bird when 'e was a'splittin' wood fer m' father, an' oh, it was a good picture. George took it out there t' th' wood pile t' show it t' 'im. That's where this fella was a'splittin' wood an' ol' Jim 'ad 'is axe way up in th' air a'ready t' come down on that block. [Walt demonstrates with his hands high above his own head.] I told George, 'Don't git any closer! Git away from there, George! What'r ya' a'doin'?' That's b'fore they knew that their picture wouldn't b' dark, s' I told 'im, 'Stop right there! or Jim Mockin'bird's gonna hit ya' with that axe.' Well, 'e didn't git no closer an' got t' keep that good picture." (See center for Apache Baskets)

Halley's Comet

A few in Walter's generation (including himself), had the privilege of being alive for two showings of Halley's Comet. As a young man he recalls some of the happenings during the first appearance. "When Halley's Comet came into view in 1910, there was singin' an' tom-tom beatin' all night long, an' I said, 'Hey, what's th' matter with ya' Indians over there?'" (See center for painting of Indian Drum.)

"'Well, we're scared an' we're askin' them spirits t' keep that thing away. That thing is gonna hit th' ground.'

"'No, no. That thing is in a orbit? It'll keep a'goin' on in that way until it comes back around agin where we can see it in 76 years.'" [Probably Walt learned the length of the orbital cycle many years later and added it to the story. One of the beauties of oral history—it grows as time passes!]

"Everyone sees it now in our telescopes. Just think o' that! M' them are powerful things – seein' that comet travelin' at that terrific speed!"

It is doubtful that Walt's assurances were of much comfort to the Natives, as they continued to pray to their gods.

As more and more people returned to the Middle Verde Reservation, The American Baptist Denomination founded a mission church. For many years, that first Baptist service of Parson Bristow's continued to be celebrated by a large multiracial group at this location. It was here that the parents of Walt's future sons-in-law, Rev. and Mrs. Perry Jackson, constructed one of three small churches serving the Yavapais and Apaches of the Verde Valley. Somehow the "Break in the Western Wave" had extra meaning when two of Parson Bristow's great-granddaughter's married Jackson boys who became ministers. Larry and Ruth became missionaries to the Navajo people, descendants of the shepherds the wagon train group had seen near Fort Wingate.

Approximately 100 years after the Bristows had arrived at Middle Verde, a special monument was placed in memory of Parson J. C. Bristow and his ministry. Here in the yard of the little stone church, beside the monument a living memorial tree was planted. A great-great-grandson, Kevin Jackson, son of F. Ruth, had the privilege of preparing the ground. Present that day were grandsons Walter Jordan and Allen Bristow with their wives, Ruth and Stella, as well as Walter's daughter Ruthie (F. Ruth). (See photo page 43)

Marker commemorating Parson Bristow's first sermon

The nomadic, hostile people found by the settlers at the breaking of the western wave, are still mostly on reservations. Here they have developed farming, lumbering, cattle raising and, more recently, casinos in attempting to improve their economic base. Although many still live below the poverty level, a large number of the younger generation are getting high school and college educations and are finding a place for themselves in off-reservation life. They have had significant roles in the armed services, in forest fire fighting, and many other parts of American society. As for the descendants of the settlers, one can only trust that they have learned to accept the natives as equals. It seems that perhaps over a century later, some of the goals of those early Indian Agents and Generals have been realized. The changes began when those in the "Break of the Western Wave" took center stage of the pageant of life being played out in the Verde Valley.

FOOTNOTES

(1) Goddard-Myhr, Margaret. <u>Jesse Goddard, One of Arizona's Last Old-Time Cowboys</u>. Suprise, AZ: Moore Graphics, 2001. 12.

(2) Trimble, Marshall. <u>Arizona, A Panoramic History of a Frontier State</u>. Garden City, NY: Doubleday & Company, Inc., 1977. 184.

(3) Hawk, Rose. "Toozigoot National Monument." Tucson: Southwest Parks & Monuments, 1995.

(4) Trimble, Marshall. <u>Arizona, A Panoramic History of a Frontier State</u>. Garden City, NY: Doubleday & Company, Inc., 1977. 49.

(5) Trimble, Marshall. <u>Arizona, A Panoramic History of a Frontier State</u>. Garden City, NY: Doubleday & Company, Inc., 1977. 182.

(6) Robinson III, Charles M. "General Crook and the Western Frontier." <u>Wild West Magazine</u> Aug. 2002: 54.

(7) Quail, Dell. Personal interview. 1949.

(8-13) Goddard, Jesse. Personal interview. 10 July 1983.

Left to right: F. Ruth, Walter, Ruth, Stella, Allen and Kevin

Chapter Four

MATCH FROM MAINE FOR ANNIE BRISTOW

On Middle Verde about five miles above the government fort at Camp Verde, Everett Jordan from Cape Elizabeth, Maine, homesteaded 160 acres on the east side of the Verde River and began writing home to persuade members of his family to join him. Ev Jordan, a cousin of W. A. Jordan, worked land right beside the homestead of Parson Bristow.

Through the eyes of Walter's memory we begin to form a picture of Will, one of the recipients of these letters. "M' father (Willie Albion, AKA Will or W. A. Jordan)[1], back in Cape Elizabeth, Maine, was gettin' news frum out West frum 'is cousin Ev Jordan. Ev wrote that it was grand country an' that th' government'd soon 'ave them wild Apaches all tamed down.

"'If possible,' th' letters said, 'Come west!'

"That appealed t' m' Dad. 'Is mother'd died an' 'is father'd remarried an' begun a second family. It seemed t' th' ones o' th' original family that th' second one was gettin' better treatment. M' Dad was anxious t' b' out on 'is own. 'E 'ad th' fever bad t' go west, but 'e waited 'til 'e was 21."

Will came by his adventuresome spirit honestly as his father, Albion, had entered into many precarious situations while serving as captain of a sailing vessel. He spent several years sailing among the east coast ports and Cuba, hauling "coal, lumber, and provisions," as recorded in his logs titled "Voyages of A. M. Jordan." On the return trips the cargo consisted mostly of rum. Captain Jordan's logs, along with letters, written between himself and family members, are in the archives of the Cape Elizabeth Museum in Maine. Through these we gain insight into his personality, leading us to believe that he was strong-minded and quite independent.

Albion's father must have warned him of the risks and dangers involved in his activities, but, as is often the case, the young feel themselves to be invincible, thus he continued. In one letter to his father, Albion describes his experience in a Cuban prison. Apparently his ship was impounded and he, plus all of the crew were imprisoned, for what offence we aren't quite sure, though it most likely was related to the fact that guns were a large part of the "provisions!" He writes that all were finally released, put back on their ship and were free to go, having lost all of their cargo and being minus all of the ship's papers. Although the documents were required to return to a port in the U. S., he very philosophically indicates that subject will be dealt with when he gets back. This epistle met with somewhat of an "I told you so" reply from his father, Isaiah. (Perhaps he was speaking from experience, as he had done "privateering in the war of 1812; was taken prisoner and paroled.")[2]

Nonetheless, from the accounts of several individuals, the major freight going south continued to be guns and returning north, rum. On one occasion the highly potent liquid served an entirely different purpose. A descendant of an early American governor in Cuba tells how Capt. Albion Jordan "came to their rescue." After all of the items were unloaded from the ship, Jordan learned of the very recent deaths of two of the governor's children. He immediately went to pay his respects and offer condolences, whereupon the governor shared his plight. He and his wife wanted the children to be buried near their home in Maine, but couldn't get the needed governmental clearance to ship the bodies. Without hesitation, the captain offered to smuggle the deceased in barrels of rum and deliver them for a proper burial. Probably many wondered at the great interest taken by the governor in the departure of this particular ship. All went as planned and Jordan had earned the deep gratitude of the official in Cuba. (After the bodies were removed from the "liquid embalmer" we are left to wonder, was the rum sold for consumption, and if so, was it served only after the drinkers were so inebriated it wouldn't matter what the secondary purpose had been?)

From other correspondence we would surmise that Captain Jordan, or Cap as he was called, was also a man who cared a great deal for family. In Jan. of 1850, while he was at sea, his first child was born. Upon reaching Philadelphia in April he received a letter from his wife Mary telling of the birth of their son. He responds, "I hope you will be very careful of yourself and also of the little stranger you wrote me about.

I would walk fifty miles to see you but I suppose I shall have to wait the appointed time for us to meet. I will try to wait patiently and you must do the same. If I had thought of being absent so long I should have left more money with you as I'm afraid you have been short."[3] He continues, telling her how he will get the money to her.

He appears to have been an independent, self-sufficient man not letting the challenges of life get him down. These traits, as well as the adventuresome spirit and a philosophical attitude, were passed down to his son Will. Some family members remember Will as "hard working, honest, reliable and independent." In addition to these qualities Ruthie recalls her Grandpa as a "gentle and kind man, family oriented, and willing to help others."

At some point Cap Jordan left the sea to become a full time farmer although he somewhat satisfied his longing for being on the water by doing a lot of fishing. He also was an accomplished hunter and Will became his shadow and companion in all of these activities. Again, we find three more of the father's attributes which developed strongly in Will—farming, hunting and fishing.

"Dad," says Walter, "told m' stories o' growin' up in Maine. Durin' th' Civil War, m' father was just a young kid an' 'e was out ridin' th' horse t' plow th' furrows fer 'is father t' sow peas. Across th' field come this friend o' m' father, an' o' course, m' grandfather knew 'im very well. Th' young man 'ad been drafted int' th' army. M' dad remained on th' horse, but Grandfather set th' bucket o' peas on th' ground.

"'Well, what did ya' pull out fer?' Cap Jordan asked.

"'Them bullets got too thick fer me? If I'd take a handful o' them peas an' throw 'em atcha, that's how much chance you'd a 'ad, an' that's how I become a traitor. I left. I'm headed fer Canada an' I'd like fer ya t' hide me out.'

"Grandfather did that until finally th' man made 'is getaway, an' 'e never heard o' 'im again. That was one story that impressed me.

"Then I heard 'im tell about huntin' wild, black ducks which are plentiful in Maine. 'E'd hunt in Bear Meetin' Bay, a favorite place fer th' clambakes Dad told me about. Th' ducks got s' smart, they knew they wouldn't b' harmed over in th' reserve, so's as soon as th' season opened with s' much shootin', over th' line they'd go. M' Dad could feed them wild, black ducks out o' 'is hand.

"Captain Sam Tyler, th' captain o' Dad's life savin' crew, was still livin' when Dad went back t' Maine in 1924. Th' Captain asked m' Dad an' 'is brother Ed t' go cod fishin'. Dad loved cod fishin' when 'e was a boy, s' they went up t' th' wharf where th' Captain kept a fine boat. That wharf 'ad been built up wonderful since Dad was there an' there was always fishermen sittin' all 'round tellin' stories, chewin' tobaccy, doin' this an' that.

"'Hey, Cap, [Tyler] where ya' goin'?'

"'We're goin' fishin'.'

"'Well, you ain't a gonna catch nothin'.'

"'Well, we're goin' out an' try anyway.'

"Uncle Ed said t' Cap, 'What th' hell do them guys know?'

"'Well, listen. Them fellers, ever'one o' them's got a good bank account now, an' Will, when ya was a boy, remember, they was looked down on. Now, them fellers are all rich. They've got big cold storage plants. They figured out when them codfish are gonna bite an' when t' go out there.'"

When they got back later that day:

"'Hey, Cap, how many fish did ya' git?'

"'We didn't git a bite.'

"Old Cap Tyler told Dad, 'Years it took 'em t' find out; ya' see, th' tide hits a high at th' full moon, an' they figured out, that that's th' best fishin' an' really made a business out o' it.'"

Leaving Maine for Arizona, 1880

"When m' Dad started fer th' leavin', it was a sad gatherin'. An awful lot o' people come t' see 'im off b'cause they just knew they'd never see 'im agin. Some o' 'em didn't git t' see 'em agin, b'cause only 'is oldest sister Clara an' 'is brother Ed were left o' 'is close relatives when 'e returned in 1924. [On his return] Everybody that could possibly git int' this big American Legion hall got in t' hear th' wild stories 'e'd tell 'em. Oh, boy! Ya could hear a pin drop all over that enormous hall when 'e told 'is Indian stories," Walt shakes his head as if he, too, wonders what will happen in that wild territory, called Arizona.

Into this suspenseful silence, in a quiet but firm tone still carrying his down-east accent, Will Jordan began, telling stories he later recorded in writing. "When I left Maine in November, 1880, my relatives and friends thought my scalp would soon be dangling from some redskin's belt, for Geronimo had not yet surrendered to General Crook; and terrible tales had been reaching us of the atrocities of marauding bands of Indians.

"Rufe Kinsman, [a friend] and I came together on an emigrant train. It took us a month and a day for the slow-going train would sidetrack for a day at a time to let other trains go by. We slept in a berth which let down from the ceiling, got meals where the train stopped, or bought food and carried it along in baskets. The only exciting incident of the whole trip was out in Wyoming past Cheyenne, where a couple of men dressed as cowboys held up the passengers."[4]

Walter, in true storyteller fashion, gives life to the incident. "I r'member Dad sayin' they [he and Rufe], 'ad a six-gun apiece under their pillows, plus their money belts each o' their sisters'd sewed t' th' inside o' their underwear. Yeah! They 'ad $360.00 apiece in them belts. Anyway, they got out there quite a ways in that rough territory goin' west. One mornin', real early, Dad an' Rufe got up an' th' crowd asked:

"'My goodness alive where'd ya' come frum?'

"'What's a matter here?' [Both were quite puzzled.]

"'Why, we were robbed ever'one o' us! Where were you?'

"They'd been sleepin', hidden away in their upper berths when all this went on. They didn't hear a thing. Them desperados robbed th' engineer, th' fireman, th' conductor, an' ever'body. Just took ever'thin' they had - jewelry, money, anythin'. Just stripped 'em all, except Dad an' Rufe. Them two come out o' bed, changed fer breakfast, just as if nothin' out o' th' ordinary 'ad happened. Say, you betcha', both were mighty glad fer them money belts Dad's sister Clara an' Rufe's sister'd sewed inside them long johns!

"I'll never fail t' remember this: frum th' flat car on the train, Dad said that men'd shoot an' kill elk an' buffalo just fer fun; no wonder them Apaches fought th' settlers. Father an' Rufe didn't like that. They got t' Truckee, Nevada. It was about noon when th' train stopped, an' there were several men out on th' pond asawin' ice. Rufe jumped down sayin', 'Let's go out an' git a job sawin' ice an' pick up a little extra money.'

"When Dad went t' follow, 'is hand stuck t' a door knob so tight that 'e 'ad t' blow on it hopin' that 'is warm breath'd help release it without takin' skin with it. 'E's reminded o' almost losin' 'is legs t' th' cold in Maine.

"'Rufe, I don't b'lieve I want any o' that cuttin' ice.'

"Father was rememberin' th' time 'e went huntin' a large white rabbit; they called it a hare back in Maine. Hares were fine eatin', s' Dad an' a friend went huntin'. When Dad come back, Grandfather Jordan says, 'Son, yer boots are frozen on yer legs. Now, don't try t' get 'em off! I've got t' git tubs o' water t' thaw yer legs out slow or they'll have t' b' amputated.'

"When Dad asked th' conductor how cold it was, th' reply was, '25 degrees below zero;' consequently, neither Dad nor Rufe cut ice that day.

"They went on. Got t' Frisco, got t' Los Angeles, an' got t' Maricopa, south o' Phoenix. This fellah down there at Maricopa asked 'em where they was a'headed. 'Camp Verde,' was th' reply.

"'Well, th' first station is Prescott, an' ye're gonna have t' git a job on one o' them freight wagons er ya' cain't get there.' They managed t' git a job - a dollar a day an' board."

They worked on the freight wagons, first to Prescott and then to Camp Verde, following the wagon road through Copper Canyon. Parts of this "trail" are still visible where it parallels the current I-17. Upon their arrival in early December of 1880, Ev Jordan met Will, and Rufe's folks met him. In the 1800's all along the Verde River, it was swampy, and malaria was so much of a problem that the fort at Camp Verde had to be moved to higher ground. The grass grew "as tall as the bellies of the cattle" in that whole valley, and one of the ways the pioneers, including Parson Bristow, supported themselves was to mow the wild grass, bale it, and sell it to the government forts.

Will Jordan started farming with Everett Jordan in the spring of 1881, right next to Parson Bristow. He farmed with him, and stayed with him for several years. Will had hoped to get his own place and send for his sweetheart back in Cape Elizabeth, but malaria sapped his energy for years, and she grew tired of waiting. His sister Clara would eventually visit with her son, who, like Will Jordan's two oldest sons, had served in WWI. Also, a half sister came out to teach, and found a husband as did many women who taught school in the Verde Valley.

Walter continues, "In th' fall, after th' harvest, Father would hunt. 'E 'ad th' folks back in Maine ship 'is ten-gage out t' 'im. That was 'is favorite gun. Dad would do the shootin', an' Ev Jordan would sometimes help b' haulin' th' ducks an' geese in, an' b' pluckin' 'em. When they got a load, they'd take 'em over t' Fort Whipple t' sell t' th' government. One winter Dad bought black powder, shells, shot wads an' everythin' t' load 'is own shells. Above expenses fer one winter's huntin', 'e made $500, an' that was pretty good money in them days.

"Dad also learned t' be a cowboy. 'E got a job punchin' cows, an' 'e learned right quick th' traits o' a trained cow horse. Now them trained cow ponies are smart critters, fer if a steer turns t' th' right, that horse is gonna follow 'im. Ya' better be ont' yer job if ya' wanta keep yer seat. Oh my, yes!! Now Dad knew this one 'green-horn' that wasn't on t' how t' do th' job, an' th' horse went after a cow an' 'e wasn't ready an' went head first int' a prickly pear cactus!" Here Walt gave a little snort b'fore continuing, "They 'ad a terrible time with that man a'tryin' t' get all them stickers out. Say, let's git back t' farmin' now.

"Dad an' Ev farmed together several years at Middle Verde, then they went up th' river t' look at this 80-acre farm owned b' a man named Wagoner an' 'is wife. It was right there acrost frum th' ole Clarkdale smelter. Dad an' Ev bought this feller out, an' Ev farmed with Dad on th' Upper Verde that year, but Ev didn't like it — willows an' stuff on it. 'E said, 'I'll sell my part t' ya' Will. I want t' go back t' m' place at Middle Verde.'

"After that, Ev sold th' ole place an' purchased 160 acres on th' east side o' th' river. Acrost th' bridge at Camp Verde an' ya' take t' th' right. I've seen Ev Jordan's place there fer years an' years. I'd be goin' down on th' west side o' th' river b' th' salt mine t' hunt ducks an' geese an' I'd see Ev Jordan's house over there. I remember s' well there was a woman teachin' school at our place in Bridgeport after we moved down there [1913] an' Everett Jordan was still unmarried an' 'e was getting' quite old. Th' teacher boarded with m' mother there at Bridgeport, an' Ev fell in love an' married 'er. They lived on that big farm o' Ev's. Sonny [Walter Jordan's son] an' I drove down there one day. Oh my, ya' wouldn't know it now! It's a subdivision! The big house is still standin', an' I think there's somebody livin' in it. My goodness alive! I never dreamed there'd be anythin' like this. Ev used t' have a beautiful farm there — rich land, an' they raised two children. One o' 'em is still livin' at Camp Verde. She comes t' ever'one o' th' Pioneer Picnics. Shirley Hopkins is 'er name; she was Shirley Jordan, an' she loves t' visit with Ruth" [Walter Jordan's wife]. As so often happens when the "old timers" are telling stories they will side track into something else.

Of the family in Maine, it seems that Clara kept the closest contact with Will and his children. Walter says, "Aunt

Submitted by Charles Jordan
Will's sister Clara and her son Harold circa 1918

Clara an' 'er son, Harold, come out here t' visit. 'E was captain o' a squadron o' airplanes in th' First War. When they come out here, I was deliverin' vegetables an' fruit t' Jerome in a truck. 'E wanted t' go with me, an' goin' up that ole' hogback an' around them hairpin curves, it just scared 'im t' death. 'E was on th' outside a lookin' down, ya see. An' 'e said, 'How in th' world cin ya go up these mountains like this?!'

"'Harold, how in th' world could ya be up in th' air an' then be scared o' this little drive? It's bad enough t' b' up there a flyin' without somebody a'shootin' at ya'!'

"It's different ya' see. It frightens 'em worse, when they ain't used t' mountains, than being up in the air with somebody a'shootin' at 'em."

Playing for the Dances

"Dad used t' play 'is piccolo or flageolet fer dances," Walter begins relaying another of his vivid memories, even doubly exciting, for as a child he knew one of the characters in the cast. "When I was a kid, Dad played in Cornville. Oh yeah, b' the way, this town was supposed t' b' called Coneville, named fer Chick Cone, a major rancher there. 'Is partner pronounced it 'corn' instead o' 'cone' sos th' post office mis-spelt it. Did ya' ever hear tell o' such?!"

At this point Walt gave a snort and a chuckle and it is difficult to tell which he thought the dumber, the partner or the post office. "Now back t' playin' fer them dances. Dad used t' tell a story 'bout one night in Cornville when Lyman Drum an' Charlie Chestnut was there.

"One time Father wanted me t' go up t' Stoneman Lake with 'im t' pick up seed potatoes that Lyman saved 'im — two sacks o' Irish Cobbler potatoes — wonderful potatoes. What impressed th' occasion on m' memory indelibly was that on our way up there, Lyman was comin' down that old road t' Camp Verde drivin' two enormous Persian horses — them horses they'd use fer loggin'. I'd heard Father tell what a man 'e was — an athlete. Oh-h-h-h, 'e was broad shouldered, and Dad told me th' first time 'e ever saw Lyman Drum was in Camp Verde in Head's store. Th' store 'ad three-gallon buckets hangin' along nails on th' rafters, an' Lyman said t' Head, 'Say, if a person kicked one o' 'em off o' there, would ya give 'im one?'

"'You bet yer life! 'E deserves one if 'e can do it.'

"Well now, Lyman just backed off an' kicked that thing right offa there. Head give 'im that bucket, too.

"Now at that Cornville dance, Charlie Chestnut was bigger than Lyman, an' 'e 'ad a nice lookin' girl there at th' dance. Lyman got t' a'dancin' with 'er. An' a fella told Lyman, 'Say, Charlie Chestnut says 'e's gonna whip th' hell outta ya fer tryin' t' steal 'is girl!'

"'If that's th' case, I'll see about it!'

"An' Lyman waited, an' after another dance, 'e went up t' Charlie Chestnut an' said, 'Say, I understand ye're gonna whip me fer tryin' t' steal yer girl. Come on outside! I'll tell ya what I'll do. I'll let th' boys tie both m' hands behind me an' I'll just kick ya t' death.'

"Charlie wouldn't do it, b'cause 'e knew what a kicker Lyman was. Whether Charlie kept 'is girl, I don't know, but there sure warn't no fight."

Obviously Will played for many dances located all over the Verde Valley for it was at Middle Verde that Annie met him. After Will and Annie married it didn't seem to matter he had become a member of a strict Baptist family, for he did not change his habits but continued his musical avocation.

Annie Bristow was Preacher Bristow's wild child. She grew to be a woman plagued by her memories of her early behaviors, in contrast to her strict religious upbringing. This conclusion was drawn partially from

Submitted by Charles Jordan
Annie Bristow Jordan early 1900

the grim photos of Annie with and without the large family she was to mother, plus discussions she had with her grandchildren. (We must note here that her expressions could also be a result of constant pain from rheumatoid arthritis, which began in her early 30s.) When granddaughter Ruthie was in high school, Annie learned that the teenager was taking square dance lessons. A lecture ensued on the proper actions of a Christian, to which Ruthie replied: "Granny I know that you met Grandpa at a dance, and it wasn't a square dance!" Naturally Ruthie felt she had won the argument, but wait! Annie's almost tearful reply settled everything, "Child, I sinned. I don't want you to sin!" What can one say to that?!

Many have said that Annie was a very beautiful girl, witty, always having a ready retort, and fun to be with. Some have even called her "the belle of the Verde Valley." She also had quite a sense of humor which was still evident even into her eighties. While Ruthie was away during the summers attending college at Arizona State University, Annie wrote her several letters teasing her about having to be away from her boyfriend, Larry Jackson.

In 1880, when her future husband, W.A. Jordan, arrived in the Verde Valley, she was only ten years old. At 16 years of age, she reputedly scandalized her family by running off with Hawkins, her sister Cumi's husband. The story goes that her father went after her and brought her back. Allen Bristow, a nephew, was not too

Annie Bristow Jordan circa 1887

clear on the subject: "Little kids standin' 'round didn't get t' hear any o' that, you know."

In May of 1887, at the age of eighteen Annie married the very handsome, talented and hardworking Will Jordan. If her father was pleased by the match, he may have had to disguise the fact; Jordan's popularity as a musician for the dances went against the letter and spirit of Baptist teaching on ideal husbands and it had been against her father's orders that Annie attended the dances. Will's musical talents were passed down to all of the children. Sons George and Sumner would become musicians, but they played and sang for church services. Sumner even wrote some of the hymns they sang to the accompaniment of his steel guitar.

Will Jordan circa 1887

Nine children born to Will and Annie

After their marriage, Will and Annie moved to his farm on Upper Verde, (later known as Clarkdale but on the east side of the river from the current slag dump.), which was near Tuzigoot Ruins. They apparently lived in the same log cabin on Rattlesnake Hill which Will and Tack Gaddis had occupied at the time of the Indian scare. Being on top of the hill, just as the Indians had built on high ground, had two major advantages. There was a view in all directions and they were above the flood waters. Walter doesn't remember much about the building of the large two story home, but he thought it incorporated the cabin. He definitely recalls the man named Carlton who built it. This nice house with many "modern" conveniences made Annie's tasks a little easier than the average. Her nephew, Allen, gives a good description of some of the difficulties encountered by a lot of the wives of settlers.

Submitted by Charles Jordan
Jordan Farm on Upper Verde, 1880s

Submitted by Charles Jordan
Jordan home Rattlesnake Hill 1890s

"When I was a kid, it was a pretty rough time fer my mother, especially th' winters — a lot o' rain. We built a little bit on t' our house an' fixed it up, an' I know m' mother put an oil cloth, cenitas, up on th' inside. She plastered that over th' inside walls, an' we nailed can lids over some o' th' knot holes. Us kids, Marie an' I, thought it was great, but my mother had a terrible hard time. She had t' draw th' water, hand over hand, outta a 90 foot well. (It seems that Will Jordan had a hand pump installed on their well.) She did the washing by hand on washboards and things. We did hire an Indian woman called Ebba -- Ebba Quail. That helped a lot. The Quails were quite a famous Indian family in the Verde Valley. There are still Quails around Camp Verde."

Helen, George's wife, remarked that "all of the kids were born in a house on a hill visible [today] from the Verde River train." (A tourist ride following the regular gauge railroad built by W. A. Clark along the Verde River. The tourist attraction was established in the 1980s)

Walter gives his version of these offspring. "All nine o' us discovered America on Rattlesnake Hill. I was th' third boy. M' brother Chester was th' oldest one. Then come Willie, also referred to as Brother Bill. Mary, Stella, Alice — they were m' sisters. George was th' fourth boy. Sumner was th' fifth an' Edgar was th' sixth. Now let's see if I got it right - Chester, Willlie, Me [Walter], George, Sumner, Edgar - yeah, that's right - six o' us. Six boys an' three girls an' I'm th' only one left o' th' nine. We buried my sister Mary at Tucson last January." (1986).

This brood of nine was almost all strongly opinionated, loud, and full of energy. A favorite evening activity was playing a card game called Pit, even their father enjoyed it. Finally one evening Annie could no longer stand the racket of everyone yelling at the top of their lungs the name of the commodity they wished to trade. Annie marched in, quickly gathered up the cards and promptly tossed them in the fireplace. "Oh Mommer, why did ya goin' do that?" Papa asked, as all of the children simultaneously shouted their objections. Thus the peace and quiet Annie was so desperately seeking was slow in arriving.

F. Ruth's impression of Granny [Annie] was that she was always fussing at Grandpa Jordan, and sort of putting him down. She remembers her grandpa as "one of the kindest, sweetest persons I ever knew. I can still see him getting up and going outside to avoid getting into an argument of any kind, especially religion or politics. When he stayed with our family the winter of my senior year in high school, he would sit in the chair, eyes closed, fingers drumming gently on the chair arm, and thinking of the early days in Maine. He often called to family members to sit near-by while he told stories of his life. Also during that winter he pruned 75 peach trees for Daddy (Walter), although recovering from a heart attack and being over 90 years of age."[5]

Helen Bristow Schmidt, daughter of Annie's brother Billy, remarked that "somehow Uncle Will was able to provide for his family so that they always had the newest things." These modern conveniences did not include a flush toilet because Annie wasn't going to have "one of those things smelling up her house!!" Crippled severely with arthritis, she insisted, until the day she died, on walking to the outhouse, or using the chamber pail. Now one is left to wonder "Which smelled worse, an indoor toilet or a chamber pail?"

In thinking about it, Will must have always earned a good living, for in those days it was almost unheard of for kids in this part of the country to go to high school, let alone to college. Three in the Jordan family, Chester, Stella, and Willie, went to college, and George to electrical engineering school in New York. All but Walter completed high school and he dropped out to help on the farm when Chester and Willie were drafted in WWI.

The Verde Copper newspaper was willing to publish any letters family received "from the front." One from Willie definitely shows the joy he felt when the war ended. He stated that he was well and had no wounds; however, not long after his return he began his battle with lifelong asthma, a result of mustard gas. (See 56 for an example of these letters.)

Jordan Family, circa 1909
Back row left to right: Alice, Walter, Willie, Chester, Mary, Stella
Front row left to right: Sumner, Edgar (on lap), Will, Annie, George

Stella became a teacher eventually returning to live with her parents to teach in Clemenceau. Sumner studied music in San Diego emphasizing steel guitar. Edgar was on his way to do the same when he was killed on the old Yuma plank highway. Chester was under the truck working on the taillights and Edgar was helping from behind the truck when another car, blinded by the setting sun, ran into the back of them. Edgar was killed instantly. Walter says, "One o' th' hardest things I ever 'ad t' do was meet that train in Prescott an' bring brother Edgar home." Yes, all would agree that Will provided well for his family, as Helen observed, "They were pretty prosperous farmers because Papa [Helen adopted her husband George's name for his father, Will] was an orchardist."

One of Annie's nephew's, Allen Bristow, shares his perspective of her husband. "I always admired Uncle Will Jordan greatly. He was a worker, an' he ran his place businesslike as far as I can remember. When I'd go t' visit George, we couldn't play or nothin' until he'd finished his chores. We'd play just a little while in th' evening before he'd be run off t' bed with th' others, or on a Saturday afternoon an' on Sunday after they'd gone t' church. Aunt Annie was th' one who made them go t' church. Uncle Will would let them off on Saturday afternoon if somebody came t' play, but any other time they were out in th' fields pulling weeds an' working. He paid them wages, an' George always had money to spend.

"George an' I visited back an' forth a lot. I'd ride my bicycle up there on that old rocky road (several miles). Walter was older, an' he was kind o' goin' with a different group o' kids. We were livin' on th' Salt Mine place then, (southwest of Camp Verde), an' sometimes I would ride th' horse up t' see George. About twice a year, my folks would hook up th' team an' wagons an' we'd go visitin'. We'd go up t' Middle Verde first an' stay with Aunt Teedie Ralston a night or two, an' then we'd go across th' river an' visit Grandpa an' maybe we'd stay there a day. Then we'd go up th' river t' th' Jordan's. Th' old road used t' go right up th' river bed. We'd stay a day or two an' we'd generally figure on goin' t' Jerome t' visit Aunt Effie. Uncle Jim Wingfield was runnin' a butcher shop there. But we only went one time because always when we'd go to leave, Aunt Annie'd issue a dire warning:

"'Oh, you better not go up t' Jerome. They're havin' another epidemic up there.'"

For some reason Annie did not want them visiting other family members. Perhaps this stemmed from her fear that others would be liked better and maybe from a little bit of jealousy. She had quite an inferiority feeling and it seems that all of her blustering was used to help cover it up.

Company was always welcome to break the regular routine, especially a visit from the preacher. According to Walt there was one exception. "I remember th' pastor down at th' Middle Verde would ride up once a month t' preach at our place. One time 'e was gonna bring 'is wife an' th' kids, an' I heard Mama say, 'Now them kids are just like pack rats. If she comes up here, I'm gonna 'ave t' put ever'thing out o' reach!'"

Allen was right that it was Annie that always made all of the children go to church. One fine Sunday morning Walter was at great odds with himself, he had to go to church but it was perfect fishing weather. Gradually he began to develop a plan, and just in case it all worked out right, he hid his fishing equipment in an easily accessible spot. He continued on to church with the others and dutifully went to his Sunday School Classroom. There his plan began to unfold, for while the teacher was praying with head bowed and eyes closed he quietly climbed out the window. With both feet on the ground it was difficult to withhold a jubilant shout, "Free at last!" Quickly he retrieved his gear and headed for Pecks Lake, found a rowboat and soon was out in the deeper water feeling he was in seventh heaven. He was so engrossed in the activity that he was totally unaware of the boat drifting. Suddenly a great buzzing around his head directed his attention to the immediate surroundings. Alas! The boat was caught in the water tulles right in the middle of a huge wasp nest. He began swatting frantically at the varmints, causing the oars to fall in the lake. Now he was truly up the proverbial creek without a paddle. Desperation set in, for he couldn't swim and he couldn't move the boat. Finally he lay flat and still in the bottom of the boat and when the wasps subsided he ventured a peek above the side of his prison. There in the distance he could see a farmer plowing the field. He began calling for help. Eventually the farmer heard the ear-splitting screams, and came to his rescue. After getting him on dry ground the neighbor took him home. There he was met with the fiery temper of his mother who offered no treatment for the numerous stings. Her statement, "Serves you right Walter Jordan! That's what you get for ditching Sunday School!" He remembers the pain, anguish, and humiliation, but most of all he remembers his mother relenting and putting baking soda plasters all over him and how good those felt.

Annie was a meticulous housekeeper and a superb cook. Even with the painful arthritis that eventually crippled her, (to the point of having to have help dressing, etc.), she would churn butter, make yeast bread and delicious cakes, her favorite being Martha Washington. Apparently she had misplaced one of her recipes and had written to a cousin in Napa, California for a copy. On January 9, 1899 the cousin responded asking about the baby, wondering if he was as fat as his picture made him look, and saying that she liked the name, Walter Everett. She also refers to their younger dancing days and to Annie's current status as a "dignified housewife" and to herself as a "school Marm."

It is difficult to imagine taking care of 5 older children and a baby (Walter), let alone having time to write and ask someone for a recipe. When would she ever have had time to make the cake?! She also made butter and sold it along with eggs, milk, and cream. Often these items were traded to Indian women for magnificently woven baskets, some of which were waterproof and large enough to use for laundry (See center for painting of baskets). As the children got older the girls helped prepare meals, clean house etc. just as the boys helped in the fields. All began chores before daylight, with a short rest coming when called to breakfast. The menu consisted of: fruit (when available), some type of meat, usually bacon or ham, eggs, hot bread or pancakes, and always oatmeal and pinto beans, plus butter, jam or honey, and milk and coffee. Right after the meal, the boys and men would return to the fields to continue working. Another break came for lunch and the bill of fare always included pinto beans. The afternoon brought more work, followed by supper or dinner, again offering the ever present beans. There seemed to always be plenty of fresh baked bread, cake and pie. Sometimes work would be resumed after the evening meal, causing one to wonder when they had time for fun including dating. Several of the boys would indulge in an evening snack of whatever pastry was available, but Will always ate some type of fruit, very ceremoniously slicing it with his pocket knife. Upon completion the knife was wiped "clean" with his large red handkerchief and returned to his pants pocket.

As a child, F. Ruth remembers going to the Verde to Granny's and Grandpa's almost every Sunday in the winter. Sumner's family, as well as Stella, lived full-time with their parents, taking care of household chores, live stock, and the farm. She states, "Aunt Evelyn (Sumner's wife) did all of the meal preparation and Aunt Stella did most of the clean-up afterwards, while Uncle Sumner played with us kids on the lawn. As we grew older we realized that out of concern and love for us Granny insisted on our coming, helped with the planning, and was responsible for sending us home with enough bread, butter, milk, and leftovers to last several days. Aunt Helen pointed out to me Granny's generosity and the boost it was to our family, (Walter's), in those depression years. Grandpa also gave us some of whatever fruits and vegetables they had. Memories of these Sunday visits are filled with love and amusement. As Will's and Annie's children became adults their penchant for arguing became a way of life. Sumner preferred to read the newspaper or go outside and play with the three of us. Holidays were always a wonderful time, being spent at various person's homes. Christmas was at Granny's with church friends being included. In the evening all would go into the parlor, (the only time anyone was allowed in that room) and the music was outstanding. All joined in, some playing instruments such as guitar, auto harp, musical saw, and of course piano. My only regret is that Grandpa never played his flagolette." (Other get together Holidays were: New Year's at Bill and Alice Gray's Coffee Creek Ranch; to celebrate Will's and Sumner's birthdays, June 15th, or a Sunday close to that date, at Mary and Jack Flannigan's in Spring Valley, north of Parks, AZ; July 4th at Helen's and George's; and Thanksgiving alternating between Helen's and Alice's. As Ruth and Walter were the only ones with children, all of the others said, "You just bring the children, so we can play with them," and the remaining family members would do everything else.)

Ruthie, Anne, Walt Jr. on Grannie's porch, circa 1939

Annie continued to want to do things for her family. Upon the news of another expected great-grand baby, Annie made immediate plans to make a special gift. Although her hands were so crippled that she could only move her thumb, she hooked one piece of the scissors over an arthritic knot, put her thumb through the other half and promptly started cutting fabric pieces. Before her granddaughter Anne's first baby was born she completed an all hand-sewn quilt for the new little one. With these knotted and crippled hands she would stick the handle of a spoon or the butter paddle between her thumb and finger joints proceeding to stir the batter in a frantic rush or swat the butter into shape. Annie can be remembered as a many talented, stalwart, and determined person.

Their home on Rattlesnake Hill was rather close to the hobo trail between Flagstaff and Jerome and occasionally one would happen to pass. Annie posted the children on the porch to watch for strangers the same as she and her siblings had been on the watch for Indians. She also relied on the kettle of scalding water for protection. Walt gives us the episode. "Well, I tell ya how it was this one day when we kids saw a Apache Indian a comin' up th' hill t'wards our house on Rattlesnake Hill. We went runnin' in yellin', 'Indian, Mama Indian!' Mama run t' th' porch, almost not b'lievin' us kids. Sure 'nuff, here come a Indian right up over that hill an' dressed in full war regalia, includin' head dress, war paint, an' everthin'. Didn't look like any o' them friendly ones livin' round us. I'm a'tellin' ya m' mother grabbed us kids in a hurry an' got us inside, an' she took that ole pot offa th' stove an' headed fer th' front porch. She yelled at that Indian t' stop, but 'e just kept a'comin' right on up that trail!

"She hollered, 'Stop, or I'll scald ya!'

"'E just kept a walkin' right up that hill straight at 'er. Mama charged down them steps with that pot o' water ready t' sling it. When all o' a sudden that Indian shouted, 'Oh Annie don't!!' It was 'er brother Billy, dressed up t' scare 'er an' when she realized it, she was s' mad she couldn't stand it. She come a flyin' down that path screamin',

"'Billy Bristow, I'm'a gonna scald you anyway!' an' th' foot race was on.

"Uncle Billy turned tail, an' took off like a shot outta a gun. She chased 'im clean t' th' bottom o' that hill. It was good fer 'im that 'e could run faster b'cause 'e barely escaped with an unburned hide."

Again Walter chuckled reliving the whole scene in his mind. It seems that this was the first and last time anyone ever tried to play that kind of a practical joke on Annie.

School was not always the favorite thing for these farm children who preferred to be outside. They tried many things to liven up the hours including playing jokes on the teachers. These could range from putting tacks on the instructor's chair, to live critters in her desk. A special raised area just large enough to hold the desk and chair provided the instructor a better view of the total classroom. One day while seated at her desk the teacher opened the top drawer, and out sprang a frog, almost into her face. She shrieked, threw herself backwards, tumbling off of the platform and landing in a heap on the floor. Walter's only regret was that just at the moment of truth he had bent down to pick up his pencil and missed the whole show!

Despite the practical jokes to break the boredom, Walter still dreamed of sitting on the river bank casting his line at the unsuspecting fish. The plan he devised this time involved his father's desire to have the ranch rid of the skunk population. One evening he set a number of traps for the varmints, feeling sure he would catch a few. The next morning at the crack of dawn he was not disappointed. He removed the dead animals, and while skinning them made sure that plenty of the scent got on him. Leaving the fields, he went directly to school, not wanting to meet any of the family members enroute. Upon his entrance to the classroom the teacher got a whiff and according to Walt exclaimed, "Walter Jordan what is that awful smell? Get outta here an' don't come back 'til ya don't stink!"

Walter feigned innocence, and slowly walked away, not wanting his jubilation to show until he was out of sight of the school. As he was coming down the lane towards home, his father saw him and reached for a willow switch. He always told the children that if they were punished at school they would get it twice as hard at home. While Walt was quickly explaining, his dad got a big breath of the stench and concurred with the teacher, and the errant son went fishing. No one ever said how long the odor lasted or how he cleared his body from it.

Life on Rattlesnake Hill was always exciting, for each of the nine had great imaginations and could constantly think of things to do besides their regular chores and work. One day Walter and George had permission to go hunting for rabbits, squirrels, etc. Walter being the older, (approximately twelve years, George nine), carried the gun over his shoulder and led the way. It is easy to visualize these two small boys in bib overalls "marching" importantly through the fields, when suddenly a shot splits the air and reverberates off of the cliffs along the Verde. Walter quickly assessed the situation, dropped the gun and raced for home. Walt picks up the story: "I charged 'crost that front porch all outta breath an' yelled 'Oh Mama! I shot George in th' head but 'e ain't dead yet!!'

"Mama was scared t' death, but managed t' yell back, 'Well, ya little dunce! Where is 'e?! Go get 'im!'"

With the help of some of the older children and his mother, George was retrieved, and cleaned up a bit before being taken immediately to Jerome to the doctor. Mercifully the bullet had just grazed the scalp, keeping the injury from being life threatening. Unfortunately some or the wadding was overlooked and the wound became infected, creating the need for removal of the stitches, another cleaning and resewing.

A large scar remained for the rest of George's life, which he covered by parting his hair on the opposite side.

On another occasion Annie had reason to again gasp and utter a silent prayer as she heard Willie scream, "Oh Mary, don't die 'til I get there!" On a quick examination of the situation she discovered that Mary had fallen from the apple tree, frightening Willie, but landing unhurt.

Alice and Mary were excellent cooks, like their mother. Their specialities included all types of candy, featuring dipped chocolates. Their older brother, Chester, felt that they were gaining too much weight and he took it upon himself to rectify this by burying a large plate of candies they had just completed. Walter continues: "When them missin' chocolates was discovered, th' girls 'pitched a fit', yellin', 'Mama, do ya know what happened t' our candy?!'

"'How should I know? But maybe ya should ask Chester.'

"When they asked 'im 'bout it, 'e wouldn't tell where 'e'd hidden it. Th' girls got their heads t'gether t' figure what they could do t' git even. Suddenly th' light dawned. Chester 'ad a very important date that evenin' an' would b' wearin' 'is good suit o' clothes. Immediately they rushed t' 'is clothes closet, removed 'is good suit o' clothes an' 'id 'em. Well, 'bout 5:00 that evenin' 'e come in frum th' field t' git cleaned up fer 'is date. A beller roared frum th' second story, 'Mama, where are m' clothes?!'

"'How should I know? Ya think 'bout it an' figger it out!'

"It only took a matter o' seconds b'fore 'e yelled, 'Mary, Alice, where are m' clothes?'

"'Where is our candy?' they hollared right back.

"This arguin' kept up until Chester finally admitted 'e couldn't git th' chocolates. Then them girls insisted there ain't no way they could git 'is clothes without th' candy first. Finally Chester 'ad t' confess that 'e took their sweets and buried their candy, an' started beggin' fer 'is clothes. B'fore givin' 'em t' 'im them girls made 'im git down on one knee, promisin' never t' touch their candy ag'in without permission!" (Both Mary and Alice continued perfecting their candy-making skills and as adults, made it for sale.)

At times even Will was in on the practical jokes. One day he was resting on the window seat after lunch, fell asleep, and began snoring. Mary quietly got the jar of the awful smelling musterole and wiped some gently in his mustache. He batted at it a few times but continued sleeping and snoring, so Mary added a bit more. This time he awakened, discovered what had happened and left the house for the field without saying a word. Walter finishes the story for us, "A few nights later, sister Mary went upstairs t' go t' bed. It weren't but just a little while when we all heard th' awfullest shriekin'. O'course we was all curious, so up them stairs we run. 'Mama, what's this thing in my bed?!' Yeah, that's right th' kids alw'ys hollered fer Mama when somethin' was wrong. Well, I betch'll never guess what we found in that bed? [For punctuation and effect, he poked the person sitting nearest him.] All eyes were on the middle o' that bed, when suddenly a great big toad frog jumped out frum under them covers an' just sat there a' lookin' an' a' croakin' at us. 'M' goodness alive, Mary, where'd that thing come frum?' asked one o' th' girls. When Mary couldn't seem t' git any idea, Mama said, 'She oughtta know. Serves her right fer puttin' that stuff in Papa's mustache!'"

With escapades like this going on almost daily, it is a wonder that Annie ever kept her sanity, let alone lived to be nearly 90.

Walter became Will's constant companion, just as Will had been with his father, so it isn't surprising that Walt could be left to accomplish many tasks by himself.

"Dad 'ad this irrigation ditch up above 'bout a mile an' a half," Walt begins, "it's where them Indian women 'ad a wonderful swimmin' hole there in th' Verde River, just right above that ditch. I was only about 13 years old, but I knew that farm, that orchard, an' how it irrigated. That mornin' Father says, 'Son, I want ya t' go up there an' irrigate that sweet potato field.'

"Th' Verde River was right along th' edge o' them two acres, an' there was brush called water moodies, just thick-thick along that edge. Ya could hide as a kid, an' I did. Oh, them women'd come down there frum them wigwams, an' get in that water. Standin' in a circle in that big swimmin' hole they'd cup their hands an' hit th' water t' make th' sound 'ahwhoomp, ahwhoomp,' like a beaver a hittin' 'is tail hard on th' water. [showing folks with his hands as he talked]. Oh, they's just a yellin' an' havin' a wonderful time. I got t' watchin' 'em an' got t' thinkin' what fun it'd b' t' scare 'em. S' I found me a rock 'bout th' size o' m' fist, [holding up his fist to demonstrate], an' I threw that thing right in th' middle o' that circle. 'Kersplash!' An' boy oh boy! Them women stopped that game in th' bat o' an eye. An' I tell ya it was so quiet I could hear m' own breathin'. Then I did a dumb fool thing. I tossed another rock out in th' middle o' that river an' they got th' direction o' me. Oh, my! Out o' that Verde they come, six Apache women, their long skirts a draggin' th' ground. I was all alone, an' sos up that sweet potato field I went. They were a throwin' rocks t' beat th' band. 'Whoof!' Right b' me. B'lieve ya me, I put on more speed. I cancelled distance an' annihilated space!! But with them wet skirts a' flappin' on their legs, they couldn't catch me. Well, I'll tell you somethin', that's the first time I saw any topless bathin' suits!"

Although farming was the main source of income, Will as an entrepreneur tried several other ventures. In the early 1900s he owned a lumber yard in Jerome and was doing quite well as the town was just beginning to grow. This venture came to a sudden standstill during one of the many fires that ravaged the community. He didn't reopen but waited for other opportunities. Around 1909 he somehow received some advertising sheets from the Atascador Land Company regarding an oil gusher down in Mexico. He showed these to the preacher (Rev. Keen), from Middle Verde and the two of them decided to go to look it over. Walter says "S' Green, [the superintendent for Atascador Co.] took 'em all over, took 'em up t' that big gusher, th' Ebonall. 'E knew all about it. They 'ad a foot bridge across th' crude oil, just a river o' oil. They didn't pump er nothin', a natural gusher! It was just a'flowin'. They couldn't make dams fast 'nuff. It was just a crawlin', an' Green said, 'Git ya a stick there, an' shove it down.' It was 3 foot deep, fillin' them big dams as fast as they could git 'em built an' runnin' off down int' th' river. Dad bought 50 acres right in that oilfield country an' then this Keen, 'e bought some there. [Buying the land must have included the oil rights, although this was never fully explained.]

"Then Green took 'em all over that whole Atascador land there, an' Father bought 150 acres o' this farmin' land. Ya could buy it cheap then b'cause that ole Diaz was on th' 'throne', an' 'e's a'cheatin' them peons. Dad paid taxes on that thing fer years an' finally this doggone Mexican overthrew th' government. Yeah, that ole Pancho Villa was one o' 'em. They declared that every American that 'ad rights there couldn't hold 'em any longer an' it went back t' th' Mexican government. 'E lost ever'thin' 'e 'ad." It is still a puzzle if he received any money from the oil during those years or not. Walt ends by saying, "There was enormous companies here in th' United Sates movin' in there an' 'ed bought it fer speculation." Through all of Will's investment ventures, including some mining ones discussed in a later chapter, the farm continued to make a profit and take care of the family.

Someone told Will and Annie that if they would move to Oregon where the climate was different that Annie's arthritis would improve. So, in 1910, Will bought a big house for the family in McMinnville, Oregon. When they moved he stayed behind to sell the farm. Although their sojourn was brief the "tribe" made quite an impression on the locals. Again, it was George and Walter that stirred up the County Fair. While walking through the exhibits Walter spied a beautiful plate of Bing Cherries. He figured the only way to judge such was to taste, so he took one, tasted it, and found it to be delicious. He then promptly scooped all into his pocket and continued walking down the aisle, eating cherries and spitting out the seeds! Imagine the distress of the poor farmer upon discovering his whole exhibit missing before the judging!

At this point he decided to find George so they both could ride the Ferris Wheel. When he tired of that activity, he went home leaving George to continue his ride alone. Upon arriving home, Annie sent him to get his brother. Back he walked, finding the wheel stopped and George in the very top seat. Walter yelled, "George Mama said fer ya' t' come down frum there right now an' git home!"

George's response in an equally loud voice, "Ya little Dunce! How do ya expect me t' git down frum here!"

At that point the operator and all within earshot burst out laughing. The operator came to their rescue, started the wheel, got George to the ground and the pair headed for home. One can imagine the annoyance felt by Stella towards her younger brothers' behavior, as she was trying to build a good reputation at her job in the 5 and 10 cent store.

None of the family liked their new surroundings, feeling closed in, tired of the rain and longing for the wide open spaces of their Arizona home. The damp weather instead of helping Annie's arthritis did just the opposite, causing her extreme pain. Put all of this together and it is no wonder that they sold the house and left after only a couple of months residence. Will had hoped to have a nursery there but he hadn't found a buyer for their Verde farm yet. Thus, before he ever was able to travel north the family was right back in the exact spot from which they had started, all delighted to be home.

Farming for coppermine

Will and Annie had a wonderfully prosperous farm and orchards, located where the Clarkdale smelter slag dump has pushed the river to the east, cutting away most of the fertile homestead land. Helen writes, "When the smelter moved from Jerome down to Clarkdale, the company town named for Senator W. A. Clark from Montana, the copper company bought up all the farms. There were 13 farms and the Jordan farm was one of them. Papa was the supervisor for a year or two; and then he found that the bookkeeper for Senator Clark, who ran the mine, was juggling the books around to make it look like the farms were losing money; whereas it wasn't true. (He didn't want the extra work of keeping another set of books.) The farms were making a profit, by Papa's accounting, and helping support Clark's smelter venture. Papa's pride as a farmer and his honesty were offended, and he said he would not work under someone who was "dishonest."

When Will Jordan quit, the company told him that three miles down the river, the smelter smoke would not kill his crops. Annie and Will Jordan bought property at Bridgeport, approximately nine miles away. A few years later the Verde Extension Mine and Smelter opened at Clemenceau, about six miles from their ranch. Smoke from both smelters killed the crops. The alfalfa leaves turned white when the smoke settled on the ground. It even killed off the earth worms, and it took sixty years for them to be gradually reintroduced into the soil.

Helen continues, "In the first air pollution law suit on the records of the U.S. Supreme Court in Washington, a confederation of Verde Valley farmers, including Papa, won their case against the mining company." (The lawsuit is discussed in chapter eight.) Walter referred to that settlement as having provided a large portion of the money used to buy the homesteads in Sedona which George and Walter worked.

Upon moving from Rattlesnake Hill, W.A. Jordan would set up his nursery on a new farm, Sam Emery's old place, in the Verde Valley near Bridgeport. The family planted another orchard with pear, plum and apple trees, and, of course, they planted hay. W.A. Jordan (Will) became known throughout the Valley and in Prescott, Flagstaff and Phoenix areas for his produce, but, almost more important, he became the Valley's nurseryman. He built a hot bed which had an area dug out underneath the planting beds that had a wood-burning stove. There were pipes running the distance of the beds and the heat circulating through them kept the plants warm during the cold springs. Valley gardeners came to depend on the Jordan nursery.

Meanwhile, in 1913, Annie had a big, two-story house built, much like the one left behind on the Upper Verde. They were able to get the same man to build for them at Bridgeport who had been their builder on Rattlesnake Hill. Walter describes some of the living conditions and activities involved during the construction.

Submitted by Charles Jordan
Jordan home Bridgeport circa 1915

"Yeah," says Walter, "Mother got 'im, th' same man t' build that built th' one on Rattlesanke Hill. 'E built that new one right 'round th' old one, right 'round it an' over it. That summer durin' th' buildin' o' th' house, us boys 'ad t' sleep out north b'hind a big pile o' redwood shingles. Th' girls stayed in th' old house. That's when th' girls threw water on us. A friend o' Stella's frum Tempe [where Stella went to college, now ASU] was up t' visit, an' we figured we'd fix 'em. We went down in th' field where there's this real swampy place that's just full o' cockleburs [egg-shaped burrs with stickers all around and about an inch long] an' we gathered a lot o' 'em. Brought 'em up t' Stella's room, an' we pulled them covers down on that bed she was a sharin' with 'er friend. We just lined that white mattress with them cockleburrs, then we put them covers an' ever'thin' back, an' we was a'listenin' in th' next room when they went t' bed.

"'My Goodness, Stella! What is this in th' bed?' [Here Walter affects a high prissy voice.]

"'Huh?'

"Ag'in, as Blanch Wellingford, Stella's guest, squirmed around tryin' t' find a comfortable spot, 'My, what in th' world is this in this bed?!' [Using the same high voice.]

"Stella went over an' turned them sheets back an' laughed, 'Ya r'member when we threw water on th' boys out there? Well, this is payin' us back.'

"M', but they 'ad a time a'gettin' them cockleburs out." And he laughs just remembering. (See center for painting of Bridgeport Home.)

The Jordan household became a regular stop for Parson Bristow after his wife's death. During one such visit he was nearly sent home early when Annie discovered the scene of her father's cogitations. He loved to sit in front of the fireplace, thinking, chewing tobacco and spitting, but as his eyesight and aim had begun to fail, he had missed the fire with a major portion of his smelly brown spew, landing it on the hearth and sides of the fireplace. His daughter came in the room and was horrified at the unsightly, stinking mess.

"You just stop that! You take that nasty habit an' go outside!" was his daughter's admonition.

Annie, with her penchant for a spotless house, did not abide messiness or dirt, even the wood cooking stove shone. It must have been extremely difficult trying to live up to those self-imposed standards with six boys and a husband working in the fields, hunting and fishing, plus the general dusty/muddy climate.

Trip to the Hot Springs with Parson Bristow

As Annie's rheumatism continued to worsen a trip to the supposedly healing waters of the Verde Hot Springs was discussed more frequently. Walter reminisces about the exciting journey. "In 1914, as I r'call, Mother wanted t' try bathin' at Verde Hot Spring fer 'er rheumatism, an' ole Grandpa Bristow an' Uncle John Will Ralston [Annie's brother-in-law] wanted t' quit chewin' tobaccy, er so they said. Th' only way int' th' Hot Springs at that time was out o' th' little town o' Mayer. It was about a hundred mile drive over rough road. We left Bridgeport in two automobiles, m' Model T an' Uncle John Bristow's Chandler. We took this windin' road around Cherry Creek t' Mayer. It was in Mayer that Grandpa an' Uncle John Will secretly put in a big supply o' full plugs o' store tobaccy. Yeah, they sure did wanta' quit! [He issues a snort for emphasis.]

"Frum Mayer we went down Big Bug Creek an' camped th' first night out on a little flat on th' Big Bug called Big Gulch. That night Uncle John, [Bristow] was on th' outside o' one bed, an' I was on th' outside o' another. M' brother Bill, [Willie] an' m' father were sleepin' on th' inside. Well, they just kicked us an' kicked us somethin' awful, an' 'bout four o'clock in th' mornin' Uncle John said, 'Well, I've 'ad enough o' this. I'm a'gettin' up.'

"Well, I'm a'gettin' outta this bed too!' An' I did. "M' Uncle John Bristow was a wonderful cowman, an' 'e knew how t' cook sos I turned th' biscuit makin' over t' 'im while I got th' potatoes, coffee, an' this an' that goin'. S' we built a big fire, an' we 'ad some good coals fer th' dutch oven. By th' light o' th' fire I saw this orange box with th' Schilling's Best Bakin' Powder can in it, an' I took it over t' Uncle John, an' 'e loaded up th' biscuits with that stuff an' put them pretty biscuits in th' dutch oven.

"After while 'e took 'is old goncho stick an' raised th' lid offa that oven t' see how they's comin' along. 'E jumped back, a'holdin' on t' that lid, 'Whew, boy, that stuff in there'll knock ya' down!'

"Them biscuits didn't rise one bit, an' were kinda' green lookin'. We made such a noise that we woke th' ladies, an' I heard my Aunt Teedie Ralston say t' m' Mother, 'I'll betcha they got int' m' washin' powder.'

"I tole Uncle John what I'd overheard an' said, 'I know there's another can with bakin' powder in that box.'

"'e whispered back, 'Well, go git it. Now, we'll have some fun.'

"'E was a great hand at makin' up jokes, playin' pranks on people. 'Let's set them green uns aside, an' we'll make a new batch with this good bakin' powder, an' we'll be a'eatin' them when they all come t' eat '

"When we 'ad everything ready, Uncle John called out like a chuckwagon cook on roundup, 'Climb a wheel! Come an' git it!'

"M' brother Bill was th' first one t' take a biscuit, an' boy, 'e yelled an' coughed an' spit. I 'ad t' keep 'im quiet, so's 'e wouldn't ruin our fun. We wanted t' fool th' rest o' 'em, an' we did. Oh boy!! What'a time we 'ad!

"That day we continued on that old rough road through Bloody Basin, which got it's name frum a terrible war between th' cattlemen an' them sheepmen in th' 1880's – th' Tewksbury an' Graham war.

"That road through Bloody Basin takes ya' over th' hills right t' th' rim where ya' drop down t' th' Verde River Hot Springs. If ya' look t' th' right there b'fore a' startin' down, ya cin see Pine Mountain. That's right at th' head o' Houston Basin. There's a big cattle outfit in there — right above where th' old Hot Spring motel burned on th' west side o' th' river.

"Frum that rim we 'ad t' go down this horrible steep road t' get t' th' hot springs, an' it was thirteen miles frum th' top t' th' bottom, an' talk 'bout crooked. Oh, it scared me t' death! That happened t' b' th' year when th' Arizona Power Company was puttin' that heavy machinery in down there t' generate electricity. They were bringin' water across frum Fossil Springs in an aqueduct t' Childs where they were buildin' th' power plant. It was a 1600 foot drop on th' east side o' th' canyon an' th' only way they 'ad t' git th' machinery in was this ole road on th' west side. They were puttin' that machinery down there with 14 mules. Th' fella drivin' that team was ridin' one o' th' two big mules at th' rear — 'wheelers' they called 'em. 'E'd use a jerk line attached t' th' lead mule an' yell out, 'Hee! Hee!' 'E'd jerk 'im t' go t' th' left. 'Haw! Haw!' 'E'd jerk 'im t' th' right.

"Just as we were 'bout t' start down, there was a fella comin' outta there with a big empty freight wagon an' drivin' 14 mules like that. They'd unload th' heavy machinery frum rail cars ont' them great big wagons at th' Blue Bell Sidin' b' Mayer where th' railroad went down t' th' mines. That heavy machinery fer th' power plant was s' huge, they 'ad t' rough lock th' wheels when they went down that terrible 13 mile hill, droppin' 3000 feet int' Verde Hot Springs. Th' power plant was bein' built on th' river about a quarter mile frum th' springs. When they went down with this heavy machinery, they 'ad t' 'rough lock' it. [A type of skid under the wheel to help brake.] They 'ad them under both wheels t' hold that load frum runnin' away. Years later in Cottonwood, I was a talkin' t' this guy named Cleave Cox. 'E'd been a cowboy fer years an' even did a little work drivin' a stagecoach fer th' movies there in Sedona in th' 1930's. 'E said, 'That could'a been me comin' up out o' there. I helped put that machinery in there at Childs.'

"'Ya' mean ya' helped t' put that machinery in there fer that power plant?'

"'I sure did!'

"He really knew how to drive them critters. [mule teams] He knew how t' drive six-up too, a team o' six horses or mules.

"There warn't no way t' get in there, only that road through Mayer an' Big Bug Creek. Now, o' course, ya' go down through Fossil Creek. The road's paved t' where ya' take off down th' six miles er so t' th' lower power house. There's two power houses above. There's a dirt road when ya' git t' th' bottom that winds t' th' right. It passes Stehr Lake. That's where th' water's settled t' git th' mud outta it. It takes off in this big pipe an' goes down 1600 feet where it kicks th' turbine. That's where th' Arizona Power's generators are there at Childs. Verde Hot Springs is only about a quarter o' a mile above Childs.

"On th' west side o' th' river there near Childs is a big cow outfit. They're still [1982] runnin' cattle in there. Th' last time I heard, a fella named Stanley was th' rancher in there, but I don't know who it is now. Anyway, right above th' power plant, an' all th' buildings, they'd made this ole road acrost th' Verde between th' hot springs an' them power house buildings. It went on, this rough road that we traveled, clear on down t' Houston Creek an' it went on clean into Bloody Basin, but it was a rough old bugger, my yes!

"These days there's a new road in there built with bulldozers. It leaves th' highway frum Phoenix right there near Cordes Junction an' goes over b' th' Dugas Ranch. Th' highway crosses Big Bug Creek right about there where th' turn-off is.

"I'll never forget drivin' that ole road outta there to Mayer. I come back outta there alone, an' I 'ad t' turn my Model T 'round an' back up that awful steep road t' get outta that deep hole. [The car had more power going in reverse than in forward.] It was gettin' int' early November an' I 'ad t' gather up th' last o' them tomatoes. Dad, Bill, (Willie), Grandpa Bristow, Uncle John Bristow, Uncle John Will, Stella, Alice, Mother an' Aunt Teedie stayed down there.

"They got ole Grandpa Bristow t' takin' them baths. 'E took about two o' 'em, an' it begun t' make 'im sick. 'E said t' m' mother, 'Annie, I don't think I'll go in there anymore. M' tobaccy just don't taste right no more.' That ole nicotine was makin' 'im sick, an' oh didn't m' mother give 'im a lecture, 'Ya come down here t' get rid o' that nasty habit, an' now yer a quittin' the baths!'

"'E just went on a chewin' an' a spittin' as long as 'e lived."

Sometimes it is difficult to understand the value systems of others. Allen sheds some light on another part of the Parson's thinking. "It'd tickle me th' way Grandpa considered a man's vices. Th' Ralston boys were laughin' so heartily about somethin' Grandpa'd said one time that they nearly fell of a their horses:

"'Lawsy me, what a shockin' thing th' way these girls dress now! Why I got t' lookin' at them an' nearly fell from Grace!'"

To which John Ralston replied, "'Grace? Why I didn't know that was his ole mare's name. I thought her name was Bessie.'" Peals of laughter followed.

Upstanding strong prejudices

Annie Jordan had a fertile mind and imagination in which the seeds of her prejudices had grown tall and strong. She was called a 'hard-shell' Baptist and a thoroughly 'Black Republican.' The necessary tools for the expression of her mind she sometimes found in the kitchen, and she loved to bake. When it came time to prepare for the Sunday visit of two Baptist preachers — one a Democrat and one a Republican — she baked a cake for each. To make known her view on the undisputable character traits of a Democratic Baptist, she included in his cake a yellow layer for cowardice.

Walter pressed her to the true test of her dual loyalties to Baptist teaching and Republican politics. Because Arizona was mainly filled with Democrats for years, he registered as a Democrat just to have a voice in the primary elections. There was only one candidate on the Republican ticket for the primary and sometimes not that. During Prohibition Days (1920s) a character from the mining town of Jerome, who openly made moonshine liquor, ran for a county office as a Republican. Walt and his mother, so the story goes, got into this big argument over for whom to vote.

"Well, Mama, even if 'e is a Republican, it would b' against yer Christian beliefs an' upstandin' strong prejudices t' vote fer 'im. I cain't see how ya would ever vote fer somebody that was a drunkard and made moonshine liquor," Walt goaded.

"'I'm here t' tell ya, Walter Jordan, that th' very worst Republican is better than th' best Democrat!'" With that settled no one ever questioned Annie again about how she marked her ballot. She truly thought a lot of Walter's quiet, peace-loving wife, Ruth, but never forgave her for being "a hot headed southern Democrat!" [As a very young child Ruth's family had migrated from Kentucky to Tempe, AZ.]

Church attendance and baptism were not on Will's "to do list." Whenever the topic of baptism by immersion was mentioned his comment was, "I'll take my bath at home." Walter remembers, "One time m' Dad asked th' pastor that'd rode up frum th' Verde t' preach at our house, 'Now, what's th' matter with me? I've raised a big family. I've provided well fer 'em.'

"'Mr. Jordan, ya done wonderful, but ya cannot go t' heaven unless ya're born again.'

"M' Dad couldn't believe that until 'e was near death. Then 'e told me, 'I look back, an' I wish I 'ad m' last fifty years t' live over.'"

The generation of grandchildren are left to wonder, just what things he would have changed simply because he had experienced the act of baptism. Although he was bedridden and couldn't be immersed, he did ask for the pastor to come shortly before he died and made a confession of faith.

Will Jordan and Annie Bristow Jordan left a legacy in the Verde Valley and Sedona of honesty, self-reliance, determination and hard work. The Match from Maine will be long remembered in center stage of the drama of the Verde Valley.

Annie and Will, late 1940s

Endnote

The homestead in Bridgeport remained in the family until about 1990, when Charles Jordan, son of Sumner, sold the farm to run the Bent River Ranch, the family farm of his wife, near old Clarkdale. Young Charles Jordan's first love had been fixing engines etc., and he spent over a year in the Air Force, as a jet plane mechanic with the Strategic Air Command. However, he returned to care for the Jordan family farm when his father died and his mother needed him. He took up his life's work to which he'd been trained from the time his legs were long enough to drive a tractor; and, as of this writing, he continues to nurture young fruit trees and bring in the hay in a field beside the river not unlike his Grandfather, Will Jordan's first homestead.

Sumner is a place name in Maine, but Sumner Jordan's full name was Charles Sumner Jordan, and he was most likely named for the American statesman and anti-slavery leader, Charles Sumner (1811-1874). As the Senator from Massachusetts in 1856, he ridiculed, in a speech to the Senate, his fellow Senator from the state of South Carolina so roundly, that the offended Senator's nephew beat Sumner with a cane in the Senate three days later. The brutality rallied the North, and Sumner went on to become a founder of the Republican party. He was at the height of his power in the Senate during the Civil War.[5]

Clemenceau: The United Verde Extension Mining Company was constructed at this location in 1917. The town was first called Verde, but due to possible confusion with other Verde post offices, the name Clemenceau was chosen to honor Georges Clemenceau., the French Minister of War during WWI. "This was done to commemorate the part which Clemenceau played in helping the Allies win the war."[6] The smelter closed permanently in January, 1937. The smokestack was imploded in the late 1940s. Other buildings currently house various businesses.

FOOTNOTES

(1) Birth records from Cape Elizabeth, Maine, vol.5, 149.

(2) <u>The Jordan Memorial</u>. Comp. Tristram F. Jordan. 2nd ed. Camden, Maine: Picton P, 1995. 390.

(3) Jordan, Albion M. Letter to His Wife. Jan. 1850. Museum Archives, Cape Elizabeth, Maine.

(4) Jordan, Will A. <u>My Only Indian Scare</u>. <u>Pioneer Stories of Arizona's Verde Valley</u>. Comp. Mrs. John Bristow, Mrs. E.W. Monroe, and Mrs. D.W. Wingfield. Camp Verde: The Verde Valley Pioneers Association, 1933. 99.

(5) Hasseltine, W B. "Sumner, Charles." Ed. Robert O. Zeleny. <u>World Book</u>. 20 vols. Chicago, Illinois: Field Enterprises Educational Corp., 1965.

(6) Barnes, Will C., and Byrd H. Granger. <u>Arizona Place Names</u>. Tucson, AZ: U. of A. P, 1960. 339.

From the Boys With the Colors

Under This Heading The Verde Copper News Will Publish Word from the Boys at the Front. Parents Who Desire the Publication of Letters Are Asked to Forward Them to This Office.

Miss Mary Wingfield has received the following letter from her cousin, William Jordan. It is dated from "Somewhere in PEACEFUL France" on November 21:

This is an answer to your and Effie's fine letters of October 2 and am glad to say since then the choicest gift of all time has been showered upon us! It is hard to realize it but it is true, for I am right here on the battlefield which less than two weeks ago was a roaring tempest of shot and shell but now as quiet as it is right there on the lawn at home. It is simply grand and I am very thankful to have lived to see the finish of the biggest of all wars. I have gone through two big drives and am unscratched from wounds and am well. In fact I am fleshier now than I have ever been.

But I feel sort of uneasy about you and the folks at home for fear you will get that awful Spanish flu which is causing so much sickness and deaths. Alice told me that Allisons had it, also Frank Stephens. She said they were having quite a bit of rain so maybe that will stop the spread of it.

The folks said you were all at the tree meeting and heard grandpa speak. I would like to have been there, you know, but my letter was there as my representative, and, Mary, let's truly hope and wish to all be together for next tree meeting time. Personally, I don't think we will be home by Christmas this year, but that is just a guess. The biggest thought in our minds is when will we sail for the "Statue of Liberty?"

I haven't had a chance to visit Abner or Chester, for they are—or at least I know Abner is—a long way from me. I have had several letters from him and have written several times.

Mary, I thank you and Effie for your good letters for it strengthens my faith in God to know you at home are praying and working for the safekeeping and provision of us boys over here. My own acquaintance with the Divine has been my closest friend and greatest source of strength through every hardship and fierce battle.

The 89th division has made good and was at the front when the firing ceased. We may be able to scan through the pages of the history of "1914-1918 world war" and find a fine record for the 89th. Our objective was set and we reached it every time. The Huns knew it; that is why they are backing up behind the Rhine.

That is why the kaiser, the coward, sneaked out of his throne and beat it like a whipped hound into good little neutral Holland. And that is why the dove of peace flies over the land heralding the sweetest note that ever struck the heart of man since the birth of our Savior himself. It has come at a time to be the most precious Christmas gift of the ages, for it is "Peace on earth, good will toward men."

These beautiful words can now be read with more meaning than ever before for there is a message in them for everyone. So let's rejoice and be glad that the time is ripe for peace negotiations.

It is getting dark in my room so will close hoping this finds all of you well. Say hello to Jim and Effie and Peggy and all my friends.

Lovingly,
COUSIN WILLIE.

Chapter Five

WILD ABUNDANCE

Above the Verde Valley, the runoff from the Colorado Plateau has cut spectacular canyons in it's descending paths to the Verde River and in this central region of Arizona a great variety and abundance of life gathered.

The most famous of the water-cut crevices in the shelf of the Colorado Plateau is Oak Creek Canyon. Stella Jordan, one of Walter's three sisters, felt so passionately about the grandeur of the canyon that she painstakingly described it in her writings. (See center for painting of Oak Creek)

"Deep in the heart of Arizona is Oak Creek Canyon. We Arizonans of this section call it the 'Enchanted Place.' A tourist, who once made the trip from Flagstaff to Prescott via the Oak Creek Route, said, 'Oak Creek Canyon is indescribable. Certainly it is the more wonderful section of scenic grandeur I have found in all my travels, and I have covered the best part of the United States.' Oak Creek Canyon is at the height of its beauty in June, [although some would say fall], when one is reminded of the Psalmists song: 'The heavens declare the glory of God; and the firmament sheweth his handywork.' Here mountains rise from low hills or plains to a sheer height of 2500 or 3000 feet above the surrounding country. The base line of these mountain pinnacles is surrounded with Arizona cypress or [locally called] the yew tree, which is found nowhere else on earth but in Arizona, unless it has been transported by man. Mingled with the yew trees is found cedar of many varieties, pinon, manzanita, buck brush, mescal or century plant, ocotillos or devil's walking cane, skunk bushes or squaw berries, algerita or Spanish currants, juniper, spruce, and balsam. Nearer the creek are quaking aspen, and Arizona Sycamores.

"This canyon offers unlimited and unexplored areas to the archaeologist and geologist, as well as ever-changing color and fantastic sculpture to the artist. [Years later her sister-in-law, Helen, would become one of these artists.] Here one may walk where flowers bloom, where the fronds of ferns serve as parasols to insect life, where the crystal-clear water ever ripples and clouds vanish into thin air in the bluest of skies. (See center for painting of abundant forest flora)

"Here and there the mountains are torn with ragged ravines in which the lairs of wild animals may be found - cougars and bear. Wild turkeys and deer are in abundance. The region might truly be considered a 'Happy Hunting Ground'."[1]

Donna Ashworth, in her book Arizona Triptych, says, that beside "the rushing water of Oak Creek, deep in its canyon,.... [even when the] sun was hot, they were cool under the moving shadows of oak and white-barked sycamore. Pine and fir trees climbed slopes that soared suddenly into colored cliffs."[2]

Submitted by Walter Jordan, Jr.
Bill Gray and Orphaned Fawn, 1930s

The abundance of wildlife in all of the Verde River watershed, including Oak Creek Canyon, enticed the forerunners of the "wave of immigrants" as they searched for food and furs. As discussed earlier, these Mountain Men did some trapping way up near the headwaters of the Verde, mainly seeking beaver pelts. The settlers and the cavalry, as well as the Indians, were somewhat dependent on the fish and wild game of the area for food. Any hunting, fishing, or just being out in the forest wilderness could have times of great danger. One of the hazards in those early days was the grizzly bear, and meeting one could, without a doubt, be a major problem.

Up until 1880, Bear Howard, famous as a bear hunter in Oak Creek Canyon, made his living selling skins. At Sterling Springs, the source of Oak Creek, the state fish and game department established two fish hatcheries specializing in trout - the wild version of which was most certainly the reason for the thriving bear population. In the early days "fisher folk" from all points north including Flagstaff (the closest railway connection), entered Oak Creek Canyon by a "zig-zag trail" laid out by Dave Hart. (Hart was a cattleman in Flagstaff who moved his family down into Oak Creek Canyon to farm. Old man Howard was their only neighbor.)[3 & 3a]

Approximately three miles north of present-day Sedona a very deep canyon, called Wilson Canyon, enters Oak Creek. According to Walter, Wilson Canyon was so named for a bear hunter, Mr. Wilson who was staying with the Thompson family, whose place was up beyond Indian Gardens (approximately 3–4 miles further). The story goes that Mr. Thompson went to Flagstaff up the steep switchback trail with his mule to get supplies, but a snow storm came, preventing his timely return. Since the family was running very, very low on supplies, Mr. Wilson said he would walk the few miles down to Sedona and get them some things. On the way he encountered a bear in this canyon, not too far up from Midgely Bridge which now crosses the gorge. As was his custom, he wounded the bear with his gun and was about to slit its throat when his knife hung-up in his scabbard. He was unable to get it out, and the bear charged him. When he didn't return after three days, folks came looking for him. When they found his remains, his little dog was sitting by him waiting for help. It appeared that he had tried to climb a large tree for his safe get-away. However, claw marks on the tree and a boot heel found near-by indicated the bear was the faster and by grabbing the heel of Mr. Wilson's boot, pulled him to his death. F. Ruth, Walter's daughter, recalled that as a very young child her Dad showed the family the tree with the claw marks. She says, "I could visualize Mr. Wilson's mauled body lying there with his faithful dog sitting mournfully beside him." (A gory scene, not to be easily forgotten, especially when each fall and spring there would be a single set of bear tracks measuring 14 inches across just outside the Jordan bedroom.) The tree that bore the claw marks stood until the flood in 1938.

Many of the early folks had a lion story or two to tell, and Jesse Goddard was no exception. "Used t' be lots o' deer in this country when I cowboyed here in th' early 1900's. See them bluffs over there? [Pointing to the mountains west of Camp Verde.] One winter a big ole' lion jumped out frum under there. My goodness! He was a whopper. We got 'im. We tracked 'im with dogs. It was a cold trail, but th' third day we got 'im. While we were after 'im, he killed a calf an' a deer an' a yearlin' filly. He didn't touch th' deer an' calf, he just killed 'em. That yearlin's belly — he ate about a quarter o' it."

"Say did I ever tell ya about that big ole' lion I shot at," began Walter. "Th' only time I ever saw one when out huntin'. I got one shot at a wild lion only that one time, a' climbin' out o' Brady Canyon in th' big oak brush. I shot right b'tween 'is ears. Brady runs int' Beaver, an' this fellah an' I were huntin' bucks up along there. 'E was a gettin' backup shots. Well, this big ole' lion was down in th' bottom, an' went right up them bluffs an' stopped in th' scrub oak right at th' top o' th' canyon — 120 yards frum me, an' oh, 'e was a big bugger. An' I went t' sit down t' make a knee rest fer m' aim, an' a Spanish Dagger [a type of agava plant] poked me right in th' rear! That made me nervous, [most likely he reared up fast, too], an' I shot that ole' lion right between th' ears about an inch too high t' kill 'im. I saw th' dust fly, an' 'e come outta that thicket an' jumped thirty feet right down over that ridge. This crazy fool I was a huntin' with, 'e went an' shot right b' th' side o' m' head. It stunned me s' bad, I couldn't shoot anymore. Now ain't that a fine howdy ya' do!! (Walter's gestures and animation always made the stories vivid and gave the listener the feeling of being in the middle of the action!).

Lion hunters with dogs, 1930s

"M' brother Chester was down below us, an' he saw that lion a'runnin'. 'E 'ad a Springfield army gun but 'e was havin' t' shoot about 500 yards. Chester didn't get 'im, an' th' lion run off int' Beaver Canyon. My cousin Jim Austin was runnin' cattle there at th' Apache Maid ranch where we was a stayin'. When 'e come in that evenin', I told 'im where this big ole' beast was, an' he says, 'That bugger's been killin' some o' my calves. I'll go over t' Harris Park [about 10 miles distant], an' I'll get Giles Goslick t' come over here with 'is hounds.'

"A day an'a half after we jumped that lion. Giles took 'is six hounds down there in this country, awful thick with cedars an' brush. This female, one o' them six hounds, she was th' best. She picked that lion's scent up, an' she went right down offa that ridge where that lion went int' Beaver Canyon. Old Giles, all 'e ever took was just a little ole sack with somethin' t' eat in it, an' 'e chased that lion, an' 'e chased that lion. 'E had a 30-30 rifle an' 'e followed them dogs. They run that bugger down int' Beaver, an' 'e went out through an' over th' Tin Roof Pasture, a big long distance, an over int' West Clear Creek. Those hounds run Giles down int' th' bottom o' that Creek an' clean over t' th' other side, mighty rough stuff. They kept a'runnin' clear on t' right near Mud Tanks where they finally caught up. There them dogs treed that ole' bugger. Giles shot 'im —a great big ole Tom, measured eleven feet frum tip t' tip. My, oh my! They chased 'im 36 hours. Jim paid Giles seventy-five dollars an' th' state paid 'im seventy-five. Oh, 'e was th' best lion hunter that was ever known.

"There was no season on huntin' lion then, just shoot 'im when ya' could. Now that crazy game department's got a season on 'em, an' you have t' pay t' git a license t' hunt 'em. Crazy damn fools! If th' lions git t' killin' th' cowmen's cattle an' calves, then they can git a permit t' kill 'em. No, it's crazy. Th' lions are on th' increase t' beat th' band. An', another thing, th' government's payin' fer men t' kill coyotes. Them dang howlin' critters 'er gettin' thicker than hawks. They come up an' eat out here b' th' house. I 'ad t' quit dumpin' them scraps right out here over Mormon Canyon there was s' many. George saw a pack o' twelve on th' ridge above 'is house. [George's and Walter's ranchers were adjoining.]. 'E counted six pups." [Walter had no objections to the coyotes being killed, but he felt that the lion population was getting too heavy also.)

"When I used t' dump them table scraps out here, th' coyotes would b' eatin' an' all, an' them dogs o' ours, m' goodness, they were just havin' a fit. Th' coyotes still come up here every once in a while. Old Tasha [their black chow] gets after 'em now! Oooowh! I remember old Shep. Oh, 'e was a big dog, as big as Tasha! 'E'd go out here t' th' brink o' th' canyon when there was a coyote gang a'yippin', an' ole Shep'd b' over there barkin' back at 'em. I'd get s' mad at 'im 'cause 'e wouldn't come back when I called 'im. One mornin' 'e went over there t' fight, an' o' all th' yellin' ya' ever heard in yer life! 'E just screamed! When Shep come back, 'e just went right under this house. I knew there was somethin' terrible wrong. Them coyotes have got th' sharpest teeth o' anythin' ya' ever saw. When they go fer a dog's leg er foot, they'll bite 'im clean through, an' that's what they did t' Shep. They bit 'im right through th' top o' 'is foot, clean through that foot. 'E'd just do anythin' I'd told 'im after that. [Walt ended the tale with a snort and chuckle.]

"When Shep was a pup, only two thirds grown, a big rattler, sank two holes int' 'im. Here's how it happened. I didn't get down on m' Model A t' oil up my big pump in th' mornin' that day, so's I went down after dinner. But, I walked through th' pass where Anne's [his oldest daughter's] house is t' do th' job an' check th' pipeline followin' Morman Canyon an' a comin' through b' Anne's. Th' dogs started t' follow me, an' I said, 'Go back, go back.'

"I thought they'd gone back t' th' house, but doggone it, they must 'ave got t' foolin' around in some bushes there east o' Anne's house. When I got back, Ruth said, 'Teddy came home but Shep didn't. Somethin' must b' th' matter.'

"So's I called an' called ole' Shep, an' finally 'e come up th' road a'crawlin' on 'is belly. Oh, my gosh! I could see somethin' terrible was wrong. So's I started t' examine 'im. That darn rattler got 'im right here on 'is throat, just under his jaw, right there. [As he points under his own chin.] It was a' startin' t' swell. Ya' know, when a pup sees a ol' rattler an' hears th' buzzin' o' its rattles, it gits curious an' gits too close. That big old bugger, 'e must 'ave been a monster b'cause it was wide between them fang marks, like 2 inches. Yeah! That's right, two inches. [Walt nods his head for emphasis.] I knew what t' do. I just kept bathin' that wound in kerosene, an' it just kept a' swellin', looked like 'e 'ad two heads. Finally th' hair all come off, an' th' swellin' went down frum around the wound. That blamed thing really swelled up, an' this here kerosene made it break an' drain, but it got swelled up three times b'fore it quit an' healed up. Ya' know that affected that dog. 'E never was as smart after that an' 'e never learned another darned thing."

As so many times, one story led to another. "Dad 'ad a shepherd dog on th' old ranch. [The one on Upper Verde, or Clarkdale.] 'E just loved t' chase bobcats, an' he'd kill rattle snakes. 'E'd rush in at one an' git 'im b' th' back o' th' neck an' 'e'd just shake 'im that a way, [demonstrating by giving his hand several hard shakes], an' kill 'im. Dad tried t break th' dog o' it, yeah. Then one day th' dog come in after 'e'd been gone fer about a week. 'E come in with mud caked on 'is nose an' face right up t' 'is eyes. 'E'd been down in th' swamp seekin' a cure on is own fer a snakebite. 'E got bit right on th' nose, an' 'e stuck 'is nose in th' mud t' bring that poison out. When it dried, 'e'd break th' blister an' then stick his nose back in th' mud until 'e got well. Ain't that somethin' — that dog knew what t' do, but 'e was 'bout t' starve t' death when 'e come home. Say, did ya' know that big strong guy, John Wetzel, that worked fer George an' me? 'E done th' same thing. Yeah, that's right. 'E was gone frum work several days an' when 'e come back 'is arm was all swelled up.

"'Hey John what's the matter with yer arm?'

"'I got bit b' an ole' rattler, an' I been settin' b' th' creek with m' arm stuck in th' mud so's that ole' red mud could suck out all o' that poison.'

"Would ya b'lieve, 'is arm got just as good as new. An' 'e never 'ad no more troubles with that thing.

"I killed a big rattlesnake m'self once up on th' ditch bank. [At their Bridgeport home.] This big rattler was coiled in th' Johnson grass. I went back t' where two Mexican families were a stayin' in that big adobe house. They lent me a shotgun. That grass was s' thick an' high, I 'ad t' part it b'fore I stepped in there t' kill that big rattler, just shot 'is head off." During his life on the farm in Sedona and his numerous hunting and fishing trips, Walter would kill many more rattlers. He even tackled a Gila Monster one time on the Verde.

Ruth, Walt's wife interrupts, "When the children were little, I couldn't let them go out to play without an adult with them because there were so many rattlesnakes. Walter killed seven in one week next to our house here in Sedona."

Many more scary rattlesnake stories could be told but there are lots of other creatures to learn about, including Gambel Quail and deer.

Willie, or Bill, was the boy closest to Walter in age and they had a lot of similar things they enjoyed doing, thus they were often together. Walter describes some of these good times, "Durin' quail huntin' season m' brother Bill an' I 'ad a good place up north frum our ole home. We'd b' gone three or four days, just us two a campin' out. Then durin' deer season we'd go back there deer huntin'. First buck I ever killed in m' life was when I was seventeen years old. I killed this ole six point buck, an' we carried it on one horse, an' we took turns ridin' th' other horse. Top o' that mountain where we got 'im frum our farm was well over ten miles, actually 12 miles. That was just b'fore their matin' season when th' bucks git terrible big, an' this buck's neck was big an' smelled pretty bad. Well, we got this one home an' skinned him. We cut some steaks offa 'im, an' Mother started t' cook 'em. Th' smell nearly run us all out o' th' house, it was s' strong! She said, 'Ya git that thing outta here! I don't want any more o' that in here!'

"So Dad give venison t' th' Indians workin' fer 'im, an' we give some t' that big family that was livin' at th' mouth o' Oak Creek. That family that 'ad lots o' bees. Oh, they thought that was wonderful venison! We didn't eat very much o' it ourselves. It was too strong."

"Did you have to have a permit to hunt deer back then?" asked Lee Jackson, one of his grandsons.

"Th' limit was two bucks a year. Yeah, there was a season, an' it was too long. They finally saw that they 'ad t' cut it down, an' they did. Now ya' got t' draw t' get a permit, an' ya' got t' hunt in a certain area. It's nothin' like it use t' b'. I'm glad I 'ad m' fun when I did. I killed forty bucks straight, in-season, with th' same rifle. I gave that old 30-30 t' George, an' it shoots right on th' money yet. I started huntin' elk an' I had t' git a bigger gun. Th' 30/30 didn't 'ave enough knock-down power. I killed three big bull elk with th' gun I got now, an' several bucks. I never did get a shot at a wild bear.

"Did I ever tell ya about me and Ed Hutchison going up this big canyon there on the south side of Mund's Mountain. [East of Sedona]. We'd been told that ya could ride up through that canyon on a burro, yeah, right on up through that canyon. Well, we's on foot, but when we got up there in that brush an' stuff, we said, ' That's th' biggest lie there ever was! Ain't no one could ride a burro up through here!'

"Well, we finally got up on top an' we wanted t' go huntin' out on Lee Mountain t' see what's out there. It's awful hard t' git frum Mund's Mountain t' Lee Mountain, even though they're right next t' each other. There's just one place ya cin git around there on it. There's a great big bluff, an' ya cin just barely git around. We got out way down on th' end an' we decided, 'Let's go down an' look there on th' ground an' see if we can't find a place t' get offa this thing instead o' goin' clear back up over Lee Mountain an' down that horrible canyon again.' We were tryin' t' git back int' Morg's Stable where I left m' pickup. [Morg's Stable is between Sedona and Village of Oak Creek where there is a series of breaks in the base of the mountain which formed rather natural stables. "Old Man Morgan" kept horses in these, thus the name Morg's Stable.]

"We looked around an' it must 'ave been 200 er 300 feet below us that water 'ad poured over that cliff there an' ground out a place in this big sandstone ledge. There's a great big pool o' cold water there. We went around t' th' other side o' th' pool an' found a crevice in th' bluff. It was just wide enough fer us t' git through, So's we took th' shells outta our rifles, an' we wedged ourselves against th' bluff an' went down through that crack about 50 feet int' Morg's Stable. Oh my! What a time we had!!"

Walter (on right) and goose, early 1920s

There was a wide variety of game along the Mogollon Rim, and all of the country surrounding it, including the Verde watershed. The Jordan brothers appeared to "know every inch" of the area and where the best places were for hunting.

"I use t' hunt in Box Canyon, down there on th' Verde. [South of Camp Verde where the ancient lake broke through.] Th' cattle come in frum th' west there, but you cain't git down there except with ladders. People go down th' ladders on th' east side yet. [circa 1985]. I use t' go down both sides, but that ladder on th' west side has deteriorated, just all rotten. I think they tore it down. Chester, Willie, (Brother Bill), an' I hunted there goin' down them ladders before WWI. [These ladders were built by Paradise Valley and North Scottsdale Water District years ago. It was hoped to use the water as an additional source for their towns. Salt River Project put a stop to the project as the Verde is a tributary to the Salt, so in a sense SRP got there first.]

"Once I went a goose huntin' alone down in there. Th' geese were at a place right near this terrible, thick patch o' water lilies, s' I crawled int' these water lilies so's that I could see 'em an' th' bushes was' s' thick I could only see two. Ya' cain't never hardly kill an'thin' a shootin' through brush like that. O' course, I 'ad that powerful shotgun an' No.2 Shot. I only shot once. That's all I could do b'cause th' brush was so thick, an' when I finally got out o' there an' ran around t' where th'

Walter with ducks and geese, 1920s

geese were, I 'ad <u>six</u> o' them buggers. [Perhaps, over the years, the number of shots he used in his story were significantly less than the amount actually fired] I 'ad t' walk a mile an' a half t' git t' where them ladders were. I 'ad a pair o' hip boots on an' a shotgun an' a coat with shells, not t' mention them geese. I took m' belt off an' wrapped it 'round their necks — six o' 'em, three in front o' me an' three b'hind me. Now, you can imagine what a load I 'ad! Them geese weighed from 10 t' 12 pounds apiece. I'd stop about every 200 t' 300 yards. Finally I got t' th' foot o' th' hill at th' bottom o' them ladders, an' I was afraid I might get in trouble with th' game warden. (I didn't just want t' leave them extras on th' ground t' rot, when somebody could use 'em fer food.) Now, by golly, I 'ad my 1947 Ford Super Deluxe Sedan parked at th' top o' them ladders. You bet, I'd drove that new car down over that terrible rough road, real easy like. I took three o' them geese on m' shoulder an' up them ladders I come. When th' coast was clear, I opened up th' trunk an' threw them three in. Then I went down th' ladder an' got them other three an' put 'em in. I struck out fer m' folks place t' give two geese t' m' brother Sumner an' two t' m' sister Alice. Then I's safe in goin' on home with th' other two."

Will loved being out hunting and fishing as long as he was physically able. When in his 80s he could no longer trail game, but he loved setting out his duck decoys and sitting in the blind waiting for the waterfowl to arrive. On several occasions he had some amusing experiences. Again, we rely on Walter to bring these to life.

"Mr. Giroux, one o' th' head minin' men in Jerome, liked t' hunt. 'E'd come down t' Peck's Lake t' hunt ducks. One time, m' father was down in under th' brink o' th' hill, outta sight in a blind, with duck decoys a settin' out in th' water. Giroux thought they was live ducks, an' 'e blasted 'em good. 'E ruined two or three o' them decoys, an' Dad yelled up at 'im. 'Hey ya dumb bunny! Watcha think ya're a'doin'?'

"Giroux knew m' father, an' 'e come down an' apologized.

"'Listen, Mr. Jordan, I'll do anything t' keep this quiet. They'd just razz m' t' death in Jerome, if they found this out.'

"Dad told 'im, 'Well, I won't say nothin' about it.'

"That was some experience, wasn't it? Another time Bertie Hawkins shot th' glass eye out o' one o' my father's decoys.

"'Look out what ya're doin'!' Dad yelled.

"When Bertie got close enough, Dad recognized 'im, an' Bertie asked how much 'e owed Dad.

"'I'll tell ya, ya're a mighty good shot with a rifle! Anybody that cin hit that duck's glass eye at that distance is a mighty good shot! It's alright. Ya keep yar money.' Yeah, 'e 'ad some good times.

"Ya' wanted t' hear some huntin' stories, s' what'd ya' think o' them?!" Walt continued. "Oh say this ain't a huntin' tale but I remember a live turkey shoot once right out there between where th' jail is now an' Lon Mason's place in Cottonwood. They 'ad them turkeys tied t' this steel pin a way down in th' dry river bottom. Th' river was beyond th' turkeys, an' I thought I'd take a chance. I got my 30/30 rifle, but my goodness, it was s' far! Why I couldn't reach 'em, an' I got mad 'cause I'd bought three shots fer a dollar. I went home t' see m' brother. Chester

From the slide collection of George Jordan

Walter and turkey, 1940s

'ad joined th' gun club an' so they issued them Springfield Army guns t' th' fellows that joined that rifle club t' practice shootin'. Them guns 'ad steel jacketed bullets, so I went down an' I got this old Springfield out. I said t' m' brother Willie, [Bill], 'Let's go out an' target shoot this thing 'bout th' distance that I think them turkeys are.'

"We put an ole five gallon can up on that flat there towards where th' Kentucky Fried Chicken is now in Cottonwood. Wasn't nobody around, an' I practiced with that ole' Springfield. It 'ad a creak trigger, ya could pull an' ya'd feel it creak, then th' least little touch an' off she goes. 'We've got that thing sighted in now,'

I said, 'Come on up an' let's shoot them turkeys.'

"So's I took about three shots. I wasted one first t' see if I'd th' range right. Shot right int' th' Verde River over th' top o' them turkeys. I fired, an' boy, it was right on the money! The ole bullet hit th' Verde River, kersplash! Well, th' next time, I got a turkey sighted in on this second shot, got th' ole peep sight lined up, took th' creak out o' that trigger an' I pulled. [Walter demonstrated holding the gun and sighting, then created a pop sound with his hands at this point in the story.] Lon Mason was down in th' river bottom away frum th' range there, an' Bruce Rickett was up where th' shooters were. 'E said, 'Why don't ya go ahead an' shoot again?'

"'Well, I'm not goin' shoot a dead turkey!'

"So they culled out that gobbler an' saw that I'd bored it right through. That steel-jacketed bullet never hurt th' meat atall. I did th' same with th' third shot. This time, th' bullet went through a turkey hen an' hit th' steel pin th' turkey was tied t', an' the'bullet ricochetted an' almost hit Roland Ricketts out there. No guns were reachin' that range except Chester's ole Springfield an' th' 22 Savage Highpower. All them men standin' around there said, 'Hey, let me shoot that gun. We're payin' good money.'

"An' ya know with that Springfield another fellah won one. Two men won turkeys an' then Bill an' I left. There was a grocery store in Cottonwood at that time an' I said, 'Bill, we don't want two turkeys. That ham's th' best.'

"It was Thanksgivin' see, an' s' I sold th' turkey gobbler. I spent a dollar t' get 'im an' I sold 'im fer three. That was right between 1914 an' when Bill went t' th' Army in 1917. That's when we shot at them turkeys. Th' law stopped us frum shootin' at them live birds an' then they 'ad clay pigeons t' shoot. Ya' remember th' time Mr. Rudd lived down here? 'E was up there t' a turkey shoot west o' Clemenceau. George woulda liked t' 'ave been in that turkey shoot, do you remember that? Well, I happened t' go over there an' Mr. Rudd was there, an' 'e 'ad a Savage shotgun just like th' one in m' clothes closet right now. Mr. Rudd said, 'Hey, Walt, ya're a good shot. Ya enter there. I'm gonna pay fer your shoot.'

"Th' first time I broke 22 out o' 25 clay pigeons. Dr. Lee Hawkins was in that shoot. 'E was in th' gun club with Dad — four o' them: Walter Miller, Dad, Lee Hawkins an' Nablock. They was th' champion clay pigeon team in th' state o' Arizona. An' ole Doc Hawkins said, 'I might'a know'd 'e'd [Walt] win it. 'E's a chip offa th' ole block.'

"Oh, m' gosh, 'e got me t' shoot again, an' I broke 23 out o' 25. O' course, this was a Savage gun. I never shot one b'fore that, but I won a turkey fer Mr. Rudd. Somebody else wanted me t' shoot an' I won one fer 'im. I don't think I ever told ya that story!"

Besides hunting, Walter and his two older brothers acquired their father's love of fishing. Some favorite places in those days were Pecks Lake, (as we learned from Walter's excapade in chapter 4), the Verde River and Oak Creek. It would take all day to go the approximate 30 miles by wagon out to Oak Creek. Up until the end of the 1900s, parts of the old wagon road which they used could still be seen paralleling hwy. 89A between Cottonwood and Sedona. There they camped for several days. The limit was 40 trout a day, and the fishermen indicated this amount could be caught in about a half a day. It is still a puzzle what they did with all of the fish, because Annie wasn't fond of cooking "the smelly things" in her kitchen.

Submitted by Cousin Mary Belle Smith

Fishing trip with cousin Art Human at Hualapai Wash, Lake Meade 1947

Years later when the population increased and the trout limit decreased to 10 per day of "them darned hatchery little, bitty things," Walt became disgusted with fishing in Oak Creek. "It ain't no fun fishin' there, a standin' on a rock just next t' somebody else, a wonderin' if a body was a gonna' git hooked when them darned greenhorns was a tryin' t' cast their lines!" To avoid the crowds he took his grandchildren to a private pond to teach them to fish.

Another chasm, breaking across the Mogollon Rim escarpment, produces a deep narrow canyon lined with red bluffs similar to Oak Creek. Its sparkling fresh water bubbling along empties into the Verde slightly south of Camp Verde. Here in this remote canyon, accessible only on foot, Walter found the solitude he so desired. During the 1950s-1960s he made many trips into West Clear Creek, walking nearly six miles before starting to fish. His daughter F. Ruth, tells of joining him on one of these excursions. "I went there on a bet with Daddy one time when I was in college. I was working as a waitress, and one morning while he and his friends were in having coffee, he bet that I couldn't go into West Clear Creek and fish with him for the day and come out, without him having to carry me back. On my next day off away we went, walking, sliding down steep banks and climbing over boulders for six miles. We fished all day and then walked out. I would have crawled on my hands and knees before I would have

Grandkids (Jackson 6) holding fish, circa 1964 Left to right Back row: Debbie, Walter. Middle row: Danny, Lee, Jacque Front row: Kevin, Jordan

let him carry me!! I wanted to win the bet, but I also remembered a time when he wanted to carry me across a stream when catching minnows, he stepped on a slick rock and dropped me in the water! In my mind having him carry me was not an option! Upon arriving at the car he gave me the $5.00. I had won the bet! He had forgotten that everyday as a waitress, I walked many miles."

On occasion he would take the grandchildren to a place up Oak Creek where they could fish in a private pond. All enjoyed showing off the catch no' matter who had been lucky enough to "reel one in."

Winter weather was no deterrent to Walter when it came to fishing. He loved to go down the river below Camp Verde and catch catfish. One cold January day away he went, stopping in Cottonwood at the hardware store to buy bait. There was something new called Power Bait and the owner convinced him to try it. After having his line in the water for awhile, "I felt this ole' fish a nibblin' at that bait. I just jiggled that line a little bit, an' 'wham'!, 'e hit it an' took off. Th' fun was on! I only 'ad a six pound test leader on th' end o' that line, s' I 'ad t' play 'im out. 'E was like a run-away freight train, an' I could see th' end o'

Submitted by Jordan Lee Jackson
Walter and big fish, mid 1940s

my line a comin' up. S' I just took off on foot down that riverbank a tryin' t' keep up with that bugger. 'Hey! Look out!' I said t' m'self. There's this great big cottonwood tree a growin' right along that bank an' in th' water an' there's no way 'round it. It only took a second fer me t' decide t' jump in that water an' follow 'im. [Amazing! He wouldn't go swimming in the summer, no matter the circumstances.] Now wouldn't that 'ave been some picture....me a swimmin' down that river with one arm an' a'holdin' m' fishin' rod up out o' th' water with th' other! My, oh my!! [And again we hear his typical chuckle.] That water was like ice there in th' middle o' January!! Well, I come t' a place where I could git up on dry land again an' that ole' fish was a'beginnin' t' tire, s' I finally landed 'im. When I looked at 'im I knew 'e 'ad t' b' some kinda record. I jumped int' that '47 Ford an' headed fer Cottonwood, t' that hardwood store. I threw 'im on th' counter, 'Hey! Looka here what that darned ole' stinkin' bait caught!' Ever'one was shocked. Th' owner o' th' store got this crazy idea in 'is head. 'Say, Walt, let's go over here t' this photography shop an' git some pictures. I'll pay fer 'em an' give ya some if ya'll let me use 'em fer advertisement.'

"'Sure I can do that. Let's go.'

"B'fore we went down th' street, we weighed that monster. *Twenty-three pounds an' two ounces!!* Th' largest silver channel catfish ever t' b' taken outta th' Verde. As far as I know that record still stands. [Mid 1980s.] Well, ya' can guess that after 'e put that picture o' that fish a restin' on them bait cans in th' store window, there was a run on that smelly ole' bait. 'E sold completely out. An' as fur as I know ain' 'nother soul ever caught a thing usin' th' stuff. Now doesn't that beat th' band!!" (More laughter, no doubt, he enjoyed reliving his own stories.)

All of the family knew that the game and fish Walter brought home certainly provided many meals that would otherwise have been quite skimpy, especially during the depression years. Even so, Ruth, who had not eaten wild meat before marrying Walt, remarked, "sometimes I'd go splurge and buy a ham in self defense!"

1957 - Walter's heart attack

It was lucky that hunting season came after all of the harvesting was completed, for it would have been a most difficult choice for Walt to make...harvest crops or hunt. "I went elk huntin' after we got th' crops all in — worked terrible hard. Been gettin' up early, early, early with Glen t' hunt, but all we were seein' was females an' we 'ad bull permits. There was one more day left in th' season, s' we got up at three in th' mornin', ate breakfast an' went out t' Jones Mountain where we 'adn't been around that season. Don Hole told m' that 'is father'd seen some bulls up there but couldn't get a shot. That darned Game Department wouldn't allow ya t' keep any shells in th' magazine o' yar gun at all. I think so's ya wouldn't git a shot at an'thin'. Darn fools! Ya 'ad t' carry th' shells in yar pocket, s' I 'ad one ready all th' time.

Walter and Glen with elk, 1957

Glen an' I went out that road that goes 'round Jones Mountain, an' I believe Don Hole's father was huntin' up on top that same time, an' scared a bull. I saw that bull acomin' down. I jumped up. I got a shell in an' I threw that gun down t' an openin' that I 'ad, only about a ten foot openin'. Like always I shot with both eyes open. When I saw that bead darken, I pulled th' ole' trigger.

"'Come on, Glen. I 'it 'im.'

"I always tried t' git their heart with th' first shot, but I was a little too low this time. We found th' blood an' followed th' trail. When we'd lose th' blood, I'd circle an' find it again. We trailed that thing about a mile an' a half when Glen saw him goin' across th' flat t' Jackson Butte. I kneeled down with that old 300, an' I got 'im this time. We worked awful hard a gettin' that great big elk outta there. M', what horns! Six points on each side an' over three feet between th' tips.

"Soon after that, I was bowlin' on a team in Clarkdale with Dr. Bright, Will Pitch, Clammer an' Dr. Bates. I don't know how I ever threw that ball down th' alley cause I was tired, but I was th' anchorman. I'd just thrown three strikes in a row when I decided I needed some water t' drink. I was a gettin' a tight feelin' in my chest, a thinkin' it was frum them wieners an' sauerkraut I ate fer supper. I 'ad t' go upstairs t' git t' th' water fountain. Now th' worst thing I could've done was t' climb them stairs. I made another strike when I come back. How in th' world I don't know. There was a screen door on th' side o' th' alley, an' I went t' that door t' git a breath o' air. Doc Bright saw me, an' he asked, 'What's wrong, Walt?'

"'I cain't hardly breathe.'

"That scared th' life out o' 'im, an' 'e said t' Dr. Bates, 'Bates, I think Walt's havin' a heart attack.'

"Cherry Wombacher, a great big fella, picked me up an' took me upstairs where Dr. Bates give me a shot o' somethin' frum th' satchell 'e 'ad in 'is car just b' chance. 'E'd stopped takin' 'is bag with 'im most places since 'e was afraid kids'd git int' it.

"I 'ad a clot in th' big artery in th' back o' my heart. They said, 'That's too much o' a shock. It would've got ya'. 'That high-powered medicine saved me. I was worn out frum th' crop an' then chasin' them elk five mornin's. Whoa! An' on top o' it m' mother died in Bridgeport.

"'Doc, I want t' go down an' see my mother, an' go t' th' funeral.'

"'Listen, your mother lived t' a good ole age, an' we don't want a young fella like ya t' die a goin' t' a funeral. No, no, no. Ya mustn't go.'

"That's when they made arrangements fer th' funeral procession t' come down th' road b' th' hospital. I got t' see it. Pretty sad! Pretty tough t' take. Anyway, they kept me in there. I'd never been in a hospital. It's just like bein' in jail. One day I said t' th' nurse, 'Are they gonna let me go home? There ain't nothin' wrong with me. I'm a' goin' t' git m' clothes on, an' I'm goin' right out that window an' catch a ride home.'

"'Ya do, an' I know where we'll find ya'. Right on th' floor!'

"M' wife, Ruth, told me, 'Ya don't have any clothes here an' ya'd look mighty funny climbin' out o' th' window an' hitchin' a ride in that sawed off night gown a flappin' open in th' rear!'

"They kept me three days more than they told me. When three weeks come around, they wanted me t' stay fer more observation. B'fore they let me go, they x-rayed m' lungs, heart, everywhere they wanted. Th' doctor told me that nature'd built a new artery in my heart, an' that if I didn't overdo, I'd last a long time - 25 years or more. It's more now." (And he continued to fish to the end; see center for picture of Walter fishing in Washington state)

He lived to just a few months short of 30 years after the heart attack. It is amazing his longevity, especially considering that he did everything he was <u>not</u> suppose to do, and nothing he was told to do. Approximately five months short of his 90th birthday while fixing a water valve so he could plant tomatoes, a massive heart attack ended a long and colorful life.

For the Jordan and Bristow families, Walter's passing ended the era of folks who had the privilege of experiencing the Wild Abundance of the Verde River watershed.

Interwoven in this time frame when game and fish were abundant were cattlemen and mining companies adding to the scenes of the Life Stage of the Verde Valley.

FOOTNOTES

(1) Jordan, Stella M., <u>Arizona's Beautiful Oak Creek Canyon</u>, personal diary, circa 1920

(2) Ashworth, Donna. <u>Arizona Triptych</u>. Flagstaff, AZ: Small Mountain Books, 1999. 205.

(3) Hart, Les. <u>Pioneer Stories of Arizona's Verde Valley</u>. Comp. Mrs. John Bristow, Mrs. E.W. Monroe, and Mrs. D.W. Wingfield. Camp Verde, AZ: The Verde Valley Pioneers Association, 1954. 167.

(3a) Thompson, Albert E. <u>History of Homesteads of Upper Oak Creek</u>. <u>Those Early Days</u>. Comp. The Book Committee of Sedona Westerners. Cottonwood, AZ: Verde Independent , 1968. 7.

Chapter Six

CATTLEMEN'S COUNTRY—RANCHING AND SCHOOL TEACHING

When I first saw the Verde Valley it was a hunter's and stockman's paradise. Wild game was everywhere and the grass was knee high and plentiful. The land was like a sponge and when it rained the water was absorbed into the ground immediately, so very little ran into the river channel and the small amount that did run into the river bed, stood in pools which became stagnant and polluted with malaria germs consequently many people were stricken with malaria, but they had to administer their own medicine, such as calomel and quinine, because there were no doctors available.

Most everybody that came to the Verde Valley brought cattle, horses or sheep with them and the stock soon trampled the spongy land down to solid ground, thus causing the rain water to run into the river channel, which was then only about 100 feet wide and the flood waters often rose to six or seven feet high, causing the river to cut into banks, change the course of the main river channel and the river bed spread to half a mile wide in places.[1]

Cattle ranching, until after WWII, was an extremely important part of Arizona's economy. In elementary school, students were required to learn the four 'C's of Arizona's economy; Cattle, Cotton, Citrus, and Copper. Later a fifth was added, climate. Of all of these, climate seemed to be the greatest detriment, prior to air conditioning. Now it is the most important economic factor of them all due to the millions of dollars realized through tourism. Sometimes vying for first place is what possibly should be the sixth 'C' - computers and electronics, or 'C' for construction. Nonetheless, as the first industry of the territory having been developed by the Spaniards, cattle was the backbone of the economy for many years. The life style and wealth of the rancheros continued until the support of the government of Spain diminished. The Apaches then overran and destroyed many of the great haciendas, leaving behind large herds of cattle. These in turn became wild and, according to some, were more dangerous than a herd of buffalo. Several years later, during the War with Mexico, the only resistance encountered by the Mormon Battalion came from wild bulls which attacked their wagon train. Mules were gored and even some of the soldiers were wounded.

Prior to the Civil War, most of the cattle in Arizona were only passing through on their way to California gold fields, the marauding Apaches deterred anyone considering ranching. However, as military attention was turned to subduing these "savages," army posts were established and the need for beef arose. In 1870 only a little over 5100 cattle could be found in the whole territory. This was going to change quickly as more and more drovers became aware of the rich grasses along the streams of the southern part of the region and the extensive ranges of the Colorado Plateau. Via many published sources, information about this great grazing land was spreading rapidly across the U. S. and Europe. Tom Miller quotes Hastings and Turner from *The Changing Mile,...* "a great ballyhoo campaign waged by railroad prospectuses, livestock journals, and territorial legislatures trumpeted to an eager public the West held easy riches and that grass was gold."[2] It seems that if a person had a "long rope" and a horse he could become a rancher. In 1885 it was "guesstimated" that within the same area there were at least 652,500 head.

One would be remiss not to mention one of the largest and longest lasting ranches started during this era, the CO Bar. This brand belongs to the Babbitt Brothers of Northern Arizona who arrived in 1886 from Cincinnati, Ohio. In Flagstaff they purchased a herd of cattle that had been trailed from Kansas. Fortunately for them the range boss was included in the transaction, as this was their first experience with the four-footed bovines. Soon they acquired a range southwest of Flagstaff, added 160 acres of leased land, and the CO Bar was born. This developed into an empire of "thousands of cattle and sheep on some 3,000,000 acres of range encompassing three southwestern states."[3] The Babbitt Brothers were able to endure through the same hardships faced by all ranchers and at the same time continue expanding. Their first experience of "hardscrabble times" came after WWI. In addition to the Post war depression, scabs, and hoof and mouth diseases caused the loss of many cattle. The rest of the herds had to be dipped, adding tremendous expense. These circumstances necessitated the sale of thousands of acres of prime land, way below the market price. Through all of this the family survived, remained a strong influence in the area and again became profitable, albeit on a much smaller scale. (It has been said that in the early 1980s their deeded and leased land totaled only 850,000 acres.)

Through Walter's oldest sister and her husband, Jack and Mary Flannigan, there was a tie between the Babbit family and the Jordans. After WWII Jack was in charge of a portion of the Babbitt herd. The winter range was northwest of Flagstaff at a lower elevation over toward the Little Colorado River. Even so, during the blizzard of the winter 1947-48 many of the cattle were stranded and he found himself riding in an army weasle to reach them. Although he individually fed and watered many, a large number were lost to the cold.

Except for the blizzards, problems for ranchers in the northern part of the territory were very similar to those of the south. These newcomers, before long, were faced with the realities of a semi-arid land and, just as gold had "played out," so did the grasslands. Overgrazing (in which the Babbitts never indulged) was bad enough, but to make matters worse, the devastating drought of 1892-1893 caused ranchers to loose fifty to seventy-five percent of their herds. Ranchers began shipping cattle out as rapidly as possible, but prices had dropped so dramatically that many became bankrupt. Edward Land, an Arizona pioneer said, "Dead cattle lay everywhere. You could actually throw a rock from one to the other."[4]

Submitted by Margaret Bristow Stover

Cowboys started young on the Bristow Ranch, Middle Verde late 1890s

Immense changes took place in ranching, including barbed wire fencing, finding additional sources of water, and limiting the number of animals allowed per acre. A majority of small outfits disappeared and the great land and cattle companies took over. Thus the dire consequences of overstocking were both economic and ecological with the effects on the land still being seen nearly a century later.

Walter underscores the role of livestock: "Oh m' yes! Cattle were mighty important t' us. I heard m' father tell 'bout th' time we'd 'ad that horrible draught - seven years o' it. Ya' could step acrost th' Verde River. It started in 1900, an' it quit in 1907, I believe. [Obviously droughts happened on somewhat of a regular basis or possibly Walter had the dates mixed-up.] I heard m' father say ya could drive over th' range there an' you'd see dead cattle ever'where, an' ya could git all ya wanted fer $5 a head, but n'body wanted 'em b'cause it was too dry – nothin' fer 'em t' eat. Well, ole Dan Marr, frum th' Verde Five, went broke. 'E was one o' th' wealthiest cowmen in th' territory o' Arizona when th' times were good b'fore th' draught hit. 'E lived down at Camp Verde.

"Dan Marr went over t' th' bank in Prescott an' asked 'is ole friend, th' manager at th' bank, 'Well, Mose, ya a gamblin' man?'

"'It all depends, Dan, on what ya want t' gamble on.'

"'Well, sir, this is quite a gamble. I wanta stock m' range agin. I just got a hunch it's goin' t' start rainin' this summer. I wanta borry $100,000 t' restock m' range.'

"'That's quite a gamble, but I'll tell ya, there ain't no man in that line o' business that knows as much 'bout cattle an' th' way th' rains act than ya. I b'lieve I'll just take that gamble with ya.'

"Th' bank loaned ole' Dan th' money, an' would ya' b'lieve, it started rainin' agin. They made barrels o' money. I've crost Lonesome Valley [northeast of Prescott] on m' way t' Phoenix when it was a good year, an' that grass was a wavin' — that wild grass, bein' two feet high. Just looked like a wheat field fer miles acrost."

Walter tells his version of the story of the Arizona Cattle Baron: "A Spaniard come t' New Spain. [With a nod of his head a wink and chuckle he continues in a matter-of-fact tone.] That's what some o' 'em educated folks called Mexico. After he'd been in Mexico fer a short period o' time, 'e found this 'ere orphan girl an' 'e took 'er name, traced it back, went back t' Spain, an' entered a monastery. 'E stayed in that monastery fer a number o' years. Ya know what that ole son-o'-a-gun did? 'E forged them critical documents in them monasteries in Spain, provin' that this girl was heir t' all this tremendous land grant. My, oh my!! It covered nearly all o' what's now Arizona. Yeah, that's right! That ole' bugger called hisself *The Baron o' Arizona*, an' laid claim t' at least half t' three-quarters o' all this here land in our state, an' it went on int' New Mexico too. Yeah! Sure did! Ya see 'e could do that 'cause 'e married that young girl in Mexico. 'E "proved up" on most o' th' land grant claims fer nearly ten years. They established farms in th' Salt River Valley area an' down around Coolidge an' Casa Grande. Th' land grants are still on record. Now ain't that some sneaky way t' get yourself some land!?"

Many of the ranchers all over the state had summer pastures in the mountains, moving the cattle or sheep to lower elevations and warmer climates in the winter. Lots of the areas bore the names of the early ranchers. One such place is Casner Mountain, located between Cottonwood and Sedona, and a bit to the west.

We experience an example of the story teller's diversion to another rather unrelated topic as Walter continues. He shares an "Old West" experience of the Casner family. "Mose an' 'is wife 'ada cabin on top o' Casner Mountain. They built this cabin t' raise mules fer th' government. Ole Bud Thompson on th' Verde River tole me one time 'e knew o' Mose Casner was a' sellin' $50,000 worth o' mules in one payment, an' 'e'd take nothin' but gold. Now that was a powerful lotta money in them days!! Ya betcha! Ever'body was a guessin' they buried it up there near that cabin. Well that's th' time them two cowboys come in one night. They'd picked just th' right time 'cause ole Mose was all alone up there on that mountain. 'Is wife happened t' b' down offa th' mountain at th' Casner place on Beaver Creek above Rim Rock an' Soda Springs. Ya see they 'ad two places. Them cowboys 'ad in mind t' git their hands on all o' that gold. Th' story goes that they kept a askin' 'im where 'e buried it an' 'e wouldn't tell. After a'bit them guys got mad an' tied Mose t' a chair, took off 'is boots an' heated themselves some brandin' irons. Then stuck them red hot irons t' Mose's feet a'tryin' t'make 'im tell where that money was. An' ya' know 'e was such a tough ole bird, 'e never did tell 'em! Now don'tcha know 'e 'ad some powerful sore feet!" Walt becomes somewhat reflective as he continues, "Kinda funny how things happen, here's Casner Mountain out there toward what we called the Red Rocks an' over here somethin' like twenty miles east is Casner Canyon comin' offa th' north end o' Munds Mountain int' Oak Creek. When ya drive up Schnebly Hill Road ya' cross that canyon, an' a rough ole bugger it is!"

Each rancher had special places he kept his horses and/or cattle. In discussing ranching, or almost any topic, folks invariably included the name of the mountain, canyon, creek or area to identify the location of the happening. It was always amazing how the narrator could immediately pick up the threads of the original tale in the exact spot where the detour was taken. In chapter three some comments were made regarding the naming of landmarks. (See map page 86). Here Walter elaborates.

"Yeah, they named places after th' pioneers, them ole timers, like Munds. Ole Johnny Mund's dad took up that place up yonder south of Mountainaire. [Between Flagstaff and Sedona, renamed Pinewood.] That's Mund's Park an' down here b' Sedona, Mund's Mountain. 'E kept horses up there. Joe Hancock kept 'is horses up on Secret Mountain. (Northwest of Sedona). That was 'is summer range. 'Is winter range is down in th' valley where 'is place is.

"Lee Mountain, that's named after ole Johnny Lee, Earl Van Deren's grandfather." Earl had a winter ranch adjacent to Walter's. Here Walt interjects another aside. . "Did ya know Iva Van Deren [Earl's sister] was born an' raised down there where Bill [Willie], Chester an' I farmed [Bridgeport] an' there was an adobe house an' a barn left. One day I was'a talking t' Iva an' she said, 'M' father [Lee Van Deren] built that big barn an' that adobe house, an' that's where I was born.'"

Much reference is made to Sedona, as it is a rather centrally located spot within the Verde watershed, and many greatly talented cowboys and ranch owners lived in that area. Today it is quite the tourist town. Sedona itself was named for a lady, Sedona Schnebly, a dear, dear person. She was the Jordan's nearest neighbor, about three-quarters of a mile away. (more about the Schnebly's in Chapter 9)

In chapter one reference was made to the Mountain Men who briefly trapped on the Upper Verde. This area was fed by springs and snow melt in such places as Woodchute Mountain, (named for the chutes built to send timbers down the mountainside to shore up the Jerome mines.), Hell's Canyon and Little Hell's Canyon, all to the northwest.

Walter continues his description of the beloved red rock area. "Sycamore Canyon comes back t' th' northeast an' turns int' th' Verde Valley. Th' Verde headwaters in Sycamore Canyon are up at Garland Prairie with th' lily ponds.

Submitted by Charles Jordan
Bill Gray (on left) and other cowboys 1920s

Mooney Trail b' Lori Butte's where th' cattlemen brought their herds down frum Garland Prairie. It'd take a couple o' days. Garland Prairie t' Coffee Creek Ranch an' vice versa. A lot o' ranchers 'ad their summer places up on the mountains like Garland Prairie, an' they all used that Mooney Trail t' move cattle. O'course, that trail was built b' a man named Mooney. It was about six miles long. Ya' know, m' sister, Alice an' her husband Bill Gray 'ad a summer place at Garland Prairie an' their winter one out in th' Red Rocks. That Coffee Creek Ranch was theirs. [Apprpxomately 15 miles northeast of Cottonwood.] They had t' sell this winter place when that dadgummed government cut their allotment 'cause it was supposedly overgrazed. That's when Dad helped 'em buy a place near Clemenceau. In them years the government fellahs would come take a "look see" at th' range, th' number o' cattle, an' supposedly check on rainfall an' a lot o' other stuff, an' then tell ya' how many head o' cattle, horses etc. ya' could run on so many acres. Well them fellahs what come out were mostly t' young t' b' dry b'hind th' ears, an' they'd never been around cattle an' 'ad only th' ole textbook t' judge b'. Darn fools didn't know nothin' about what they were a'doin'. All them cowmen 'ad trouble with 'em.

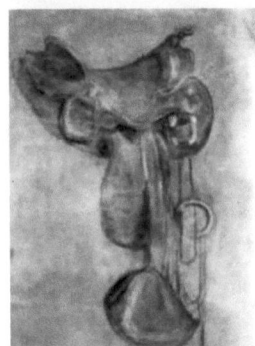

Western saddle charcoal by Helen Jordan

"Anyway, Bill an' th' fellahs'd git them cattle rounded up, git 'em all out o' th' brush an' canyons an' Alice'd ride with 'em and th' herd — down Mooney Trail in th' fall an' up th' trail in th' spring. She rode it every time, but not on the round-ups. Oshea Mulligan was th' only woman I ever knew that rode with them cowboys on th' roundup, an' she was one o' th' best riders o' th' bunch. Say, did ya know that that doctor that delivered Alice's baby boy that was dead, said th' reason they couldn't save th' baby was b'cause Alice'd spent s' much time in th' saddle a'grippin' th' horse's sides with 'er knees, that 'er muscles wouldn't give an' let th' baby through. He woulda been 'bout a year older than m' oldest daoughter, Anne. That was really sad! They never 'ad no more children." Here Walt pauses blinks his eyes and swallows a couple of times before continuing. "It was up there at th' Garland Prairie place that Ruth got 'er one an' only buckin' off." When he paused to laugh, Ruth gave him a hard look and said, "Well you just better tell them why I got bucked off. That back cinch was too loose and worked into the horse's flank!" Walt had to agree that that was the situation and that Bill was shocked for the horse was extremely gentle.

"Say, ya know that m' sister Mary married a cowman too. That was Jack Flannigan an' they 'ad their main range up there in Spring Valley. They's north o' that little place called Parks an' Alice was south o' it. Ya know 'bout half way b'tween Flagstaff an' Williams on I-40. Their winter range was kinda off t' th' northwest at a lower elevation, but even then that 'orrible winter o' '47-'48 was too bad. Seems t' me they had six to eight feet o' snow on th' level an 20 foot drifts. Why m' sister said she almost 'ad t' dig tunnels frum th' house t' th' barn an' chicken house. After several days b' using old army weasels Jack was able t' git t' part o' 'is herd an' part o' th' Babbitt herd 'e was a tendin'. 'E tole me that many were frozen frum th' knees down an' couldn't move. Others 'ad icicles hangin' frum their noses t' th' ground cause a their breath. B' takin' feed and water t' each o' them stranded cows 'e saved a bunch o' 'em.

Leather saddle made by John Bristow, circa 1910

"Now let's git back to drivin' them cattle. It would take quite a few days up in them Mogollon Rim Mountains to get all o' them cows gathered up. That's why th' foreman would usually divide th' cowboys int' pairs. 'Ya two fellahs, ya ride that section there, an' ya two ride this'un.' They'd go in ever' which direction ridin' up t' ten miles frum headquarters b'fore they'd move that ole' chuckwagon. Thata way they could cover ever' bit o' th' range. Sometimes they'd miss a few in them terrible thickets. An' oh, my! If them cowboys didn't wear them leather chaps their legs'd been all tore up frum them Cat's Claw an' other bushes. (See center for Old Cowboy painting)

"Over at Secret Canyon an' Houston Basin, they never could git some o' 'em cattle out. Earl Van Deren an' Irie [Ira Smith] went over there in Secret Canyon an' got out some o' them ole' wild devils that'd been in there quite a number o' years. An' over in Houston Basin when I was a huntin' quail with Ray Steel just b'low Pots Spring, I heard dogs a'bawlin' an' saw three riders a'comin' through th' saddle o' th' ridge, down 'bout a mile frum where I was. I thought mayb' they was lion hunters, an' I wanted t' see if they'd caught any, sos I high-tailed it down outta there on a shortcut an' got t' 'em b'fore they got t' th' river. As it turned out, they waren't a'huntin' lions a'tall, they was a'chasin' wild cattle outta there.

"'Them that we cain't tie up overnight, we kill an' butcher,' one o' them cowboys told me.

"I was a'tellin' this story t' Rue Marshall, a lion hunter up in Flag, ('E worked fer Babbitt in th' heavy duty machinery department), an' 'e knew 'bout th' cattle operation in Houston Basin. 'E told me they'd killed an' butchered sixty o' them darn wild cattle in th' past spring. Sometimes th' cowboy cin git 'em out t' where they can b' roped. If they won't lead, they tie 'em up overnight. Then usually they'll lead.

"Irie Smith, born an' raised on Oak Creek an' one o' th' greatest cowboys in th' state o' Arizona, worked as foreman fer a big cattle outfit headquartered at Rogers Lake that drove the cattle on Mooney Trail. Why, I r'member when 'e was breakin' horses fer th' Trigger 2 Bar Cattle Ranch, I saw 'im ride some o' th' wickedest broncs alive. Cowboys like 'e was 'ave t' b' born an' raised in cattle country. 'E musta got it frum his father. Link [Lincoln] Smith, was a'other one o' th' greatest cowmen we 'ad. Irie 'ad a friend, Earl Van

Deren, also born in Oak Creek. Th' two o' 'em together was a pair! My, oh my!! There was none equal t' them two in th' whole Mogollon an' Oak Creek country. Earl 'ad that place just t' th' south o' us, an' I can r'member hearin' them cattle a'bawlin' way off in th' distance when they'd b' a bringin' 'em down fer th' winter. We all use t' stand out in th' back yard a watchin' an' a'waitin' t' see 'em a'comin' down over Brins Mesa. Do ya kids r'member that?!"

Walter would turn to whichever of his three children would be listening in this particular storytelling session, and chuckle with pleasure as they nodded affirmatively.

"A cowboy's main job use t' b' roundup in th' spring an' fall. They'd brand them calves an' drive th' whole bunch t' new pasture or t' market. Now, I suppose tendin' fence is one o' th' big jobs, but in th' early days there waren't no fences on th' range. Th' government forced them cowmen t' build them darned fences. B'fore th' fences all th' cattlemen'd git together at roundup time, each one 'ad t' share in th' ridin' with th' rest o' 'em on this, an' they elected a foreman. Th' foreman chose 'is cook fer th' roundup chuck wagon, an' if an'body ever attended a roundup, 'e never forgot them cooks. They'd make 'doughgods,' as they called them biscuits, an' th' steaks, beans, gravy an' coffee was like none other, an' all done over an open fire an' in a dutch oven."

These were the meals of the 20th century and usually would also include potatoes, vegetable, dessert, and in some camps salad. In earlier years one would more likely find just beans, biscuits, coffee and sometimes steak. Most outfits often had extras dropping by the chuck wagon at mealtime and in practically all instances the cowhands were glad to see folks. However, Marshal Trimble tells of a couple of ladies who had worn out their welcome at the CO Bar roundup camps.

"One chuck wagon cook, whose gourmet talents were widely recognized, took exception to a couple of eastern ladies who dropped in for a meal one time too many. He was busy kneading the biscuit dough when they arrived. After offering a friendly 'howdy', he casually spat a brown stream of tobacco juice into his hands, rubbed them together vigorously, and submerged them into the fresh dough. The ladies, a little green, suddenly remembered a previous commitment and quickly departed the camp."[5]

Walter explains a "special technique" used in the trade of the cowhands. "When them cowboys are a'drivin' that herd, there's one o' 'em brutes that's th' leader. There're riders called cowpunchers that ride along b'side th' leaders. Them fellahs'd force th' leaders, an' all o' th' herd would follow right b'hind."

As with every person, each has his/her own story of personal experiences to tell. Jesse Goddard, who herded horses up on Mud Tank Mesa when he was a boy, plus helping with cattle, recalls the territory he loved and a very special roundup. "I was raised on Clear Creek, an' one o' m' fondest memories is o' takin' a boat up th' creek t' th' Bullpen Ranch t' pick fruit. They 'ad a fine orchard up there. There were wild horses an' antelope all over this country then. I bet there was seven t' eight hundred [antelope] when I worked here. A ranger told me there was 12 on this whole mesa last year, an' now th' cattle ya see in here are owned b' th' big money people. I say let 'em have 'em.

"I was thirteen years old when I first rode roundup. Used t' b' a little ole cabin down that draw where we'd camp. They built a lot o' tanks out here an' that corral is fer shippin' th' cattle. It was up there b' th' side o th' pump house, we were holdin' 1200 head one night with two guys a guardin' when somethin' 'capped 'em off.' B' gosh, you talk about a stampede! We 'ad cattle all over that country that night. Cowboys ever'where, an' nobody knew where th' other was. B' golly, next mornin' when we came back int' camp, we counted only a very few head. Them cattle were panicky that night. Ya'd git 50 head t'gether, an' some'd b'gin t' run agin. We 'ad about eight or ten cowboys on that roundup." Jesse doesn't relate how and when they recovered the whole herd.

Walter talks about night herders. "They 'ad night herders, night riders t' watch th' herd on them roundups. Didn't want nothin' t' spook that bunch. Yeah! Them cowboys'd even sing at night as they'd ride 'round that herd sos as t' keep 'em from a goin' t' sleep."

"If they went t' sleep", says Jesse, "they were likely t' b' startled b' noises in th' night. A horse shakin' 'is saddle, darn near anythin'd set 'em off when they were tired. Once they're frightened, they'd run an' run. Ya'd learn t' keep 'em goin' up hill if ya could. Don't let 'em jump down! Ya' might wind up down near th' river.

"Normally in a stampede, th' cowboys'd run their horses just as fast as they could run t' git t' th' leaders an' turn 'em. If they couldn't g't t' them leaders, they'd holler an' holler an' lots o' time shoot their pistols a'tryin' t' swing th' herd int' a circle, an' finally th' herd would calm down again. That was some job. Lots o' times fellahs got hurt an' even killed in them stampedes. Them cowboys 'ad an awful dangerous job there. They 'ad t' know what they were a doin' t' turn th' leaders."

Lightning and thunder storms were always one of a cowpuncher's worst fears when tending a herd, for many a stampede was caused by acts of nature. A number of ballads, books, stories and movies have been written about stampedes, cattle drives, working on the range, and the life of cowboys.

It was mentioned that Will Jordan wanted to learn "cowboying." Apparently he was quite proficient at it as shown in another of Walter's stories. "I'll never fergit th' story m' father use t' tell 'bout wantin' t' b' a cowboy in th' early 1880's. 'E hired out t' a cattleman named Hewlett. They were drivin' a herd o' 'bout 400 head over t' Show Low about 75 miles t' th' east o' where they'd rounded 'em up in th' Verde Valley an' cut th' ones ready fer market. They got up as fur as Mormon Lake, which use' t' b' about three miles acrost, an' it was terrible dry. Why it was s' dry there was big cracks in it where the mud'd dried. Father said ya' 'ad t' b' careful ta' not trip yer horse in them cracks. Hewlett says, 'We gotta git water fer them steers or we're not a gonna make it.'

"Mormon Spring was th' only water within miles. If them fellahs didn't git water fer that bunch there they'd loose a awful lot o' them cattle before th' next waterin' place at Show Low. 'E said, 'I've heard them Mormons up there at Mormon Dairy Spring are a guardin' that water an' they's awful mean.' That was on th' northwest side o' th' lake where they 'ad a dairy an' a big spring." [Most likely he is referring to Lot Smith. "An iron-fisted, temperamental man,…one of Brigham Young's captains, led a party of colonists to the Mormon Lake area…. This ranch, the Mormon Dairy, was known by its Circle S brand."6] Hewlett 'ad 'eard a number o' stories 'bout them Mormons an' how mean they was. One o' them stories was that they'd promise ya that ya could water th' herd, an' ya'd 'ave 'em all bedded down waitin' t' water 'em th' next mornin'. That's when them Mormons'd stampede that herd an' git a lot o' cattle. So Hewlett warned all them cowboys t' keep their guns right under their heads when they's a sleepin' an' 'is last orders was, 'Ya' all b' saddled up an' ready t' go.' They 'ad th' night riders workin' 'round th' herd all night o'course, but nothin' happened, not a bit o' trouble. Th' next mornin' Hewlett said, 'I'll tell ya' just what I gotta do. I gotta go up an' see that headman o' Mormon Dairy Spring an' this dairy.' That's when 'e asked Dad t' go with 'im. Ya know, Dad was quite a arbitrator an' 'e'd keep a level head. [Will's even-tempered disposition was also noted by the interviewer for Vital Statistics in approximately 1914, 'Believe he is not very radical personality, but is forced into this position by his wife and his sons…'7]

"'E went up an' talked t' th' guy 'bout it an' said, 'We just gotta have water, an' I'm willin' t' pay ya' a'plenty. We gotta 'ave water fer them cattle or we can't make it t' Show Low.'

"An' that fellah at th' spring said, 'Well, ya just bring yer herd right on up here an' water' em. That's just fine.'

"So they all figured them Mormons would stampede th' cattle while they was a'drinkin'. But they didn't 'ave a bit o' trouble at all. Them Mormons was very good t' 'em, an' th' headman says, 'We wish ya' good luck on yer way. No, ya' certainly don't owe us a penny.' Hewlett, m', 'e was elated, thanked m' dad an' they drove th' herd right on t' Show Low.

"The cattlemen would sell in th' spring an' fall. They 'ad two roundups. They'd brand in th' spring an' brand in th' fall. After th' brandin', they'd take t' market most o' th' good heifers an' steers weighin' 'round 500 pounds."

The cattle sold could be of various ages, as Jesse explains. "Well ya'd git s' much fer yearlings, s' much fer two year olds, an' s' much fer three. About a ten dollar spread in th' prices. Th' three year olds would bring about twice as much as th' yearlin's. They're sold b' th' pound now.

"We always drove our cattle int' Clarkdale. They 'ad a long main gate there, an' we never 'ad any trouble, but up at Flagstaff, they always 'ad a bunch o' trouble. I r'member [in Flagstaff], there was two big pine trees right there at th' gate. Almost ever'time ya'd git 'em right up there t' th' gate, an' they'd b'gin millin' 'round in a tight wad until a train would come 'round th' bend an' blow its dadgum whistle. Away they'd go...oh, boy! We'd ride int' that little wad an' try t' break th' millin'. Once some o' 'em start through th' gate, why th' rest o' 'em' follow, but we always 'ad trouble there. Another thing, t' git t' th' stockyards, ya'd have t' cross Bitter Creek, which was a little narrow ditch used as a sewer. Ya' could smell it a quarter o' a mile b'fore ya' got t' it. Don't ya think, we 'adda hell o' a time gittin' them cattle t' cross that son-o'-a-gun."

"Another thing them cowmen 'ad t' contend with was rustlers". Walter shakes his head in disgust as he continues, "M', yes! A friend o' mine, Frank Waldrup, who 'ad cattle just west o' Apache Maid Mountain was appointed cook fer th' roundup one spring. 'E never'd any trouble b'fore. This was after th' government made 'im put fences up. I think 'e tole me 'e run about 100 head. Now that wasn't a very big spread at that time, but it meant a lot t' 'im, an' it was a good livin'. 'E was on th' roundup that spring when them dadgummed rustlers cut through 'is fence on th' south side. There's a big mountain there right next t' Beaver Creek west o' Apache Maid Mountain in 'is allotment called Hog Hill. It was awful rough country down b'low on th' west side o' Hog Hill, s' they cut 'is fence on th' south side an' took nearly all o' his cattle. H' only 'd about 25 head left. 'E was planin' t' drive 'bout 75 head t' market. Them rustlers drove them cattle down through them thick cedars, down t' where they could git 'em off o' th' mountain t' a truck. 'E never found a one o' 'em. Now ain't that somethin' awful!

They'd change th' darned brand. They'd brand 'em out with a certain kind o' brandin' iron, called it ventin' th' brand. Pretty hard t' do it, but they did it. They 'ad lots o' time.

"Even with th' ear marks they use now a'days, there's rustlin' goin' on today [1982]. We got it goin' on right over here at Prescott. Ya betcha! They caught two o' 'em over in them rough mountains west o' Prescott south o' Seligman. Them two rustlers did it slow like, over quite awhile, until th' rancher finally noticed 'is herd was a gettin' smaller, an' 'e reported it t' th' law. Th' sheriff put men out t' watch an' they caught them two. Their case is about t' come up b'fore th' court in Prescott.

"They're doin' it kinda different than in th' old days, not exactly th' same as 100 years ago. They git trucks in there real close, herd th' cattle int' th' trucks an' away they go. No way t' trace 'em. Ya 'ave t' catch 'em at it. Some've said them rustlers 'ave even been a usin' helicopters t' run 'em down th' canyons int' th' trucks."

The venting of brands was usually done in a remote area, and one of these places is in the Bradshaw Mountains above Crown King. It is called "Horse Thief Basin", and can be reached from I-17 by taking the dirt road. A campground has been established there, although driving to it is difficult. In the early 1900s it was nearly inaccessible.

Going back again to his childhood memories Walter talks of other experiences involving cowboys. "When I's a kid on th' Upper Verde, our school was 'bout a half a mile frum our home. We walked that distance, an' there were several families, well I'd say only three er four, some o' 'em 'ad t' walk as fur as three miles t' git t' school. Our school buildin' was only just two er three hundred yards frum th' river. In th' spring th' snow would be a meltin' in th' mountains, an' th' river'd b' a runnin' quite high. S' sometimes when th' cattlemen were bringin' them herds down t' ship 'em t' market b' train frum Jerome, (where W.A. Clark 'ad built a small narrow gauge railroad in frum th' main line t' supply 'is mine), they'd 'ave a tough time. That was th' nearest transportation, an' th' cowboys 'ad t' git them cattle acrost that Verde River t' Jerome Junction which'd take 'em on t' th' main line an' then t' market. So's, when they started t' drive them cattle acrost this river, they'd whoop an' yell loud as they could t' git them leaders t' go in. If they could git 'em t' go in, th' others'd follow an' swim that ole Verde. O'course, them cowboys'd 'ave t' git 'em started, an' swim acrost too t' keep them cows in a herd once't they'd got acrost th' river.

"The first time I ever saw this I r'member very well. They began a whoopin' an' yellin', an' we kida jumped outta our seats an' almost busted out th' windows o' th' schoolhouse a tryin' t' see what was a goin' on. Th' teacher shouted, 'Sit down, sit down! That's only them cowboys a drivin' th' cattle acrost th' Verde!' That time we didn't go down t' th' river, but we saw 'em drive them herds right b' th' school. Th' next time we heard them cowboys a whoopin' an' a yellin', we didn't wait. We jumped outta them seats an' away we went. Th' teacher, she 'ad t' go too. [He chuckles at the remembrance.] Them cowboys were a whoopin' an' a yellin' on th' other side o' that river, a tryin' t' git them steers in that terrible swift water. We just kept on a watchin' until they 'ad all o' them cattle acrost b' yellin' that-a-way.

"Another time when they were comin' frum th' other side, th' river was extra high, an' them cattle knew it. They weren't about t' go swimmin', but this one sort a small cowboy — he was about half organized, I think – 'e yelled, 'I'll get 'em acrost there,' an' 'e pulled a bottle o' whiskey outta 'is chap pocket. 'E waved it t' th' crowd – th' schoolteacher an' all o' us kids on th' opposite side o' th' river. 'E began a yippin' an' a yellin' at them steers until four o' 'em jumped in an' th' cowboy with 'em, but th' water was s' swift, they just turned 'round an' swam right back t' shore. The cowboy an' his horse might a gone on down th' river, never t' b' seen, if 'e 'adn't a slid outta that saddle an' held ont' th' horse's tail. Back on shore, 'e reached down in 'is chap pocket, held up that bottle, an' waved it again, 'Well, I got m' bottle yet.' Them cattle 'ad more sense than 'e did. They knew good an' well they couldn't swim that thing. It was too swift. It was too high. I still r'member that cowboy's name, Billy Strahan, it impressed me s' much.

"Onct down at Camp Verde quite a crowd gathered on both sides o' th' Verde River t' watch this crazy cowboy swim th' river when it was swollen in th' spring. Th' river was up really high. 'E swum it on 'is horse, but then 'e said, 'Now, I'll show ya' I cin swim it with m' chaps on.' Well, that made it too heavy fer th' horse t' swim acrost. Th' horse went down, an' 'e 'ad t' swim off. By golly, 'e's a carried down th' river an' drowned. They found 'im about a mile b'low an' th' horse too – both drowned. Th' horse got int' th' quicksand. There's a lotta quicksand along th' Verde. Ya' 'ave t' b' mighty careful if yer a swimmin' in that river. That was at Camp Verde where th' south bridge is now. There warn't any bridge at that time.

"Say, th' other day I was tellin' Don Hanson, who reads th' meters, about a time 'is father tried t' swim th' river when it was up, t' show off fer some ladies we were ridin' with. 'Is dad, Louie Hanson, was frum back East but 'e b'come pretty good on a horse b'cause 'e'd ride with Paul Tissaw, who'd been a bulldogger in th' rodeos until 'e broke 'is ribs." [Bulldoggers ride out beside a steer, jump from their horse and grab the steer by the horns to twist his head and pull him to the ground.]

"At th' time I was goin' with Helen Shopper at Camp Verde. She an' 'er sister Margaret were teachers over in Clarkdale an' were frum New Jersey. Louis got acquainted with Margaret. They [the girls] were crazy about ridin' horses an' absolutely 'ad t' 'ave chaps. So Louie'd wear chaps, an' I got a pair somewhere. Billy Blue, who'd ride with us an' bring 'is lady, a teacher frum somewhere b'low Bridgeport, also 'ad chaps. There were six o' us that'd go ridin' different places. We went an' rode out t' House Mountain one Sunday an' picked strawberries at Johnny Hurst's place an' 'ad a big strawberry feed. Louie's swim, I's gonna tell ya 'bout, took place on one o' our rides in th' spring when that ole river was a'comin' down with that snow water, an' it was pretty high. It was higher than Louie should try, but 'e was a wantin' t' show off fer 'is lady friend an' t' show off fer th' crowd. An' I told 'im, 'Louie ya' better not go in there. That water's too high!' Well, th' chump, went on an' went. Th' horse an' 'e went under an' with 'im a'wearin' them heavy wet chaps, but 'e knew enough t' slide outta th' saddle an' catch th horse b' the'tail. That's all that saved 'em both frum drownin'. That ole horse just turned 'round an' come right back t' our side. An' ole Louie was drownin' wet, an' th' rest o' us sure did laugh. Louie's son got a kick outta that story."

The "real" cowboy of the family was John Bristow, Annie's brother and Allen's father. Allen gives his perspective of his Dad's "cowboying," but first he, as many of the old timers did, establishes the locale and a few facts which were important to him: "I was born up on Clear Creek, [in 1900], just b'low where the bridge crosses t' go t' Payson. [South of Camp Verde.]. Out in there is what's called Verde Lakes today. Well, Verde Lakes is down in th' creek bottom from where we were at a little place there. [A few years later], we were livin' about eight miles b'low Camp Verde on th' west side o' th' river. We called it th' Squaw Peak place b'cause it was right under th' shadow o' Squaw Peak. The road on the west side o' th' river wasn't there then a tall. Th' road t' go down there, we had t' ford th' river, cross th' river on th ford, just south o' Camp Verde above where the so-called white bridge is. Then went down an' over a kind o' a plateau, an' down b' th' old Belle place, an' across the big sand flat an' then on t' a crossin' down there. It's a wonder anyone ever found our place! My dad [John Bristow] was runnin' th' H Bar Y cattle at that time. His range was up in th' triangle that is bounded by the Verde an' Clear Creek an' Fossil Creek in that wild area down there called Towel Peaks an' Sally Mae."

Life for the women living in these remote areas and trying to raise a family was difficult, at best. Perhaps this contributed to his family living outside of Arizona for awhile.

"My mother was expectin' my brother Woody," says Allen. "An' well, I don't know. There was some story that she left my dad an' went to' California."

"She told me she did!," Allen's wife Stella interjects.

"She had a sister that lived in Los Angeles," Allen continues, "an' she went there an' stayed with her a while. Marie an' I were with her. I was less than two years old. Then she lived with Aunt Cumi Wilbur in Fulton, California, that's where my brother Woody was born. That's when my dad sold the H Bar Y's cattle t' Arthur Heath an' came out t' California t' join us. I knew he was lookin' for work. He went over t' th' cement plant, but they were layin' people off b'cause th' rope was broken that hoists th' ore up t' th' mouth o' th' grinders. My father said, 'Well, maybe I can fix it.' The hoist had a great big grass rope, an' he was an expert with ropes. He spliced that rope an' put 'em back in business again in no time. They gave him a job sittin' there watchin' that rope. If it looked like it was gonna break, m' Dad was t' splice it again. That was 1902, in th' spring right after my brother was born in June an' I was a little over two.

"I don't know how long my dad worked at th' cement plant, but he like t' went nuts sittin' there watchin' that rope, just doin' nothin' else, so we come back t' Arizona an' stayed a couple o' weeks er a month with Grandpa an' Grandma Bristow at Middle Verde. They had a house with a basement or cellar [which was much nicer than the one built upon their arrival in the Valley], where Grandma kept a lot o' stuff. I fell down them stairs one time. She brought me back up an' kind o' fixed me up an' gave me some bread an' jam. She used t' make the darndest biscuits you ever saw. They were good! She an' Aunt Teedie made great big, yeller soda biscuits in th' Dutch oven. She had a big fireplace there, but no cook stove. She'd fix up a lot o' coals, rake them out on th' hearth an' cook with th' Dutch oven, pots, pans an' coffee pot there in th' fireplace.

"We stayed there, an' I played around outside. I remember bein' stooped in th' grass by a pretty good size ditch. [Probably the irrigation ditch Parson Bristow talked of building soon after his arrival.] I was just watchin' the sticks go by when Uncle Charlie [Parson Bristow's youngest] came out an' scared me from behind. I jumped an' fell in th' ditch. I guess I'd a drowned if he hadn't pulled me out b'cause it was pretty deep. He pulled me out o' there. I remember that. Then, my father bought th' H Bar Y back from Heath, an' we moved down there t' a little house, south o' Camp Verde. It was pretty sparse. We did have a cook stove out in th' front room. It was one o' those houses — window, window, door, [Using his hands he draws the semblance of the house in the air.] - that looked just like so many o' th' houses made by th' settlers. There was kind o' a little community called Offman down there while there was mining activity. A family by th' name o' Hopper had th' store an' post office. This was just east o' Squaw Peak.

"It was fall o' 1902 when we moved into that little place, an' it was pretty tough goin'. My mother had a small baby, my brother, an' he wasn't healthy. He was a blue baby an' wasn't expected t' live. James Elwood was his real name, but everybody called him 'Woody', except my father. He never called him Woody. He called him Jim.

"We didn't even have kerosene lamps. We used candles for light. Pretty primitive. [A more complete description of the house and living situation is given in Chapter 4.] My brother Frank was born down in that little old house. He was quite badly retarded. Could'a been th' same hereditary factor that caused Woody t' be a blue baby. We did hire an Indian woman, Ebba Quail, t' help my mother. [The Quails were quite a well known Indian family, and there are still Quails living around Camp Verde. The same family as Dell Quail referred to in Chapter 3.] My dad would be gone a week or so at a time, [taking care of the cattle]. I remember seein' him head out int' th' wilderness on his saddle horse with two pack horses trailin' b'hind.

"He lost quite a few cattle t' rustlers. They would go out there an' butcher them right on th' range. Some pretty ornery people lived around there at that time. My dad carried a telescope. He'd go up on a hillside where he could see a lot of country, lay down under a tree, an' pick up this telescope. It was a mariner's telescope about three feet long an' he always carried it on the back o' his saddle. Th' cattlemen called it his 'long eyes,' an' he could see th' brand on a cow with it. My dad also carried a six shooter, an' he was pretty good with it.

"Once he spied some o' these people stealin' his cattle, I won't name any names, an' he went down an' caught 'em. They talked round an' round, but he won th' argument, an' they took off. I don't know if he preferred any charges against them or not, but they were mad at him. So, once when we were gone, somebody came an' stole that telescope an' a big tarpaulin that he had for his campin' outfit. We always figured it was that particular set o' thieves. You know, my dad tried and tried to find another telescope that was as good as the one that they stole, but he never could buy one that focused as good. He did get one though an' went out t' try an' catch more rustlers. In those days if people went out an' butchered a beef to eat, th' cattlemen didn't pay much attention t' it. A lot o' people did it. Old Mose Casner, he was famous for that. He lived offa th' other guy's beef. That's the story anyway.

"We stayed at th' Squaw Peak place until th' spring o' 1906 when my mother couldn't hardly take it any longer. There was a farm for sale across th' river, north toward Camp Verde. You only had t' ford th' river once t' get t' that farm, an' it had a little better house on it. My mother talked my dad into sellin' th' cattle again t' Arthur Heath. Heath, Colonel Monroe, an' some others made a lot o' money off th' rest o' th' people in th' Verde Valley. But you can look at it two ways, o'course. One way those men were just opportunists; th' other way, they helped people like my folks when times were bad. They'd buy th' cattle an' turn right around an' sell cattle back t' th' same people for more, but if it hadn't been for them, why who knows what would'a happened t' ones like my folks.

"I don't really know where Heath an' Monroe came from or when they came. My folks were in the valley before they came in. They may have been attracted t' come in the 1880's an' 1890's, when th' big English syndicate came out an' established cattle companies. There were about three or four o' them in th' Verde Valley. Th' Diamond S down where Clear Creek enters th' valley was one big outfit. Another one was Lee's up at Middle Verde. They put cattle on there like you wouldn't believe. It was so lush an' green, an' th' rains were so good. My father worked for them an' he said they would roundup several thousand cattle in a day down on those big mesas like Wingfield Mesa down b'low th' Verde. Those mesas were just like big pastures — thick with grass. Well, it only lasted about ten years. They grazed it so much that th' big companies couldn't survive any longer, an' they b'gan t' sell out an' split up. But th' range was already over-grazed an' spoiled. When my folks first came here, th' river never flooded. It was just a series o' lagoons an' rivulets - beautiful. There were canyons, o'course, but it was more level country, an' there were little springs here, there an' everywhere. Just lots of water all over.

"There was a benefit from all th' over-grazing. With all that water, th' valley was full o' mosquitoes, an' many people died o' malaria. Th' over-grazin' caused th' river t' cut a channel an' flood, washin' th' mosquitoes away. That was a true benefit from th' overgrazin'. It created th' big washes an' floods, but it saved lives."

It is sad that the range has never recovered. The problem of overgrazing was compounded by the smelter smoke drifting over the area. Although it has been over fifty years since the smelters shut down, very little grass has come back. One wonders how long, or if ever, the countryside will be like it was. (See center for cowboy paintings)

Allen's father continued riding the range for quite

some time, but it wasn't always on horseback. Allen tells his version of "modern day" cowboying. "He, (John), an' Walt drove out on th' Miller Valley Road t' see about some cattle. That road used t' go out in th' country, an' there was a couple o' ole bulls fightin'. My dad knew that when bulls are fightin' you want t' give 'em a lot o' room b'cause when one gets th' best o' th' other, th' loser's bound t' run, an' he'll run right over anything that's in his way. Both bulls are mad, o'course, an' they'll charge anything. So, he was drivin' out there, an' he came around this turn an' here them bulls were fightin'. My dad came t' a stop an' one o' them bulls began t' charge. But instead o' steppin' on th' clutch t' down shift, or on th' throttle, my Dad just spurred at th' driver's seat o' th' car, knockin' a dent in it under the seat. The bull hit th' rear fender an' dented it before my dad could get out o' th' way. He'd have been clear of it, if he'd a'stepped on th' gas, but outta habit, he spurred that car like it was a horse." [Here Allen stopped to have a good laugh.]

Vintage car a little older than John's

Allen continues, reverting back to many years prior. "My folks got out o' th' cattle business an' moved up ont' a farm in 1906. We called it the Maxwell Place. I think they bought it from Lee Maxwell, I'm not sure, but anyway Maxwell was our neighbor. Dale, th' bee man, lived just below us, just south o' us. We had about 60 or 80 acres t' farm, an' my folks raised alfalfa, corn an' vegetables. They did pretty good. I had already started first grade at Squaw Peak School an' finished th' school year — about a month or two left — when we moved in th' spring o' 1906. After that, I went t' th' Clear Creek School, [south of Camp Verde], down where th' Old Stone Church is. There's a big cemetery down there now, an' th' Camp Verde Historical Society took that church over t' rebuild it. They use it for meetin's. When we were livin' down at th' Maxwell Place, church services were not regularly held, only sometimes, an' they'd hold funeral services, meetin's an' get-togethers there.

"My father worked awful hard on th' Maxwell Place until he sold it at a good profit in th' summer o' 1909. Then he bought th' place on th' Salt Mine Road below Camp Verde, which he kept until he died in 1934. My mother lived in that house with my brothers until she died in 1944. She an' my brothers couldn't run th' farm, so she rented th' land out. Yeah, ya' know Woody was too fat an' couldn't work. He couldn't only walk but a hundred yards. My mother got him int' sellin' Watkins products. He made a little spendin' money I guess. Frank worked around for wages. People were awful nice t' hire him t' irrigate. After my mother died, Frank an' Woody stayed on in th' house an' monkeyed around. Stella [Allen's wife] an' I helped 'em, gave 'em all th' money we could afford. [Rather regularly the two brothers would go up to Sedona and have Sunday dinner with either Walter's or George's families.] We'd come over from California an' help 'em rent th' land. They scrabbled along like that for a couple years. Then we sold th' place in 1946.

"Ya' know I never got up t' Sedona until 1922 when Stella an' I were on our honeymoon. Grandma Hart [no relation - some called her Aunt Delia] had a little grocery store up in there then. Th' road from Cottonwood had a bridge across th' Verde an' we drove my father's car, not the one he had spurred, but a 1920 model. I took a photo o' Stella down on th' rocks where Tlaquepaque is now in Sedona. When I was a kid growin' up, we just called it 'up in the red rocks.' People used t' come up from th' valley t' visit an' 'run th' 'chuck line', which was my dad's term for spongin' offa relatives. They would talk about this one couple that would visit in Camp Verde an' then go up t' visit a brother up in th' red rocks. Th' wife was awful nice. She'd help my mother cook an' wash an' all that when she'd visit, but accordin' t' Uncle Buddie, [Lazarus] her husband would sneak off t' talk socialism with a neighbor. That's my only childhood association with th' country up around Sedona, exceptin' that I could see it on a clear day walkin' t' school. I'd see th' red rocks an' th' San Francisco Peaks, all snow clad, standin' up above. You know there was perpetual snow on them Peaks until th' [nineteen] thirties."

When Allen was young and observing the "red rocks" little did he imagine that he and Stella would retire there and spend the last years of their lives in a country he had admired from a distance.

We return to cattle ranching while listening to Walter tell of some time he spent on one of these ranches. "When I did leave home, I learned a little cowboyin'. I went up t' th' Woods Ranch on th' Mogollon Mountain, an' I leased five acres o' land [1927] frum a cousin o' mine an' 'er husband, Dutch Dickison, who 'ad a cattle ranch. I wanted t' experiment with growin' lettuce fer th' Phoenix market in th' summer when th' Phoenix farmers couldn't grow nothin', 'cause it was s' hot. M' cousin Dora an' 'er husband were roundin' up th' cattle an' they made their headquarters at th' old Woods Ranch. Today the interstate highway, I-17, crosses Woods Canyon right there where that cabin is on that ole Woods Ranch.

"When I got my garden planted, Dutch asked me if I was able t' go down on th' fence line an' help th' fellas build a fence clear down t' Cedar Tank Canyon, which is about eight miles from the ranch. An' s' I went down there an' helped. They were buildin' a drift fence, which's four strands o' barbed wire pulled t' 150 pounds pressure. They called it a drift fence b'cause it kept the cattle from driftin' off a cattleman's allotted range. I helped ole Dutch Dickison build his fence clear down t' th' bluffs at Cedar Tank Canyon. Th' cattle couldn't git 'round them high bluffs. Usually, we could find a tree right on th' edge o' th' canyon that th' cattle couldn't git 'round t' fasten th' wire t'. Out in th' forest lots o' times, ya' could fasten th' fence on cedar trees an' pine trees.

"I never knew how th' ranchers built them drift fences until I helped Dutch build that'un. They cut an oak tree, with big limbs about six inches in diameter int' a 'v' shape. Then they'd drill holes in that thing, [the tree], two on each side fer th' big pins they'd pound int' them holes, an' them pins'd hold th' four rolls o' barbed wire. Each roll weighed about a hundred pounds. One mule'd pull the whole rig over that rough country – four rolls o' wire in th' wagon an' all other tools, that's a lot fer one mule. T' stretch that wire, they'd anchor it 'round them pins, jack up a wagon wheel an' pull th' wire 'round it. They'd git on them spokes an' pull down, turnin' it 'round th' wheel 'til that wire was s' tight it'd sing if ya' hit it. Once ya' got it stretched, th' men'd tack it with staples t' th' trees er posts. We'd always 'ave an awful good anchor t' start with. If we didn't 'ave trees, we'd have t' put in braces at the startin' point. We'd stretch 'bout a quarter a mile at a time. That's goin' some. We went down over rocks an' stretched that wire down through th' roughest country ya' ever saw. That fence we built back in 1927 is still there. [Circa 1983]

"While I was a workin' out there m' cousin Dora sent word that I was needed back home fer somethin', I fergit what it was. A fellah come out with a horse fer me t' ride back. Ever'body always carried a slicker, made o' an oily cloth. In th' summer time them big storms were liable t' come up. Well, one did, an' I got that slicker off a b'hind m' saddle an' put it on. I couldn't get it on too quick b'cause them storms come in a hurry. An' that's when I saw static electricity playin' on my horse's mane. That scared me. I didn't dare stop. I just kept out in th' middle o' this road, away from them pine trees. It come pretty close t' me as it was. Bang! That ole' lightnin'd come under them trees! [Walt emphasized the thunder with a loud clap of his hands and his spellbound listeners jumped in their seats!] Pretty scary trip! I'd t' ride about five miles back t' th' ranch. I just stayed right in th' open road, an' it just poured!"

At this point in the storytelling session Walt launches into another tale of lightning and thunder. "Another storm in 1917 down at Bridgeport crosses m' mind. Th' storm was a gatherin' while I was a talkin' with them Mexican workers livin' in th' big adobe house. Th' one I already told ya' about, th' one where Iva Van Deren was born. Well, we were standin' in th' yard, an' Bang! [More demonstration, but the listeners were more prepared for it this time.] This streak o' lightnin' hit 'bout forty feet in front o' us. Oh, it knocked us t' our knees. I could smell th' brimstone strong. Our farmhand, Kelly, wasn't s' lucky. We'd 'bout eight tons o' hay in our big barn, an' 'e liked t' sleep up in there. 'E was sittin' on th' end o' them bales in the draft, b'tween two windows, when th' lightnin' frum that same bolt struck 'im in th' head an' killed 'im dead. When we looked there was smoke a pourin' outta them windows. We'd t' run fast down there an' git 'im out s' we could take all a that hay outta there an' git t' th' bottom an' put out th' fire. That ole lightnin' followed them balin' wires clean t' th' ground at th' bottom o' that barn!"

Here he jumps back to the Woods Canyon setting. "I never even got wet up there at Woods Canyon with that slicker an' a big hat rolled at th' brim so th' water'd run off." The hat he is describing protruded out over the neck of the slicker when worn correctly so there was no opportunity for water to run down the collar.

"Oh, say! Ya' know what happened t' that field o' lettuce? Well, I'll just tell ya'. Later in th' summer when I was 'bout ready t' harvest that crop another one o' them big thunderstorms come a wham-bangin' through th' place. Why it was s' hard an' loud on them tin roofs, a fellah'd thought a whole army was a'shootin'. One crack o' lightnin' an' clap o' thunder come s' close I thought it hit th' ranch house. Even 'ad th' big ole' ranch dog s' scairt that when I opened th' bunkhouse door t' look at th' house, 'e like t' knocked me down racin' in through m' legs! 'E run right under m' bed like a shot outta gun. Well, anyway, that rain was s' bad it just pounded that terrible black dirt int' my lettuce s' bad I couldn't wash it out. I just 'ad t' leave it all in th' field an' fergit it. That ended m' farmin' on th' mountain."

Ranch families were always willing to help each other as shown in an excerpt from *Christmas Eve on a Cow Ranch at Cherry Creek in 1927*, written by Esther Henderson, daughter of early settlers. Esther and her mom had spent the day baking and preparing for the next day's dinner. "…It was about 3pm now, we heard a knock on the front door and as Dad was nearer than the rest of us, Mom called to him to answer the door. Pretty soon he appeared with a neighbor (10 miles away) 'Sam' I call him, had gone to Camp Verde the day before with fifty dollars for groceries and the three kids' Christmas things. To make a long story short, there was a poker game in progress at one of the local saloons, so Sam decided,

'Hey, maybe I can make a little extra money,' instead he lost it all. He didn't even have gas money to come home on, so he hitched a ride to Cherry Creek. He came to our house to get my Dad to take him home to get a few dollars they were saving for their taxes and to get his brother-in-law to take him back to Camp Verde for his pick-up. He still didn't have enough money for all that they needed. Dad said, 'Well it's too late now to go to Camp Verde and get back, so we'll fix something for you.'

"…We came up with a book of paper dolls, a book, *The Three Little Pigs*, a small strand of pink beads and hair ribbons, a pair of blue mittens, and two hair barrettes for the oldest girl. For the little one we had an ABC coloring book, a small box of crayons, a red toboggan cap, a small copper bracelet, some hair ribbons, and two barrettes. For the little boy, my brother divided his marbles, found a grey sweater slipover he had outgrown, a pocket comb, a new toy top, and a brand new yellow pencil."[8]

Dude Ranches and Ranch School Teaching

Dude ranches were a natural outgrowth of cattle ranches, as easterners became enthralled with the western way of life. Dudes were city folk who usually knew nothing about horses or cattle, but liked to pretend.

Soda Springs guest ranch, 1920s

Cowboys were romanticized by movies, ballads and Wild West shows, causing many to fantasize about riding carefree on horseback. Rarely did these would-be cowpokes have a clue about the hard work, grueling weather and dangers involved in working cattle. Ranchers realized there was money to be made by offering good accommodations and meals along with modified activities, i.e. trail rides, cookouts etc. Thus began a whole new industry focusing on a group of "want-a-be's," and usually somewhat wealthy people, who quickly became known to the locals as, "dudes, city slickers, and tenderfeet." Of course officially they were recognized as guests. Many were lovely people just seeking a peaceful place to relax and vacation. Only a few behaved in the manner to evoke these somewhat derogatory titles.

Although Wickenburg became the "dude ranch capital" of Arizona overflowing with guests, particularly in the winter, there were other smaller ranches with great reputations. Among these was Soda Springs, which was simply a working cattle ranch until the mid 1920s. This property was ideal for evolving into a Dude ranch with part of its charm being the year-round stream, Beaver Creek, which flowed through the land near the guest lodges and the large ranch house. The stream was lined with huge cottonwood trees giving wonderful shade and atmosphere to the grounds. Adding to its enchantment was a spring with such a high soda content that folks would "bob around like a cork," and a large size swimming pool built during this decade. These amenities, plus Spanish Hacienda style buildings with western décor, cattle, horseback riding and the perceived "romance" of cowboys, brought many out-of-state guests to this locale. It was to this place Ruth Woolf (Jordan) came from Tempe in about 1922-23 to teach at the Beaver Creek School. It was her good fortune to board at Soda Springs Guest Ranch. She shares some of her memories:

"Upon arriving at the ranch I knew I needed to learn to ride. I had never been around horses or cows before." Ruth continues her story of living at Soda Springs. "My first experience was helping with the roundup. What an initiation to being astride a horse! In later years I was asked how in the world did I ever get out of my bedroll let alone climb back on the horse the next day. My reply, 'Very slowly and very carefully!'"

"There were a few rooms for guests on the Soda Springs Ranch in the early 1920's. Beaver Creek had an ideal climate, not too hot in the summer, not too cold in the winter, and the change of the seasons is always a very beautiful time of the year. Back in the 1880's sometime, it [the area] began to be settled up with people who had small farms or large cattle ranches, and the cattle ran in herds on the range. Many had homes along Beaver Creek and

Virginia Finney Loudermilk, 1930s

changed the cattle from winter [here in the valley], to summer [up in the mountains]. Then visitors gradually came in, and saw how attractive it was. The area was such a wonderful place to ride horseback year round, that outsiders became interested in developing it as a place for people who could afford to come and spend long vacations there. Even in the very early twenties, people came and spent their short vacations at places like the Soda Springs Ranch where I was living while I taught school. In about 1924, a group of men from Pennsylvania came west to look over a suitable location to develop, and the Beaver Creek Ranch, which had been farmed for years and produced wonderful fruit, became the first really commercial dude ranch in the area. The Pennsylvania bunch offered trips to many interesting places and horseback riding everyday if one wanted it. After the Beaver Creek guest ranch began business, Romaine Loudermilk, who was running a dude ranch in Wickenburg, would bring his guests up through the Beaver Creek country to spend the night at the Soda Springs Ranch. He would take his guests on to Grand Canyon. Later he and Virginia Finney, who was born and lived on the Soda Springs Ranch with her parents and had helped to entertain and work with the guests, would marry. For awhile they even sang and entertained at the prestigious Biltmore Hotel in Phoenix where Virginia served as Social Director and hostess. Prior to marrying, Virginia showed him a place on a hilltop that she thought would make a good building site for another guest ranch. It was near the schoolhouse at Beaver Creek. She gave it the name of Rim Rock Ranch, and they ran it together for several years. When Virginia's family could no longer run the Soda Springs Ranch, they, [Virginia and her husband], moved back to it and developed it as the third guest ranch in the area. Eventually she established a summer ranch near the Apache Maid Mountain called Coyote Basin. [Soon Virginia and Romaine divorced and in the mid 1940s she married Paul Webb. For twenty years they continued running the guest ranch and after that as a working cattle ranch until the mid 1990s.]

"The guests enjoyed visiting back and forth between the ranches and having parties together. They were within a few miles of each other, but it was a good horseback ride for a day's visit. As they became available, cars sometimes replaced the horses as transportation. It was easy to have parties together at night. Occasionally outside entertainment was available, but mainly they created their own consisting of singing, guitar playing, western music — songs that had been sung by the cowboys around the campfire. The visitors at the different guest ranches also enjoyed attending community entertainment, parties and dances at the schoolhouse or wherever. They'd see a lot of local color at these activities. Many frequently rode horseback to interesting places like Indian ruins. Guests were fortunate if they were visiting during roundup or some special occasion like a rodeo. Each guest ranch had it's own large living room in which to entertain and another room where the meals were served family style, mixing cowhands and guests together."

Sometimes the entertainment included groups from "town" coming out to join the locals. One such group, the young adults from the Verde Baptist Church, arrived at the schoolhouse for an evening of "fun and fellowship." Although Ruth knew Walter's sister Stella from Tempe Normal School, it was at this particular social event where she met Walter. After several hours of playing games and enjoying refreshments, it was departure time for the guests. Upon returning to their cars, all were shocked to discover none would start, neither were there any headlights working. Finally it was discovered that while all were inside playing, singing, and eating, someone had "slipped up an' cut all o' them wires in our cars!" Walt stated in disgust. Ruth said that her greatest worry was that Walter would never come back. But he did! His excuse for returning was to show her his brand new Model A Ford, and of course take her for a ride.

Who was this petite, pretty schoolteacher? She had to be quite special to capture and hold the interest of one of the most eligible bachelors of the Verde Valley.

Ruth Marie Woolf was born in Crittendon County, Ky., on Nov. 7, 1902, the youngest of Franklin and Fannie Woolf's three children. Her brother Jesse was nine years older and her sister Lena was five years Ruth's senior. Partly due to the wide age differences, it has been said that Lena and her mother would prefer to have Ruth sit on a stool and read to them while they would do the housework. It also seems they felt they could do the chore much faster, thus she was never really good at cleaning house, cooking or doing dishes. Her preference was helping with the fruit, teaching children, or visiting with folks. As her daughter, Anne, once said, "She never made a difference between a governor or the town drunk. She always saw the best side of everyone."

When Ruth was nearly ten years old the family moved to Tempe, AZ, (1912) just after the territory gained statehood. Her father had been encouraged to come "west" by relatives who had already relocated. To assist in his semi-retirement, Franklin bought stock in the Hayden Flour Mill, which many years later became the controlling stock between two "warring" factions. (Another story for another time) Here they settled in a large home with a big canal passing in front of the house and a railroad track along the back edge of the property. The canal, with huge trees along it, plus the two foot thick adobe walls, helped keep the inside cool in the high temperatures of the summer. She always chuckled when telling that during the hot months they could go out front, jump in the canal with all of their clothes on, and come back into the house. Dripping dry didn't hurt the linoleum flooring and this method provided one's own private evaporative cooling system. (ASU has built a dormitory on the spot where their house stood.) The entire family was very active in the Tempe Baptist church, teaching classes, taking leadership responsibilities and serving on various boards. Ruth specifically, was an officer in the youth programs and a teacher. Her desire to be a schoolteacher, surfacing at a young age, lead to her attending Tempe Normal School, now Arizona State University. After her graduation in 1922 she arrived at Beaver Creek, fulfilling a childhood dream of living in the country, having her own horse, and teaching in a one teacher school, earning $50.00 a month. Although in the book, *By the Banks of Beaver Creek*, there is another teacher mentioned who taught there at the same time and states a salary of $150.00 a month, Ruth always told it as stated above.

Her sense of humor would make her blue eyes sparkle and caused one to wonder just what joke or trick she had "up her sleeve." Her enthusiasm for acting in plays found an outlet in her one-room-school as she coached her students in a variety of performances. All of the folks in the surrounding area came to attend and enjoy these. One in particular stage play that Ruth loved to recall was *Mrs. Wiggs and the Cabbage Patch*. The cast required more girls than she had female students, thus the challenge became to convince some of the boys to take the role of girls. Her strategy was to inform the fellows that it took a lot more talent for a boy to play the part of a girl than for a girl to portray a guy. It worked, and for years it was a production which many remembered with fondness.

At recess time she took part in games and activities, having as much fun as the "kids." Softball, dodge ball, or jump rope, it didn't matter, she would give it a try. One year, word that some of the older ones were planning to "play hooky" reached her ears. Instead of giving a lecture about not "ditching school," she discovered what day it was to be, talked the school board into approving a day off for everyone, and informed them she was "playing hooky" with them. At this point, her riding companion a first grader, asked, "Miss Woolf, how do you play hooky?" The day for their planned absence dawned and they all rode their horses to the prescribed rendezvous, continuing on to some Indian ruins. Here she showed them artifacts and talked about the ancient ones who had lived in this area.

After a picnic lunch and some rest time, they returned feeling great for having "played hooky," not even realizing she had turned it into a great learning experience. (Today it would be considered a field trip!)

It was this tiny, many talented, highly respected teacher that Walter wanted to get to know better, or in the verbiage of the twenties, he wanted to "court" her.

Ruth soon learned that as a teacher in a one-room school, she not only taught, but did janitorial duties including building the fire in the large wood stove in the center of the room. Her students came from miles around and were a wide range of ages. Some were in their late teens and taller then she. These were boys who had had classes on an intermittent basis due to being needed for roundups, planting or other ranch work. Her youngest student was a six-year-old first grader who lived farther away from the school than Ruth did. Someone from the little girl's family would ride with her to Soda Springs where she would continue her journey with Ruth. Obviously the youngster needed to stay at school until the teacher was ready to start home. One afternoon while they were still at the school a cowboy stopped by to invite Ruth to the upcoming ice cream social. Before she could answer, she felt a tug on her skirt and heard a small voice emphatically saying, "Miss Woolf, we are not going to the ice cream social with him!"

Ruth was also concerned about the students' lives away from school and when they were absent without her knowing why she would check with the families. After all of the children from one family had been absent for several days she rode over to their place to see if help was needed. Apparently the father was away working and as several were ill there were things she could do to be of assistance. Upon leaving, she was riding up the trail that the children used to walk to school. Suddenly she saw a large rattlesnake across the path. She felt compelled to rid the children of that particular danger. Backtracking a short distance, she tethered her horse to a mesquite bush, gathered some rocks and proceeded to throw them at the snake. Soon there were enough rocks in a pile from her throws to resemble a small monument. It was amazing, that she was able to kill it, because it appeared she would have been a better catcher on a ball team than a pitcher. Nonetheless, she succeeded, and then began to wonder if the cowboys back at the ranch would believe her when she told them she had killed a rattler. Convinced they would not, she decided to put the snake in one of her long leather riding gloves and tie it to her saddle horn. Fortunately for her, her horse, Pet, was extremely gentle, because no one had informed her that horses are very skittish around snakes. Upon arriving back at the ranch she told the fellas she had killed a rattlesnake. Just as she had suspected, no one believed her and the kidding started. She immediately took her glove loose, withdrew the snake and held it up with a "so there!" attitude. In unison the cowpokes dropped their jaws. Finally one recovered enough to say, "Ruthie, [their nickname for her] we would have believed you killed it, but we never would have believed you brought it home!!".

Times were hard on a lot of these ranchers, especially during the depression years. Ruth wanted to brighten lives a bit so decided to bring home each student at least once a year to eat and spend the night at the Guest Ranch. (A more dignified term for Dude Ranch.) One evening at the dinner table the little boy whom she had brought with her kept eating, and eating. She became concerned that he would be sick from overeating, so she mentioned something about it to him. His reply, "Oh, Miss Woolf, it's so good to be full!"

She also learned that having an adequate water supply was often quite a challenge for the ranch families. One little boy had been wearing the same shirt for quite awhile and it was beginning to look dirty. She suggested that he needed to take a bath and put on a clean shirt. He arrived the next day wearing a different one. When this happened a couple of times she realized that the body didn't smell cleaner and on further inspection noticed several types of collars lined up the back of his neck. It was then she recognized that he had just been putting one shirt on top of another. She soon came up with an idea to partially assist. Each week she would have water brought to the school and heat it on the wood stove. She then helped all of them shampoo their hair and gave haircuts to all of the boys who would let her. These were a whole bundle of new experiences for a girl who had lived all of her life in the "city."

Ruth continues remembering. "Riding (3 miles) from Soda Springs Ranch where I lived in the 1920's to my one room schoolhouse at Beaver Creek, I got a lot of wear out of my hat, leather skirt and spurs that Ruthie, our daughter, wears when she gives her tours of Arizona and the Southwest. (1983-1992 – See picture on back cover, Ruthie wearing mother's skirt, hat, and holding quirt.) I had acquired a Tom Mix style hat with the high crown from J. C. Penney's in Jerome, and paid $50.00 (a month's salary), to a man in Prescott to make a divided leather skirt for me. I looked like a cowgirl and in my last year of teaching I got a lot of practice yelling, because I had such a large class. (Now I even sounded like a cowboy. They often had to holler at the cattle.) In the one room school, [at Beaver Creek] I had at least six grades at a time. I would gather each grade separately around me and talk very softly. But my last year when I was engaged to be married, I lived in Tempe with my parents and wound up taking a job with 52 fourth graders. They were so jammed into that room that if I wanted to get from one side of the room to the other, I'd have to ask the children to stand so I could side-step between the seats. [That was really crowded because Ruth was about five feet tall and weighed only ninety-five pounds.] That last semester, I would begin the week with a strong voice, but by Wednesday, I could only whisper. So on the weekends, I wouldn't go anywhere, or talk to anybody. I'd just motion to my parents and say as few words as possible, so I could start in again on Monday. That's how I made it through the last year."

Taking guests at the cattle ranches enabled a number of the owners to stay for a while longer in the "business of cows" than would have been possible otherwise. Even so, after World War II the cattle business underwent another change. Arizona began attracting tourists and with the development of air conditioning more and more permanent residents were arriving. All of these folks wanted to explore and experience many areas of natural beauty within the state that heretofore had been rough country inhabited by wild animals and cattle. Real estate developers gobbled up any land available, thousands of acres being patented land. Communities with fancy names, such as Mesa del Caballo on Horse Mesa north of Payson, replaced what had been grazing land. Homes of all types, permanent and temporary, sprang up all through the mountains of northern Arizona, plus large portions of the National Forest became recreation sites and camp grounds. Suddenly, areas previously used for summer grazing had fences to keep cattle out instead of in and the cowmen were left wondering what to do. One old retired rancher said "…Why nowadays these foreigners …are mostly interested in land deals."[9]

Although the cattle ranches are being squeezed so tightly some have not been able to survive, at the end of the 20th century some small ranchers continue and other large outfits, such as CO Bar are still operating. For now, a small piece of the romance of the Old West lingers on and continues to be a live scene playing on the stage of human drama in Arizona.

FOOTNOTES

(1) Willard, Charles D. Charles Douglas Willard. Pioneer Stories of Arizona's Verde Valley. Comp. Mrs. John Bristow,

Mrs. E.W. Monroe, and Mrs. D.W. Wingfield. Camp Verde, AZ: The Verde Valley Pioneers Association, 1954. 150.

(2) Arizona: the Land and the People. Ed. Tom Miller. Tucson, AZ: U. of A. P, 1986. 222.

(3) Trimble, Marshall. CO BAR. Flagstaff, AZ: Northland P, 1982. 22.

(4) Ibid, p. 10

(5) Ibid, p. 49

(6) Ibid, p. 32

(7) Arizona. Bureau of Vital Statistics, Agricultural Branch. NO. 106. Flagstaff, AZ: NAU Archives-
SCA, MS 199 Box 8 Folder 85, 1914.

(8) Henderson, Esther. Christmas Eve on a Cow Ranch at Cherry Creek in 1927. Dewey, AZ: n.p., 1999.

(9) Arizona: the Land and the People. Ed. Tom Miller. Tucson, AZ: U. of A. P, 1986. 225.

Geographical Sites

DUTCH OVEN COOKING

By

Mary Smith Wyatt

Daughter of Ira Smith, Early cowboy and an expert Dutch Oven cook. (Her grandfather Lincoln, A.K.A. Link, was half-brother to Luranda Caroline Smith Bristow)

Dutch ovens are a three–legged [iron] pot with a lid that has a lip to hold the coals. It came from Europe and the early settlers used it to do all of their cooking. As people came west on the wagon trails and by horseback, the Dutch oven came with them. They were in all sizes but the ones that were about three inches deep were called bread ovens. Most people had three or four of various sizes but sometimes a lone cowboy would only have one. He would cook his bread first, then when it was done he would cook the rest of the meal.

On the round-ups the cook would have a helper that got the wood and packed the water and helped around the camp. A lot of cowboys got their start by working as the cook's helper. A good round-up cook could always get a job in the spring and the fall when the cattle were being moved from the summer or winter range.

To cook in the Dutch Oven you would need good hardwood coals, a shovel and a chuck box. The chuck box was put in the back of the wagon and when the lid was opened it made a table. The cook and his helper were up early and had the cook-fire going and the water heating long before daylight. Once the ovens were hot and one could smell the coffee and bacon or side meat and the biscuits were cooking, the cowboys did not have to be called. They were already up feeding the horses and were standing around the morning fire just waiting to hear "Come and git it b'fore I throw it out!" Some had a dinner bell they rang also.

How to Cook in the Dutch Oven

First get the pot and lid hot on the main fire, then put a shovel full, or so of coals on the ground away from the main fire and set the Dutch Oven on the coals. Next put in the meat, eggs, bread, or whatever. For the bread put the lid on if it isn't hot enough put some coals on top, letting it cook 10-15 minutes. Some cooks have an iron rack and hang the pot on it over the coals. When needing to use more than one pot they can be stacked on the lids with the largest one on the bottom, graduating sizes until the smallest is on top. If necessary more coals are put on the top lid. This method saves on the amount of coals used. Here in central Arizona we had mesquite and oak hardwoods so most cooked right on the ground. Without the lid it was just like cooking in a pan on the stove and putting on the lid made it like the oven of a stove. Pies, cobblers, and cakes could be made in it. My father, Ira Smith and Earl Van Deren [another local cowboy] would put a pudding pan in side the Dutch Oven to bake in. This kept the sugar from getting on the iron oven. To clean it one did not use much soap and water, but instead would burn it real good on the fire and take a gunny sack [made from burlap] and wipe the oven clean.

A cowboy breakfast would be made of side meat, bacon or steak with biscuit, gravy, eggs and sometimes pancakes, often called flap jacks. Biscuits could be made faster, a lot at a time, and were good as leftovers. A lot of cooks would mix the biscuit dough right in the flour sack by making a little hole in the flour, putting in some baking powder, salt, shortening and water or milk and mixing to the right consistency. Some would pull off a little dough at a time and put it in the hot Dutch Oven, others would put all of the dough on a floured board, roll it out and cut it with a biscuit cutter usually made from a tin can. Often a beer or wine bottle would be used as a rolling pin. In the end they all came out the same, very good and would stick to your ribs all day. As a little girl I remember taking a biscuit with pieces of bacon in it, wrapping it in some wax paper and putting it in my shirt or jacket pocket to eat around noon, as the cowboys I worked with did not come in for lunch. We ate a good breakfast, then rode all day and had supper that evening after all of the stock had been fed and watered for the night.

In the 1970s and early 80s I was riding with my Dad out on the Windmill ranch west of Sedona. We would leave Sedona with the horses in the trailer just as the sky was getting light in the east, getting out to the Windmill at daylight and we would saddle up. By the time the sun came up we would have been way up the trail. Mom would make us lunch that we carried in our saddlebags and she made the best lunches I ever ate out in the woods, always included a banana, orange or apple. We carried a canteen with water as the springs were no longer good for drinking. In the early days we just drank from the water holes. I have many great memories of being with my Dad riding trail, helping with roundup and cooking in a Dutch Oven.

Dutch Oven Biscuit Recipe   (the updated way)

Measure desired amount Bisquick

Add enough beer to make a soft dough

Roll out on a floured board and cut

Melt a small spoon of shortening in a heated Dutch Oven

Place biscuits inside and cover with a hot lid

Put Dutch Oven back onto the coals for 10-15 min.

Check once or twice to see if biscuits are browning on top, if not put a few hot coals on top of the lid. Serve with butter and jam   ENJOY

Introduction and Biography – Helen the Artist
Examples of her work

Helen in her studio circa 1985

Self portrait from snap shot on location

White Bear Fredricks- Hopi Chief & Sedona resident circa 1970

Charcoal of Tony Coburn Sedona resident circa 1975

Sculpture of Navajo Woman

Oil- Landscape of Red Rock Crossing and Courthouse Rock (renamed Cathedral Rock)

Introduction and Biography

Oil- Still Life

Iris

Etching

Pastel

Watercolor

Decoration on wooden cabinet

First oil painting, Walter & Ruth Jordan's Ranch circa 1945

HELEN THE ARTIST - EXAMPLES OF HER WORK

Chapter One

Pastel – Montezuma Castle

Chapter Two

Oil – Sycamores at Beaver Head Point

Oil – Navajo Sheep Herders

Chapter Three

Oil – Indian Drum

Oil – Apache Crown Dancers

Photo of Ruth Jordan and Jesse Goddard at the Battle site of the Big Dry Wash circa 1985

Chapter Four

Oil – Annie and Will Jordan's Home at Bridgeport

Oil – Apache Baskets – on Navajo Rug

Chapter Five

Watercolor - Fisherman

Oil – Oak Creek

Walter with fish on the line at Yellowstone Lake in 1978
(81 years old)

Oil – Abundance of Forest Growth

HELEN THE ARTIST - EXAMPLES OF HER WORK

Chapter Six

Bell Rock and Big Park (now Village of Oak Creek)
was great cattle country
Photo through car windshield circa 1948

Watercolor - Cowboy

Cartoon and Poem of Bill Gray circa 1943
By Helen Jordan
"Oh Bill is a gay cavalier-o
He gracefully rides on his mule
His cattle are fat
His horses sway backed
And he knows how to peddle the bull-o"

Oil – Cow Puncher

Chapter Seven

Oil – a street in Jerome

Oil – a house in Jerome

Chapter Eight

Oil – West end of Twin Buttes where smelter smoke was sometimes visible

Oil – Identified by Helen as Schnebly's very first house

Chapter Nine

Oil – Sedona Schnebly

Watercolor – Jordan Road 1940s

Chapter Nine (cont'd)

Walter's Peach Orchard
Picture by Bob Bradshaw 1950s

Walter holding his apples 1940s

Chapter Ten

Oil –Icicles on water wheel

Oil – water wheel

Photo from George Jordan's slide collection
Walter's Reservoir 1960s

83

Chapter Seven
CONGREGATIONS ABOVE THE VALLEY; MINERS GATHER ON CLEOPATRA HILL

While Parson Bristow was gathering his congregations down in the valley along the river at Middle Verde and Upper Verde, another type of congregation was forming up on the side of the Black Mountains. An area that was soon to be known as Cleopatra Hill, was beckoning to those who were seeking their fortune in the rocks of "them thar' hills." It is interesting that though folks came from near and far, the place of settlement was on the west side of the fertile and rich Valley. As these folks' "western star" settled over Cleopatra Hill, the curtain was rising on scene V of the human drama of the Verde Valley.

Red, on the geology map of the mining districts in these mountains to the west of the Verde Valley, indicates the economic mineralization. These rocks, suggesting a potential richness, attracted men to look closer for the precious metals in the massive sulphides in the Black Mountains rising 4,500 feet above the western edge of the Verde River's flood plain. In one of the late geologic periods of volcanic activity, a break in the ridge - the Verde Fault - divided one extraordinarily large and rich mass of sulphide ore. One portion was exposed and the other displaced, setting the backdrop for the exciting new drama in this verdant valley.

The ancient pueblo dwellers, the 16th Century Spanish explorers, the ranchers, farmers, and U.S. Cavalry officers, (specifically Al Seiber who filed several claims), had recognized the signs of a major mineral event in the Black Mountains. In the Verde Valley stories of the early salt mines, and caves, which harbored skeletons and weapons reminded new settlers of mining's strife. In this chapter are the mining stories of Will Jordan's son Walter and Walter's family; of Allen Bristow, son of Annie Bristow's brother John; and of Jerome natives - John McMillan and his wife, who were interviewed in the mid 1980s.

Walter related most of his mining stories on a trip taken with his daughter (F. Ruth) and wife (Mrs. Ruth Jordan) into the mountains where legendary Jerome is perched. They had arranged a meeting with John McMillan who worked 16 years underground in Jerome's "Glory Hole," and at the time of the visit was working as caretaker for the property of Phelps Dodge Corporation, a job he kept into his eighties. Allen Bristow's stories were recorded on another outing.

Jerome, when its rise on the line of human history began, was just another hole in the ground among dozens of mining ventures and many of the smaller operations were dug into the country rock of the ridges south of the gathering of little shacks and tents. At the turn of the twentieth century as exploration continued and mines opened along the Verde Fault, nothing could stop the development of one of the richest little mining towns in the West: Jerome, referred to as The Billion Dollar Copper Camp.

Red peppering on the map marks the presence of rich ore in free milling gold and silver veins and pockets in numerous mines that honeycomb the mountain. Names of many of these lingered on the tongues of those early settlers for their entire lifetime - Leghorn Mine, the Sitting Bull, the Federal, the Bunker, Cherry King, Blackhawk, Sunnybrook, Golden Idol, Conger and Gold Bullion Mine among numerous others. The pattern of development had been "discovery, the arrastre stage [grinding ores by means of a heavy stone], the sinking of a shaft to a depth of 200 or 300 feet, followed by the erection of a small mill, and ... usually a prolonged rest, with a watchman in charge."[1]

More than veins were sometimes encountered in the diggings and mines just below the Verde Fault or on the rock cliffs of nearby canyons like Gaddes and Goddard, named for early anglo investigators. Two types of ore bodies had been formed: those created by the massive sulphides requiring smelting, like the ones at Jerome existing on rock shelves; and the free-milling precious metals which could be extracted without smelting. Lead and zinc ores at the Iron King mine and copper ores at Jerome helped sustain the mining enterprises. For copper to be profitable, millions of dollars had to be invested, thus effectively eliminating the individual prospector.

The first small boom in the area, with a one furnace smelter, lasted from 1882-1884, with another brief operation in 1887. W. A. Clark's entry on the scene in 1888 revived the town of Jerome. As a commissioner at the New Orleans Exposition in 1885, Clark viewed a fine copper collection on display from the United Verde Mine. Clark had made a "good grubstake" freighting food and supplies to miners in Montana before buying into the Anaconda operation and becoming wealthy. He had always wanted to be a Senator and in 1899 he was "elected" by spending over a million dollars in bribes. The Senate Elections and Privileges Committee would not allow him to be seated so he ran again and was again elected in 1902. After acquiring his desire as a politician he decided he didn't like public service and did not run for re-election. (It would be surmised that his unethical practices were the basis for people in Montana to express derogatory feelings to F. Ruth while visiting a mining museum there. They literally scoffed when she referred to him as "Senator.")

In the meantime, Clark purchased the United Verde Mine paying the asking price of $300,000 plus paying off the current indebtedness of $60,000. The McKinnon Brothers, William and John, did the first work to develop the property. In 1884 it was owned by a company presided over by a Mr. McDonald and a man by the name of Thomas was superintendent. After about two years, they (McDonald and Thomas) thought the best ore had been mined out, but Frank Murphy, whom all old timers well remember was able to interest Clark. Using only two 35-ton furnaces (jackets), Clark was able in his first year of operation "to replace the $60,000 back in his pocket and paid for the balance of the mine."[2] Prior to Clark's purchase, Phelps Dodge had sent Dr. James Douglas to evaluate the site. Dr. Douglas, a highly knowledgeable mining man who had discovered a new method for extracting ore, felt there were plenty of minerals present but that the area was completely lacking in transportation. The company (Phelps Dodge) considered the owners (McDonald and Thomas) to be "over a barrel" and offered $30,000. However, for some reason the management of Phelps Dodge changed their minds and offered full price, one day after Clark had completed the purchase! "Phelps-Dodge would acquire the property many years later, paying twenty-million dollars, after millions of dollars of ore had already been extracted."[3]

Clark brought Joseph L. Giroux with him from Montana and the first ore was brought up, putting the mines in business again. Clark kept extremely tight control of everything, owning most of the businesses in town, restraining the newspapers by withholding advertising if he didn't like what was printed, and firing miners if they told those above ground anything about what they knew was down below. From many he earned the title of "villain."

In 1914, James "Rawhide" Douglas (Son of Dr. James Douglas) gambled on the Little Daisy Mine, the mine that was to become the other major one of the area. In it the Verde Fault had taken a big bite out of the lower ore body of Clark's United Verde Company, opening the door for other companies. Before Jerome's glory ended, the mining enterprises of Clark and Douglas at Jerome would account for 99% of the recorded metal wealth extracted from the region. Douglas finished his Jerome operations in 1938, Clark in 1953. Although Jerome mines were shut down, Arizona continued into the mid 1970s to produced one-half of the nation's copper, accounting for the state's major single income and source of taxes.

As the these episodes unfolded, the geologists and mining engineers sampled, measured, weighed and otherwise noted refinements of their theories, but mining remained largely a game of chance. The homesteaders in the region, like Will Jordan, took that chance with limited return on their investments.

Walter describes one of these situations: "One day when Dad was in Jerome unloadin' fruit an' vegetables, a hobo come along an' said 'e 'ad 1500 shares in th' Little Daisy that 'e'd sell fer 15 cents a share. Dad told 'im, 'You wait. I'm gonna talk t' this friend o' mine.'

"Dad's friend advised 'im not t' buy th' Little Daisy but instead t' buy shares in th' Hanes mine on th' northwest side o' th' mountain, adjoining the big United Verde mine, an' that's what 'e did.

"Dad bought 1000 shares o' Hanes, paid a dollar a share, an' 'e got only six cents a share back outta that. If 'e'd a bought frum that hobo, 'e could o' sold fer $51 a share. Just think o' that! B'fore they got th' tunnel built int' th' mine t' bring th' ore down here easily t' th' Clemenceau smelter, United Verde Extension ran a tramway frum th' mine up there an' hauled their ore t' Jimmy Douglas' smelter in th' southern part o' th' state." [Douglas, AZ. The smelter there was still operating at the end of the twentieth century.]

"I r'member th' big ore bins when my brother Chester an' I were haulin' hay up there t' th' slaughter house. [Located between Jerome and Clarkdale.] When we saw this big ore bin right there by th' United Verde Extension Railroad, we went up t' it an' picked up a great big rock that 'ad bounced out o' th' bin. Ya' could see th' pure copper in it, but like chumps, we didn't buy any o' that stock either. It was $3.00 a share at that time. A friend o' mine, who went t' work up here in Jerome in 1913, raked up all th' United Verde Extension stock 'e could possibly git. When 'e left, 'e sold fer $51.00. That's how 'e got 'is start up in Oregon an' Washington in th' fruit business."

Undeniably, the success of their agricultural enterprises was linked to the phenomenon of Jerome. When Clark's United Verde Copper Company was being sued by the Jordan Family and other farmers in the valley for smelter smoke damages to their crops, the company's agricultural experts liked to point out that the mining community was the chief farmer's market in the region and the reason for the growth of farming. The conflict between the farmer's and the smelter smoke is described in the following chapter.

The geology of the land and mining has always attracted human activity. The salt mines, located on the west side of the Verde River between Middle Verde and Squaw Peak, were important for Indians settling in this area and later for settlers who mined soda, as well as salt for preserving food. Allen recalls other ways in which the contents of this mine were used:

"You know that's not sodium chloride in that salt mine there near Camp Verde. That's sodium sulphate. They mined it t' make glass. They also used it in paper-makin' and in makin' ammunition. Now, whether they ran big at the start o' the Second World War, or whether they had it goin' before then, I'm not sure because I went to California to finish high school in 1919, before the mine started, but I remember the salt mine as a kid. My Dad used t' take us there. We were runnin' cattle, and we used t' go up and get chunks of salt and put it out on th' range.
"We'd dig it out with picks an' shovels. No one back then made a minin' project out of it. It was just the same as where that big gypsum plant is in th' valley. Th' people used t' go up there when they'd build. If we needed t' mix plaster or something, we'd go there an' get a load o' quick lime, [a misnomer used by the old timers to refer to gypsum] or what you call gypsum, out o' that pit. We'd mix it in th' plaster an' in th' mortar for our buildings.

"I had a friend that used t' drive truck for th' mine in there. When I'd come back t' visit the folks, I'd visit him. He'd be drivin' truck for th' salt mine, an' we went on up an' watched them work. They had a lot o' conveyor belts, tunnels, an' machinery t' do the digging. He told me about runnin' into an old tunnel with a skeleton with a tomahawk still lodged in th' back o' th' skull. Maybe th' ancients fought over who would claim th' huntin' rights t' a spot attractive t' wild animals that came t' lick th' salt."

The minerals used for building were often community property in the early days of settlement. The precious metals were another story, and a set of mining laws was created by the prospectors in the gold fields of California and adopted by the federal government in 1866 to keep the greed and violence in check.

Walter explained part of the process. "If ya held a minin' claim, ya 'ad t' do assessment work, a hundred dollars on each claim. [Assessment Work in the U.S. code of mining laws is any work or investment which helps to define or outline the deposit of mineral or lead to it's eventual extraction at a profit.] When we were doin' this work one Sunday, I walked up that steep mountain there, an' I found a ledge o' quartz, free-millin' gold quartz. [Needing only to be crushed, the gold did not need to be freed from a complex ore by smelting.] I brought some back t' th' camp where I 'ad a pan. I crushed th' rock with a hammer an' panned out some gold. I told George about it one day. 'E was crazy about gold minin', an' 'e said, 'I want you t' take me up there someday.'

"Well, I said, 'George, that's a horrible climb.'
"But he says: 'I can make it.'

"I kept seein' this quartz broken off th' ledge an' floatin' down th' hill, an' I followed it up. That's th' way I found that ledge o' quartz. We took up 26 claims at th' foot o' th' mountain, an' I helped do th' assessment work on 'em. We eventually dropped them claims when th' boom blew up in two or three years. It would take lots o' money t' develop them claims int' a big mine. There's lots o' mineral though, in them mountains. It's still there, you bet in them mountains, kinda t' th' south part o' Mingus Mountain!" [Named for brothers Jake and Bill Mingus who operated a sawmill on their mountain.]

"Dad once 'ad an interest in a mine over in th' Black Canyon country. They took a lotta gold out o' there. That has quite a history. My father owned one third o' that an' the Iron King at one time. He went in on it with two Camp Verde men. They found a big boulder mighty rich in silver an' shipped a ton o' it on pack horse out through Baker's Pass, t' th' railroad. It netted them $300 above all expenses an' one o' them men at Camp Verde, one o' th' owners, 'e couldn't keep 'is danged mouth shut about it; so ole' Johnny Dukes in Prescott gotta a man t' go up there an' jump them claims. When Father heard about it, 'e was told, 'Ya better be ready fer 'em. They plan t' run ya off.'

"Well, m' Dad 'ad a double-barreled ten-gauge shotgun loaded with buckshot, an' 'e was workin' doin' assessment work on th' claim when this feller walked up an' said, 'Ya're on our claims.'

"'Well, all right, an'time ya git ready fer me, I'm ready.'

"Dad made sure that feller got a good look at that ole ten-gauge."

"'Oh, no. We didn't want t' cause any trouble.'
"'Listen, you don't own these claims.'

"So the thing went t' a lawsuit an' W. A. Clark, one o' th' owners o' th' mines in Jerome, took part an' footed th' bill fer lawyers fer m' Dad an' 'is two partners. They were in court in Prescott over that thing fer a year an' a half. Finally, they compromised it: Clark took th' lower half, called Iron King; Johnny Duke an' his partners took th' Copper Chief, an' that's th' way it settled. W. A. Clark give m' father an' 'is two partners $2500 apiece." [Due to the settlement one can easily surmise that Clark's motive for "helping" Will and his partners, wasn't kindness and charity! The Iron King mine contained gold, silver, lead and zinc.] "Johnny Duke got enough outta th' Copper Chief t' build th' St. Michael Hotel in Prescott. Ain't that somethin'! There was a fortune there, an' Dad lost it. If only them guys 'ad a just kept their darned fool mouths shut!"

With her father, F. Ruth visited the St. Michael's Hotel after its renovation. While being given a guided tour through the facility, Walter announced to everybody, "This here place never would'a been built if that ole Johnny Duke 'adn't a stole m' Dad's mine. Guess ya' could say this was built with money that b'longed t' m' Dad!"

When asked about the amount of mineral taken from the Copper Chief, Walt's answer could cause a major case of depression for the "almost heirs." "Oh my goodness! They took $2,000,000 out o' there, [in the early 1900s, imagine its worth in year 2000] and Frank Derrick, [a friend of Walt's who worked for the copper company], says they never even touched th'bulk o' it. 'E said that when he was minin', 'e found great big chunks there just like th' ones up here at th' Glory Hole. They call that Jerome mine th' Glory Hole b'cause th' gold by itself paid fer more than all the expenses t' run th' smelter an' the mine. It was so rich!

"Sometimes it wasn't all that glorious. Th' original big underground mine 'ad s' much sulphur at th' 200 foot level that it caught fire. In order t' go ahead, they 'ad t' put in what was called bulkheads t' keep th' fire back so's they could go ahead an' mine. It got s' bad that they finally decided t' take all o' that top burden [soil and rock] off, all 200 foot o' it. So's t' git t' that ore body an' put out th' fire. [Some have called it the 160 Foot level and others refer to it as 400 foot.] Th' Glory Hole's on th' south side o' this big open pit an' ya' can still see that whole area up t' th' west. They 'ad t' shoot off th' whole top o' that thing t' get down t' th' fire."

Walter has been relating all of these stories during the first twenty miles on the journey from Sedona. Daughter F. Ruth, Walt and his wife, Ruth, were on their way to visit John McMillan and his wife in Jerome. As they neared the small community formerly known as Clemenceau, Walter really "comes to life" pointing to the many things which he is describing. First in Clemenceau he indicates a large group of buildings which in recent years housed a mattress factory, exclusive clothing factory and other shops, etc. "That was the Clemenceau Smelter. Th' big machine shop was down there an' different things fer th' smelter. An' down below was th' coolin' pond where th' water was sprayed out t' cool th' pond. They had t' keep that water cool. Over here [pointing to the south side of hwy. 89A] was th' smelter an' stack. Sister, ya remember when they blew that stack down. [He turns to his daughter] Yeah, we all come t' watch it, that was somewhere in the 1940s. This United Verde Extension got their smelter int' operation in th' 1920's, an' they took out millions an' millions o' dollars worth o' ore b'fore it played out." Walt shakes his head and gives a snort. "They claimed it 'played out,' but there's worlds o' ore in there that could b' run through this new process they've got. They can process ore now that only runs 4.5% copper an' make millions o' dollars when they open pit mine and run thousands o' tons a day.

"All that ore they smelted at th' United Verde Extension come outta that Little Daisy mine Dad didn't put 'is money in. That great big mine's right under th' smelter that use t' b' part way up towards Jerome frum Clarkdale. It was kinda in th' gulch, near where th' slaughter house was later, where it was moved when they blew off that overburden. W. A. Clark's geologists missed it. They didn't calculate that there was any more ore in that body b'cause part o' it'd slipped upwards. They just plain missed it, an' that's how Jimmy Douglas gotta hold o' it. 'E heard about them prospectors that'd struck a pretty rich spot, 600 feet b'low th' surface, in what they called th' Little Daisy, but they run out o' money."

Marshall Trimble states, "His [Jimmy Douglas's] mine hit a vein of pure copper five feet thick, the richest ever found in American mining."[4]

Just after driving through Clarkdale, Walter points toward Jerome. "Here ya' kin see th' tunnel that C. B. Hopkins engineered int' th' mine at th' 1000 foot level. M' Dad said that Hopkins surveyed that in so accurate that when th' crew o' men workin' toward th' new tunnel frum inside th' mine broke through t' th' second crew that'd been tunnelin' frum outside, th' two lengths o' th' tunnel fit together perfect. That's where Hopkins got th' feather in 'is cap. 'E was such a fine engineer, 'e 'ad that tunnel designed t' th' fraction o' an inch through them rough hills.

"Here's th' Texas Shaft. Now Jimmy Douglas wanted t' finish that tunnel in a hurry t' 'ave it ready fer th' new smelter. First they tunneled t' th' center - that's this Texas Shaft – t' work both ways frum there, an' they'd a crew on both ends - four crews workin' on that tunnel at once. I was deliverin' fruits an' vegetables t' a man an' 'is wife who run th' restaurant there fer th' workmen, that's how I heard about it. The main tunnel, th' Josephine, is three miles long.

"Oh, say did I ever tell ya' that just before startin' up th' Hogback, [so named because the road runs along a narrow ridge, both sides dropping steeply into canyons] Dad use t' own a lime kiln. The old pioneers took that lime an' made lye in that kiln. They 'ad t' burn it."

As the years passed, more people arrived and Jerome began to grow up as a town. "Them people built churches, an' we 'ad th' school, an' a really good hospital. Then fraternal orders 'ad meetin' houses in town too. I never b'longed t' a lodge, but I made up m' mind that if I ever did, I'd join them Odd Fellows," Walt continued.

Founded in England, the Odd Fellows was one of the largest fraternal and benevolent orders in the

Jerome, 1930s

United States. The first American Order was organized in Baltimore in 1819. Working people often organized fraternal societies to provide sickness and death benefits for members.

"That ole Elk's Lodge 'ad th' wildest parties up here. The Masons weren't s' bad, but I use' t' bowl with an Odd Fellow an' 'e told me one day, 'The reason I joined them Odd Fellows is they're clean. They don't 'ave no such parties as that dad-gum Elk's Lodge.'"

Walter's voice dropped to a conspiratorial whisper as he told this story. "M' cousin b'longed t' them Elks. 'E liked t' play poker at th' lodge. This was b'fore 'e converted, mind you. 'E'd drink with 'em, an' one o' 'em went t' Las Vegas an' got a woman. O' course, they 'ad t' pay 'er a lotta money. She stripped off naked an' danced. There wasn't nothin' goin' on but a poker game as far as th' law was concerned, s' long as everythin' was quiet." Here Walter gave a big snicker, obviously enjoying the tale all over again.

Among the several houses of worship that were built was the Mexican Methodist Church. It was constructed over a period of three years, (1939-1941) single handedly by Sabino Gonzales, the pastor. He spent the mornings as a barber at his shop in the Central Hotel, the afternoons constructing the church. Old mine timbers were used for footings and beams, powder boxes for wall sheathing. Locals referred to it as the "powder box church." In Richard Snodgrass's, *Ballad of Laughing Mountain*, Pastor Sabino is quoted, "Christ, the great teacher. I know nothing of carpentry, masonry, plastering when I begin. He taught me. People say I am crazy in the beginning, but He guides me each path. With a black and blue thumb occasionally, yes; never-the-less, He guides me. After the morning of the first service, people no long say 'There goes Loco Sabino.'"[5]

His final sermon was delivered in late 1952 to a congregation of 7, having shrunk from 63, when the mines were booming. As he locked the front door, he was not only closing a building but ending an era in which he had fulfilled his dream.

Highway 89A makes a hairpin curve swinging northeast as it begins the extremely steep climb up to the Hogback. Then at the top of this stretch, (but only a short distance up Cleopatra Hill), another corner just as sharp heads in the other direction. At the apex of the hairpin, replacing a former service station, is a viewpoint. Here the trio made a brief stop to gaze across the Verde Valley to Oak Creek, over forty miles to the east.

"Right here is where I stopped t' fill up m' truck with gasoline one night when I was a goin' t' Phoenix with a load o' produce," Walt points while talking. "Th' fella that owned that station 'ad already closed up, an' 'e 'ad this big police dog a comin' out o' there after me, s' I left in a hurry! I was lucky t' git some gas at another station around here. See where that says 'Sports-crafts?' [He points to a place slightly around the hill.] That's where I got gasoline that night."

All of the Verde Valley stretches out before the eye from this popular vantage spot at the point of the hill. The red rocks below the cleft of Oak Creek Canyon are only slightly visible, hidden for the most part by the mountains and the high plateau. The communities and industry of Clarkdale, Cottonwood and Camp Verde seen across the valley, form the sprawl tucked along the foot of our mountain perch. An oasis of marsh greenery marks the remainder of Peck's Lake between the foothills and the river. Through the carved and barren mounds of lakebed sediment snakes the desert river's path, a reminder of the violent water sometimes shed from the purple ridges on the far horizon, including the often snow-covered San Francisco Peaks - a lordly presence in the far sky and the highest elevation in Arizona. (12,696 feet)

Looking east from Jerome

Continuing around the curve, and passing the million dollar high school, (last graduating class approximately 1950), Walter points out two of the major buildings to the right. "Down there's Jimmy Douglas's mansion an' th' Little Daisy Hotel an' where th' restaurants use' t' be fer th' miners. Th' Douglas Mansion's a museum now, [an Arizona State Park] an' they tour people through it. [The mansion is one of the few fully restored buildings in the town. All that is left of the hotel is concrete walls and floors and the "porch" with gorgeous cement arches. During the nineteen fifties a church group from Sedona had a Halloween Party in the Little Daisy, but failed to inform the Jerome fire department. It was quite a surprise when the fire truck rolled up to the front with sirens wailing!] Back to Walt: "When I's a kid, th' general manager was a friend o' m' Dad's, an' 'e invited our whole family t' tour th' mansion. I went along, an' I'll never fergit that."

The road leading down over the hill and around to the mansion passes an area known as "the cribs," and an old head frame for one of the shafts. Continuing on past the intersection a short distance, Ruth asks how long the Methodist church had been there. Walter's answer moves into describing more of the town as the drive follows 89A through the section where the highway separates; one street for uphill traffic and another for downhill. "It [the church] was operatin' when my Uncle Jim Wingfield an' Aunt Effie [Annie Bristow Jordan's older sister] was a'livin' in a big house right there. They was members o' that church. [The date never was stated].

"There's th' old Jerome Motel, right there where th' 89A Highway marker is – th' same route we used. Right here on th' left use t' be th' jail." Currently the jail is several hundred feet down hill on the right side of the road. An old miner is quoted in Snodgrass' book, "Never be another mine like it — never be another slide like the one in the mid -Twenties. Years of blasting in the tunnels beneath Jerome — there are 85 miles of them — loosened a geologic fault, slid two city blocks of buildings across Hall Avenue. Among the buildings to go was the jail, which now has a sign on the door '*Danger Keep Out!*'[6] In the early nineteen fifties the Saturday Evening Post published an article on Jerome stating that this is the only town in the U. S. with a sign posted on it saying "Danger Keep Out!"

Walt continues, "J. C. Penney was on that side, [the east] an' now I'm goin' t' show ya where th' road went 'round t' this red light district. We use t' have a bank right across th' street frum our farmer's market, an' T.F. Miller Company 'ad a big store. Right there where that big hole is."

"I think I still have a dress I bought there. We used to come to Jerome to do our main shopping at Penney's," [approximately 35 miles from Sedona.] Walter's wife interjects.

Walt picks up the conversation again. "That's th' old road we use t' take up t' Prescott, an' th' Hampton House use t' b right there - a big motel. Now you see that little road goin' out over th' hill there? Ya can go on over t' Chino Valley on it." Walter gestures to the west while describing the territory. "That use t' b' th' narrow-gage railroad, an' th' railroad come in on top b'fore this thing was blasted out. Now we're goin' over here on th' right where Jimmy Douglas's old office is up on th' hill. See it? There's th' big hoist int' th' Glory Hole on th' left there. Boy, that's really somethin'! Go 'round where that road goes t' th' old United Verde headquarters. That's where John's waitin'."

At the time of the following interview (approximately 1984) John McMillan was working as caretaker of the Phelps Dodge mining company property at Jerome. Many old photos of the mining operation and Jerome were on display in his office. F. Ruth asks John to explain the ownership of the mines at Jerome. "W. A. Clark and Jimmy Douglas ran the two different outfits up here. The Little Daisy mine was owned by the Douglas family. W. A. Clark, better known as Senator Clark from Montana, was owner of the old United Verde Copper Company and this is it. Phelps Dodge bought it in 1935 after W. A. Clark III was killed in a plane accident down here in the valley at Cottonwood. W. A. Clark III had his planes at that airport, [Clemenceau airport] in fact, he helped improve that area. He had a co-pilot, and the day he was killed, they were out practicing spins, which used to be a requirement to be able to spin a plane and pull it out. He was practicing spins under the hood - blind flying - and for some reason they didn't come out of it. His co-pilot was supposed to keep him out of trouble, but for some reason he didn't. He wasn't under the hood, you see, that's the reason. They don't know just what ... well they have their theory about it. That was the situation anyway. The United Verde was Clark's operation, United Verde Extension was Douglas' Little Daisy. Clark's smelter was at Clarkdale and Douglas' down at Clemenceau. W. A. Clark's mine was known as the Big Hole. Douglas' mine was known as the Little Daisy."

John points out that an enormous amount of ore was taken from theses two holes. "In the neighborhood of $475,000,000 worth of copper, gold and silver came out of the Big Hole, and from the Little Daisy in the area of $125,000,000. Just imagine what that would amount to 50-100 years later! There is a certain amount of ore left in both. The price of wages kept getting higher, so they bypassed a lot of the lower grade ores that they used to mine, when it stopped paying because of the higher wages. This mine here still has a large deposit of zinc, and someday if there were demand and the price were right, they may come back and mine it. There are places in the pit here that run as high as three ounces of gold per ton and have over two hundred ounces in silver, but mostly copper. There's a possibility it could be opened up. Open pit mining is the least expensive nowadays. Underground mining is quite expensive."

F. Ruth remarks, "When I was in high school, (about 1950), just before they closed down the smelter, the talk was that the company was closing the smelter just to be able to buy Jerome and make it a big open pit. People speculated and talked about that for a long, long time.."

"Yeah," John comments, "That was the story they got out. A mining community is usually the breeder of all kinds of rumors. That's my conclusion after living in one all my life."

He continues with the history of the mine. "This building was built by W. A. Clark as a mine office. Look at these pictures of the original mine and smelter up where the pit is today. Back in 1896 or thereabouts, the ore body down on the 160 foot level caught fire. [The depth of the shaft containing the fire varies according to the person telling the story. Perhaps the fact that there was more than one fire accounts for the differences.] There were four shafts that caught fire going down into the mines. They don't know just what caused the rock to catch fire - friction from slippage in the earth or a blast or something of that nature. They do know what kept the rock burning - its high sulphur content. For nearly 20 years, they fought that fire before they decided to build a new smelter in the valley, (Clarkdale), and move the old smelter off so they could strip mine."

While looking at the pictures on the wall, F. Ruth points to one. "This picture shows Grandpa Jordan's farm and where the slag dump pushed the river east. It pretty much cut away his farm."

John confirms this," Washed it all away."

Ruth (Mrs. Jordan) reflects, "The foundations of the old home are still there up on the hill. The river didn't sweep that away, but there is no tillable land down there anymore. I understand the home burned due to the owner going to sleep smoking a cigarette."

Back to mining and smelting operations. "Checking the map here, the slag dump covers the area [as large as] of Peck's Lake - 653 acres. The slag, I would say, averages close to 75 feet thick. There's a lot of ore in it, and someday the slag may be mined. It runs a half percent copper, two percent zinc, and thirty to thirty-five percent iron."

Moving to another picture he continues, "This picture was taken when they started stripping. You see this big shovel. It's at the 300 ft level right down below us. This house in the picture was replaced by the office we're in now. That was a dining hall and down on this level, out of sight here, was a big dormitory. And this was a big steam shovel that was designed and built to go to the Panama Canal. Later it did this stripping at Jerome. This is in 1919 after they'd been at it for quite a while. It was a slow proposition."

In reply to Ruth's (Mrs. Jordan's) wondering, "Where did they haul all that stuff to?" he points to another picture. "All the overburden is out in this area. In the 1920's, some of the officials here were baseball crazy, and they built a beautiful baseball diamond back up here on the overburden."

Mrs. Jordan recalls, "I visited Jerome around 1920, and one of the things that everyone said I must see was the new baseball field."

"I was in high school up here then, and that's where we played baseball, football, and what have you," John remembers.

"And it looked like a rainbow," Ruth chimed in. "That's what I remember. It was something that people liked to show off. I had just graduated from old Tempe Normal school, [now ASU] and I think it was that summer that I came up here and stayed a couple of weeks in July. I had to see the baseball field and the new road going to Prescott."

All of the folks in the area were mighty proud of that athletic field. John continues, "It was a handmade field, and at one time I saw a newspaper that was printed back east that was tailored strictly to baseball. In the center of about a four or five column spread was a picture of the diamond and the field taken from up above. The caption was something to this effect: 'A handmade baseball field and the fastest in the world.' The surface of the field was a certain kind of rock they had up here, crushed rock, spread out and smoothed by wetting it down and running a big roller over it. That made it real hard and awfully fast. When we fell playing football on there, we would slide along and take off a lot of hide."

Walter tells, "Them baseball teams traveled all over th' state. The team was playin' over in Prescott one time on th' Fourth o' July. That Prescott team was an awful good one, but we beat 'em. An' our pitcher - oh, 'e was a wonderful pitcher! 'E sprung a leak in 'is heart, an' 'e 'ad t' quit pitchin'.

"Th' company got them semi-professionals frum California t' work fer them so's they could b' on their team. They [management] 'ad 'em doin' office work or somethin' like that, easy work. Them boys were in Jerome t' play baseball an' pretty much nothin' else."

Pointing to another picture John explains, "Those are water tanks and those, incidentally, are the reservoirs for the town of Jerome and the mine. The water comes from about seven different springs strung along the side of Mingus Mountain. It all comes in by gravity. Right now we have two steel tanks up there replacing those wooden tanks."

The question was asked if they hauled ore from Jerome to Clarkdale when they started smelting down there.

"Yes, the underground operation and on the thousand foot level, which is actually about 700 foot below us, has a main ore haulage tunnel about a mile long under the pit. The tunnel had a standard gauge railroad that took the ore out from the diggings and dumped it into ore bins in a gully down there. Ore from the bins would be taken to the smelter, and then the train would wind its way up here with a string of empty ore cars to go back into the tunnel."

Walt wants to know, "When was it that Clark put in th' railroad?" [referring to the narrow gauge out to Jerome Junction.]

John replies, "The first thing W. A. Clark did after he purchased the mine in this area was to build a railroad."

Walt elaborates, "'E put in a narrow-gauge railroad, twenty-seven miles long, frum th' main line, th' Santa Fe, t' bring in the supplies." At the Junction, Clark also built a brick factory and these were hauled inbound and used in his smelters.

The point of connection was known as Jerome Junction, 15 miles north of Prescott on highway 89, and today is called Chino Valley. The main purpose of this three-foot wide gauge railway was transporting copper out of the remote area, bringing back supplies and materials. An added plus was the ability to carry passengers. Russell Wahmann states, "A railroad could haul greater loads at cheaper rates, carry revenue producing passengers, and, as a human factor, reduce the remoteness."[7]

After six years of using mule trains to haul ore, W. A. Clark had the railroad constructed in 1894. (Some authors say 1892). The first thirteen miles follow around the north side of Woodchute Mountain, with 126 curves, some of them 45 degrees! Wahmann summarizes the narrow gauge's reason for being, "They came as a necessity; to penetrate mountain regions impervious to the standard gauge."[8]

John tells what it was like prior to the new railroad. "Up to that point, there were only a couple of roads into here. One of them came from Granite Dells near Prescott. [Over Mingus Mountain and down through Yaeger Canyon.] I talked to an old timer whose father was a trader that bought freight over in the Dells. They had a siding on the Santa Fe where they set out cars to be unloaded for Jerome. These freighters would unload the cars there and before Clark's railroad, would use mules and wagons to come across Lonesome Valley and wind their way up over Mingus Mountain and down into Jerome. Part of that old road still exists.

"The reason the first paved road was not put through following the pioneer wagon routes, such as Copper Canyon, the present route of I-17, was because it did not go through Jerome. The biggest need at the time of the paving was for a road from Prescott to Jerome, over Mingus and then down into the Verde Valley to Clarkdale and the smelters."

John directs the attention of the group to outside the building. "You see that thing right out there on the banister? That's a gizmo used to keep freight wagons from running away going downhill. I'll show you how it works. You see how it's all worn? The freighters kept one of these chained to the wagon bottom. They kept it on a hook under there. When the wagon would start down a hill, the drivers would take this gizmo off the hook and drop it down in front of a rear wheel. The wheel would roll up on it and begin to slide and act as a brake. You see they had brakes on the wagons but they weren't too good if they had a big, heavy load. They used them on just one side. There're grooves in the old road caused by these slides."

Turning and pointing to another building, he continues, "That was an assay office and the little building beyond was the bucking room where the sampler processed rock he had taken off the blast faces. Every time a miner put in a round and blasted, the sampler came in and took samples off of the face. The samples were brought up here and processed in the little building and then assayed in the big building. They also had an assay office at the smelter. After a time they did away with this one and turned it into a guest house. Since I've been here, it's been used as a storage place."

His wife recalls, "I remember when, for the guest house, the company had a Chinese cook with his own vegetable garden. The guest house was used to entertain people that came to town. "

F. Ruth asks Mrs. McMillan, "How long have you and John lived in Jerome?

"John and I have been married only a little over three years. He lost his first wife. I grew up in Jerome. My family, the Darcy's, came in 1919. My father was a mining man and came to Jerome in 1917. It took him a while to find us a house.

"When I married, I left for 40 years, but I came back here to retire, and one year after I returned John and I married. Both of our families lived on the hogback at one time. Then after my father became superintendent of the Little Daisy mine, we moved to a house provided for mine officials. Ours was next door to the Little Daisy Hotel. The Bells live there now."

Several people were remembered by name in the ensuing conversation, including a friend of Walter Jordan's who had worked underground for many years.

Walter describes the job his friend did. "'E worked down t' th' 4200 ft level where they 'ad t' keep an air compressor standin' by in case somethin' happened. 'E said they'd have t' git it goin' in a hurry b'cause you'd die pretty quick at 4200 feet [underground] without air. Hey, John what was the deepest tunnel here?"

"4,560 feet was the deepest tunnel. It just went down. Oh, there's drifts back. When I say drift, that means tunnel. There's a hole over there up on the side of the wall that comes out in the gulch below the Prescott Highway in Jerome."

Walter made use of some of the pipe from inside a tunnel when one of the mines closed. "I bought 2,500 feet o' pipe that used t' run back int' th' Verde Central b'fore it closed down. That was 2,500 feet so I could help run that pipeline frum Oak Creek up t' m' reservoir t' irrigate – 5,000 ft distance – an' I got half o' it frum th' tunnel fer two bits [a quarter] a foot. Henry Farley, you remember him?"

"Yeah" John answers.

"Well, 'e hauled all that stuff fer me. Now, John, perhaps you could clarify fer me th' difficulty with loadin' th' holes with powder at th' 4,200 foot level. I was told it was s' hot that they 'ad t' load them holes with powder under water."

"They were loaded under water all right, but it wasn't because they needed or wanted to, exactly. I was running hoist on that job. The water was there because they were drilling down or 'sinking the holes,' as they call it, and when you sink a hole, the water naturally runs in. Anytime you get down below the surface of the earth, you start getting water. This mine had pumping stations about 500 feet apart, starting at the bottom. They'd lift the water up 500 feet to another level where they had what they called a big sump. They'd dump the water there and then had another big pump that would bring the water out at about the 1,000 foot level where it ran down to the river."

Moving back to the pictures John indicates one with smoke. "That smoke is from a coyote blast. You see that little black dot right there? That's a tunnel that went back in there about 75 feet to where they 'drifted' to the left and to the right. Then they loaded about 2,000-3,000 pounds of black powder in pockets, which they dug all the way across that face to make what is called a coyote blast. These pictures are in a series to show the result of the blast. You can see it brought down a good amount of muck, and that big shovel that they use to build the Panama Canal, it was the one that would pick that up. They were removing the overburden off of the ore body and hauling that overburden out here on the dumps." All of this was done to get down to the fires and extinguish them.

"Say John," Walter inquires, "Didn't one o' them big shovels blow apart? I hauled some hay t' a Mexican down here in lower Jerome, an' 'e says, 'Come in here in m' basement an' I want t' show ya a piece o' that shovel.' An' 'e did. It'd been s' hot 'e couldn't touch it, an' it just missed 'is two boys in bed."

"That was Frank, wasn't it?"

"Year, I think so," Walter answers. "Another piece went through th' corner hotel, an' another blew clear t' th' slaughter house. [3-4 miles away] Ya remember that?"

"Yes I do. It killed two men. Dad was the undertaker and I saw what was left of them. I was sleeping or I'd just gone to bed down on the lower Hogback, and I heard the steel flying through the air. It was a coyote blast gone wrong. One of those pockets of powder with maybe two ton of black powder didn't go off with the rest. They would use electrical hookups to set the powder off, but one of the wires got cut or something, and the pocket didn't go off as it should have. The shovel dug into it and set off the powder. The two men running the shovel were killed. There was very little left of the man at the bottom of the boom because he was right over the top of the blast. There was at least 15 working around the pit. They all just happened to be where none of them got hit by the rock or anything. They eventually repaired the shovel."

"I remember talkin' t' yer Dad when I was haulin' fruit t' Phoenix. I just stopped t' git a sandwich here in Jerome one evenin', an' I talked t' yer Dad on th' corner. 'E told me 'e use t' be a railroad engineer."

"Yeah," John remarked. "Dad had been an engineer."

The group said its goodbye's and proceeded to the mining museum in Jerome. Across the street was Sullivan's Saloon and Walter Jordan began his father's stories of Jerome with a little coaching from his daughter.

"Thane was one o' th' main men on m' Dad's farm, an' ever' six months er s', 'e'd come t' Jerome on a tear. 'E'd git drunk an' 'e'd leave all o' 'is money with Sullivan. [the bar owner] Thane'd b' gone 'bout a month b'fore Dad 'ad t' go t' Jerome, an' Sullivan'd say, 'Hey, Will, you gotta take Charlie home. 'e's spent all o' 'is money.'

"Dad'd 'ave quite a time gettin' ole Charlie t' go home. 'E'd 'ave t' show him a half a gallon of whiskey.

"There's another thing that happened at that same saloon, only it was called Tony's Saloon then. Sullivan didn't own it at that time. Up above th' mine there's' a mountain called Woodchute. They named it that b'cause they 'ad men cuttin' logs up there an' sendin' 'em down a chute t' timber th' mine. There 's a feller b' th' name o' Gallagher keepin' books on that operation. 'E was very well educated but 'e 'ad a terrible habit o' drinkin'. Jerome was a wild place, an' they 'ad a bar up there near th' 'chute' called th' Bend where Gallagher 'ad a habit o' gettin' drunk. Well, this Gallagher got up there, an' 'e got drunk. An' my father was takin' vegetables up t' th' Montana Hotel when this thing happened. Gallagher, 'e'd git pretty mean when 'e got drunk. 'E was a'havin' a big time just a'shootin' out th' lights an' this thing an' that, so's th' saloon keeper called down t' th' main part o' town t'git th' sheriff.

"'Come on, Gallagher. Come on!'

"'No, I ain't a goin'!'

"Well, Hawkins [the sheriff] 'ad t' deputize two great big Austrian miners there. An' 'e said t' my father, 'Jordan, I want ya' t' haul 'im down t' Tony's Place.' (Jerome didn't have a jail yet.)

"Gallagher picked up a rock t' hit th' sheriff an' said, 'Jim, I'll kill ya' fer this!'

"Th' big Austrians pulled 'im away an' Gallagher said t' m' father, who knew Gallagher well, 'Don't worry! I don't blame ya', but I'm a gonna kill that Jim Hawkins!'

"S' m' father took Gallagher down t' Tony's saloon an' warned Jim, 'Now you watch that fella or he'll kill ya'. He's dangerous.'

"'Oh no, Will, 'e'll be all right when 'e sobers up. We'll take 'im over t' Prescott. 'E'll be all right.'

"They left Gallagher there, under th' charge o' th' saloon keeper, Tony. Well, ole man Thompson was up at th' saloon that night frum Indian Gardens in Oak Creek Canyon, Tater Thompson as we called 'im, [because he grew a lot of potatoes] an' 'e loved t' play poker. Just after midnight, Tony says, 'Thompson, I'm goin' t' leave Gallagher in yer charge. You watch 'im now.'

"Well, Gallagher knew that Tony kept a six shooter under th' bar, s' when Thompson got interested in that card game, Gallagher slipped 'round that bar an' stole th' gun.

"Next mornin', Jim Hawkins come t' git Gallagher t' take 'im t' Prescott. 'E was walkin' out in th front o' Gallagher, not t' th' side, an' Gallagher killed 'im. Shot him dead, right out there in th' street. Terrible, terrible!" Walt ducks his head and shakes it several times from side to side, emphasizing how bad he felt about it.

"Gallagher ran up t'wards th' mine t' a big coke pile under a shed at th' smelter. Frum under there Gallagher defied an'body t' come an' git 'im. Well, th' copper company 'ad a deputy that they sent up t' arrest Gallagher.

"'If ya' come any closer I'll kill ya!' says Gallagher, th' deputy retreated. So's 'e went back down an' 'e told 'em, 'I don't want any part o' that.' That's when they called in this fella who was workin' at th' time on top o' th' woodchute helpin' git logs down int' th' mine. 'E 'ad a tough reputation, an' they sent a man up t' th' 'chute' t' ask 'im if 'e'd come down an' arrest Gallagher.

"'Yeah, I'll come down. I'll get 'im.'

"'E 'ad a six shooter on, but 'e didn't even pull it. 'E just walked up t' where Gallagher was an' called 'im.

"'Ya' come any closer, I'll kill ya'.'

"'Well,' 'e said, 'ya' just better start a'shootin' b'cause I'm a comin'!' An' 'e walked right up there, brave as that an' arrested Gallagher.

"'Ye're a mighty brave man. There was only one shot in that gun, an' I already used that'un t' kill Jim Hawkins.'

"When they took Gallagher t' court, 'is folks got him outta that dirty, bloody crime, with their money. It cost only five thousand dollars t' exonerate 'im. Can ya' beat that!? But 'e didn't stay in Jerome. 'E would'a been killed, but this was all b'fore I was born.

"Th' copper company appointed Gallagher's captor sheriff o' Jerome immediately. M' father give 'im th' money t' b' bonded, bein' s' brave as that, an' m' father got t' know 'im some. 'E'd ridden a mule from Virginia an' on th' way stumbled on a battle o' th' famous Pleasant Valley War b'tween them Grahams an' them Tewksburys. 'E was a'ridin' through that part near Bloody Basin an' it was a gettin' dark when 'e sees this here cabin. 'E went over an' said, 'Say fellas, reckon a guy could bed down fer th' night?'

"'Why sure. It's okay with us, if'n ya don't mind some excitement b'fore mornin'.'

"'Well just what kinda excitement are ya' expectin'?'

"'There's these fellas out there that don't like us too good an' sometimes they start a shootin' at us.'

"Well, that traveler decided t' stay, an' 'e told Dad that just as it got dark th' fireworks opened up. All night they was a shootin' back an' forth at each other. This guy looked around an' discovered that there was a high adobe foundation all 'round that cabin, yeah, about 3 foot high. S' he just got himself over next t' th' side where th' shootin' was a comin' frum an' lay snug against it an' tight t' th' floor. 'Bout sunup everythin' got real quiet, an' th' gunmen inside put up their guns an' said, 'That's all fer tonight. Nothin' else'll happen until night time.' Both groups were hired gunmen, but Dad never did say which was a fightin' for the Tewksburys an' which fer th' Grahams. Now don't that feller frum Virginia have a knack fer comin' out alive when them bullets were a'flyin'?!

"Oh say! Did ya' know that at one time m' Dad 'ad a lumber business in Jerome with a man named Pugh? They were doin' a pretty good business when th' big fire struck that nearly wiped Jerome out. Th' story is that a man livin' in a tent outside th' mill knocked over 'is lantern. The tent burned, an' th' wind spread th' fire t' th' lumber yard an' int' Jerome. They dynamited th' buildin's down ahead o' th' fire tryin' t' stop it, but with no fire department, th' lumber yard was wiped out, an' m' father quit that business an' stayed with th' farmin' in th' valley. When Dad lost money in a business venture 'e just sorta shook th' dust off o' 'is feet' an' went on with life. Farmin' kept th' family goin'"

This fire, most likely, is the one on Sept. 11, 1898, that Herb Young refers to in his book, *They Came to Jerome; the Billion Dollar Copper Camp*. He gives a bit different version of the start of the fire, quoting from a letter written by H. J. Allen, town manager, to W. A. Clark:

"The fire started about 7:15 this morning at the extreme north end of Hull Avenue, and was caused by a drunken Austrian, so the story goes, attempting to kindle a fire with kerosene." [Another version is that a hobo caught his coattail on fire standing in front of his campfire and then the tent was ignited.] "At 9:30 the entire site of the stores was waste. The works were shut down at the alarm and our men fought fire as well as they could with insufficient water supply, and with dynamite and giant powder..."[9]

Even having admitted the lack of water was a major problem and knowing most of the burned buildings were company owned, Allen resisted incorporation which would provide funding for a fire department and increased water. He didn't want any interference with his running of the town. He was reflecting Clark's attitude of wanting nothing from the outside to affect his community, which he considered to be his kingdom. This was carried to the extreme when after this great devastation, Prescott, a neighboring town, took up a large collection of money to help. Part of the group traveled over the mountain and tried to give it to Allen. Their offer was totally refused and they were sent back home. This rejection of their kind and generous offer of aid sparked resentment which could be seen nearly 100 years later in bitter rivalry between the towns. The county Board of Supervisors voted for Jerome's incorporation early in 1899. It still took another fire in May of that year, the third in seventeen months, to get the citizenry motivated into actually providing money through a bond issue for high-pressure lines, hydrants, tanks, etc.

There are many Jerome fire stories. Walter used to tell another one about a young schoolteacher bound for Camp Verde and Beaver Creek. "She 'ad t' leave 'er trunk in Jerome after she got off o' th' train, an' she ask a little Mexican boy t' take care o' it while she took a wagon t' Camp Verde. She promised t' pay 'im a certain amount that seemed mighty big t' 'im, if th' trunk was still there an' safe when she come back fer it. B'fore she got back Jerome burned. That little boy moved that ole trunk several times durin' th' night t' stay in front o' th' fire. Oh! That fire was a real humdinger, burnin' hot an' fast. When th' teacher got back with a ranch family t' pick up her trunk, she was terrible upset t' find th' whole town in ashes. She started askin' around an' somebody told 'er they'd seen a kid draggin' a big trunk, stayin' ahead o' that fire. At last th' cowboy who'd brung 'er in spotted somebody a sittin' on somethin' clear across th' gulch frum th' Hog Back. There perched on th' ole trunk, was that boy she'd hired. Everythin' was all right an' she paid 'im what she'd promised. 'E sure wanted that money awful bad, an' believe you me, 'e sure 'nough earned it." Nearly 50 years later, when Walt's youngest daughter visited with friends in Pasadena CA, she met a former schoolteacher. Although quite elderly, the lady told the same story of her arrival in the Verde Valley. It was quite impressive meeting the actual person who had featured in one of Walt's stories.

A few years later the town burned again but this time there was water available, and they pumped lots and lots of it onto the fire. This saturation of the clay bed beneath the town could have been another contributing factor to the previously described slippage.

Allen Bristow shares his memories of Jerome:

"People in Jerome would die o' scarlet fever an' diphtheria, an' typhoid. That was th' nastiest place you ever saw. You can't imagine. They had no sewer system, so everyone had a little out-house behind their place. I know Aunt Effie did, and guys would come around an' clean out the holes under the out-houses with long handled shovels. They'd put that stuff in wagons with two by four bottom boards that they could turn t' dump out the load in a gulch. Naturally, since the boards in the bottom o' the wagon were loose for dumpin', when the wagons went down the rough streets of Jerome, why the wagon would leak, an' you could smell Jerome miles before you got to it. [Here he enjoyed a chuckle.] It was the most awful place you ever saw, an' that's why they had so many epidemics. It was quite an experience t' visit th' graveyard: grave after grave marked with 1909, an' there were other epidemics too. You name it! They had it! You know there were thousands o' people who lived there right on top o' each other - as many as 17,000 people when the mine was runnin' full blast." There was only enough space for about 5,000, so folks built lean-tos on their houses and some have said that the same room would be rented to three different men, one for each shift. Because they were taking turns using the tiny rooms, "miners used to walk the four-mile grade between Clarkdale and Jerome on cold winter nights just to keep warm."[10]

Allen continues, "Jerome burned several times. The 1903, [not sure this date is correct] fire may have been the first one or the worst one; I don't know, but I saw for myself the gulch burn where the ladies of ill-fame lived. They used to have what they called cribs, you know, little shacks, one room maybe eight by ten feet where the girls lived. You can see the foundations as you turn an' go up that hill - just little bitty foundations all over that hillside.

"It would've been the summer of 1913, [perhaps

95

he is referring to the 1911 fire], when they built the Clarkdale smelter, that I was up at Middle Verde one time visitin' my second cousin Harold, Aunt Cumi (Bristow) Hawkins' grandson. We went down t' the river t' go swimmin', an' we stole ourselves a watermelon which we were eatin' while we watched the dumpin' o' slag from th' Jerome smelter. This was just before they moved th' smeltin' operation from Jerome down t' the new smelter at Clarkdale in 1914. Harold an' I were eatin' that watermelon when we saw a great flame sweep up th' mountainside. We sat there an' watched it until it died down. When I told my father about it, he said, 'Oh, that must have been the slag you saw.'

"'No, sir. The gulch burned.'

"Next day, my Dad went up t' Camp Verde an' heard the news o' the fire in Jerome. I think it was 87 little shacks, an' several people burned to death too. The fire just swept up the side o' the mountain, an' they never rebuilt that."

It is easy to see that each event has a different slant according to the memory of the individual storyteller. Nonetheless, the fact is that all of these things did occur, in some fashion or other, and the folklore surrounding each telling is typically, fascinatingly "Old West".

Often the suspense, excitement and glamour of these fabulous stories overshadows how mining shaped the state and the politics. This industry, more than any other, propagated Anglo settlement of Arizona. It was the main connection between corporate America of the East and the Arizona frontier, and was responsible for the building of railroads and the Gadsden Purchase. It was in the mines that organized labor first got its hold in the state, becoming the basis for a major fight between labor and management. Governor George W. P. Hunt, who had grown up in and around the Globe mines, had great empathy for the miner against "dollar despotism" and "profiteering patrioteers." He fought the copper companies on every level possible, including the courts, the press, and the legislature, only to be forced to watch these companies seize total control of Arizona.

James Byrkit referred to this control as the forging of the "Copper Collar" which broke the unions and intimidated the miners, effectively destroying any liberal influence. Douglas managed to used the WWI fear of Germans to his advantage by branding all union men as Wobblies (members of the radical Industrial Workers of the World). Other tactics used to strengthen the "Copper Collar" included: buying off law enforcement officials, seducing law makers, frightening newspaper editors, threatening ministers, and rigging elections.

Jerome became the practice ground for much greater injustices in Bisbee, as 200 vigilantes captured 67 supposed Wobblies and deported them to Kingman. This effort was supported by the copper company and local law enforcement agencies. Later in the Bisbee Deportation of 1917 only 100 of the 400 deported were Wobblies, the others were union members.

Walter Douglas was the President of Phelps Dodge Corporation, and Chairman of the Board of the Southern Pacific Railroad. He also controlled most of the newspapers. The power he had is described in *Arizona, the Land of the People*. "Douglas pulled the strings in a way Hunt never could, carefully manipulating public opinion against the unions, mobilizing the often antagonistic copper companies to unite against their common enemy, recapturing county and state governments and even the governorship itself in order to break the unions during the First World War."[11]

Although the "Glory Days" of Jerome have passed and the mining era of the Verde Valley drama has closed, some lights still twinkle on the slope of Cleopatra Hill, beckoning adventurers to again "Follow Their Westward Star" and visit the shops and artists of the town that refused to become a ghost town. (See center for Jerome paintings)

FOOTNOTES

(1) Lingren, Waldemar, 1926, page

(2) Jerome Reporter 28 Dec. 1899.

(3) Trimble, Marshall. Roadside History of Arizona. Missoula, Montana: Montanta P Co., 1986. 358-359.

(4) Ibid, p. 239

(5) Snodgrass, Richard. Ballad of Laughing Mountain. Tempe, AZ: Counterpoint Productions, 1957. 32.

(6) Ibid, p. 29

(7) Wahmann, Russell. Follow the Narrow Guage from Jerome to Jerome Junction. Jerome, AZ: Robert Des Granges & Russell Wahmann, 1982. 1.

(8) Ibid

(9) Young, Herb. They Came to Jerome, the Billion Dollar Copper Camp. Jerome, AZ: Jerome Historical Society, 1972. 60.

(10) Trimble, Marshall. Roadside History of Arizona. Missoula, Montana: Montanta P Co., 1986. 358-359.

(11) Arizona: the Land and the People. Ed. Miller Tom. Tucson, AZ: U. of A. P, 1986. 231.

Chapter Eight

HAYSEED JUSTICE

In 1911, Jordan Sr. arranged to sell his Upper Verde Valley homestead, buildings, and equipment to W. A. Clark, as the copper company was buying up all of the farms. Will Jordan was hired to be the farm superintendent for a year or two, keeping the farms productive and adding to the coffers of Mr. Clark. According to Walter his Dad then discovered that the bookkeeper for Senator Clark was juggling the books to make it look as if the farms were losing money. (According to handwritten records in Northern Arizona University files the deficit for the year Feb. 1, 1912 to Feb. 15, 1913 was $20,000.00) Walt says that Will knew the farms were making a profit and said he would not work under someone who was dishonest, so he quit. (The same records as mentioned above state that he was "discharged as superintendent" and asked to vacate the house.) Being aware of some of the happenings during the suit, it would appear that Walter's version is the most accurate. Perhaps the bookkeeper didn't want the extra work of keeping an additional set of books. Also United Verde Copper Company may have been counting on Will Jordan to resign, because soon afterward, the company broke ground for a new smelter on former Jordan farmland. The town of Clarkdale would be laid out in 1914, and the first furnace began operating on May 26, 1915. WWI (1914-1918) was on, and metals deposited in the Verde Valley fault were in demand.

The smelter's slag dump would eventually move the river to cover the old farm. During the same time period the house was burned to the ground having been ignited by the then current occupant smoking in bed. Thus with the farm buried and the house gone, the Jordan home on Rattlesnake Hill became another set of ruins along a river that nurtured many settlements in ages past. Today the site of the house where all the Jordan children were born is visible from Verde River Railroad's tour train.

The family now needed to determine where they would like to relocate. Walter said, "Dad went to an old friend who had been superintendent of the Clarkdale smelter and asked how far he thought the killing effect of the smoke would go down the valley.

"'Oh, about three miles.'

"'Well, we're safe in going down six miles then.'

"'Oh, yes. Yeah, that's safe.'"

It is unknown why Will and Annie purchased property separately, but it remained that way the rest of their lives. Records show that on May 31, 1913 Annie T. Jordan purchased 48 plus acres in the Bridgeport area. This was the land considered to be "Mama's." Walter says, "We actually smelled smoke on Mother's farm at Bridgeport even before we, [he and his brothers], bought any land. He continues, "M' Dad an' two brothers an' I went in together there an' bought 193 acres right adjoinin' m' mother's old place." This ranch included an old apple orchard. On it they started the Jordan Farm and Cattle Company, AKA W. A. Jordan and Sons. The Bridgeport property was approximately nine miles down river from the Clarkdale smelter and the land where Ev (E. A. Jordan) and Will Jordan first ranched together.

After getting advice on the distance to move it is easy to empathize with Walter's feelings when the smelters began coughing out their smoke. "United Verde got th' dad-burned smelter goin' in May o' 1915 an' b' September we smelled smoke," Walt relates.

His sister Stella's diary reinforces Walt's recollections. "September 17, 1915. I rose this morning to the usual sound of Mamma in the kitchen. Temperatures are cooling a bit now that we're well into September. I noticed a haze and a stench when I scattered feed and fetched the morning eggs."[1]

"The smoke consisted of large concentrations of sulfur dioxide. Dew would settle at night, and when the sulfur dioxide mixed with the water, it produced sulfuric acid."[2] This created a serious poisonous effect on crops and people.

Walter continues, "Two years later Jimmy Douglas finished 'is tunnel fer Little Daisy ore t' come down th' hill an' built 'is smelter at Clemenceau. We knew we'd had it, but th' real killer smoke didn't come until a year after th' war ended."

When WWI began in 1914, the older Jordan boys went off to fight. Walter Jordan was about 16 years old at the time and was needed to do battle as a "gentle hayseed" attempting to keep crops producing against the smoke in the atmosphere. This was an insurmountable task because during the war the extremely high demand for copper kept the smelters puffing at full blast. Fortunately for the farmers, prior to 1918 wind currents had kept the smoke from Clark's operation traveling upstream during the critical times for the crops. However a wind shift could mean disaster, and a closer and more pronounced danger erupted with the opening of the United Verde Extension smelter. Environmental destruction would become a subtle development from World War I.

By the time both the Clarkdale and Clemenceau smelters (1917) were regularly sending clouds of sulphur dioxide down river, Will Jordan and family had, in addition to livestock, 648 apple trees, 316 peach trees, 90 pear trees, 27 cherry trees, 24 plum trees, 15 prune trees, 7 apricot trees, and fields planted in lettuce, sweet peppers, tomato, alfalfa, sweet potatoes, Irish potatoes, watermelon and cantaloupe. Near the house they cultivated 6 English walnut trees, two black walnuts, two almond, two purple leaf plums, one persimmon, an apricot, two peach, one fig, a date palm, two quince trees, seven pomegranate and 108 grape vines. Neighboring farmers reported crops of sweet corn, carrots, squash, pumpkins, beets, onions, beans, celery, cucumbers, parsnips, turnips, spinach, and strawberries. These, along with many others, were very prosperous farms in a fertile river valley and all were feeling the negative effects of the smoke.

On Nov. 27, 1917 the *Jerome Sun* published an article stating, "...the fact that is daily being brought home to the cattlemen is that the browsing is about gone...This is doubtless due to some chemical action of the smoke and dews and probably this is the reason why the oak leaves are not growing this fall."[3] Some even were adamant that the smoke also killed off the earth worms.

The Jordan's had an alfalfa field that was standing about three feet high, a beautiful field, ready for harvest, and they were planning to cut the hay the next morning. Alas, when they went out to begin harvesting, it had all turned white and was lying flat on the ground. The wind had changed in the night and extremely toxic smoke had come down river. It killed the crops and provided primary evidence to win the farmers' plea for damages under the law. Walter and Will went out and collected some of that blighted alfalfa and baled it. When tested it contained double the amount of sulfur considered to be "healthy." According to Walter, that bale of hay and his Mother's diaries were the major things that helped win the suit.

Walter continued, "That must 'ave been 1919 or 1920," and the Phoenix law firm of Gust and Smith filed documents against both the United Verde Copper Company and the United Verde Extension Mining Company Aug. 17, 1920 in the Superior Court of Arizona in Yavapai County. It was alleged that the defendant discharged "...noxious, foul, and poisonous gases, smoke, fumes and flue dust and other dangerous, injurious and poisonous materials ...upon the premises of plaintiffs...between the 16th of August 1918 and the first day of January, 1920 [which] killed, injured, burned, parched, scorched, seared and destroyed plaintiffs' orchards, trees, vegetables, fruits, alfalfa and other crops... ."[4] The stage was set for one of the first air pollution suits to be brought to the U.S. Supreme Court.

Prior to the filing of the law suit approximately 110 farmers began to organize the Verde Valley Protective Association. They were concerned about the negative economic impact of the smoke on their livelihood. Meetings were held and experts contacted to advise them as the best way to proceed. However, the companies immediately weakened the group by offering to buy up the damaged farms on one condition, that they would sign a release stating that they would never sue. Most agreed, leaving only thirteen families in the group, of which W. A. Jordan and Sons became the driving force.

For some reason after the suit was filed a different lawyer was engaged. Early in 1921 Walter says, "Our lawyer, Robert Morrison, 'ad meetin's with us, an' 'e told us, [the group of Verde Valley farmers who banded together to bring the law suit against the smelters] t' keep book count from 1921. That's when they shut th' smelters down fer repair. That gave us a chance, t' have a year without smoke an' compare. That's when Morrison told us, 'Keep strict account o' every plant ya set out an' th' amount ya harvest frum 'em. 'Ave it in yer book fer 'em when ya git on that stand.' Frum then on we went t' bat. We kept everythin' strict.

"Morrison called Dr. Thomas down frum Midvale, Utah, a little over a year b'fore th' trial began. 'E was t' b' our expert witness, an' I helped 'im count th' leaves in that bale. 'E told us, 'Keep that bale o' hay locked up, an' b' sure ya 'ave it with ya in th' courtroom.'

"When Thomas saw that ole Model T truck I 'ad fer cuttin' wood, 'e said t' me, 'Ya know o' any automobile we could use fer a test I need t' do? I want t' drill int' th' intake manifold an' put a valve in there t' suck th' air all out o' this big glass bottle, so's we can git a sample o' that smoke.'

"I volunteered th' truck an' got a mechanic t' do th' work. Thomas took a rubber hose an' connected up with a valve on a rubber cork in this great big glass bottle, about a five gallon bottle. [A vacuum bottle was created.] 'E started that ole engine an' sucked

Smoke drifting north away from farms

all th' air out o' it-whoosh!" [Here Walt makes a loud sucking noise to demonstrate his point.] "Then one mornin' when there was a lot o' smoke comin' down 'e yanked that ole cork right outta there an' that nasty air went in. 'E poured some iodine int' that jar 'cause ya see 'e used a centimeter gauge an' iodine solution t' make 'is measurements. That iodine turned int' a pink lookin' gas. Accordin' t' the tables 'e 'ad there was a million parts o' oxygen t' 25 parts o' sulfur dioxide. I said, 'Say Doc what's that mean?'

"An' 'e said, 'That means that a plant livin' in that kinda atmosphere wouldn't b' much good after 30 minutes.'

"This was another one o' our most convincin' pieces o' evidence we 'ad in them trials.

"Say, did I ever tell ya what them dirty sons-o'-a-gun done?" Walter continued. "While this here investigation was agoin' on several fellas were sent t' inspect them fields. I went out there with 'em, an' as they were a walkin' through them fields, I noticed them fellas kept on a'rubbin' their heels together. When I said, 'Hey what're ya guys a'doin'?', they wouldn't answer. So's, I just bent down an' turned down them cuffs o' their levis. Them cuffs were filled with spiders an' mites an' other bugs that they were a'tryin' t' git t' fall int' them fields so's that they could say that it was bugs that'd killed all o' them crops an' not th' smoke. Why, did ya' ever hear o' such! Them dirty low down skunks!"

From some of the reports written by investigators hired by the copper company, it is evident that the feeling of animosity was mutual, as shown in the report of W. W. Jones, April 10, 1921. "Last year [during the investigation of the farms} Walter Jordan treated me more disrespectfully and was more insolent than any person I met in the valley. He was always unreasonable in regard to his statements and in his interpretations of natural conditions."[5] On Sept. 24th of the same year another investigator H. Brisley reported, "We were confronted by Mrs. Jordan and Willie Jordan at the entrance to the house. They seemed to be in a poor frame of mind and were evidently not at all friendly toward representatives from the smelter. They told us…that they had decided to shut down completely on all smelter representatives, saying that during the Biles-Wells trial, Mr. Jordan's place had been so successfully lied about, that he had decided it was not to his advantage to let us go on with investigations."[6]

Actions like this apparently made Will skeptical of nearly everyone. From the following incident involving a long time trusted friend, it is obvious he should have been even more careful. In a letter to a smelter official on Feb. 26, 1925 Walter Miller refers to the "hipocracy of the whole Jordan outfit" plus relaying a happening told to him by Dr. Hawkins. "…W. A. Jordan asked Hawkins if he was wearing a copper collar-and if not he would like for Hawkins to go down to his ranch and make some color pictures. Doc remarked that while the copper companies had always been his best friends, yet he was willing to make the pictures for an old friend.

"They went to the Jordan ranch, and Doc was taken from place to place, photographing the few dead trees in colors. Doc made a lot of inquiries about picturing the good trees, but Jordan would have none of it. Hawkins says that the number of dead trees was nothing unusual, that in his personal experience raised on and in orchards all his life, that the number of dead trees was as was to be expected.

"If you want it, I think that Doc will give you some more of the same as above."[7]

The smelter smoke wasn't the only difficulty for the farmers at the time. Mother Nature had some challenges in store. Again Walter gives us some insight. "Times were hard. We 'ad some terrific floods 'round about 1919-20. Ole Johnny Hearst's place washed clear away. It took us a month t' git th' drift frum that thing outta th' big apple orchard at Mother's place."

In some of the reports by the smelter investigators they commented that there was smoke damage, but definitely hesitated to indicate that it was of any great value. "We noted many marks of apparent smelter smoke injury upon the pig weed, rag weed, Cenothara, fleabane, wild morning glory and Heterotheca subaxillarus. These markings were more noticeable along the ditch banks, and in parts of the fields that had been kept damp. However, we found no indications of damage of any economic importance on any of the cultivated crops."[8]

On April 10, 1921 W. W. Jones noted in his report that he had been asked about the smelter's using methods as were used in Salt Lake City and other areas. Due to the topography of the Verde Valley, Mr. Jones assured Walter "…that there was no reason to think that higher stacks and heaters would materially change the course of the smoke in this valley."[9]

Perhaps it was these devices used in the stacks in Salt Lake City that caused the Bingham Press in Utah to write, "That a truce will be patched up between the farmers and the smelters there is no doubt, and the smelters will continue to do the business at the same old stand, and the gentle hayseed will continue…"[10] No such truce was on the horizon for the smelters and farmers of the Verde Valley.

Walter readily admitted that frost had been a problem as well as thrip, blight, and other insects and diseases. He told Mr. Jones "...that the Jordans were very fair and open minded and always admitted insect injuries and plant diseases and that they thought the smoke men ought to be as willing to admit smoke injury."[11] However, it was obvious as the years progressed and the court date drew nearer both groups became more accusatory.

The human factor often presented problems in getting an undamaged crop to market. This is brought out in another of his stories, focusing on the animosity between farming kids and mining/town kids. Although some "grown-up farming kids," had gone to work at the smelters, there was still friction and these "kids'" sympathies were with the farmers.

"One afternoon I seen them fellas frum th' smelters a goin' through our field a'cuttin' watermelons an' pluggin' 'em too. I went down there an' told 'em t' git out an' leave them melons alone. Ya' know it ain't s' bad if they just pick one er two, take 'em an' leave. But pluggin', just cuttin' a chunk outta the top t' see if they's ripe, ruins 'em. Why, a few fellas can ruin a whole field in nothin' flat! Well, all that talkin' t' did was make 'em do their stealin' at night. There's this friend o' mine that worked at th' smelter an' 'e knew what them fellas were adoin'. 'E come t' me an' said, 'Hey, Walt, I'll help ya' catch them guys, if ya' want me t'. I know who's gittin' in yar field.'

"'My goodness alive. O'course I want cha t' help!'

"Then we figgered our little scheme. 'E let me know when they's all plannin' t' come down, an' it was a wonderful bright moonlight night. I hurried up an' got m'self down in th' middle o' that field an' I just laid down there flat in a ditch with m' good ole Winchester. Pretty soon, here they come. 'Ad their bright lights on just a drivin' right on up t' that fence. They all jumped out, makin' s' much noise ya'da thought they owned the place. They's a talkin' an' a laughin' an' 'avin' a great time. I waited until I figgered they's pretty well spread out acrost that field. An' then, <u>'ker'bam!'</u> I let that ole gun go puttin' a few shots up int' th' air. Oh my! Ya' should'a seen them people scatter in ever' which direction. They's a leavin' all kinds o' parts o' their clothes on that barbed wire fence." Pausing a moment to chuckle he continued, "I could hardly keep from laughin' right out loud, but I jumped up an' run acrost t' th' lane tryin' t' head 'em off. Then all o' a sudden here they turned around an' were a comin' back. I run out in front o' 'em a wavin' that ole gun in their faces!

"'Hey, fellas! Were ya th' guys that was just out there in m' watermelon field? I think ya' are!'

"'Oh no! We don't know nothin' about a watermelon field. We're just drivin' down th' road.'

"'Well, I think ya' do know about it. I oughtta go call th' law. I'll tell ya what I'm a goin' do. If ya' know anythin' about it or anyone who knows about it ya' just tell 'em I'll be a waitin' out there fer 'em with m' gun!' I could see m' friend a sittin' in th' rumble seat with 'is 'at pulled down over 'is face a tryin' not t' laugh!

"Well they just took off an' I didn't learn until quite a lot later that two o' 'em were real close t' me lookin' at th' same melon, when I shot an' they jumped s' hard they banged their heads t'gether an' knocked both o' 'em out. When they didn't git back t' th' car with th' rest o' th' party, they's all scared t' death that I'd killed 'em. But after meetin' me on th' road nobody 'ad th' nerve t' go back in that field an' try t' find 'em. T' this day I don't know how them two got home. 'Bout a year later somehow them fellas found out it was a setup an' they made m' friend buy 'em a keg o' beer. But none o' that bunch ever tried to steal watermelons agin." At this point he enjoyed another good laugh.

While "the wheels of justice" ground slowly along, the lives of the farmers continued in much the same patterns — planting, trying to protect crops from smoke damage, and harvesting. The children grew up, some went to war, others married, a few went to college and one or two tried life in the big cities of California and New York. Through Allen and Walter we catch a glimpse of a few family members during these years:

"I went to school in Flagstaff at the Northern Arizona Normal School in the summer of 1917," Allen recalls, "an' in th' winter of 1917 an' '18 to catch up. I started again in Flagstaff in the fall of 1918. Dr. Bloom was gone an' I didn't get along with his replacement. He had promised me a job an' didn't give it to me, so I quit an' went home. I took the train down through Ashfork. Then at Drake I took the narrow gauge down to Clarkdale. I had my bicycle with me on the train, so I started to ride it home. When the tire went flat, I threw it in a bush an' walked the rest of the way [probably 15-20 miles]. I got there about two o'clock in the morning, an' my mother was all shook up. She didn't know what to do. Netty Gilbert, Aunt Cumi's daughter, was visitin' at the time, an' she said, `Why don't you let him come out an' stay with us an' finish high school.'

"I wanted to go to Tempe, but my mother had heard about some scandal in Tempe. Some boys an' girls gettin' together too much. Netty said, `He won't get in any trouble in Riverside [CA] because the boys go to one school an' the girls to another.'

"An' so I was sent to live with Jim and Netty Gilbert. Jim Gilbert worked for Pacific Electric Railway. George went out to Riverside with me. He didn't want to be a farmer, an' he was lookin' for a job. When he couldn't find one in Riverside, he went on down to San Diego an' got a job until he heard Pacific Electric was hirin'. He come back up to Riverside, an' he went to work for the Pacific Electric while I was goin' to school. That same fall I had influenza. I like to died, an' th' school was closed. I graduated in 1919.

"I come back home an' worked that summer on th' thrashin' machine. George was still workin' in Riverside, an' I'd put in an application for a job with the Pacific Electric, too. Well, I got a telegram from George at the end of the summer. It said, 'Come on out. Job is waitin'.' I went to work for them - 22nd of August, 1919. Before I retired in 1965, I'd been the superintendent of Pacific Electric's automotive maintenance in Los Angeles, in charge of all the buses for nine divisions from my office on Baker Street. When Pacific Electric sold out in 1954, I ran El Monte an' went over to an office in West Hollywood where I had my heart attack. But that was after the formation of the Transit Authority. When I got a little better an' got back t' work, I went out t' Van Nuys for th' Transit Authority an' ran that division fer about eight years before I retired in 1965."

George was only in Los Angeles a short time before he went to New York. Allen seemed to regret that George was there just "…months, not more than months. He and I boarded together until he quit the streetcar business. He made up his mind he was goin' to work until he saved up a thousand dollars, an' he did." [There was also some discussion within the family regarding quite an electrical shock George received while working on top of the streetcars. It seems that this may have hastened his decision to quit.] "He had his mind made up he was goin' to Electrical Engineering School. He was there in 1920 and 1921. When he graduated, he went down an' he worked with Uncle Will [George's father] on the ranch in Bridgeport. [He didn't actually complete the course in NY because he came home to help his Dad on the Sedona place.] An' then he opened a garage. Now, exactly the dates I don't know. He wrote me about it. George and I corresponded all our lives. He was runnin' this garage in Sedona, not doin' very well, but the settlement of that suit against the smelter companies changed all that."

While George and Allen were out of state "gittin' educated" and working, and the older brothers were fighting in WWI, Walter continued farming and finding a "lady friend." "M' mother bought Sam Emery's place — 48 acres next t' us in Bridgeport — when Sam gave up farmin' an' went down t' Phoenix country right away. I was plannin' t' marry 'is daughter Mary as soon as I got outta that blamed lawsuit against th' smelter people. She'd come up an' visit Melvin Farro's sister. They were great friends, an' she'd come up an' stay with her. (I used to go fishin' with Melvin, an' 'e worked in th' Clemenceau smelter.) Well, anyway, I got acquainted with Mary when I was farmin' there.

"In th' meantime, she left Phoenix an' went t' Salome t' teach school. Harry, her youngest brother, was livin' with 'er. She wrote lots o' letters t' me. We were goin' t' 'ave this lawsuit th' next year, near as I could figure. Then she wrote me a letter sayin', 'Now I'm goin' with a fella here, an' 'e wants t' git married, but you're first choice an' he's second choice.'

"I didn't like them words 'first an' second choice'. If there was any 'second choice', well… Th' main thing was that I wasn't 'bout t' git married knowin' that I was a goin' int' a big lawsuit. It'd be crazy — foolish, so I told Mary that I couldn't make arrangements that a'way, an' that I was goin' t' come over an' see fer m'self. On th' way t' Salome, lo an' b'hold, I spotted brother Willie an' Hazel [his wife], in their old Model T on th' road ahead. They was goin' home t' California after a visit, an' I waved 'em down. They knew I was a goin' over t' see Mary t' decide what we was gonna do.

"'Well, are you an' Mary gonna get married ?'

"'No, no, far from it, Willie.'

"'Why? Mary's a fine girl.'

"'Yes, ya bet she is a fine girl, but, I'd b' crazy t' git married now with that lawsuit comin' up.'

"That was after Willie went int' war because it was after th' war that 'e married Hazel, an' 'e was livin' over in California. Well, I didn't go with any girl fer a long time after that. It hurt me s' bad, an' it was 1923 b'fore we started th' trial. We didn't git it int' court quicker b'cause o' that son-o'-a-gun judge down in Tucson. We thought maybe th' copper companies bought him off. He just lingered along, lingered along. [The farmers could have been correct regarding a payoff. As noted in the previous chapter, the copper companies were in control of nearly all state government through bribes and payoffs, the infamous 'copper collar'. Walter Douglas, in Bisbee, was the power behind most of it and with Jimmy Douglas being a part of the suit and a relative, we are left to draw our own conclusions.] We got Robert Morrison, our lawyer, t' call a meetin' t' insist that th' thing b' tried. We told Morrison, 'If that judge's got a toothache an' cain't come, git someone else!'

"Well, th' powers-that-be listened t' Morrison, an' they got a judge from Duke, Montana, down here t' try th' case. [Interesting, especially since W. A. Clark was from Montana, and his United Verde Co. was named in the suit.] That was th' best thing in th' world b'cause they couldn't buy that judge off. No, sir! An' 'e didn't show any partiality. I was th' first one on th' witness stand. I'd been farmin' there at Bridgeport about fourteen years o' th' best part o' m' life, battlin' that dang smoke t' help payoff a mortgage. Mama's diary an' that bale o' hay we saved was brought in too. In one week's time, th' thing went t' th' jury. Th' evidence we 'ad, it was strong. But on th' first vote, th' jury only brought in "normal" [nominal] damages. Th' foreman told us afterwards that 'e knew good an' well that two jurymen'd been bought off, so's 'e just bawled 'em out real good b'fore takin' th second vote.

"'With this evidence s' strong against these copper companies, why vote "normal" damages? That means one dollar. Ya' know better than that! Put ya'selves in these farmers' places an' let's vote ag'in. Give these farmers a just decision!'

"When they voted ag'in, they brought in a decision o' $33,000, [1/3 of the amount being sought] an' Chris Sailor heard ole Leroy Anderson, th' big lawyer fer th' United Verde, tell th' three jurymen right ahead o' Chris, 'Well, gentlemen, ya' did all right under th' circumstances.' This left no doubt that the "smokemen" had promised these three a large sum of money to vote as they did the first time,

The Federal Reporter shows an appeal was filed in District Court D, Arizona, November 14, 1925 and a new trial denied.[11] Again both companies appealed, this time to the Circuit of Appeals, Ninth Circuit on August 2, 1926, with a rehearing being denied on September 7, 1926.[12] Walter elaborated: "Anderson [the lawyer for the smelters] appealed t' th' 9th District Court o' Appeals in San Francisco. Morrison took all o' 'is paper an' ever'thin' over, an' 'e beat 'em on ever' point. Then them dirty guys tried t' git another hearin' an' that judge wouldn't do it. Noneo' us 'ad t' go t' that."

"That was in 1926, a year an' a half after th' judgment in Prescott, s' th' companies 'ad t' pay 6% interest on $33,000 fer a year an' a half. I was secretary an' treasurer o' th' farmers association. When I got that check frum them copper companies, I 'ad t' write a check t' each one o' them farmers fer their share. When we took it t' court, each o' th' thirteen farmers 'ad t' pay accordin' t' th' number o' acres 'e was actually cultivatin' an' irrigatin'. [To cover expenses.] So, we 'ad it all figured out. I drew a check t' each one o' them farmers fer their amount o' that damage. O'course, W. A. Jordan an' sons got th' biggest share. There were five o' us: Chester, Bill, (Willie) Dad, Mother an' me. Th' court also ordered that th' smelters b' fitted with filters, but t' m' knowledge th' filters weren't never put on. [In 1950-51 the last of the smelters closed and still no filter bags.] Chester found th' court report on that case. Goodness alive, every word fer word was printed in that federal court record, you bet it was!"

The Jordans and the farmers who joined them in the lawsuit were principally concerned with recouping monetary loss and did not articulate environmental reasons for pressing the first air pollution suit to reach the U.S. Supreme Court. The Verde Valley farmers pointed to the smelters in Utah, which they believed had employed the latest in air filter technology to allow the farmers to live in economic harmony with the mining barons. Ecology had not yet become a household word. The unspoken hope of the pioneer farmers of the Verde Valley was that they were establishing farms around which a community would grow and flourish for their children, grandchildren and decendants. The smelter smoke settled mortality upon the cultivated fields, and the farmers let die the vineyards and the orchards.

In another time those holding the "Copper Collar", as James Byrkit referred to the industry in his book, *Forging The Copper Collar*, might have used their wealth to sustain and cultivate the communities they created. However, in the 1880s and early 1900s there were railroads to carry the precious metals out of the struggling territory to the cities in the East, allowing the welfare of the local communities to be ignored. The mansion home Jimmy Douglas built at Jerome remains like a castle on the side of the mountain, a State Historical Museum, where visitors presumably learn from history.

"Uncle Will came up an' bought a place in Sedona in 1926", says Allen, "I can remember that. Maybe he came up an' ran it alone a little while, but pretty soon George was livin' with him an' ran th' place. George married Helen, of course, in 1928, an' Walter who had been runnin' th' places down in the Verde Valley came up in 1929 to try dry farmin' the Sedona property with his dad."

After the lawsuit was completed Will said that he was going to go so far away that smoke would never find him. He went 20 miles to Sedona, purchasing property along Oak Creek plus a smaller portion approximately one mile to the west of the creek. Ironically there were days the smoke would be visible coming around the southern side of Sedona by Twin Buttes, but never enough to bother any crops. (See center for painting of Twin Buttes.)

Will also continued farming at Bridgeport without quite as many problems, because by the time the suit was settled, it seemed the Clemenceau smelter wasn't belching out nearly as much smoke. Although, that smelter closed in 1937, the smokestack wasn't imploded until into the mid to late 1940s. The operation at Clarkdale continued for another decade. One day during daughter Ruth's senior year of high school, (1950-51), all of the students were allowed to sit out in the schoolyard and watch as the Clarkdale smelter gave its final gasps, with whisps of smoke dissipating on the horizon. For years, the silent, stalwart stacks stood over the valley as sentinels guarding secrets of an era which brought wealth to a few and heartbreak to many.

The economic promise in the red of the geology map had become history - Will Jordan's history. From the death of his dream and the monetary settlement of the mining company, his sons, Walter and George, would write their own history in the red rocks of Sedona. Here they had moved as farmers to escape the smelter, but in turn, their red rock countryside would become the residence of wealthy retirees and of the Sedona Historical Museum.

Although mining and smelting continued beyond the 1920s, justice for the "hayseeds" or farmers had been received. Thus, one era closed and the drama of the Verde Valley shifts to scenes set on the eastern portion of the watershed, - Oak Creek and Sedona.

FOOTNOTES

(1) Jordan, Stella M. Personal Diary, 17 Sept. 1915.

(2) Beard, Christine D. "People and Their Environment: An Historical Overview of the Middle Verde Valley". Unpublished Thesis, 1987. 2.

(3) *Jerome Sun,* Smelter Smoke is Ruining Valley Vegetation. 27 Nov. 1917.

(4) W.A. Jordan and Sons and Annie T. Jordan v. United Verde Extension Mining Company and United Verde Copper Company. N0. 7930 & 7931 NAU Cline Library, Special Collections and Archives, M.S. 199, Box 2, Folder F 3-4. Super. Ct. of the State of Arizona in and for the County of Yavapai 1926.

(5) W.A. Jordan Place, Property No. 29 Investigation by W.W. Jones. NAU Cline Library, Special Collections and Archives, M.S. 199, Box 32, Folder 10 1-2. Super. Ct. of the State of Arizona, in and for the County of Yavapai 10 April 1921.

(6) W.A. Jordan Place, Property No. 29 Investigation by H. Brisley & R.A. Channel. NAU Cline Library, Special Collections and Archives, M.S. 199, Box 32, Folder 10 Super. of the State of Arizona, in and for the County of Yavapai 24 Sept. 1921.

(7) Miller, Walter C. Letter to Bob. 26 Feb. 1925. Information to the Copper Co.. NAU Cline Library, Special Collections and Archives, M.S. 199, Box 32 Book 2, Flagstaff, AZ.

(8) W.A. Jordan Place Investigation by H. Brisley, R.A. Channel & J.W. Johnson. NAU Cline Library, Special Collections and Archives, M.S. 199, Box 32, Folder 10 3. Super. Ct. of the State of Arizona, in and for the County of Yavapai 31 Aug. 1920.

(9) W.A. Jordan Place, Property No. 29 Investigation by W.W. Jones. NAU Cline Library, Special Collections and Archives, M.S. 199, Box 32, Folder 10 1-2. Super. Ct. of the State of Arizona, in and for the County of Yavapai 10 April 1921. p. 1-2.

(10) Bingham Press Utah. "The Smelter Smoke Fakers." Jerome Mining News 27 Apr. 1907:

(11) Ibid, p. 2

(12) United Verde Copper Co. v. Jordan et. al. and United Verde Extension Mining Co. v. Jordan et. al.. Doc. No. 4735 & 4746 14 Federal Reporter, 2d Series 299-307. Circuit Ct. of Appeals, 9th Circuit 7 Sept. 1926.

(13) United Verde Copper Company v. W.A. Jordan, W.E. Jordan, C.A. Jordan, et. al., etc., & United Verde Extension Mining Co. v. W.A. Jordan, W.E. Jordan, C.A. Jordan, et. al., etc.. No. 692 & 693 47 Supreme Court Reporter Memorandum Decisions 243. United States Circuit Ct. of Appeals 29 Nov. 1926.

Chapter Nine

FARMING AND FRUIT TREES IN SEDONA

The drama on the center stage of the Verde Valley was paralleled by the developing scenes in the extended wings of the Red Rock Country as the Thompson family began homesteading approximately 20 miles east of the main stage.

The wonderfully fertile and iron-rich soil, plus a steady water supply, made the area along Oak Creek ideal for farming. The earlier settlers found and utilized some of the same spots that the Yavapais and Apaches had cultivated for decades. In one of these select spots, known as Bacon Rind Park, John James (Jim) Thompson, along with B. F. Copple took up the first squatters' rights in 1876. Jim wrote to the Abraham James family of Southern Nevada telling them of the great opportunities and advantages of the Red Rock country, and in 1878 they made the long trek to establish a farm on Lower Oak Creek near Page Springs. A year later they moved up the creek about 10 miles to become the first settlers of the area which would later be known as Sedona. In 1880 Jim married Margaret James and built a cabin on land that, some forty years later, would become the George Jordan place. Here their oldest son, Frank, arrived in 1882, the first anglo child to be born in Sedona. The family remained at this place until 1887 when Jim brought them to his original homestead at Indian Gardens, formerly Bacon Rind Park.

Gradually others discovered this piece of paradise and began building homes, among them T.C. (Carl) and Sedona Schnebly. In 1901 they, along with Carl's brother Ellsworth, arrived from Missouri, settling near Oak Creek (See center for painting of Schnebly's first house). Eventually an eleven room, two story house was built offering a warm welcome to many travelers. Paula Schnebly Hokanson refers to it as "Sedona's first 'Bed and Breakfast' and Grandpa [T. C.] as the first 'Chamber of Commerce president' as he used to visit with anyone in an out-of-state car and bring them home for tea."[1]

Sedona Miller Schnebly with her background and education must have made a charming hostess (See center for painting of Sedona Schnebly). Paula eloquently describes her: "Gramma was very well polished coming from a family of Academy students and proper, and probably cut a pretty good pose in those days. She was talented — played piano and organ, spoke German, had taught school, had elocution lessons, was beautifully dressed and groomed of well-to-do parents — eyes that could knock your socks off!!!!" She also states that, "Grandpa, whose father was a doctor, was quite well educated for that time."[2] Coupling T. C.'s feeling that the Oak Creek area was "God's Country" and Sedona's gracious hospitality, they were ideal host and hostess for those passing through.

From Helen Jordan's collection
Sedona Miller Schnebly 1940s

From Helen Jordan's collection
T.C. and Sedona Schnebly late 1940s

As the community grew and a postal station was established the need for a name arose. T. C., the first postmaster and Ellsworth suggested to the U. S. Postal National office several names including Schnebly Station and Oak Creek Crossing. The response declared both names too long, so Ellswroth suggested naming it after his sister-in-law, Sedona. The name was accepted and in 1902 Sedona in Arizona Territory became a reality.

Along with farming they also had some cattle. One evening Sedona, son Ellsworth and five year old Pearl rode out to bring in the cattle. For some unknown reason Pearl had attached her lasso to herself with the other end fastened to the saddle horn. As all cow ponies are trained to do, when a cow darted around a bush her horse quickly followed it. The unsuspected move caught Pearl off-guard, causing her to fall from the saddle. The frightened animal raced for home, dragging her behind it. This tragedy in 1905 was more than the family could bear and so they returned to Missouri, staying until approximately 1910-1911. At this time they purchased property in Lincoln County of Eastern Colorado, built another lovely home, which is still standing. It is interesting nearly simultaneously with their move to CO. their beautiful former home on the creek in Sedona burned. At the ranch in Colorado, tragedy struck again in the form of Anthrax disease, causing T. C. to have to burn all of their cattle. (It would seem that most people never heard of Anthrax until after Sept. 11, 2001, but here it was in the 1920s-1930s.) Following this in the early 1930s, they once more came to Arizona, and having lost everything in the way of property and income, T. C. worked for several of the local people.

Besides naming the community, another contribution of the Schnebly brothers, was assisting in contacting the Board of Supervisors and in the paper work to get

Schnebly Hill Road, 1930s

things moving for the road up Schnebly Hill. Many of the families, including the Thompsons, contributed finances and labor to make this alternate route to Flagstaff a reality. Allen shares his remembrances of the amazing way in which the road was engineered. "Schnebly, [Ellsworth with the help of his brother T. C. aka Carl] laid out th' road up that mountain, just eyeballed it in without any instruments. 'E tied ribbons on bushes all th' way up there. Schnebly picked out a route for th' road an' that's how th' hill was named after th' family."

Paula remembers her Grandparents as folks who "always seemed to have such a humble, honest dignity about them and love for their community,"[3]

Although the Jordans were in no way among the early settlers, arriving approximately 50 years after Jim Thompson and the James family homesteaded, they definitely had an impact on the growth and development of the community. Some of their areas of involvement included: employing local residents, developing water systems for themselves and the community and assisting other farmers. The influence of their wives was felt in community activities, school teaching, programs for youth, music, drama and through leadership in the Sunday School.

Walter Wedding photo

After completing his water system, Walter grew vegetables to provide an income while the fruit trees were growing to maturity and fruit-bearing age. During this time he and Ruth decided to be married. He suggested November as a date for the wedding. His plan was to harvest the first crop, which would provide some reserve finances, plus by waiting until fall he would have the time to build a dwelling. However, she eventually convinced him it was "crazy" for her to spend the summer in hot Tempe while he was farming in the cooler climes. George and Helen solved the dilemma of housing by offering their spare bedroom, so, all objections having been met, Walter conceded to move the date to an earlier time. The search was on to find a time to fit around farm duties and Ruth's commitment to being maid-of-honor at the wedding of her best friend. (Ruth Faulkerson and Ted Howard). With everything already basically planned for that eventful day, it seemed the logical thing to do was to have a double wedding. Ruth even wore the lovely dress that she had previously purchased to wear as an attendant. So at 5:00 a.m. (probably the earliest Ruth ever arose in her life!) on July 20, 1930, Ruth Marie Woolf and Walter Everett Jordan became man and wife. Due to the hour of the ceremony, the newlyweds were able to reach higher elevations and cooler temperatures

Ruth Wedding photo

early in the day, escaping the unbearable heat of the valley afternoons. Traveling in their Model A Ford, their honeymoon consisted of a short stop in Bridgeport to visit Walter's family and an overnight at the Grand Canyon. Then it was back to Sedona to accept the hospitality of George and Helen, and continue with the crops.

Due to distances and road conditions, marketing was definitely a challenge for all of the farmers in the area. Helen recalls: "To market the fruit and vegetables, it was necessary to travel very narrow dirt roads. The old Schnebly Road to Flagstaff was unsurfaced, so there was lots of dust in summer, and mud up to the fenders when it stormed, and the canyon road was little more than a trail. It followed Jordan Road, [so named circa late 1950s, formerly known as "The lane", or "County Road"], north around Steamboat Rock, and was a real one-way road. The road to Cottonwood was surfaced, but melting snow or a rainstorm could cause Spring Creek and Dry Creek to become rivers, and sometimes it took a long time for the flood stage to subside enough for a car to be able to ford the streams. (See picture of Oak Creek Canyon road at end of chapter.)

"When we were first married, we had a little old car, and we used the Schnebly grade road. George would get up real early in the morning to go up to Flagstaff to peddle stuff to the grocery stores. We used to have to carry our own shovels to dig ourselves out of the mud. He took a flashlight and held it out the window and took another run at the steep grade. We'd see trucks stuck up there that would unload and go to the top with part of the load and come back for the rest. CCC boys built the new road and that little thin white line at an angle on the face of the hill is all that is left of the old Schnebly road. George wanted to show me the scenery up there and we did it once. We had to back down some to make the curve and go around."[4]

Walter and George would take turns driving George's truck up Schnebly Hill while the other one would stay to continue the work at the farm. Walter tells, "Sometimes when we'd be'a drivin' up that ole steep road, an' th' rear-end o' th' truck'd just give out. So's whoever was a'drivin'd just have t' high-tail it up t' Foxboro Ranch t' use th' telephone, they had a Forest Service phone. That was about a 5 mile hike. Well, when thatun'd git there 'e'd call th' Sedona Forest Ranger Station, 'cause ya know nobody here 'ad phones in them days. Then th' ranger'd go tell whoever was home that we's broken down on that awful grade, an' th' other un'd bring a new rear-end up, an' we'd change th' dad-blamed thing right there on th' side o' th' mountain. We always kept an extra at George's place 'cause we's always needin' it. Anyway, sometimes it'd still be dark an' we'd use great big flashlights an' even have t' build a big ole fire t' give us enough light t' see t' change that bugger. When we got all done one o' us would go ont' Flag, [Flagstaff], an' th' other'd head home. We 'ad t' git that produce up there b'fore it spoiled." Walt shakes his head ending the tale, "My, oh my! Them was some times!"

Both brothers had a great propensity to work extra long hours when situations required it. Helen continues sharing, "One time George's sister Alice and her husband, Bill Gray, came to stay all night with us. We had a lot of ripe tomatoes which had to be packed and loaded on the truck, so we worked long after dark out in the yard under a big light, with my brother helping us. Next Day, Bill, who loved to tease and joke, said to Dad Hart, [another early settler who opened the first grocery store] 'sure don't take long to stay all night at the Jordan's. About midnight Helen went to bed, and at one o'clock her brother Paul came in. Then at two, George came in, took off his pants, shook them, put them back on and went to Flagstaff.' (See photo of their ranch at end of chapter.)

"During the depression, the prices of farm produce reached a new low, and with each farmer trying to compete with his neighbor, you could hardly give it away. We decided to form a cooperative. The farmers brought their fruit to our packing shed where we packed it uniformly, and George did the marketing for everyone. He made regular trips each week to Cottonwood, Clarkdale, Jerome, and Prescott, [60 miles] and also to Flagstaff, Williams and Ashfork, and even to Winslow and Holbrook, [120 miles] each time taking orders for the next trip. He would get home late and would work till midnight, and after that get the truck loaded for an early start the next morning. This brought about a much better market. It was grueling, but George was determined to have a ranch."[5]

After a strenuous summer of hard work for Ruth and Walter, the carrots were ready to be harvested. Walter considered taking them to neighboring towns, but thought the best opportunity for him to market independently was in Phoenix. Although he knew it would take all night to get to the Salt River Valley, he felt it would be better than using Schnebly Hill road, as George had to do when taking fruit and vegetables to northern towns. In addition, he didn't want to disrupt the market which George had worked so hard to establish. Next step was how to transport the produce, for in the past he and George had used the same truck, but that was no longer an option. He solved the situation by removing the rumble seat of the Model A Ford and replacing it with a homemade small stake back. Carrots were brought from the fields, tied in bunches of five or six with cotton twine, twelve of these were bundled together and tied with binder twine, then stacked on a wooden platform, washed, and kept moist for freshness. All of the work was done by hand and fingers could become mighty sore. Walter kept instructing those tying the single bunches that it was simple, "just use a Granny knot!" However he never did explain just what he meant by a "Granny knot". In order to get the binder twine tight around the dozen bunches Walter would place them between his knees freeing both hands for tying it tightly. When enough were ready for the ten to twelve hour trip to Phoenix, he would load them, put a canvas over the top and drive all night. The first few years Ruth went with him to be the peddler while he returned to get another load. The carrots were piled in the yard of an elderly friend in Tempe, who loaded the carrots into his Model T Ford, taking them and Ruth to the kitchen doors of restaurants and hotels of prospective buyers. (One of these, the famous Westward Ho in central Phoenix, is still in business, although 75 years later it is a residence for Seniors, not an exclusive hotel.) Jumping ahead a couple of years Ruth recalls, "It was very difficult for me to arrive before dawn

Fannie Woolf (Ruth's mother), Ruthie, Anne, Walt Jr. with carrots ready for market, circa 1938

at those places, smell the food cooking, plus the garbage outside, and complete the business transaction before running behind the Model T and vomiting. Mr. Ashworth [the owner of the Model T] would hold my head and help me get myself regrouped, before going to the next place. I was about two months pregnant with Anne, our oldest child, and was having rather severe morning sickness."

Walter relates an experience on one of these trips: "We was a'drivin' acrost Pepples Valley in th' middle o' th' night with a load o' them carrots, an' Ruth was asleep lyin' down in th' seat, when I seen these two armed men up ahead a wavin' their guns in th' air a wantin' me t' stop. I knew right away they's lawmen. S' I stopped, rolled down th' window, an' o'course Ruth came t' life an' sat up just as this feller was a walkin' up t' my window with 'is big ole gun. When he poked 'is head in th' window an' demanded, 'What'cha got in th' back there?' Ruth was a plenty scared, believe ya me. Well I just said, 'Them's complexion powders I'm a'takin' t' Phoenix.'

From Helen Jordan's collection

George's peach orchard

"'Where're ya a'comin' frum?'" He was mighty gruff th' way 'e talked.

"'Sedona,' I told 'im.

"Then 'e wanted t' take a look, so's I got out an' showed 'im what was under that ole canvas. That's when 'e told me there'd been a bank robbery in Clarkdale an' th' authorities thought they's a'headed this way. 'Be careful an' keep yer eye peeled. These fellers are mighty dangerous,' 'e told us an' then waved us on our way.

"When we got goin' agin Ruth asked me, 'How on earth could ya possibly joke with 'im when 'e ad a gun in yer face?!'

"'My goodness alive! Couldn't ya tell what they was? I saw right off that 'e was a officer.' Ya see she thought we was bein' held up b' some bad guys."

After the carrots were all harvested, building a 14 by 20 foot cabin was the first order of business, which in the early 1990s became the "cabin room" of the Sedona Heritage Museum. Then Walter turned his attention to getting fruit trees planted, for unlike his brother he was "starting from scratch." (George already had quite a good-sized orchard that was bearing fruit when he bought out his father.) In the fall, Walt ordered small trees from one of the major nurseries and "heeled them in." This required digging a ditch about 10 inches deep, placing the young trees on their sides with the bare roots in the ditch and covering them with dirt. These were left until spring when it was warm enough to set them out. By that time he had the planting area all "laid out" to his specifications. Ruth and Walt's Dad did a major portion of the planting, protecting each little tree from rabbits, deer and porcupines with a round of chicken wire. The young trees had been selected for strength and disease resistant qualities of the stock. The chosen variety for fruit was then budded or grafted into the nursery stock and Walt, with his father's help, did all of this. He could have purchased trees which had had the marketable variety already introduced into the stock, but he preferred to do it himself. "That'a way I know fer sure exactly what I got!" he explained.

Budding is defined in a dictionary as "...inserting a single bud into the stock."[6] He had a rather unique method which he and his father had found successful over the years. After preparing their materials, they first carefully made a slit low on the small stem with a "mighty" sharp knife. Next the desired leaf bud was precisely removed from its branch and placed in the slit. Beeswax (as in most budding techniques), was used to initially hold the tiny interloper securely in place. The next step was where their process deviated from the norm by involving resin to assist the bud in its attachment and growth. The resin was heated in a bucket and either cheesecloth or burlap strips were dipped in the gooey mess. These strips were then bound around the area snuggly, leaving the tiny bud with its "head" sticking out. The bud then began to grow into the branch or stock of the young host tree with the budding material being either absorbed or disintegrated. Both orchardists liked using the resin because it increased the number of buds that "took," or grew. It seems they had approximately a 95% success rate with the whole tree becoming the induced variety.

Even something with as specific a role as a beeswax and resin bucket can find itself in a new setting with a distinctly different task to perform. Walter, Ruth and a couple of friends were going hunting and Walt hastily grabbed a bucket in which to boil coffee over a campfire. That evening after dinner several poured their coffee, took a big swig and promptly began sputtering, spitting and yelling. "Walt, whatever did ya put in that coffee. It'd gag a maggot!!" "Oh, I betcha' I know what happened!" he retorted. "I betcha' a hunnert bucks I grabbed that ole bucket we's been a'mixin' beeswax an' resin in." Upon closer inspection of the offending bucket and coffee they discovered he was correct. Walt continues the story: "About that time that big feller, John Wetzel I told ya' about with th' rattlesnake bite, come a'walkin' int' our camp. I winked at them others an' asked 'im if 'e'd like a cup o' hot coffee? Fresh made. An' o'course 'e did. So's I poured 'im a big cup o' that nasty coffee an' wouldn't ya' know, 'e never even flinched. 'E just chugged down that whole cup without a word. About that time we figgered th' joke was on us!"

Walter's illustration of grafting, 1980s

Grafting is defined as the process when "a bud, shoot, or scion of a plant [is] inserted in a groove, slit or the like in a stem or stock of another plant in which it continues to grow."[7] Walt always used the term in reference to placing a shoot, not a bud into the stock. Much the same process was used as in budding. This was called the Beideman Graft, being named after the gentleman who designed it. (See illustration on previous page)

In the early 1930s Walter and Ruth again borrowed money from Ruth's family to expand the tillable land. Walter knew that when the trees began producing fruit he no longer could plant vegetables between the rows, and when the opportunity arose to buy 55 acres south of their house he felt he should take advantage of it for his "truck garden." He worried about repaying the loan and what he would do if a crop failed. In his words, "I 'ad t' fill in a gully that run right through th' middle o' th' best part o' th' land. T' do that I 'ad t' take that team o' horses an' a small scoop an' dig out a'nuff dirt t' make me a small reservoir up there at the back [west] o' that orchard t'

Anne and Ruthie playing in reservoir built to contain gully run-off

stop water from runnin' down there. I could also store water that I pumped up there in that tank an' use it fer irrigatin'. After I got that gulley all filled up I just loaded that land with barnyard in th' fall an' disced it under good, an' left it fer a year. Th' next spring I planted them wonderful Kentucky Wonder Pole beans. Oh my!! Them's th' most wonderful beans I ever grew. Why! Some o' 'em was fourteen inches long an' Ruth 'ad t' bend 'em over t' git 'em in a half gallon sized jar when she was a cannin'. Well,

Walter and Anne on borrowed tractor, 1933

off a one acre o' them beans I made more'n a'nuff t' pay off that $950.00 loan. My, oh my! Was that ever a big relief. Ya' betcha it was!"

The orchards of the Jordan brothers flourished and provided an abundance of fruit. Helen explains, "We found that Sedona had the perfect climate for the fruit grower, and our trees produced so much fruit that we needed a packing house other than the canvas-sided shed we had been using. We also needed a cold storage to take care of the fruit properly. George hauled lumber with which to build the packing house from a mill near Mormon Lake. [Happy Jack] This was during the depression, and the mill owner offered the lumber at a very low price, otherwise we could not have afforded it. The old truck would be loaded to capacity for each trip. Stones piled on the running boards and fenders kept the front end on the ground, and with the help of two carpenters, one being Jim Farley, the packing house was built." George also hauled windows from one of the old mine buildings in Jerome. The building was constructed on a hill beside their house, with space for the trucks to come between the two buildings (see page v in the introduction for picture of packing house). Here, on a platform at the second story, boxes of apples from the fields were unloaded, put through the "wiper" for cleaning, sorted in the new grading machine, packed into

New fruit market on Highway 89A

proper shipping boxes and sent down the tin-lined chute to the lower level to be placed in the cold storage. All of the community kids felt the main purpose of the chute was for them to use as a slide. George allowed this activity anytime that fruit wasn't being processed, for the peaches were handled downstairs and to have a live body suddenly land in the middle of a box being packed with fruit would most definitely anger the ladies packing and hamper progress. Often, when Helen was needed downstairs, she used the chute as a short cut rather than taking the outside stairs and walking all of the way around. Any observers got a big laugh out of watching her and she always landed with a giggle. The lower area also served as a "farmers' market" providing passers-by and neighbors a place to purchase fruit and vegetables. Helen was delighted to move the operation away from the house, as many customers would walk in her kitchen and lift the lids off pots on the stove to see what was cooking. Soon it became evident that the customers' main way of determining ripeness of any fruit was to firmly squeeze each item, often leaving it unsalable. George quickly made an attempt to alter this by designing a large sign that Helen lettered: "If you must squeeze something, squeeze one of the hired hands!" In later years when nieces, Anne and F. Ruth would be working as clerks, many older gents would eyeball the sign and with a lecherous grin, start towards them with outstretched arms. Fortunately,

Helen standing by sign

Anne devised a great stopper: "We're not hired hands, we're relatives!" Looking rapidly around searching for another likely person on whom they could bestow their squeeze, they could only see a couple of well-worn farm workers. As their faces fell, they halted mid-stride, attempted to regroup themselves and with much disappointment returned to the fruit buying. (See end of chapter for sales flyer and sample ledger)

While George continued with the co-op, selling fruit in northern Arizona towns and at his packing shed, Walter expanded his Phoenix market until Mr. Quinn of J. R. Quinn Produce placed a standing order for any fruit and vegetables that the Jordans grew. He offered them at least a cent a pound higher than was being paid to any other suppliers. This certainly made the long haul worthwhile. The Model A was no longer adequate, so in 1938 Walt purchased a 1937 Ford truck of the economy series, identified by a Scottie dog painted on the doors. (The thinking of Ford Motor Company was, that a Scottie came from Scotland and the Scottish were known for their thriftiness, thus the dog represented economy.)

Anne, Walter, and Ruthie on tractor, circa 1937

This vehicle had four speeds forward plus a "Brownie Under" which had been added to the transmission. This gave an additional lower gear to each of the forward ones allowing the ability to haul heavier loads up steeper grades.

During the years following the setting out of the trees, Walter continued to grow bush beans, pinto beans, pole beans, carrots and strawberries. Much work involving cultivating, pruning, smudging, and many other tasks, kept him constantly busy. Although the peaches had begun producing fruit a few years sooner, it was the summer of 1942 that the apple trees bore their first fruit with an enormous crop. (It takes 8 years for an apple tree to begin bearing.) Walter, with the occasional help of a relief driver along, was making the trip several times a week. He would work in the fields all day, load the truck and leave between five and six p.m. for the all night run, arriving at the Phoenix market by five a.m. One morning he was a bit surprised when Mr. Quinn said, "Say, Walt, we just had a request from the government to provide one thousand boxes [a box was approximately a bushel] of apples in one week to be shipped to the armed forces in Europe. Can you do it?" Walter agreed realizing that this was his opportunity to show his patriotism. He had felt a bit guilty for not doing his part in WWI because when the older boys went to war he had to stay home to help on the farm, and he was considered too old at age 45 to go into the forces in WWII. Never mind the shortage of available help, or just the one truck and all of the other produce, plus peaches to move, he was

Apple trees and smudge pots, 1942-1970

determined to get the job done. To add to the difficulties, this was the summer flood water had inundated his pump and generator. When he arrived home that evening he discussed all of it with Ruth, knowing that this would intensify her duties as "straw boss." She had always been completely in charge of the harvesting and packing operations in his absence — quite a change for a city girl who had never planted or grown anything before her marriage. In the early years when the children were small she would take to the fields, all eighty pounds and five feet of her, with one of the girls hanging onto each of her Levi hip pockets. It is a wonder that their little legs could keep up or that her pants stayed on with them dragging behind.

A whirlwind of a week began, trying to find extra help and packing both peaches and apples late into the night. The packing shed, which normally functioned as the tractor garage had one wall lined with wooden tables built especially to keep the fruit boxes slanted. The packers placed the field boxes of fruit in the center of their space with at least two empties on each side to accommodate different sizes of their precious cargo. A major skill of a packer was the ability to eye-ball each piece of fruit, make a rapid and accurate decision as to the size, and place it in the proper box. (When Anne and Ruthie were helping they would get upset when they nearly had a box completed and their Dad would come in, start grabbing fruit and rearrange everything. When he did it to the adult lady packers, they told him to get out in no uncertain terms!) Prior to reaching the packers the apples were wiped clean of spray by youngsters wearing cotton gloves and rubbing each one until it shone. Often the shine had a short life due to the soft dirt floor in the shed and the dust "kicked up" when walking in the area, then the packers had to at least wipe the top layer clean.

Walter and the crew put extensions on the top of the sideboards of the truck to accommodate extra boxes of fruit and then loaded beans and carrots above that, using special care not to damage the fruit. A heavy water proof tarp tightly tied down covered all of the top and most of the sides. Ruth would hold her breath and offer a silent prayer when he made the turn leaving the loading place, as the top would weave to the side even at this extremely slow speed and level ground. She reflected briefly on the numerous twists and turns over the three mountain ranges and the seven to seven and a half tons on this ton and a half truck. Her strong faith in God and His power of protection certainly was upheld, for Walt, truck and load were spared from several near misses resulting from Walter's driving eight nights straight without going to bed. At one point he didn't lie down at all to sleep for forty-eight hours, and his shoes had to be cut off of his swollen feet.

On one occasion he awakened at the wheel to realize he was going to completely miss the New River Bridge. He steered back onto the road as sharply as possible without rolling the truck and managed to barely get back in time to enter the bridge, but the whole right side of the truck scraped the inside of the railing. The truck bore the evidence of this close encounter for as long as he owned it. When telling this episode he always ended by saying, "B'lieve ya' me, I sure was awake after that, an' I didn't git sleepy all th' rest o' th' way t' Phoenix! But I did have t' pull over an' sit fer awhile 'til I got through shakin'. My, oh my!"

Other experiences included him being jolted into awareness by the loud honking of a horn. Recognizing that he had crossed the centerline and was headed directly towards a woman and her car, all movements became automatic. Again, he was able to avert an accident and continue up the mountain road until he could find a place to safely pull over and regroup his nerves. It was during these episodes that he restarted his former smoking habit, thinking it would help prevent drowsiness. Those good old Camels remained a part of his life until a heart attack at age 60, and then after a few months of not lighting up, he began again, against the doctor's advice.

The week continued in a frenzy of activity as all were exerting extra energy to meet the deadline. Walter would arrive back at the ranch in the late afternoon, time depending on whether or not he had to drive across Phoenix to get a load of apple boxes and/or peach lugs. (In those years all were wooden.) Ruth and her crew were supposed to have a full load ready for him to start putting in the truck as soon as he drove up the drive. After getting everything loaded and the huge heavy, waterproof tarp tied on over the top, he would go to the house, cleanup, "eat a bite" and start out all over again. However, on some days the summer monsoon rains had delayed the picking as peaches cannot be handled when wet or they will mold. Although the packers would often join the pickers in the field if rain threatened, (in order to stockpile fruit for packing while it stormed), there still would be times without enough packed boxes ready for him to begin loading. One such day was the eighth and the last of the back-to-back runs. The workers stayed quite a bit later than usual assisting in the remaining monumental task. By eleven p.m. family members were the only ones still packing fruit by lantern light and putting boxes into the truck. Walter asked his two girls (8 and 9 years old) if they had had supper. "No" was the answer so he said, "Anne ya' an' sister go on t' th' house an' eat an' go on t' bed. Mother [Ruth] an' I'll finish." At two a.m. they completed getting everything ready and the truck loaded. Walt told Ruth, "I've just gotta lie down a few minutes b'fore I start drivin' agin." There in the tractor garage/packing shed, he stretched out on an army cot, she sat down on an apple box and they both fell sound asleep. Something awakened them two hours later, and in his words, "With a start I jumped up right quick, run t' that ole truck, jumped in, an' started 'er engine, yelled goo'bye at Ruth an' was on my way. B'fore I got t' Phoenix m' buyer, Mr. Quinn, 'ad sent a truck out a'lookin' fer me. They thought fer sure that I'd gone over a bluff somewhere's. Well, we did git all o' them apples t' th' train that week, as well as all o' them peaches an' vegetables t' th' market. I did have t' git a driver t' help one night when we 'ad extra stuff. George lent me 'is big truck an' that sure did help out. After we's all done, lots o' folks told me they didn't think we could do it. Ever'body pitched in an' did their share fer them boys a'fightin' in that awful war. We couldn't 'ave done it without all o' their help."

Wild happenings and danger were not limited to the eight days and nights of 1942. Walter enjoys reliving some of these as he regales his listeners: "One night I 'ad a big load on that ole truck, ya' know th' one that 'ad them Scottie dogs on th' doors when I bought it an' b'fore I put my name on there instead. Well, I made m' way up through Jerome on that old hogback about two miles an hour, an' on t' th' top o' Mingus Mountain where I pulled off t' check ever'thing. Lo an' b'hold, here somebody'd cut a darned hole in th' top o' that heavy canvas an' thrown out about a hundred dozen bunches o' carrots. Goodness alive was I ever mad! I figgurd it 'ad t' 'ave happened grindin' up that awful steep hogback. [Approximately a 15% grade.] Well, I made up m' mind that was th' last time that'd ever happen, so on m' way back I stopped in at th' police station in Jerome an' tole 'em what went on an' that I suspect a bunch o' no-goods 'ad jumped on when I was a 'goin' s' slow. I said, 'Gentlemen frum now on when I'm a'haulin' through here I want a police escort up that steep part!'

"'Oh mercy goodness alive, ya' don't expect us t' be able t' escort ever' truck that comes up that hill, now do ya'?'

"'O. K. fellas if that's th' way ya' feel about it, just spread th' word I'm a'carryin' m' gun an' when I shoot it ain't a'gonna be fer practice!' Amazin' ain't it, now-a-days they'd a put me in jail just fer sayin' that, let alone fer actually totin' one.

"Well, that's exactly what I done. Th' next trip I 'ad Ed Jackson with me, no relation t' m' future sons-in-law. Anyway, this here Ed, he just loved t' fight an' as we was a'crawlin' up along th' ridge o' th' hill past th' high school on th' hogback, an' we both seen a bunch o' heads pop up over th' edge o' th' road just after our headlights got by. Ole Ed says, 'Keep agoin' Walt I'm a gonna go see what damage I cin do.' Wouldn't ya' know he jumped out right quick an' started fightin' that whole darn bunch! I b'gun t' git worried 'cause it seemed 'e's gone too long, so's I just left that dang ole truck in th' lowest gear with that ole Brownie Under an' let it keep a chuggin', 'bout 2 miles an hour. When I stepped out on th' runnin' board, 'Zing!' a rock come a'sailin' right past m' head! That's when I decided that was enough so's I reached in under th' seat an' got out that blamed ole forty-five an' fired a few shots int' th' air. Like a flash them fellers cleared outta there an' Ed got back in th' truck just a'laughin' 'is fool head off. 'E thought it'd been great fun. Well let me tell ya, I never 'ad a bit more trouble goin' up through Jerome!

"Then on another night we 'ad a extra big load an' was goin' down th' backside o' Mingus Mountain an' come around this curve an' here they was a'workin' on th' road. I stopped t' wait fer 'em t' move a great huge boulder outta m' way. It was right smack in th' middle o' th' highway. Them darn fools kept a wavin' an' hollerin' fer me t' go on around it. I yelled back, 'That's too steep an' leanin' t'wards th' canyon. I'm top heavy an' if I try t' go over there I'm a'gonin' t' turn over!' Th' dumb bunnies wouldn't listen so's I finally 'ad t' give it a try. I told Ed, 'Ya' git out an' stand on that right side just above them rear duals an' if I start t' roll, jump as fer as y' cin t' git clear o' th' truck. As I eased that ole truck 'round there I felt them rear wheels lift off o' th' ground an' I know'd there wasn't nothin' I could do. So's I just turned th' front end t' go down with it int' th' canyon th' same direction th' top was a'goin' an' as th' front got down hill a bit, them rear wheels settled back down. By th' time I got ever'thin' under control an' stopped, I was quite a ways down in there. Boy, I was a hoppin' mad! I jumped outta that truck an' bellered at them damn fools t' bring their dadgummed bulldozer down there an' pull me out. B' th' time this operation was finished them buggers was a wishin' they'd a moved th' damned boulder in th' first place. But we didn't hurt th' fruit none a tall. Now wasn't that somethin'!" His hand gestures brought the whole scene to life for the listeners.

"Oh, yeah! There's this time when I was a sleepin' an' Ed was a drivin' comin' offa Yarnell Hill, just after makin' th' hairpin bend at th' bottom an' goin' straight on that long downhill just after gettin' down on th' desert. Somethin' woke me up. It was 'im a down shiftin' an' startin' t' slow down. 'My goodness alive man, what'er ya' doin'?!'

"'Look up there, there's a man a lyin' in th' middle o' our side o' th' road!'

"I'd heard some other drivers a talking about some kinda holdups with a guy lyin' in th' road t' git em t' stop. So's I yelled at Ed, 'Gun it! Gun it! Give 'er all she's got! If 'e don't move take th' other side o' th' road, but I'll betcha 'e runs off!' That's just exactly what happened too. 'E jumped up an' run off s' fast ya'da thought 'is britches was on fire! It's a good thing I woke up 'cause if Ed'd stopped we'd a been robbed fer sure." Walt paused for a good laugh as he could still see in his mind's eye the whole scenario.

"Now I'm a gonna tell ya' one more o' these hair raisin' tales an' then quit. Ya've heard enough an'way ain't ya'?" At this point the listeners always begged for more. "B' th' time this'un took place I 'ad that big GMC truck (2-1/2 ton), we could haul 500 lugs [of peaches]. An' we usually'd haul about six or seven tons easy on that ole Chevy. Them were scary nights when we hauled th' fruit t' market. This particular event happened down near th' top o' Yarnell Hill. That road in them years was cut right outta th' face o' th' mountain [only 2 lanes wide] an' dropped close t' three thousand feet in about seven or eight miles with that hairpin curve at th' bottom I was a'talkin' about. We alwa's stopped at a little café down there at Peeples Valley near Yarnell an' 'ad coffee an' a sandwich. While we's in there th' waitress ast where we's a headed. 'Phoenix,' I said. 'Well, ya won't be goin' fur,' she told us.

"'Why not? I gotta git them peaches t' market.'

"'Well. ya' cain't.'

"'What's a matter?'

"'There's a semi full o' copper frum th' smelter jack knifed part way down in th' middle o' one o' them big turns an' th' Highway Patrol ain't a lettin' nobody go through.'

"I couldn't just sit there s' I said, 'Come on Ed. Let's go have a look. We'll just take 'er easy an' go on down there an' look 'er over.' That was one o'clock in th' mornin'. Seems like Ed was with me on th' most o' them excitin' times. We got down there an' sure 'nuff this big ole truck was a'layin' on its side clean acrost th' road. Big old diesel truck, th' fella drivin' was a greenhorn. They was haulin' th' copper frum Clarkdale smelter t' San Pedro an' shippin' it t' Japan. They 'ad 12 an' a half tons on th' truck, an' 12 and a half on th' trailer, an' 'e started down. 'E didn't git int' 'is low gears when 'e left th' top an' th' emergency brake on that thing was on th' drive shaft, an' 'e burnt that out an' 'e still couldn't git it in a lower gear. 'E saw that 'e 'ad t' telescope it an' 'e run it int' th' bluff, an' that smashed th' diesel engine (It was a wonder it didn't kill 'im. Didn't hurt 'im much.) an' that just threw th' trailer clean acrost th' road. My goodness, an' th' lady'd said they didn't have a wrecker big 'nuff up here, an' it would b' three o'clock in th' mornin' b'fore they got one frum Phoenix. O' course th' patrolman stopped us an' told us we'd 'ave t' wait 'til after th' wrecker moved ever'thin'.

"'Good gracious man! I cain't sit here all night with them peaches. They'll git too ripe a'sittin' out here. I 'ave t' git through here an' on t' Phoenix! I don't plan on deliverin' peach jam t' m' buyer!'

"'Ed,' I said, ' We've got t' figger a way t' git 'round this thing. Let's measure frum th' end o' that semi t' th' edge o' th' bluff, an' then we'll 'ave t' measure m' truck t' see if we've got room t' spare or if we can git 'round a tall without takin' a short cut t' Phoenix goin' right over th' cliff.' Then I checked out them bluffs, an' they was that kind o' rock that's as solid as any ya' ever could see. It was straight up an' down there fer a length o' about 2000 feet, just solid, almost solid rock er I wouldn't a tackled it a tall. While we's a doin' this, that lawman was a gittin' mighty huffy, tellin' me that if I tried what it looked like I was a gona try 'e'd write me a great big ticket.

"'Start writin' officer,' I told 'im, 'b'cause I'm comin' through.' From our measurement, don't remember just how we went about measurin', Ed an' I figgered we'd 'ave about two inches width left o' them outside duals on good ground an' th' rest hangin' over th' cliff, an' that was with me scrapin' th' end o' that semi with m' truck. 'Well, Ed, I tell ya' what I'm a'gonna do. I'll git in there an' put it in th' lowest gear I got an' just barely crawl an' ya tell me where I'm at.' By Golly, with 'im a directin', I just kept on a easin' forward, an' gradually we got 'er past th' end o' that semi with them outside duals a hangin' off o' that darned ole cliff. We just eased through that thing. Was I ever r'lieved. I was a sweatin' all over when that patrolman come t' m' window shakin' 'is head. 'Well I wouldn't 'ave believed it if I 'adn't a'seen it! I'm not a gonna write that ticket after all. Someone that good don't need no ticket.'

"Now, I told ya' that's all I was tellin' this time an' I'm done. Oh yes, Ruth, yer right! There was a truck that turned over one time. Okay, I'll tell th' rest o' ya' about it.

"That time we's a comin' slow just about t' git t' th' bottom o' that awful steep section o' Yarnell Hill when we saw a big truck load o' apples off o' th' road. It was down there at that big curve at th' bottom o' this long straight part just gittin' off o' that darned grade. If yer not careful when ya' come off o' th' main mountain, ya' git t' goin' a little too fast t' make th' curve. That fella'd eight tons o' loose apples frum Colorado all over th' road, an' that truck was down offa th' side. We saw a light still on, so's we stopped an' went down there, but there wasn't a soul around."

His wife, Ruth, adds, "George called me on our country phone that night to ask if Walter had gone with a load, and I told him that you had left at the usual time. George said he'd heard that a truckload of apples turned over down toward the foot of Yarnell Hill. So that's all the news I had all that night. There was no way for Walter to let me know. We had no regular telephone."

Hearing stories like these it is no wonder that Ruth

offered a silent prayer for his protection when he left, and one of gratitude when he returned. She even got to the place she could recognize the sound of the engine of his truck as he geared down coming from Grasshopper Flat (now West Sedona) into Sedona. Although it was at least 3 miles distance as the crow flies, the afternoon air currents carried sounds well. While out in the fields and orchards, she would pause briefly to listen as trucks came down the hill. All knew when it was Walter's truck, for a slight smile would cross her face and she would urge workers to hurry because, "Walter's nearly home." Years later Walter discovered the reason everyone was hustling and ready to meet him as he drove up the lane. He was a determined, strong character, and she, his steady and constant helpmate.

Much to the surprise of many, producing delicious fruits and vegetables is a year-round occupation. When asked by his grandson what tasks were done throughout the year, Walter started describing farming activities that happen in the fall just after harvesting is completed and continued explaining work that took place throughout the rest of the year.

"In th' fall, in October, I put a good coat o' barnyard on th' ground an' git it stirred in good. That gives that barnyard plenty o' time t' decompose. Next spring ya've got plant available fertilizer. But if ya' don't want t' put it in that fall, ya' can git quick action on it in th' spring b' spreadin' a good coat o' barnyard on th' ground an' then a coat o' 1620 commercial fertilizer. That's 16% nitrogen an' 20% phosphate. That causes th' barnyard t' break down right away an' b'come plant available sooner. If ya' don't decompose barnyard, it takes three years fer th' soil t' finally take all th' use out o' it. I always put that barnyard in there in th' winter in th' place I'm gonna put th' tomatoes. An' fer th' string beans, it's better t' put a good coat o' barnyard on in th' fall, about October fer orchards an' other garden vegetables. Now a winter like this last one, o' course, I 'ad t' wet it down quite a bit b'cause we didn't have hardly any moisture. I al'a'ys hauled that barnyard frum Camp Verde where th' Wingfields 'ad a big dairy. (Wingfield's would ship quite a bit o' their milk t' Phoenix. That was back when th' Verde Valley was still mostly ranches an' farms. Wingfield's was producin' even after the Black Canyon Highway, I-17, went through t' Phoenix in the 1950's.) They'd use a front loader t' git m' big truck filled up. I put on them short sideboards I'd made, about a foot high. That ole barnyard's s' heavy ya' cain't pile it very high. When I'd git back up here somebody'd git up on th' top o' that smelly stuff an' shovel it off while somebody else stayed in th' cab an' was a'drivin' from spot t' spot. A lot o' times Anne or Ruthie'd drive while Son [Walter Jr.] an' me'd do th' shovelin'. Them two sure felt lucky that they's girls an' didn't 'ave t' b' back there with that awful stinky mess!" Here Walt stopped to snicker.

"After I visited m' friend Frank Ames up in Washington in 1956, I b'gan sewin' alfalfa in m' orchards. I went t' school with Ames. His Dad 'ad a farm next t' us. I 'adn't seen 'im since 1913. 'E took me around 'is big peach orchards, an' I asked 'bout th' alfalfa 'e 'ad growin' in there with them trees. 'E tole me that alfalfa draws th' nitrogen out o' th' air an' puts it down in th' soil. Up there 'e left th' alfalfa until it got pretty good size. Then 'e'd use a big machine with revolvin' blades t' cut that alfalfa down int' th' soil about two inches deep. That'll git ya' some rich soil. Ya've got yer nitrogen frum th' air an' yer organic matter. Up there in Washington they never harvest that alfalfa an' clover off o' there. It all goes in the ground, an' that's why I wanted t' go up and see how they did it. That's th' biggest orchard state in th' union. When I went up there an' saw what they's a doin', I come back an' sowed all th' orchard in thick alfalfa.

"Frank Ames didn't 'ave t' use hardly any commercial fertilizer a tall, an' e never moved pruned limbs. 'E left 'em on th' ground all 'round th' trees. 'E 'ad a machine that would grind 'em up an' just put that ole organic matter right back in th' soil. I bought one o' them machines an' stopped haulin' th' pruned limbs outta th' orchard t' burn. I still use a orchard disc on th' peach trees, but I quit usin' it on th' apples alt'gether. On m' small orchard, I use a rototiller t' keep th' ground broken up. It don't go deep a'nuff t' hurt th' feeders. Two inches don't hurt. Sometimes I'll run this big orchard disk in there, but when I do I slant them discs so's they don't cut very deep.

"I once 'ad ten acres o' peaches that started gettin' yellow leaves. We 'ad a wonderful state entomologist who was with th' extension agency fer forty-one years. 'E was th' best authority there was fer farmers, so I showed 'im th' trees an' told 'im I thought they 'ad a disease called Texas Peach Yellows.

"'No, no. That's iron deficiency.'

"Whatta ya' mean, Doc? This soil's made out o' them red sandstone mountains all 'round. It's decomposed sandstone an' full o' iron. It shows up black in th' furrows half-a-day after I irrigate.'

"'That's true. It's full o' iron, but that iron's locked up. It ain't plant-available. Ya' need t' git yerself some iron sulphate. Then take a bar, poke down about ten inches, three feet out frum th' trunk o' th' tree, ever' two feet 'round th' tree, put a tablespoon full o' iron sulphate in each hole an' kick th' dirt in.'

"That was in February. Well, I didn't put much faith in it, so's b'fore I went t' all th' expense o' doin' th' whole orchard, I took four trees an' tried it. Them leaves come out, oh, great big dark green leaves. Doc knew what 'e was talkin' 'bout. I did th' whole orchard, an' it worked. That dadblamed ole iron was locked up, all right. Th' lady down here 'ad some Pyrocantha bushes with yellow leaves. I tole 'er what t' do, an' th' green leaves come out fer her too. I only 'ad t' do th' orchard that one time fer th' iron t' become plant available - didn't have t' do it agin. This winter I'll do it t' some o' th' trees in a young orchard I've got.

"With th' orchard, ya' don't have t' use a commercial fertilizer if ya've got a'nuff alfalfa or clover in there an' ya' knock it down in th' summer. M' friend up in Washington, 'e use t' give 'is orchards a boost in th' spring with five pounds o' '1620' t' th' peach tree. An' my, I'll tell ya', them orchards 'ad big, green leaves. They 'ad plenty o' food, see. If ya' put plenty o' food in there, you'll have success. If ya don't 'ave th' ground rich a'nuff, all th' insects in th' world will attack them plants. If th' plant's strong an' healthy, they don't bother ya' near as much. That's a fact with orchards. Wheat's another story. Insects'll jump on healthy wheat an' eat it up. Kind o' strange, but I'll tell ya' if ya' want t' b' in th' gardenin' business or th' orchard business, ya' got t' keep th' ground built up. Ya' deplete yer ground o' organic matter ye're not goin' t' b' successful."

To his grandson's question on how to build up depleted soil, Walter replied, "I ask Dr. Bartlett frum th' University o' Arizona that very question when I started in farmin' here on Oak Creek. I sent soil int' th' government agricultural extension service at th' University. They analyzed th' soil t' tell me what I lacked. Their report said I 'ad ever'thin' but organic matter. That's when I asked th' doc ('E'd alwa's come up here t' Oak Creek t' fish.) what I could do other than haulin' barnyard which was too fer t' make a lot o' trips. 'E tole me t' sow alfalfa really thick.

"'Cut it an' leave it an' in two years time ya' plow it all under. Ya"ll b' able t' grow anythin' that'll grow in yer climate.'

"So's, I put two acres in o' thick alfalfa t' try it out."

Then his grandson wanted to know if the dry grass was a fire hazard. Walt continued, "Now that's th' question I ask m' friend Frank Ames up in Washington when I saw alfalfa two foot high in 'is orchards. I said, 'Frank, ya've got a terrible fire hazard here, ain't ya'? When ya' cut that?' 'E took me out t' 'is implement shed an' showed me a big machine called a culti-cutter that 'e'd use t' cut it all down. If ya' don't cut it down usin' somethin' like that, ya'd have a fire hazard. When I saw that operation in Washington, I went straight int' Yakima t' th' Edwards Implement Company an' bought one o' them machines. It's seven foot wide. They use th' ten foot wide up there. Ya' travel 'bout five miles an hour on that piece o' machinery, an' it really cuts 'er down. That's what we did all th' time when Robert [his former son-in-law] farmed with me.

"But at th' first when I was just tryin' t' build up my soil on them two acres, I done what Doc told me fer two years. When I plowed that alfalfa under, it changed th' whole texture o' th' soil. It b'come real loose. Talk about a vegetable garden! I 'ad string beans a foot long - Kentucky Wonders. One picker picked 700 pounds workin' frum nine in th' mornin' t' three in th' afternoon. Imagine that! Seven hundred pounds!" This was the crop which was mentioned earlier that repaid the loan to his father-in-Law.

December and part of January was spent repairing equipment and catching up on loose ends, for pruning started as soon as it was warm enough to be outside, even for a part of the day. Walter preferred to be completely finished with this chore before the trees started blooming; however, there were many times that the task spilled into March with the blooms already open. In the early years before buying the culti-cutter, the trimmed branches were gathered and removed from the field. This job fell to the three children. There was also a twofold purpose for it was at this time that Ruth would replenish her supply of

Ruthie and Anne help Walter and Ed Jackson (on ladder) prune peach trees

"switches." Knowing that the cuttings collected for their Mother would most likely be used on them in the near future, it is amazing that the children competed with each other to provide the best branches. It was a matter of pride to have one of theirs chosen to join the cadre lying on the deer antlers in the cabin.

Walter pruned the peach trees so the branches would be rather low and wide with the center of each tree quite open. This made it much easier for the pickers. However, apple trees were trained to grow taller with limbs left longer forming a canopy that came almost to the ground. This method was devised by Walt to provide shade for the majority of the fruit, thus protecting them from the hot September weather and preventing them from sun burning. Mary Smith Wyatt, daughter of cowboy Ira Smith, recalls Walter teaching her father this method when they were experiencing trouble with sunburn on their apples. Acquiring the desired shape was accomplished by finding the bud pointing in the direction in which one wanted the tree to grow. This was called the leader bud. Folks were always surprised at how rapidly Walter and his Dad could look at a branch and start cutting. Some trees needed to be strengthened by being pruned very heavily, even taking out some big limbs. The next growing season's new growth could be as much as 6 feet high. The peaches always bloomed earlier than the apples making them more susceptible to frost, so these were trimmed first. He preferred to complete the pruning before preparing to protect the fruit from freezing. However, when the fruit bloomed early, this job had to be interrupted to provide time to bring the smudge pots/heaters into the field on the sled behind the diesel caterpillar tractor. One of these would be placed next to each tree. (See center for photos of peach trees and smudge pots)

After getting all of the pots into the orchards, tops needed to be removed, and dampers opened and cleaned, before filling them with diesel. Walter would call the Shell Oil distributor in Clarkdale, (about 25 miles away), to bring his truck out full of diesel. The truck would be driven through the fields with two persons following behind, each carrying one of the large hoses over his/her shoulder, squirting the thick, black liquid into the containers. With this part of the preparations completed, someone then went through the orchards putting lids back on and closing the dampers to prevent dust and dirt from getting inside. On evenings that were getting colder rapidly and firing the "pots" seemed inevitable, one of the teenagers would be sent out to open the dampers. At the onset of his smudging career, Walter waited to open dampers until beginning to light the heaters, only to find them frozen shut. A blowtorch was necessary to warm each one sufficiently to continue with the job and in the meantime fruit was lost to the cold. Hard experiences, such as this, producing financial loss were lessons never to be forgotten or ignored. Thus dampers were always opened before they became stuck closed. If temperatures hovered all night just above the point of firing, someone simply had to close them again in the morning. The type of these temperature raisers owned by Walt evolved from the small, approximately two gallon size with a "spider" across the top and no damper, to 5-10 gallon ones with a smoke stack and damper, to the larger, taller, more sophisticated, and much easier to regulate, smoke recirculating heaters.

As soon as the buds on the trees began to swell, Walter kept an "eagle eye" on the weather. He kept meticulous records and to some extent got a feel for what might be happening by comparing the current conditions with years past. He soon realized that when the wind blew from the northwest it was considerably colder than when it came from the northeast having moved across Oak Creek. The thermometers were checked regularly during the night when smudging was imminent or in progress to determine if a drop of water on a saucer was forming a skim of ice at 32 degrees. If not, was it at a colder or warmer temperature? With this information and knowing the killing temperature for each stage of blossom, he could adjust the point at which heaters had to be lighted and how many degrees to raise the temperature. Another hard lesson was learned when he discovered that there was a wide variance of temperature from one part of the ranch to another. One night after monitoring everything in his homemade weather station near the house, he determined that it was time to begin warming up the trees. Upon arriving in the northwest section of the orchard he was dismayed to find temperatures below killing level. And yes, nearly the whole crop was gone. A very tough way to discover that portion of his place was several degrees colder at all times than that at the house, which was approximately in the center of the property. The eastern part was much warmer due to the breeze coming from the creek via a gap in the hills and cutting across part of that property. This area could be protected by simply running water through the rows all night.

Ruth would check the thermometers, (no less than three side by side) every hour during the early part of the night but as it grew colder the alarm was set for every thirty minutes. She was to call Walter when it reached his specified temperature, which was always about two degrees above killing and varied according to the stage of the blooms. Many times the thermometer would see-saw up and down just above the danger mark, so he would get a full night's sleep and she very little. When he was called usually she went to bed after fixing sandwiches for the "smudging crew." It was almost like a roulette game for there was quite a chance being taken by waiting to the last minute to start. However, it was necessary to conserve oil as much as possible. On several occasions when having to fire early the oil did not last until sunrise, then the tractor with the sled was used to bring diesel and "pots" were filled by hand with five gallon buckets. As just prior to sunrise is the coldest time of the night, enough fuel was needed to enable him to open the dampers wider.

The torches consisted of a container for the gasoline and kerosene mix, with a long spout encasing the wick and a series of small screens for protection of the user. Walt had heard of a person who became impatient with his torch, removed the screens and when the wick was lit the flame moved rapidly into the main container, exploding and killing the individual. When the word was "Go!" each person took his/her torch, rammed it into the opening of the heaters, and ran to the next tree as soon as the whoosh and orange flame showed it was burning. F. Ruth(ie) committed another big no, no one night when only she and her Dad were firing pots in the fifteen acres of peaches. One was particularly slow to light, so after several attempts she stood on tip-toe, with torch still inserted, placed her face over the stack to try and discover the problem. Just at that moment it decided to ignite and whaaam, she was quickly minus eyebrows, and was sporting singed hair. Her unladylike verbage brought a scolding from Walt who was only a few trees away.

After all smudge pots were lit Walt informed the crew of the temperature he wanted maintained and the remainder of the night was spent monitoring thermometers in and outside the field and adjusting dampers. The crew would take turns going inside to have a bite to eat and a cup of coffee. Just at daybreak everyone was back in the orchards fighting that last gasp of cold from the atmosphere. As the sun peeked over the gorgeous red mountains a cheer would arise and all were rushing to close everything down to stop the burning and save oil. Then it was time to start the cycle over again, opening, cleaning, filling, closing and offering a "Thank you" for protecting the fruit one more time, along with a silent request for warmer weather the next night.

Temperature box, circa 1940

Walter felt that there must be a way to monitor the temperature without Ruth having to get up and go outside to check. To solve this he devised a thermostat that operated on dry cell batteries. As the weather became colder, two needles were drawn closer and closer together, until making contact, which rang a buzzer beside Walt's bed. Depending on the stage of the blossoms the setting would vary between twenty-eight and thirty-four degrees. This allowed everyone to get more sleep. To protect this apparatus, he built a small, covered platform with three sides enclosed by slats to allow the air to flow through. Originally he had only the thermometers placed on the side of a post.

Whenever discussing the smudging, he has a hearty laugh recalling one of Ruth's escapades. Let's first set the scene: the night was unusually cold early and Ruth was watching the thermometers. She was dressed in her regular bedtime attire, flannel pajamas, knee socks pulled up over the pants legs, a wool bandana tied up over her head, a wool scarf pinned around her neck, and a calf-length light blue robe. (With almost no fat on her tiny frame, she was nearly always cold. Also when her head was in a draft or cold she had violent headaches.) When going outside she topped off the outfit with a slightly shorter pink robe, Walter's heavy red and black mackinaw and gloves. Quite a colorful sight to behold!! Now, let the tale begin! Walt says, "I rushed in frum that peach orchard an' urgently yelled, 'Ruth come quick! I gotta 'ave yer help!'

"Naturally, that scared 'er an' Ruth come a'runnin' t' see what was th' matter. 'My goodness Walter, what's wrong? Is anybody hurt?'

"'No!' I told her, 'that damned ole temperature's a droppin' too fast! We ain't got a'nuff help t' light them big heaters fast a'nuff t' save that crop. Go quick an' see if ya' cin find anyone t' help me!' With that I turned on m' heel and headed back t' that field on a dead run!"

Here Ruth interrupts, "I knew that I had no time to change clothes so I grabbed the pink housecoat and heavy mackinaw, struggled into them, donned my gloves, snatched the keys to the big truck and ran out the door. You see, in those years we had no telephones so I had to go try to awaken some of the neighbors who had helped at other times. As I drove down the lane, I thought whose house should I go to first. Suddenly a bright idea dawned, maybe the bar was still open. I roared up to the front of the Oak Creek Bar, jumped out and ran to the entrance. As I stepped through the door I said in a rather loud voice, 'Is anyone in here sober enough to come help Walter smudge!?' Everyone turned to look at me and immediately all mouths fell open in unison. I do believe that they thought they were seeing 'pink elephants!' Well anyway I got two who came and worked all night in the orchard."

Walter continues, "I couldn't figger out what kept them fellers a laughin' most o' th' night when one o' 'em finally told me. Now don't ya think I was plenty embarrassed? Well, I sure was! When I come back t' th' house I said t' Ruth, 'M' Goodness alive woman! What on earth did ya do?! Don't ya know them men are al'ays gonna be a laughin' at me?'

"'Oh quit yer worryin' about it,' she tole me. 'I got yer help didn't I!?'" Walt starts laughing again while remembering the episode.

There was no question as to when pots and heaters were put in the field and were made ready. However, it was a bit more difficult decide on the removal date. Walter had two signs of nature upon which he relied heavily –one was when all of the snow was gone from Mingus Mountain and the other was when the leaves of the Mesquite trees had come out. However, one year not even these could be trusted as is noted in a letter written by Lawrence Jackson. "I worked for Walter last Saturday thinning Peaches. Walter is displeased about the lie the Mesquite trees told him. He took smudge pots out a week ago Sunday and had to put them in the next day to smudge that night. He also had to smudge the night of May 7."[8]

For three consecutive years in the early fifties nearly all of their peach crop was killed because it was so cold that even with all heaters and smudge pots roaring full blast the temperature couldn't be raised sufficiently. On night two he borrowed extra pots and night three started burning old tires in the orchard. Still the cold was so intense that very little of the fruit was saved. After rechecking his records, Walt discovered that all of these extreme temperatures came on the third night following an atomic test blast in southern Nevada. Feeling certain that this was the problem he wrote to the national weather service asking if was possible for those test to affect the weather so dramatically. Their reply assured him that it was so. He then asked what reimbursement was possible for the loss of the crops. Needless to say he was quite upset when the response was "None." This financial loss triggered the decision to begin selling part of his land for the incredible price of two thousand dollars an acre. Soon fifty acres became a subdivision. (George loudly and lengthily protested to Walter about underselling, for the younger brother was getting five thousand an acre along highway 89A, the year 1953)

When asked about his irrigation schedule, Walter began explaining. "Well, that depends on th' temperature. We 'ad terrific hot weather here too soon - 100 degrees, [referring to the current year in the mid 1980s]. I 'ad t' sprinkle here ever' week or five or six days. If ya' cultivate an' keep that soil loosened up, th' wind won't dry it out s' fast. S' I cultivate lots when we're a havin' t' do irrigation real often. If ya' let that dirt pack down an' git crushed over hard on top, ya'll have t' wet it twice as much. Broken up soil cin hold th' moisture twice as long. It's good t' have th' sprinklin' system 'cause if we 'ad t' still irrigate in furrows we couldn't come in an' disc an' mess up them ditches. And the peach orchard — the same thing. We don't use any big disks in them orchards an'more a tall. I've learned that frum experience up in th' northwest. They were destroyin' th' root system, an' they quit usin' th' big disks entirely. Them feeders come right up t' th' top. That's where th' richest soil's at — frum th' top down t' a foot.

"We'd irrigate them orchards ever' two weeks in June, July an' August. Ya' cain't let that orchard git dry. If ya' do, ya've stunted yer crop, yer apple or peach, an' you never cin build it up ag'in. We'd run that sprinklin' system 12 hours in a set b'fore we'd move it. That ground 'ad t' b' wet. If ya' put a shovel down int' th' ground after a good irrigatin' ya' shouldn't bring up any dry dirt. Ya' want that sandy, loam that we've got 'round here saturated down t' about 15 inches. Th' way t' know if ya've irrigated long a'nuff is t' dig down one foot frum th' top o' th' ground. Take a handful o' that dirt, press it in yer hand, then let yer fingers loose right quick like, an' if that dirt crumbles an' rolls off in a hurry, it ain't wet a'nuff an' certainly needs water. If it sticks together when ya' press tight an' doesn't fall away, it's moist a'nuff. If ya' let that soil git dryer than that, it's no good 'cause them feeders come right up t' th' top o' that ground in any soil. That's th' nature o' them fruit trees.

"When ya' irrigate, ya' also have t' fertilize b'cause th' water carries fertility in th' rich topsoil down through that sandy loam. Plantin' alfalfa or clover in th' orchard can really help with that. Alfalfa is what they use in th' state o' Washington. It won't deteriorate. Ya cain't hardly destroy alfalfa. I put that sprinklin' system in when I got back frum Washington b'cause ya' want that sprinklin' system t' rot th' leguminous organic matter. Up 'til that time, I'd been usin' th' capillary system – runnin' water int' deep furrows – t' irrigate. Sprinklin's a lot easier than th' capillary system. Fer instance in irrigatin' ya'll have them dang gopher holes. Ya' cain't keep 'em all killed out, an' yer water's agoin' down them gopher holes. Ya've got t' go find 'em an' plug 'em up. Terrible lot o' work! With th' sprinkler, th' holes don't make no difference. Th' water keeps agoin' on down an' down ever'where even like. That's why I use this sprinklin' system out here - this little plaything I got." His plaything was the small orchard of dwarf trees he had planted after selling the orchards for a subdivision.

"Now with vegetables ya do things kinda different. T' git ya'r root system down fairly deep when ya'r plantin' vegetables like beans an' corn, don't put th' seed down any deeper b'low th' furrow th'n two inches an' leave th' furrow open. [A small amount of dirt was placed over the seeds to prevent sunburn and blowing away.] Th' wind blows th' soil over, an' I may bring some in gradually as plants start growin'. By th' time th' ground is level, ya'll 'ave ya'r root system down pretty deep. I dig th' furrow 'bout four inches below th' surface an' just gradually build 'er up.

"With somethin' like carrots, if I'm goin' t' use th' sprinklin' system, I just sow in rows an' leave th' ground level. If ya'r are goin' t' use th' capillary system – waterin' with ditches - why, I plant two rows on top o' them ridges. That's th' way they do in them big fields with carrots. I'd say th' rows on top ought t' be six inches apart on th' ridge. Th' furrows or ditches fer th' water should be about two an' a half t' three feet apart. It depends, they 'ave t' make them furrows exactly t' fit their machinery. That's th' way they 'ave t' do with cotton. They 'ave t' plant that cotton th' width t' match them cultivators, an' they got t' b' plenty even or ya'll tear them plants up.

"Ya'd have t' thin them carrots t' a little over an inch apart. That's th' way I used t' do 'em, an' I'd haul 'em t' Phoenix. They liked carrots about one inch in diameter an' about eight inches long. Th' Danvers Half Longs were th' best variety I 'ad.

"With tomatoes, th' best way I've found frum experience t' keep them tomatoes frum catchin' southern blight frum dry, hot winds, is t' sew them seeds in a hill, right where ya' want t' leave them, so's ya never disturb th' root system. When they git big a'nuff, about three inches tall, don't leave more'un two tomato plants t' a hill. Th' reason I put two, is b'cause sometimes one will die o' th' southern blight an' th' other one won't.

"When I git plants t' set out, I like t' 'ave six er eight inch tall plants. I put th' root system down deep like settin' out a tree. They do fine that a way. If ya' buy th' big, thick plants frum a nursery an' they ain't left 'em out in th' cool t' git 'em use t' it, they're no good at all. I wouldn't 'ave 'em if they give 'em t' me!

"I use' t' grow lots o' cucumbers. We plant two kinds o' squash now - zucchini and crookneck. Them're th' ones we like best, but we used t' sell a lot o' summer squash - the little, flat, white squash. We'd plant th' squash down about two inches deep, three foot apart. Ya put about five seeds t' a hole, but don't put 'em all in one bunch. Scatter 'em out in a six inch distance, so's they won't b' all t'gether.

"Now I have a string bean that I've tried, an' it's a marvelous bean. I learned frum this man Taller in California. 'E grows pole beans. It's a type o' a pole bean. Ya don't 'ave t' put poles up er any fence er no'thin'. 'E wrote t' me about it. I saw 'is name on a crate o' beans in th' Bayless market one day - Taller Farms, s' I wrote t' 'im. 'E wrote me a long letter, an' 'e tole me t' plant them beans about an inch apart. That's very thick, but they hold each other up thata way. S', I planted them beans. They're an early bean: they'll come up frum seven t' ten days, an' they're bearin' beans ready t' eat in 51 days. That's what I've been a plantin' ever since.

"I use' t' grow worlds o' bush beans, an' I'd put th' big disc on th' bush bean field [turning them under] after th' plants quit bearin'. I'd git that stuff under th' ground as quick as I could b'cause beans are leguminous plants that draw nitrogen. Th' same thing with corn. I learned that frum Tom Pendley. [The Pendleys had a ranch further up Oak Creek at Slide Rock.] I couldn't see how 'e'd keep growin' corn in th' same place year after year. Just as soon as 'e got that crop off, 'e put down a big disk an' buried them big corn stalks under th' ground. 'E's got a bunch o' organic matter there without puttin' barnyard on. Then 'e'd use th' commercial fertilizer when 'is corn got t' b' twelve or fourteen inches high. 'E used 42% an' that's awful strong!, an' I think 'e tole me 'e used 200 pounds t' th' acre. 'E did grow th' corn! Now if 'e depended on straight commercial fertilizer entirely, in about three years 'e would've drawn all o' th' organic matter out o' th' soil, an' it wouldn't 'ave grown a thing. Wouldn't even grow black-eyed peas. I couldn't figure out how in th' world 'e was gittin' a'nuff organic matter, but 'e seemed t' an' them stalk's were pretty high. 'E didn't grow a real early corn b'cause it didn' git as big. 'E grew th' 85 day corn t' git th' great big ears. Pendley knew th' importance o' discin' 'is fields under as quick as possible after harvestin'. With th' corn I also 'ave t' go along an' pull suckers off. Some types o' hybrid corn sucker terrible. Now that means another shoot coming up at th' base that will take strength out o' th' main stalk. Oh, there's a lot t' this here gardenin'!"

Walter also grew strawberries between the fruit trees when the trees were young. In fact when their second daughter arrived, he waited to go to Flagstaff to see the newborn and Ruth until he had a load of strawberries picked. He then peddled them to grocers in town to help pay the doctor's bill. The physician also took some berries for part of his fees. It is rather ironic that this daughter grew up loving this particular fruit. So much so that when helping pick at age five or six she got into trouble with her Dad. Walt paid ten cents a basket to the pickers, and each basket was filled level full with loose berries. Then an extra big one was placed in each corner followed by filling in the side edges first and building like a pyramid until at the top of the center tier another large one was arranged. F. Ruth(ie) was picking and was about half way down the long row when Walter came to check on everyone. He looked in her basket seeing only a few berries and exclaimed, "My goodness alive, Sister! Is that all o' th' berries ya've picked. What 'ave ya' been a'doin'? Eatin' 'em all?" With eyes cast down and tears starting to well-up, she meekly gave a slight nod of her head. "Well, I cain't afford t' 'ave ya' eatin' all o' th' profits. Ya' come with me, an' I'm a'goin' t' 'ave ya' start weedin' carrots." This happened to be her least favorite job on the whole ranch, so she determined right then and there as soon as she was allowed back in the strawberry field, she would use all available willpower to not eat any until the picking was finished. As an adult she looked on the experience as not being too bad, because it did add to the development of a strong will which served her well in later years, and she still loved strawberries.

As with all other plants, strawberries thrived with

care particularly suited to their needs. When asked about this Walter replied, "Oh yes, I 'ad lots o' strawberries. I 'ad 'em out on th' ridges, set th' plants about two feet apart, an' let th' vines git thick all over that ridge. I went out t' visit th' strawberry fields in Alhambra, California, t' see how th' Japanese do it. They're about th' best there is in growin' truck gardens, ya' know. They use a special band saw t' keep them vines frum runnin' all over th' ridge. They keep cuttin' 'em back until they 'ave big, bushy plants about 12 or 14 inches apart. They'd take this band saw that they've rigged in a circle an' come down over that plant choppin' th' runners off. Them plants spread out 14 inches around, an' they really 'ad th' strawberries. That cuttin' throws more strength on th' berries instead o' lettin' them vines be too thick."

In the spring all three children would anxiously await Walter's return from his daily excursions into the strawberry patch. Disappointment reigned if he could be seen with his hat on his head, but excitement exploded if he was carrying his hat in his hands. This indicated that the first berries had ripened and he had picked them, placing the luscious fruit in his hat while walking to the house.

Insects and pests were a constant challenge for any farmer or gardener. "Ya' sure gotta dust fer insects with them tomato seedlings, an' them carrots, or th' insects'll eat 'em all up. With th' corn ya' 'ave t' watch fer worms when th' silks starts a comin' on th' ear. I use a chemical called 'Sevin' - liquid Sevin - on th' corn. On th' tomato plants I'll use Sevin dust. I use th' liquid on th' corn b'cause it soaks int' th' silk better an' it'll stop them worms. I spray about three times b'cause some o' them ears ain't in silk an' if you don't spray in th' silk, yer're not goin' t' stop that worm. If ya' wait too long, th' egg's in there an' th' damage is already done.

"We'd a bird that was terrible in them peach orchards. I tried everythin' I ever heard o' t' keep them birds outta there. We hung fruit jars lids in th' branches so's when there was a breeze they'd hit together an' make a tinklin' sound; we hired kids, t' walk up an' down through them rows bangin' on pans an' them danged ole birds'd just fly over a couple o' trees an' start a peckin' on peaches there, well ya r'member, 'cause ya were some o' them kids that done that; we even put up a carbide gun that went off ever' few minutes, but them awful things'd just look at it an' even sit on top o' it after they got use t' it. We didn't find n'thin' that'd work 100 percent. After we sold them orchards, they come out with a plastic nettin' t' keep them pesky birds offa th' trees. Well, since I only 'ave 'bout eleven trees now, I bought a'nuff o' them bird nets t' go over th' top an' we pile dirt all around th' bottom an' it keeps them birds off. [The whole family got a huge laugh from watching Walt storm out of the house and into the orchard when he had spotted a bird inside the netting. Crawling under the netting he began chasing the intruder, swatting at it with a shovel, assisted by much yelling, some cursing, and a lot of arm waving.] It sure is expensive t' do it thata way t' keep 'em off. O' course ya only 'ave t' b' out th' big expense onct b'cause ya take th' nets off an' roll 'em up an' save 'em fer th' next year, an' them birds don't bother us a tall."

Thrip are another insect that can ruin a crop, and it seemed the apples were especially susceptible. After the blossoms have been attacked, the small stem turns brown and the petals and tiny unpollinated fruit drop off. Spraying was the only solution, and over the years Walt used a variety of chemicals. "That Black Leaf Forty was th' best stuff fer killin' them little fellers. But it was sure tough on th' bees. Then th' government outlawed th' use o' it, so's then we used DDT. It was outlawed an' we went t' another kind o' spray that didn't really do th' job. We always 'ad a big problem with them awful spring winds. We'd 'ave t' git up terrible early t' get th' sprayin' done b'fore th' wind got t' blowin'. Ya r'member Anne'd drive that Farmall Tractor that pulled the sprayer. [We all learned to drive the tractors, then the Model A, next the car and last, but not least, the trucks.] When it's really blowin' them bees won't fly a'tall so's th' blossoms couldn't git pollinated."

In planning the layout of the apple orchard one major consideration was which trees were self-pollinators and were the others close enough for the bees to carry pollen to them. As bees work over a bloom the pollen sticks to their legs so that when moving to another bloom some of the original pollen is carried and deposited there. This cross-pollination is necessary for the nonself-pollinator varieties to produce fruit. When purchasing the apple trees he asked Stark Brothers Nursery what was their best self-pollinating tree. The reply was "Jonathan." Thus he had many Jonathan trees near the Stark's Red Delicious for the purpose of pollination. In his words, "Low an' b'hold them darned ole' Jonathan come int' bloom ahead o' them delicious. I 'ad other pollinators in that orchard but they's a too far away. I figger'd I better do somethin' quick if I was a gonna have any crop a tall. So's I come t' th' house an' asked Ruth what she thought o' th' idee o' me a takin' an' cuttin' some blooms offa them pollinators an' a hangin' 'em up in them Red Delicious trees. That's what I done. I hung what I called bees' buckets in th' middle o' them trees. They looked like big bouquets o' apple blossoms. I'd drive nails on either side o' a big tree about in th' middle an' string a wire acrost t' hang a can o' water on. Then I put in a bouquet o' a different variety so's th' bees would cross-pollinate. Th' state agent who come out never'd seen anythin' like that done b'fore.

"Well, I done somethin' else too. I'd go t' this here beeman down towards Cornville an' git 'im t' bring some o' 'is hives up here an' put 'em out in that apple orchard. Thata way them bees don't 'ave s' fer t' fly an' on windy days they could work at least a little bit.

"I needed t' protect m' strawberries from quail, so's one year I went down t' see what Mr. Spain down in Buckeye [west of Phoenix approximately 35 miles], was a'doin'. 'E showed me how t' make this trap. 'One time,' 'e said, 'I caught 12 dozen quail in this thing.'

O' course, 'e 'ad a large trap. I didn't want t' make one near that large, so's I could set it up in th' bushes. Ya want me t' tell what happened? [Naturally the listeners answered in the affirmative.] Well, all right. I 'ad that trap settin' in them bushes an' th' next day I went back t' see what 'ad happened. M' father went with me t' look at th' trap, an' we 'ad twelve quail in there. Since I'd left a place so's I could stick m' arm in t' catch 'em, I'd grab one an' pull it out. Then I wrung their necks – took them heads right off. Father said, 'Son, I don't like t' see ya do that. Somethin' is liable to happen.'

"I told father, 'Well they's eatin' them strawberry blooms off. What am I agoin' do? Let 'em eat m' crop up?'

"'Well, son, I sure don't like t' see ya' do that. Somethin' awful's gonna happen.'

"Well, it did happen, just like Dad said somethin' would. Th' next year we 'ad this migratory grasshopper called th' Mexicayla, which was known t' go through two states in one summer, an' they were terrible thick. Th' government man come up frum Tempe an' made a check, an' there was an average o' 36 grasshoppers per square yard. I called our farm agent in Flagstaff. 'E come down. 'Is name was Luker, an' 'e said let's go over an' meet th' head man o' th' CCC Camp. [Civilian Conservation Corps] That was where th' King's Ransom is today. [Originally built for movie filming personnel, including actors and actresses. Later it became a Quality Inn.] We went on over there an' th' boys tole th' fellas they 'ad a Dodge truck. They put men in th' back o' th' truck, an' they 'ad a hopper in b'hind th' truck. They fixed it so's that when they put that poison bran in there an' traveled about 15 miles an hour, it would scatter th' poison bran a width o' about 60 feet. And where they couldn't get t' it with the truck, them boys took th' poison bran an' scattered it b' hand. Our ditches where I irrigated were just full o' worlds o' them dead grasshoppers, an' it killed 'em all, but one thing I noticed, b'fore we'd poisoned 'em, at least 300 feet all 'round m' big reservoir, I noticed there weren't no grasshoppers a tall. Not even a single one. I b'gan t' investigate an' I discovered, lo an' b'hold, there was two big families o' quail an' they 'ad their little ones with 'em an' they'd simply annihilated them grasshoppers fer at least 300 feet around that reservoir in any direction. So, I did what m' father'd said t' do. 'Don't kill them quail, son.'

"When I discovered what them quail were a'doin', I figured they was doin' me more good than they were damage, so I never killed anymore o' them quail."

As often happened when telling things he would backtrack to a previous subject. "Now this here's somethin' I forgot t' tell ya' about them orchards. Ya know there's a lot o' science t' keepin' them orchards. We 'ad t' thin th' fruit on them trees as soon as th' apple drop was over. That's when th' apple's formed an' th' king bloom is th' center one. 'E's alwa's th' strongest. That's how nature provided for thinnin', that center one'll be left when them others fall off, Ya'll do injury if ya don't wait until after th' apple drop in about th' middle o' May. Th' up-t'-date thinnin' method is with chemicals spayed on. It's too danged expensive t' hire hand-thinners an'more, an' through scientific research we know th' exact strength o' chemical necessary. If ya' don't git 'em thinned quickly, ya' won't 'ave much o' a crop th' next year b'cause all fruit trees sets their fruit fer th' next year in June. Th' chemical thinnin's so quick that production has really increased. Th' fruit buds that ya' 'ave in June are there all winter. Both them apples an' peaches set their fruit buds in th' spring. If ya' hand thin, ya' got t' know th' difference b'tween th' leaf buds an' th' fruit buds. Them fruit buds is round an' plump lookin'. Th' leaf bud's sharp."

When asked, "How far apart did you thin the apples?" he replied, "About six inches. A little more if ya' want 'em bigger. Six inches will give ya' apples that'll pack 88 t' a box. They'll be right around three inches acrost. Mr. Quinn used t' sell t' th' Arizona Club an' th' Westward Ho. Them fancy places wanted them great big ones.

"Th' biggest apple we ever growed, well, it weighed better than a pound. It wouldn't go through th' chute. [Meaning the apple wiper and grading machine.] Th' biggest peach was one an' a half pounds. That's th' Alberta peach (correctly spelled and pronounced Elberta) yer mother 'ad on display in th' store. It was th' biggest peach I ever saw er ever heard o'. While she 'ad it on display, one quite old lady, sittin' in th' rockin' chair while Ruth waited on several other folks in there, ast if she could buy that peach. There was one place on it that was startin' t' spoil, an' I knew it wasn't goin' t' keep fer long, so's when I found out she was frum Sun City, I said, 'Well, it ain't fer sale but I'll tell ya what I'm agoin' t' do. I'll give it t' ya if ya'll take it down t' Sun City an' show it 'round. Tell 'em how th' Jordans grow big peaches up here in Oak

Creek Canyon.' Oh, she was tickled t' death an' I told 'er that I'd been in th' fruit business all m' life an' that was th' largest peach I ever seen er ever heard o'. (See center for picture of Walter and his apples.)

"We let th' peaches grow larger than th' apples. Sixty peaches t' a box was fair but 48 t' a box was what we were aimin' fer. Four an' a halves' we use' t' call them big fellas b'cause o' how far acrost they measured an' how many'd fit acrost a lug box. We thinned 'em never less than six inches, staggerin' 'em around th' limb like we did with th' apples. Th' reason we 'ad such big Alberta peaches that one year was b'cause th' frost killed quite a few o' 'em. After that frost, they was ten inches er a foot apart. When ya see 'em grow so much bigger, it's b'cause they git so much more sap. If ya' leave them peaches or apples on a tree just as thick as they'll stick, ya' won't git big uns."

Even with all of the thinning the apple branches would be so heavy they'd start drooping too much and to prevent the branches from breaking he put props, wooden 2X4s fastened together, under the most heavily laden limbs. One year, despite all of his precautions, a big apple tree with an enormous crop split right down the middle of the trunk. Walter got a man to help him fasten steel plates to the opposite sides of the trunk, then drilled it and ran a heavy cable all the way through. He brought the two tractors and secured one end of the cable to each machine. He and his helper drove their tractor in opposite directions, gradually pulling that huge tree back together. As Walt says, "That dadgummed ole tree didn't even know th' difference. Why it just kept right on agrowin' an' was still producin' apples when I sold that part o' th' orchard!"

"Shippin' them peaches down t' Phoenix sure was improved b' th' cup separators in them boxes. We could git 'em down there in s' much better condition. We were also shippin' th' biggest, 3 1/2's maybe some 4 1/2's t' Charlie Ward at Brown an' Bigelow in Rochester Minn. fer their advertisin'. 'E tole ever'body that 'e grew 'em on 'is ranch, Rancho Roco Rojo. Why, we even 'ad t' stick in on top o' every flat [same size as a lug only instead of two layers there was only one] a paper peach-shaped bib givin' that name! We didn't care what name was in there fer 'e paid big money. We packed 'em only one layer deep with excelsior on top an' bottom, then nailed a top over that flat. We hauled them t' Flagstaff where we loaded 'em int' refrigerated boxcars.

"One year I 'ad too many fer m' own cold storage so I rented some space frum George. 'E 'ad refrigeration down there, but it wouldn't lower th' temperature b'low 42 degrees. We needed 36 degrees t' really preserve peaches fer th' trip t' market. If Bill Bevens 'adn't come up an' bought s' many ripe peaches, we woulda lost a lot. I remember tellin' yer mother, 'Why 'e'll 'ave peach jam all over th' road cause 'e was a'haulin' 'em loose.' Well, lo an' b'hold next mornin' about 10 o'clock, 'e called me.

"'Jordan, 'ave ya' got any more o' them peaches?'

"'Why, yes! We got plenty o' 'em. What in th' world did ya do? Ya ain't sold all o' them peaches a'ready?'

"'I called m' best customers an' tole 'em if they wanted peaches frum Oak Creek, they'd better git over here fast. They swarmed m' place an' cleaned me out in a little over an hour.'

"'E bought 75 lugs in th' first load an' ordered 100 more t' b' picked up th' next day. 'E sold 'em s' fast 'e was back th' day after that fer another 100 lugs. I think I let 'im 'ave 375 lugs total an' Ruth was a'sellin' 'em like fury outta th' store."

Walter had a similar experience with the apples one summer after a very severe hailstorm. Amazing, but true, a green apple is softer than a green peach, so when the hail comes in June or July a large portion of the apples left on the trees are lumpy and soft in spots. A man came from Phoenix looking for inexpensive Oak Creek Fruit and for three days in a row dumped 120 boxes into his pickup, paying $1.00 a box. It was enough to help pay the hired help those days.

"Ruth's sister, Lena, lived in Tempe an' she 'ad folks who was just crazy t' git Oak Creek peaches, s' she 'ad me bring th' seconds o' both peaches an' apples t' her an' she sold 'em off o' her front porch. Most o' th' time she 'ad more orders ahead than we could fill.

"There's this one variety o' apple that we grew, it was a marvelous cookin' apple an' that 'un was called th' Stayman Winesap, but it 'ad a bad peculiarity. When ya 'ad lots o' moisture, rain in th' summer, an' th' fruit got 'bout half growed, them apples'd start t' crackin' open. T' stop that from happenin', we mixed a powder called Bordeaux in water an' sprayed it on th' trees. Bordeaux's a mixture o' copper sulphate, an' we hated t' use it b'cause it'd stunt th' growth o' th' apple. I use a chemical called Stay Fast t' keep them apples frum fallin' off o' th' trees. By usin' that properly, ya' cain't hardly push them apples off with yer thumb an' finger when they git ripe. If ya' don't use it up here, th' wind'll 'ave half o' yer crop on th' ground. I usually spray that Stay Fast 'bout th' first o' September. Sometimes we 'ad t' use it twice when it was terrible hot an' dry.

"Now ya' see, this here orchard business an' commercial gardenin's a full time job, an' ya' 'ave t' b' on yer toes all th' time a'learnin' all ya' cin. My, oh my, th' things I've done in m' lifetime! Why they'd fill a book!"

With a sigh Walt indicated he would, in some

ways, like to step back in time to his younger years of greater activity. However he was quick to add he didn't miss a lot of the hard work. "Yeah," he said, "I guess this ole man's gotta 'nuff t' do in this little orchard an' garden." Ending his session with his grandsons, he "headed out" to his "miniature farm" to examine the soil for moisture and the plants to be sure no insects had taken up residence. Even though the remaining area of fruit trees and vegetables was small, the same activity schedule was necessary. Summarizing his discussion of tasks done in certain months, it is easy to understand the year-round job, although some months involved much more work than others:

January: catching up on additional repairs on equipment and buildings, starting the pruning if weather permitted.

February: pruning and some specialized fertilizer for the peaches.

March: complete pruning and put smudge pots into the orchards. (Depending on the weather, this could be done in Feb.) Constant watching of the weather and smudging.

April: begin thinning peaches, cleaning ditch that fed the pump and power plant, trimming strawberry plants and possibly smudging.

May: putting buckets of blooms in apple trees, bringing beehives, removing smudge pots, irrigating could start as well as cultivating, picking strawberries, spraying, and planting vegetables.

June: thinning continued, knocking down alfalfa growing between trees, cultivating, thinning carrots, spraying vegetables and fruit.

July: starting to pick peaches and maybe some beans, irrigating every two weeks, fertilizing some due to regular irrigating, making wooden boxes for fruit, (mostly peach lugs) and preparing to begin major harvest.

August: harvesting peaches, a few apples and beans, marketing in Phoenix, and dusting corn.

September: completing harvesting of peaches and beans, spraying Stay Fast on apples, major harvesting of apples begun.

October: fertilizing all of fields, or the planting of alfalfa, harvesting carrots and a few apples.

November: continuing carrot harvest, hauling wood for the house.

December: repairing farm equipment, buildings, pumping and generating equipment.

Walter and his father could be described as true orchardists learning from each other, plus continually experimenting and finding new methods that enabled them to be more successful.

It is evident from Walt's attempt to dry farm with his Dad that water is an important commodity in almost all types of farming and raising of fruit. Some of Walter's numerous challenges in getting water to his ranch are described in the next chapter, Wheeling the Water, and the drama of Oak Creek Canyon continued.

FOOTNOTES

(1) Hokanson, Paula, personal letter to F. Ruth, July 26, 2002

(2) Ibid

(3) Hokanson, Paula e-mail to F. Ruth August 1, 2002

(4) Jordan, Helen unpublished diaries

(5) Ibid

(6) The Random House College Dictionary, revised edition, Random House Publishers, NY, 1975, page 176

(7) Ibid, p. 572

(8) Jackson, Lawrence. Letter written to Perry and Robert Jackson, May 9, 1950,   Paragraph 5

Submitted by Marybelle Human Smith

Tunnel along road in Oak Creek Canyon, 1929 Art Human (son of Mary E. Bristow and James W. Human), daughter Marybelle in back of truck

George's and Helen's ranch, circa 1929, currently in uptown Sedona (Helen's paint smudges)

One of George's sales flyers, 1940s

1946 - Elsie here
1947 - Bldg. all finished
Iron stove

1948

June	19			5 00
	20	Sunday		17 25
	21			13 45
	22			11 50
	23			9 47
	24			10 83
	25	Friday		16 20
		Week's Sales		83 70
June	26	Saturday		31 52
	27	SUNDAY		41 72
	28	closed most of day (went to Flag.)		3 05
	29	" (Red Bird Clinic)		1 17
	30			9 3
July	1			19 00
	2	Pd out. Berries etc.	26 00	26 53
		Weeks Sales		118 8
July	3	Sat.		36 94
	4	Sun		94 93
	5	Mon. Picnic		1 43 12
	6	Tues. aunt stayed		33 4
	7	Wed. this week		31 60
	8	Thurs.		3 36
	9	Fri. Pd out	47 82	25 26
		Total for week		350 91

Sample of Helen's sales ledger mid 1940s

Chapter Ten
WHEELING THE WATER

All of the variations of the origin of the name, Arizona, relate to water, or the lack of it. Appropriately so, for undeniably, water is the one most sought after resource in the territory/state. From the ancient dwellers to present humankind the challenges of storing and channeling this essential commodity have been a constant and unparalleled effort. The Hohokams built large ditches to transport river water to irrigate their fields, with many of the current canals in the Salt River Valley following the same routes. The settlers constructed earthen dams across creeks and arroyos in the attempt to catch and store as much as possible of the run-off from the higher areas. Battles have been fought and lives lost over the rights to watering holes. Coupled with the need for storage reservoirs was their desire to control the yearly flooding, triggered by melting snow in the high mountains to the north and east. The need for storage was magnified by a five-year record drought which was dashing the dreams of many, and causing a major exodus from the Salt River Valley. Some days departing wagon trains stretched as far as the eye could see. Eventually the remaining folks began exploring ways to tame the river and preserve the water.

As individuals, or even as communities and towns, they lacked the resources to accomplish this seemingly insurmountable task. Fortunately, President Teddy Roosevelt understood the situation that confronted not only Phoenix, but other areas of the west as well. "In 1902, he signed the National Reclamation Act, which allowed the federal government to harness the arid frontier's water with a system of dams and reservoirs."[1] Unlike a century later, the government wasn't just handing out money — they wanted a guarantee on a long-term loan for construction. The Salt River having been chosen as one of the first five projects, residents now had their answer within their grasp, but how to underwrite a loan of several million dollars was another huge dilemma. At last valley leaders realized their only option was to pledge "all the land they owned."[2] On Feb. 7, 1903, they took this big leap of faith, forming a co-op for water and power that later became known as The Salt River Project. (A hundred years later SRP continues as a public utility, the third largest in the nation. The dam cost twice the estimated amount, totaling $10 million, the final loan payment being made in 1955.) With the loan guaranteed, construction could begin. Built by Italian masons using rock, it is the highest masonry dam in the world and during the 1990s was extended 70 feet higher. In March 1911, Theodore Roosevelt dedicated the dam bearing his name. This became the first, as well as the furthest upstream, in a chain of four dams to be built on the Salt River. The next one to be constructed is Horseshoe Dam that backs up Apache Lake. The third is Mormon Flat Dam, named for the Mormon people who established a tent village of about 4000 people who lived in the area now buried by Canyon Lake which formed behind this dam. The last one to be completed is Stewart Mountain Dam, constraining Saguaro Lake. These four structures not only gave flood protection, but also provided water and hydro-generated power for the Phoenix area. The wide variety of recreational opportunities available at the lakes continues to be an added bonus.

The power of the flooding prior to the building of the system of dams became evident in 1979 and 1980. Warm rains on top of a deep snow pack in the mountains filled the reservoirs along both the Verde and the Salt to overflowing, causing all of the flood gates to be opened. The Salt River (into which the Verde River feeds) was sending one hundred eighty-six thousand cubic feet of water per second through Phoenix. None of the river crossings had been made to accommodate torrents of that magnitude. The only full bridge that could be used was the old Mill Avenue Bridge in Tempe. This bridge had been built in the 1930's by prisoners from Florence State Prison, and folks joked that it must have been the "free labor" that made it so strong. By closer examination credit had to be given to the geology of the area, recognizing that this was the only bridge constructed where the pilings could reach to bedrock. Other partial available crossings were the westbound lanes of Interstate-10 and the Central Avenue bridge.

With the completion of the dams on the Salt River, water became a much more steady resource, but an additional problem was created. The water table began to drop throughout the Valley since it was not being replenished by the flooding, thus the farmers had to drill their wells deeper. The decreasing ground water table has been an issue for a long time.

In the late 1940s, Arizona congressmen began lobbying to get Colorado River water to the desert towns and farms of Arizona. A few years later a relative newcomer to congress from Arizona, John J. Rhodes Jr., became the champion of the project. The Arizona Republic newspaper states: "...former Interior Secretary Stewart Udall said Monday [Aug. 25, 2003] from his home in Santa Fe, 'He [Rhodes] was the single most important person in the authorizing and construction of the Central Arizona project.'"[3] It was largely through his efforts that in 1968 President Lyndon Johnson signed a bill approving funding and construction of the CAP. Approximately twelve years later [nearly forty years since its inception] the first water flowed through the Central Arizona Project Canal into the Salt River Valley. Why so long? Because of the battle between Arizona and California, each insisting on a larger share of the water, and the electricity generated at Hoover Dam on the Colorado River. Arizona felt short-changed in both areas, pointing to the division of power, as evidenced by the sizes of the substations. After crossing over the Hoover Dam, driving toward Las Vegas, there is a huge substation on the north side of the highway. That's for electricity going to Los Angeles. A little bit further, on the other side of the road there's a little tiny substation. That's for electricity bound for both Arizona and Nevada. The struggle for adequate water and electricity continues and can only become worse as long as there remain no constraints placed on building, growth and development. In Sedona, the Jordan family was intimately involved with "wheeling the water" and power into place. Walter and his family had water rights on the Verde River. When he started his ranch in Sedona in 1928, he needed water. Although he had tried dry farming for one year with his father, it just wasn't satisfactory. He was able, after many months of trying and several appearances before the state water commission, to have the water rights he had on an acre parcel along the Verde River transferred to Sedona. This was possible as Oak Creek was a tributary to the Verde.

> In [1926], Jordan, Sr. [Will Jordan] acquired extensive acreage in what is now the main part of Sedona. He was joined in its operation by sons Walter and George. In 1929, George bought the original 175 Sedona acres from his father, and for a while operated the tract with his brother, Walter.
>
> In [1928], Walter Jordan took over 65 acres of a nearby dry farm, which his father had acquired in a trade with Jesse Purtymun. Walter then fought for and won water rights for the area, and from that time on the brothers operated the two farms separately.
>
> When Highway 89A was put through Sedona in the 1930's, the Sedona area began to grow, and in the early 1940's George Jordan put in the first public water system here. He operated this until his retirement six years ago.[4]

Walter gives the specifics of the Jordan's arrival in Sedona. "M' father paid Claude Black fer 175 acres at th' mouth o' Oak Creek Canyon. There was about 3 acres on th' lower end that Father 'ad t' give up. That left about 172 acres o' land, an' there was quite a lot o' it down in th' creek bottoms. Father stayed there that summer in 1926. (Water for this ranch was provided by the Owenby Ditch, which had its head approximately one and one-half miles up the creek. Among those who were provided water from this source were Purtymuns above Jordans and Farleys below.) There was some trees, but 'e set out a good number more o' trees down there, an' 'e irrigated 'em an' harvested. But, oh my! 'E got terrible, terrible homesick b' livin' there alone, an' 'e said that that ole wind'd come down th' canyon ever' night, it'd rattle all them windows an' keep 'im awake. 'E got awful lonesome, so m' oldest brother Chester come up fer a time t' run th' place, but that left Father runnin' th' Verde place without a son t' help. I don't remember where Chester's wife, Pauline, stayed. That was b'fore they moved t' California. I was up at th' Woods Ranch an' George was back in New York goin' t' school. 'E was takin' a electrical engineerin' course, an' 'e was about half through it. 'E thought too much o' Dad bein' there on th' Verde alone, so's 'e quit 'is engineerin' course. 'E come out t' Sedona an' went in with Dad."

When George and Helen married in the early part of 1928, they came to Sedona and moved into the house that George's father had lived in. Helen was thankful for "running water" in the house, but it did have its drawbacks. "Our water supply for the farm came from the creek down the irrigation ditch, and a hydraulic ram pumped it directly to the kitchen faucet, which made it bad when the ditch was being cleaned, or the creek was muddy."[5]

Walter refers to the time spent on the Woods ranch as he explains how he became involved in Sedona. "I come off o' th' mountain in 1927. I'd experimented with growin' vegetables there fer th' Phoenix market It didn't pay off, an' I give it up. Father owned a 65-acre dry farm that he'd traded fer with Jess Purtymun. [This was located about one and a half miles west of Oak Creek.] Jess wanted a smaller farm down near th' creek s' my Dad cut 12 acres off o' 'is 172 acres, includin' th' creek an' give 'im $1000 t' boot fer th' 65-acres. When I come down off o' th' mountain, 'e asked me what I was goinna do. I told 'm I didn't know. I didn't have nothin' o' m' own right then.'

"'Well, why don't ya come in with me here on this 65 acre dry farm? We'll put out a big orchard an' grape vines.'

"'I told 'im I didn't like dry-farmin', an' 'e told me how Charlie Willard 'ad a big orchard out 15 miles t' th' west o' us.'

"'Yes, but that place is different than this. There's water! Lots o' water comes offa them bluffs. That place is self-irrigated, lots o' it,' I tole 'im.'

"Some o' them old timers dug wells. They didn't have t' go down much more than 50 feet deep fer water, maybe a 100, but very rarely b'cause they 'ad t' b' han' dug. Then they 'ad t' use cut stone t' wall th' sides o' th' well t' keep it frum cavin' in. [It does seem incredible that the settlers could dig down 100 feet with out a major disaster from cave ins.] Now [1980's] they have t' go down 600 t' 800 feet most places. Th' only other source o' water at th' time I put in th' pump an' turbine was a cistern or reservoir back b' Hancock's place fer catchin' water offa' th' mountain.

"Well, anyway, 'e persuaded me t' go in with 'im, an' 'e give me half interest. I rented George Black's Fortune tractor an' 'ad t' do a lot o' work t' git that place in shape. Dad furnished th' trees - 600 peach trees, 5000 grapevines, an' I helped put 'em all out. Th' first thing we 'ad t' contend with was them darned ole jackrabbits. We'd t' put a chicken wire fence all around th' whole dang thing t' keep them buggers out. Then th' deer jumped that dadgummed fence, an' we 'ad trouble with 'em. Then there was th' drought. Oh, it was terrible, terrible dry. I knew it wouldn't pay, an' I told Dad I wasn't gonna stay there another year without a way t' irrigate them crops.

"B'fore my first summer o' dry farmin' here was over, I'd begun contactin' big companies that were in th' line o' makin' water wheels an' turbines, an' I got lots o' data an' learned how t' measure water in miner's inches usin' a weir. That's a dam ya put across where

Water wheel almost completed early 1930s

ya're gonna run th' water. Ya cut a openin' a certain width, an' ya' measure th' pond ya' backed up with th' dam. Then ya' turn your water in, so many gallons a minute, or miner's inches. Th' Arizona rule is 11 gallons o' water per minute t' a miner's inch.

"From a'studyin' m' books on pipe lines an' such, I settled on a Fitz Overshot Wheel made in Hanover, Pennsylvania, as th' thing we needed. Th' company wanted $10,000 fer th' wheel an' th' pump would'a been $1,125 in Seneca, New York. Dad said that was way too much.

"'Ya'd have more in the water system than I paid George Black fer th' first 172 acres by th' creek!'

"S' George took th' pattern fer our wheel off'a th' picture in m' Fitz Waterwheel Catalog. 'E built it after I got th' pump in an' ended up keepin' it at 'is place."

The actual building of this wheel not only involved George but Helen as well, if only for her patience. She was an excellent housekeeper, "with a place for everything, and everything in its place." She remembered with pride George's talents to build many types of things, but it is easy to imagine her frustration with the process. "When we cleared more land and planted a large orchard above the ditch, George decided to build a water wheel to pump the water to a large open reservoir above the orchard, and also to a large storage tank for the house. He built an overshot wheel, 20 feet in diameter, which was powered by the ditch water. He built the wheel on the living room floor over the winter. He cut the buckets for the wheel, and riveted them by hand. This water wheel worked perfectly for many years and was a favorite subject for photographers."[6] (See center for paintings of water wheel) [Part of the time-share development of Arroyo Robles encompasses the area where the water wheel serviced the farm and community for over 40 years.] Helen briefly states reasons for George's involvement in developing the "city" water system: "We eventually got good roads. The highway from Phoenix came through to Sedona in 1940, and more people came to Sedona to live, but the town needed a good water supply in order to grow, so George was persuaded to dig a well and start a water system for the community. The well was approved by the health department, but it was a difficult task to get the pipe lines to the scattered settlement through the rocky terrain, and even hard to find good pipe during war time. As more and more people came, and subdivisions were developed, the pipeline was extended across the creek and on down to the Broken Arrow subdivision. This was the beginning of the Sedona Water system which is now the Arizona Water Company."[7] After starting the water company for the community, George also used the wheel as a booster pump to assist in lifting water to the tanks Helen mentioned. While he was out digging trenches, laying pipelines, and setting meters, her task was to watch the white flags on the outside of the redwood tanks, high on Water Tank Hill. These were attached to floats on the inside and as the water went down the flags went up. When these reached a certain height, Helen would go start the electric pumps in the well and the water wheel to replenish the supply.

Walter's pumping station and generator was approximately one mile north of Sedona. The settling pond and penstock are still visible along the side of highway 89A where a funny little rock house sits right over the edge of the bluff. (This was added by some other folks around 1980). Beside it is a fountain and that looks like a big waterfall - that is the excess water from the ditch, returning to the creek. Before going over the cliff, the water rests in a small pond, which has been covered over. At first Walter left the pond open and accessible to passersby. He knew that the road up Oak Creek Canyon was, at best, steep and precarious, often causing car radiators to boil over. He felt that this gave folks an opportunity to easily replenish their water supply. One morning upon arriving to oil the pump and clean the settling pond he found people washing their feet in the water and another time someone was washing dirty diapers. He promptly informed all that the water was used for drinking and asked that they only use it for their cars or human consumption. After the diaper episode he had Helen paint a large metal sign stating it was drinking water, etc. This was welded to a metal two-inch pipe and cemented into the ground. Very shortly he discovered the whole thing missing. He was certain that in order to remove the sign and pipe someone had to have pulled it with a very strong vehicle, probably a tractor. This ended his generosity with the water and he put a heavy plank cover over the complete pond. The real purpose of this was a settling pond for leaves, trash etc. so these could collect in a grate, thus protecting the pumping equipment. Every morning and evening, before oiling the pump, Walter would take a special rake with teeth made to match the grate and remove the debris. The water was pumped from here on Oak Creek at one hundred fifty gallons per minute in a six-inch pipe, through a tunnel under the highway and straight up Mormon Canyon, a mile and a half to Walter's ranch. He had nearly a mile and a half of concrete ditch and a half mile of 24-inch steel pipe upstream from the "pour-over" and settling pond. To the south of this was the division box diverting water for Walter into the penstock, with the remainder continuing on to George and other families. Under the cliff about 30 feet were the pump and turbine. The pressure of the falling water coming through the penstock turned the turbine, which powered the pump and the generator. Walt's three children loved going to the site and climbing down the ladder with him to oil the pump. They were fascinated watching him get his arm in rhythm with the up and down motion of the pistons in order to place the oil can on top of the oilers and squirt oil into the mechanism. The generator produced their electricity until after WWII, with the pump providing water for irrigation into the 1970's. When floodwater came down Mormon Canyon and through the road tunnel, inundating all of the equipment, there would be no lights or water for long periods. Fortunately, this usually occurred in the summertime, or monsoon season, when the fields didn't need irrigating and the kids thought it was great to go to the creek everyday for a bath. Being without electricity was a different matter, although kerosene lamps and Coleman lanterns were available. Packing fruit after dark by lantern light was a difficult chore.

Walter continues telling about the acquiring of equipment and the building of the power station. It was to be constructed back a short distance from the creek to the north side of the mouth of the tunnel for Mormon Canyon and on nearly solid rock. "T' find th' pump, I went int' Phoenix. I knew Gilbert Hardware Company did lots o' dealin' with th' mines all over th' state o' Arizona, an' I thought I might get a used pump frum 'em, which I did. I ast Jack Gilbert, th' manager if b' chance 'e 'ad a used, six inch, triplex dual pump, an' 'e pointed out on th' platform t' one that'd just come in. Th' price was right, $350, s' I said, 'Jack, figure that's bought.' (See end of chapter for cost of materials twenty years later)

"'What're ya goin' t' use fer fall?' [Jack wanted to know.]

"'A six overshot wheel.'

"'Well, I can save ya a lotta' money with a turbine that a minin' operation in California never used at their millsite. They were goin' t' generate power there.'

"'Well, will it work under a 32 foot head [fall]?'

"Jack called 'em on th' telephone an' got me that turbine fer $625, an' I hired Henry Farley t' haul that machinery. Now, I 'ad th' ditch ready fer th' water an' I 'ad th' machinery but' I didn't have no station built. I hired Frank an' Jim Derrick frum Clarkdale, but they was too slow. They put some shots [dynamite] off, an' on Friday evenin' they went back down t' Clarkdale sayin' they'd b' back Monday mornin'. On Saturday I ast a friend, John Wetzel, who'd a lot o' experience with dynamite, what 'e thought about an idea I 'ad t' do th' job m'self. I wanted t' take a turn drill I 'ad an' drill a hole down there about eight, nine, feet t' th' bottom an' spring it with a lot o' dynamite t' blow th' center first an' then th' corners. John thought it'd work.

"We used fifteen sticks o' dynamite, mind ya'! O'course, we drilled th' holes int' th' side o' th' cliff first – th' big one in th' center where I wanted th' station t' sit an', then th' corner holes. We cut them fuses so's th' first t' blow'd b' th' middle. Then th' others'd 'ave a chance t' do a lot o' good work - blow it out this'a way an' then that. [Through hand movements he shows the listener how it's done.] Ya alw'ys cut th' fuses different lengths so's ya cin count 'em. If ya don't, two could blow at once an' ya'd have t' wait t' go back t' a missed hole fer a long, long time. Our blasts blew tons o' rock clear out acrost th' creek. When them boys come back t' work on Monday mornin', my, was they amazed. S' we got th' job done.

"Ruth, m' wife, an' I 'ad a job makin' them blueprints fer th' draft tube. It 'ad t' b' six inch concrete reinforced with steel an' tapered t' eighteen inches at th' turbine base afittin' frum more'n two foot acrost where th' tube ended in th' water. I 'ad t' blast a great big hole out in th' bottom o' th' powerhouse t' put this draft tube down under water. Ya'd git more power with th' water pullin' through that tube accordin' t' them instructions. Oh, I worked. We 'ad t' measure th' holes on th' base o' th' turbine t' git th' bolts t' fit an' th' hole in th' floor 'round th' tube 'ad t' b' sealed perfect symmetrical. Th' tube was only three foot high but it 'ad t' b' made exact.

"Then we put that turbine in there. Talk about a job! We put th' pump in first. I took George's mule up Wilson Canyon, an' I cut them good, big timbers an' drug 'em down th' road t' th' powerhouse. I got old Gus Ericson, 'e's th' guy that drilled Mother's well an' lots o' others, t' help me install that pump. 'E was a awful good machinery man, an' I knew 'e understood pumps, an' m' friends th' Blacks, George an' Sally, boarded an' roomed 'im while 'e was a'workin' with me.

"Ever'thin' was ready on th' eastside o' th' powerhouse room, with bolts in th' cement t' fit that big triplex dual pump. We got that machinery in there on poles an' skids. We dug a big ole deep hole on th' top fer th' dead man t' hold th' machinery, so's it wouldn't get banged goin' down there. An' we put them logs in there usin' a winch with a cable 'round th' deadman. Gus got everythin' all set. 'Now we can let that machinery down there with one hand an' a block an' tackle,' Gus told us. We've got pictures o' Mr. Pyle standin' there a'watchin' us put that machinery down. I 'ad John Wetzel helpin'. 'E was a big strong man, oh my yes! We got that pump down. Then we 'ad t' use a block an' tackle on th' big timber acrost th' top t' pull that big pump up offa' th' skid an' place it on them bolts. It was some job! But ole Gus sure knew how t' handle it. That pump 'ad a crankshaft four inches acrost, an' goodness, them big pistons, — six inches in diameter, eight inch strokes — that thing was heavy. We set it right down with th' holes in th' base right on top o' them bolts in th' station floor, an' just like that, we 'ad that big pump in. Can ya imagine that!? Th' next thing was t' git that big turbine down in there in that station. It was about eight foot long, includin' th' shaft, a two an' a half inch shaft, a foot an' a half wide. We 'ad th' draft tube an' bolts fer that turbine already set in th' cement. We just set that turbine down on there, right on top o' all that, an' that thing fit perfect, just perfect. Then we was t' put this steel tank together over th' turbine, an' there's an eighteen inch manhole right there on top. I got Joe Derrick t' weld th' steel tank t' b' exact. I think it was seven foot long, four foot wide an' four foot high."

From inside the pumping station Walter continues his explanation. "Another thing ole Joe done was t' weld that eighteen inch penstock that went up th' bluff. Ya remember th' division box I showed ya yesterday up on top o' th' hill b'low th' ditch? Remember it's got a 18-inch pipe runnin' t' George's place an' th' pipe runs 850 foot t' Jess Purtymun's house. The penstock goes inside that box. It's just smooth, straight pipe an' it went right on th' top o' this turbine tank with an elbow t' go down. Frum up on top there ya could always see that curved part about ten foot down t' th' top o' th' turbine. Over here we 'ad t' make bolts in this solid rock fer them great big dynamo bearings, fer that two an' a half inch shaft t' go through. [He takes the listener over a short distance to show the location of the bolts.] One bearin' just outside o' th' turbine tank, then another one over here about four foot out on th' end. An' in th' north end o' that turbine, there's a great big thing — eighteen inches in diameter — with holes about half inch in diameter fer th' water t' come in. Th' disk with them holes 'round it equalized th' pressure an' kept th' shaft frum goin' too far thata' way. I put it in accordin' t' th' blueprints. We bolted 'er down an' put heavy cement all 'round th' bottom b'cause Gus said, 'It's goin' t' have awful pressure.'

"I turned th' water in it an' th' tank filled up, an' I 'ad a hold o' that control that worked th' gates t' th' penstock. It was gonna take 225 miners inches o' water goin' through th' turbine t' git m' power. Fer that amount th' penstock 'ad t' b' full. That's an awful lot o' water t' keep that amount goin' through but still full, see, t' git th' weight. Th' control was a wheel about four inches acrost. I watched that water, I heard that water agushin' through there, an' I saw th' side o' that turbine tank start abulgin' out just like a great big toad. Goodness alive! I threw that pressure off in a hurry, but it'd already done th' damage. Th' seal was busted along th' bottom o' th' tank. O'course, immediately I called Jack Gilbert.

"'Good land, Jack, this thing never held atall!'

"'Ya drill two holes on each end o' that big tank, sixteen inches deep. Ya got solid rock there. Tomorrow, I'll send a welder an' a pump manual.'

"Lo an' b'hold, that welder was Johnny O'Neill. I knew 'im years ago when 'e was a'doin' 'is apprenticeship over at th' Clarkdale smelter. I knew, 'e knew what 'e was a doin', an' 'e went about reinforcin' that tank t' take off that terrific pressure. 'E did a wonderful job."

It is certainly true that the reinforcement was done well for it held for over 50 years of nearly constant use. It did create some difficulty, however, for anytime Walter and crew had to go inside the casing for repairs or maintenance they had to crawl over and around all of the extra supports. Much verbiage, that turned the air blue, could be heard being emitted from the bowels of the turbine at these times. When climbing down the ladder to enter the pump house, one landed on the top of the turbine. Here there was a very narrow space on which a person could walk around the penstock, over the end near the generator and get down to the floor. The reinforcement beams and almost no light presented additional obstacles creating a greater need for caution when moving around on top of the tank. This narrow ledge was the delegated spot for all observers and a very favorite place for the three children.

Walter continues describing the process, simultaneously expecting his listeners to remember all as well as he did. "Don'cha remember that pour over tank I 'ad there? Well, sure ya do. Th' water would go back int' th' creek when I closed th' gate on th' turbine. Ya' know that big waterfall, comin' out o' th' settlin' pond? Well, th' only time it ran was when I 'ad that pump shut off an' that's where th' backup fell down int' th' creek. It never bothered George's gate a bit, an' I put in a big steel gate t' cut that water offa m' turbine entirely.

"The ditch we first put in run about a mile. We had t' cement 2000 feet o' it, where those skunks an' ring tailed cats were a'diggin' in th' banks an' lettin' th' water out. We went below th' grade o' th' ditch about four inches, an' we took three foot chicken wire an' lined th' banks an' put about a half a inch o' cement all th' way along fer 2000 feet t' stop that."

"How far does the ditch go above where it crosses Wilson Canyon?" asked one of the listeners.

"Oh, it's over a quarter o' a mile. It's close t' a half a mile th' way it runs in under th' bridge an' then acrost that Wilson Canyon. When Robert was in with me, [Robert Jackson was a partner and son-in-law for a few years.] we took my four-wheel drive truck, that biggest one I 'ad, th' three quarter ton. 'E 'ad a trailer, an' we bought these 36 inch road covers t' put acrost that, t' run our water across ole Wilson Canyon. Floods 'ad kept a'washin' our ditch out. T' git down there we went down th' old road an' made a road down through th' river bottom. Ya' cin see that ole road frum th' bridge at Wilson Canyon [Midgely Bridge] down under th' bluff. [He points, looking up the canyon.] It goes down t' th' river bottom, an' we crost over one channel there where our water was a'comin' down. We 'ad t' make a road down in there int' that awful place. We put a pipeline through there an' cemented it in. Shorty Newton helped us at th' head o' that pipeline. We piled river rocks all 'round th' entrance an' poured a thin mix o' cement over it. Th' cement ran all through them loose rocks an' cemented 'em all t'gether. Them floods never washed it out ag'in after that. We also put in them culverts acrost Wilson Canyon, an' they're still there. [Approximately 25 years.] Now there was other things that gave us trouble, like people rollin' boulders down frum up on top. They didn't know that ditch was down there, they was just tryin' t' see if one o' them boulders would travel clean down t' th' creek. Th' last time I 'ad t' fix that ole bugger was when I was nearly eighty years old, just after I'd 'ad cataract surgery, not too long b'fore I sold th' rest o' them orchards. I'd gone down t' clean th' grate an' oil th' pump an' there warn't very much water comin' down, so's I started out t' find out what th' trouble was. About a mile up some darn fools'd pushed a bunch o' them big rocks over th' edge an' they'd busted out th' side o' m' ditch an' all th' water was just a'runnin' right back int' th' creek. Well, I come home plenty mad an' told Ruth I'd 'ave t' 'ave 'er help me. I still wasn't seein' so good an' we was gonna 'ave t' go down that awful steep Huckabee trail. We got dynamite, caps an' cement, an' Ruth got 'erse'f a strong ole' walkin' stick. We struck out down that bugger o' a trail. My goodness sakes alive, what a picture we made — Ruth a leadin' th' way usin' that stick, an' me a holdin' ont' her shoulder t' see where I was a walkin' an' I 'ad them dynamite sticks an' caps, an' fuses stuck in m' pockets, with that bag o' cement on m' shoulder. I don't know how we made it with Ruth bein' such a little bitty thing. But we got down there an' I blasted out them big boulders an' cemented that darn hole, an' saw th' water was a'runnin' good. So's back up th' hill we come." [Here Walt pauses to chuckle and shake his head as he is reliving the episode.]

"Then there was th' time I went down t' oil up early one mornin' several years ago an' there wasn't a drop o' water runnin' int' that settlin' pond. So's, I struck out on foot as fast as I could go followin' that ditch. It wasn't long 'til I come around a corner there above Purtymun's place an' lo an' b'hold here was a car seat lyin' plumb across that ditch. I thought t' m'self, 'Uh-oh! Somethin's bad wrong up here!' Sure a'nuff, just a little further on there was a woman a lyin' in th' water in that ditch. Ya' see, th' car seat'd acted like a dam an' was holdin' back th' water. Anyway, I went up t' 'er an' there wasn't nothin' I could do, b'cause she was already dead. Then I thought I heard somethin', kinda like a groan. An' I got t' lookin' 'round there an' my, oh my, was I ever in fer a shock! Here, caught up in th' branches o' a tree was a feller I knew real well. 'My goodness alive man! What in th' world happened?!' 'E told me that he an' 'is lady friend'd been comin' down th' canyon an' somethin' went wrong an' 'e missed th' big curve an' run over th' bluff an' 'e was thrown way outta th' car. It was a good 200 feet down t' where they landed. I told 'im I'd go get help, an' I took outta there in an awful rush. Well, after th' ambulance got 'im t' th' hospital, they found out 'e'd broke 'is back. That's just one o' my experiences.

"Well I better git back t' busines here. I was a'tellin' ya' about puttin' that pump down there an' startin' that turbine. One o' th' hardest jobs I 'ad t' do t' keep that pump a'runnin' was t' adjust th' thrust on th' turbine. Th' shaft was goin' too fur over t'wards th' water equalization disk. Th' shaft was cuttin' th' gate an' ruinin' it. So's, I got on th' phone with Gilbert Hardware again. Ya' betcha I did!

"'Jack, this thrust's goin' th' wrong way, it's no good.'

"'I'll tell ya what I think's th' matter. That machine was made fer a 54 foot drop an' you've only got a 32. Ya're goin' t' 'ave t' git that plate outta th' back end an' drill th' holes in it t' one inch instead o' one half inch. That's double th' amount o' water in there t' equalize that thrust. Th' shaft's goin' too fur one way.'

"I 'ad t' go in there around them thick reinforcement rods an' get this great big disk out. I took it t' th' Clemenceau smelter where I knew one o' them machinists, Howard Owens. 'E drilled them holes, an' I put that heavy ole part back in place. It worked pretty good. But one day Carl Richards, [a local mechanic], an' I made a few improvements t' make th' machine run smoother an' take less water t' operate th' pump.

"We put thrust bearings from m' old Model T on th' end o' that two an' a half inch shaft. Carl put a file on that shaft an' ground that down so's that bearin' would have a collar. We got them bearin's on there. One o' 'em would take care o' th' thrust goin' one way, an' th' other one kept it from goin' back th' other way — double thrust bearings with an oil box on th' bottom. We didn't care if that thing on th' back end o' th' thrust worked or not. I drove wooden plugs in that back end so's it would take less water t' operate th' pump.

"Finally, George said, 'Let's put another pulley on this shaft. We've got enough water t' run a generator.' So's, that's what we did. George knew how t' hook it up. 'E'd been goin' t' electrical school, ya know. An' we put that seven kilowatt generator in there an' used that in 'is house an' mine fer fifteen years. I put a 'lectric line down there. Remember that? I think we put that generator in b'fore th' war."

George had electricity from the REA power company before WWII, but for Walt's place, they only got the pole hauled in for the line and the hole dug on Friday before Pearl Harbor. All construction on the line came to a screeching halt until the war ended and Arizona Public Service finished the job. George had REA power all during those years and many times Walter's family wished they had it also. Walter describes some of the problems the new company was having.

"I r'member talkin' t' Mr. Bridgewater over there where they was a hookin' up some houses t' 'lectricity on th' Purtymun place, an' they were havin' low voltage problems. Th' line 'round th' hill was burnin' motors up, an' 'e was gonna 'ave t' do somethin'. I went over there t' ask about 'avin' our line put in frum th' generator. 'E pointed t' th' transformers they was puttin' in an' told me 'e could give me a free right-o'-way t' put our lines on 'is poles. I was athinkin' that was in th' early forties."

During the years that the two families shared the direct current, Helen and Ruth scheduled all tasks which required extra power, i.e. washing, and ironing. If either were going to deviate from the set routine the other had to be notified, as the voltage was too low to accommodate more than one of these activities at a time. Helen had a gas refrigerator but Ruth made do with an ice box and a burlap cooler under a large shade tree. This was a small cupboard-like structure, with burlap all around which had to be kept wet to provide coolness. The family cat made a habit of tearing through the cloth and helping himself to the food.

One summer in the early forties, a big thunderstorm roared through the area dumping large amounts of water, particularly at the headwaters of Mormon Canyon, creating flood conditions. Trees were uprooted, and combined with other debris, crashed along as the raging, rushing, torrent tumbled through the canyon on its way to join Oak Creek. Standing in the way of this onslaught was the large culvert and rock fill provided for highway 89A. Here the larger items spun around until they were crosswise of the tunnel, blocking the water's flow which caused it to change course and filter through the rock and into Walter's pumping station and power house. All of the equipment was inundated with water and silt, ruining everything. Because of the war it was most difficult to get the materials to repair the damage, leaving the farm and family without water or electricity for the remainder of the summer. This was one of those storms mentioned early in this chapter, which occurred in the summertime, with the monsoon rains providing plenty of moisture for the trees. However, all water for household use had to be hauled. As mentioned previously, Ruth loaded the children on the converted flat bed of the Model A Ford and headed to the creek, along with a bar of soap and a towel for their daily baths, thus minimizing the amount of water needed in the house. Naturally, all of the younger generation felt this was great fun, not minding the "icy" temperature a bit. In later years as adults they wondered how they were able to put any more than a big toe in that cold stream!

Coleman lanterns and kerosene lamps were used in the house and the packing sheds, ironing was done with irons heated on the stove, and most likely washing was done at Helen's house. After several months, Walter was able to get the generator rewound with copper wiring at the Clarkdale smelter and to get the pump repaired. Following a major mucking out of the station, the equipment was reinstalled and things were definitely improved.

The fickleness of the weather in the southwest causes great variance from drought to floods. Allen comments on Mother Nature: "During the 1930's, Dust Bowl time, there was a long, hot dry spell. Flagstaff had to ship in water because they were dependent on melting snow. That was lovely drinking water from that snow - so pure. I remember when I was going to school up there in 1917-1918, that water almost tasted like distilled water."

Walter felt some type of flood control was needed and he thought dams might be the answer. However, those didn't get built, but some other things were tried. He explains: "Frum about 1938 until th' beginnin' o' WWII, we 'ad them CCC boys in here. There was a big flood in Oak Creek in 1938. Th' WPA put lots o' boys t' work doin' things that we knew wouldn't answer th' purpose such as puttin' wire nettin' in th' canyons an' washes an' fillin' it with rocks t' make soil erosion dams. They spent thousands an' thousands o' dollars out here. Dad Hart, who was runnin' a little store out here, made fun o' it. 'E said, 'Just look at where our taxes are a'goin'.'

"'Yup, but in order t' git good times, we've got t' put these men t' work.'

"I did git tired o' newcomers who'd ignore th' advice o' ole-timers t' build above th' high-water mark b'cause Oak Creek ain't th' innocent little ole stream it appears t' b'. Them newcomers t' Sedona was alw'ys underestimatin' th' power o' Oak Creek. A lot o' 'em would build where they pleased an' then call fer help when them floods come."

Walter's son remarked; "Recently there were two dams planned— one below Camp Verde at the Box Canyon, and one at the upper Box Canyon up near Sedona. Salt River Power company blocked that project. They didn't want those dams built, and they claimed to have a prior water right."

"That's right," Walter interjects. "They claimed t' 'ave th' water rights goin' back b'fore 1917." This could be done because both the Verde and Oak Creek are tributaries to the Salt River.

"After the war I dug that big new reservoir an' my of my, I 'ad plenty o' water fer irragatin' then. It'd hold enuff water t' irrigate this whole place." (See center for photo of reservoir) Sometimes dams were desired for other reasons, as Walter discovered. "Them movie people that come up int' Sedona sometimes needed temporary dams. When they made that picture "Johnny Guitar," they wanted t' back Oak Creek up an' that's exactly what they done. They paid me fer 20 steel drums fer that dam. They built a stairway down th' bank t' git down frum where they 'ad th' camera up on th' hill down t' where th' dam crost th' creek. They paid me an' George big money t' weld nipples on six-inch valves that we put in that big steel pipe t' bring water down over this tunnel [Mormon Canyon under highway 89A] fer th' movie. It was where Joan Crawford went through that water in th' last o' th' film. It was suppose t' b' a waterfall hidin' a secret get-away. Sure did look natural in th' movie."

When Walter sold the remaining orchards in the 1970s the buyer also purchased the water rights and pumping machinery. Due to financial problems the new owner was unable to develop the area as planned, so the buildings and surrounding cliffs and boulders were secured with a strong fence. Many times Walter would stand looking over the edge, and comment rather sadly that it wasn't being used. "[Mr.] McClinchy," Walter comments, "as fer as I know still owns it. [Circa 1982]. They've got bolted boards blockin' any entrance t' that operation now." The converted settling pond, the little stone house surrounding the division box, and the stalwart looking penstock remain as silent reminders of an era soon to be forgotten in the saga of developing the West.

FOOTNOTES

(1) McKinnon, Shaun, Enriching the Desert: The Story of SRP, *The Arizona Republic*, Feb. 5, 2003, page A10

(2) Same as above, page A1

(3) Sexton, Connie Cone, John J. Rhodes 1916-2003: An Effective, Humble Leader, *The Arizona Republic*, Tuesday, August 26, 2003, page A14

(4) Rigby, Elizabeth, Valley Native George Jordan Dies, *Verde Independent*, 1964

(5) Jordan, Helen unpublished diaries

(6) Ibid

(7) Ibid

CONCRETE CONDUIT COMPANY
CENTRIFUGAL CONCRETE PIPE, SEWER PIPE
IRRIGATION PIPE, DRAIN PIPE

224 SOUTH 23RD STREET
PHOENIX, ARIZONA
PHONE 4-4703   P. O. BOX 2670

November 13, 1953

Mr. W. E. Jordan
Box 15
Sedona, Arizona

Dear Sir:

Replying to your letter of November 9, 1953 we quote you herewith on Screw pressure gates and Model K Kanal gates in available sizes. The Model 20 Gate is a special gate which is quoted to us on application to the factory. If you will advise the size and quantity we will be glad to get prices and delivery dates on this gate.

Size	Screw Pressure Gate	Kanal Gate 4' Frame	Kanal Gate 6' Frame	Kanal Gate 8' Frame
10	34.20	30.52		
12	43.20	33.05		
14	66.00	36.57		
15	79.20	38.28		
16	98.20	52.57		
18		57.03		
20		62.75		
24		73.31		
30			114.07	
36			137.02	
42				208.61
48				251.79

The prices quoted are F.O.B. Phoenix, Arizona.

Yours very truly,

CONCRETE CONDUIT COMPANY

Manager

WCH/gh

CONCRETE CONDUIT COMPANY

CENTRIFUGAL CONCRETE PIPE, SEWER PIPE
IRRIGATION PIPE, DRAIN PIPE

4242 W. Buckeye Road

PHOENIX, ARIZONA

PHONE P. O. Box 2670
Ap 8-3526

Dec. 8, 1953

Mr. W. E. Jordan
Box 15
Sedona, Arizona

Dear Sir:

Replying to your letter of Dec. 7, we can order the parts for Model K 18" Flat Back Kanal Gate for you and the prices are as follows:

1	Part A Frame	22.82
1	Part B Lid	23.21
2	Part P-1 upper Wedge bolt @.50	1.00
2	Part P-2 lower " " @.66	1.32
1	Part WL left wedge	1.81
1	Part WR right wedge	1.81
		51.97

Plus 2% State Sales Tax
F.O.B. Phoenix, Ariz.

So far as we know we can get immediate delivery o these parts and if you will advise us method of shipme to you from Phoenix we will be pleased to proceed with your order.

Yours truly,

CONCRETE CONDUIT CO.

W. C. Harford
Manager

WCH-H

Chapter Eleven
WINTER RIDE DOWN MEMORY LANE

December 23, 1983

Walter was in his mid-eighties when he suggested to his daughter F. Ruth(ie) that they take a drive from Sedona through Bridgeport, Cottonwood, Clarkdale and on to Peck's Lake near Rattlesnake Hill where he was born. It appeared he wanted to have one last look at the areas in which his life took shape, plus a deep desire to share many of his fond memories. This family excursion is a series of glimpses into the hours and years of some of Walter's life experiences.

The drive had barely begun when Walt started pointing to spots of significance to him. In West Sedona he indicated the dome-shaped, gray mountain to the north called Grayback. (Newcomers call it Capital Dome.)

"Oh my! How I r'member th' night we all got t'gether t' carry Gene Ash offa that mountain. 'E'd been up there with another feller lookin' at them Indian ruins when 'e lost 'is footin' an' fell 'bout twenty feet a landin' on 'is back. [Walter was frequently called on to help with search and rescue for he knew "every inch o' that country", was surefooted and quick thinking.]

A few miles further, when crossing the bridge over Dry Creek, he began to chuckle. "I alw'ys 'ave t' laugh when I think 'bout what John Wetzel an' I done t' that ole road. Them darn fool highway engineers put a 6-12 inch concrete wall acrost th' lower side o' where th' road crosst through that creek bottom instead o' puttin' it on th' upper side where it b'longed. When ever it'd rain an' that ole creek started runnin', why, we'd 'ave th' awfullest pond o' water all over that road, an' it waren't safe t' try t' cross it neither. Ole John, 'e come t' me an' said 'Say Walt, I think we'd better go down there an' help that road crew fix that Dry Creek crossin' proper like.' So's t' make a long story short, we waited 'til after dark an' borr'yed some dynamite caps an' fuses right outta that road construction camp. We figgered them guy's messed it up s' their supplies could fix it! We took them things down there an' got 'er all fixed up an' when we lit them fuses — Cerwham!! Out went th' wall an whoosh all o' that water that was built up b'hind just poured out! Ya betcha, we 'ad that ole thing dry as a bone. Now wouldn't ya know, them fools put it right back th' same way. Here come ole John ag'in wantin' t' go fix it a'other time, but I said , [with an emphatic shake of his head] 'No, John, I don't think so. I think they might be awatchin' t' see who done it afore an' I don't wanta git caught.'"

From White Flat he pointed to the northwest and recalled, "Way over there in Sycamore Basin, Duane Miller's father bought a thousand acres fer nearly nothin'. Just a few days ago 'e died in Phoenix. Th' paper said 'e was 83 years old. My goodness, th' big things 'e was in! Four hundred acres in cotton, an' 'e was in th' cattle business. At one time 'e 'ad a 1400 head permit – th' DK Cattle Company. 'E owned that, an' Duane went in with 'im. They traded th' Forest Service that thousand acres over there in Sycamore Basin fer this land over here. Duane's making millions out o' it.

"Norman Fain, same thing, 'is dad just left a fortune in 'is lap. Dan Fain built that subdivision just this side o' Prescott called Prescott Village, I believe. [Prescott Valley]

"Oh yeah, here we are at that Page Spring turn off. [Just past the southwest end of White Flat.] Jim Page was one o' th' old timers, 'e come in there. I don't know who 'e got that place frum, but ever since I was growin' up, 'e owned it.

"Edgar Page an' young Jimmy Page, named after 'is grandfather, 'ad a beautiful farm there at Page Spring. Edgar drilled an' got artesian water t' irrigate that farm. Oh, it was wonderful! Jimmy is there livin' yet. Finally, Edgar sold ever'thin' on his farm t' th' State Game Department. All that over where th' big fish ponds are fer th' hatchery was where Edgar farmed. Jimmy kept a place on th' north side o' th' road, an' 'e put in that store an' trailer park down near th' bridge. [Lolamai] Th' water frum that artesian well goes up int' th' air when they turn on th' valve without puttin' any pressure on it, without pumpin'. Jimmy showed me one time. Goodness, 'e 'ad world's o' pressure!

"Johnny Hurst owned a place right on down below th' fish hatchery. 'E 'ad a big, beautiful farm there with strawberries an' tomatoes. That terrible flood in February o' 1920 practically washed all that beautiful farm away. There'd been a freak snow in November o' that winter. It even snowed down here on th' Verde. A warm spell come right after an' washed away th' forms fer a bridge that Williams was 'bout t' pour. [At Bridgeport, across the Verde] 'E salvaged a lot o' them timbers frum down in th' river bed an' was ready t' pour them forms a second time when that February flood come that took most o' Johnny Hurst's place. Bill, our neighbor with th' bee hives, woke me up just at daylight: 'Come look at this river!' 'Why, land o' th' livin'! [Walt exclaimed] It was all over our farm down there runnin' int' th' swill just east o' where Charles' barn is now. [Charles Jordan, grandson of Will Jordan, farmed the old Bridgeport ranch for years and still farms at

139

the Bent River Ranch upon this writing.] When th' floodin' washed Williams' bridge forms away fer th' second time, 'e told th' state that 'e's broke, an' they'd have t' finish th' bridge theirselves.

"Looka there. There's where th' springs come up t' give this creek its name, Spring Creek. That's where ya went with me t' catch them minnows b'fore we went a fishin'. 'Member when I was a carryin' ya acrost t' git t' m' favorite spot, an' oh my! When I stepped on a slick rock we both went down kersplash an' got wet all over. My, ya sure was mad at me!" Walt paused to chuckle and enjoy the memory.

"The old road used t' go acrost just north o' that bridge back there on Spring Creek. I'll never fergit th' day yer Mama an' me was acomin' back frum m' mother's place there on th' Verde. We got up t' here an' ya wouldn' b'lieve th' number o' cars lined up on both sides o' this creek fer nearly a half mile. There'd been a terrible storm up in them mountains t'ards Barney Pasture. Well I parked that Model A an' went down there an' stuck a stick at th' edge o' th' water. I kept awatchin' that fer about twenty minutes an' I seen that that water was a goin' down, then I knew I could cross it. I just lifted th' hood on m' Model A an' dropped m' fan belt sos it wouldn't spray water all over that distributor. I started th' engine an' drove past all o' them folks right down t' th' edge o' that water. I poked m' head outta th' window an' hollered, 'Look out over there! I'm comin' acrost!' They couldn't imagine me a tryin' t' cross a stream that high but we just went right on over t' th' other side, no trouble, no trouble atall, 'cept I think Ruth was kinda scared. When I got acrost t' th' other side, them folks yelled at me, 'Whatcha got there? A submarine?!' I just waved an' smiled. I didn't want t' give way m' secret sos I went down th' road a little b'fore puttin' th' fan belt back on. An' I didn't hang around either t' see if any o' 'em got stuck in th' middle. Ya know ya 'ave t' stop yer fan frum turnin' er ya'll b' stuck out there in th' middle. One time that creek come down an' washed a great big Cadillac car down 'bout a half a mile. They 'ad t' take that fancy car all t' pieces an' clean th' dirt outta it." His daughter reminds him that when the family was on their way to visit the folks at Soda Springs Ranch that Woods Canyon was running big and had taken out the bridge. Walt picks up the story: "Oh yeah. We 'ad t' wait quite a long time an' I drew pictures in th' sand fer ya an' Anne t' keep ya entertained. Son was just a baby. After while I saw that water was recedin' sos we went down t' a little better crossin', dropped th' fan belt an' went acrost. I kinda think ya was scared when that muddy water was a swirlin' in at yer feet!"

Approaching the Cornville turn-off something else caught his eye. "Hey! See that over there. They're sellin' raw honey at that place. We use t' git raw honey frum ole man Solomon when m' sister Alice was alive. 'E didn't doctor up 'is honey none. It was wonderful catsclaw honey, an' it would sugar right away. That's what Ruth loved, an' I use' t' buy 'er a half gallon when I'd buy a gallon o' th' regular. Now 'e adds glucose t' it so's it won't go t' sugar. It's catsclaw honey, but it ain't what we liked so well.

"See acrost th' Verde over there t' our right? That hill's called Sugar Loaf 'cause it's s' round an' usually white - all limestone, lookin' kinda like a pile o' sugar. Now it looks like somebody planted grass all over it. That's 'cause we've 'ad s' much rain. An' last year, too. I looked up th' record fer rainfall yesterday. [He had a book in which he kept quite complete weather records, along with specific measures to be taken to enhance the crop. These were used for comparison to current years and assisted him in making decisions.] "Boy, we 'ad lots more rain at this time last year, than we've 'ad in November an' December o' this year. Lots more! M' records show it, yeah.

"On th' east side o' th' river frum Sugar Loaf's where I use t' own some land that 'ad water rights. That's where I transferred them water rights frum t' git water in Sedona. M' mother's place was just acrost th' river an' m' sister Stella's th' one 'at named that hill an' m' mother's place Sugar Loaf Ranch.

"They's sure got a beautiful bridge here acrossin' th' Verde. Ya know this's Bridgeport, don'tcha? That's th' bridge that finally got built after them floods I's a tellin' ya about."

Approaching Clarkdale, east of highway 89A the tailings are just as they were nearly forty years prior when smelting operations ended. "Th' copper company bought up all o' them farms an' they pumped them tailings frum th' Clarkdale smelter an' filled up that big farm. Ah, looka there how much they filled in that beautiful farm with them stinkin' tailings. Ain't that awful! My, oh my !! That was quite a sight fer a young feller t' witness." He interrupts the reminiscing to give directions to the driver. "Now take it slow right acrost th' bridge. We turn t' th' left at th' sign. That's it. If we went to the right up here, we'd go t' th' Tuzigoot ruins on th' paved road. We'll be on a gravel road here pretty quick. Right here, see it. This here road goes clear over t' Sycamore Basin. I've been all over in here. In that sharp pointed hill, there are cliff dwellin's right up behind Clark's Mansion up there. Ya see 'em?"

As they turned right onto a narrow dirt road he pointed slightly to the northeast, "Aw, right out there's where I saw m' Uncle Billy courtin' Frances. There's a hollow place in th' top o' that hill, an' I was a trappin' animals when I heard a noise over there. I snuck up an' peeked over th' top an' I caught 'im kissin' 'er!" Naturally this revelation brought a great laugh. Frances Miller was the teacher for the one-room school, and as always the students were most interested in the personal life of their teachers.

"There's them flag tules [bullrushes] with them cat tails on 'em. That was th' ole Petchard place. Oh, how this takes m' back. Quite th' memories! Th' Verde River use t' b' frum Tuzigoot solid, clear acrost. It come right through here an' clear around east o' Tuzigoot back int' th' channel. B'fore any pioneers ever got here, it washed itself through, took thousands o' years ago. Th' river use' t' run clear 'round through this. Ya cin see where th' ole river chanel run. Ya know this's what them ole timers called Upper Verde. An' there's Peck's Lake."

..PECK'S LAKE - Yavapai County, Elevation 3332 feet

This lake may have been named for Edmund George Peck. The Yavapai name is Hatalacva ("crooked water") because of the shape of the lake. According to an unidentified clipping at the Sharlot Hall Museum, this lake was formed when workmen removed hundreds of tons of earth to turn the Verde River from its natural channel.

Edmund George Peck (b. Dec. 28, 1830, Canada; d. Dec. 13, 1910) arrived in Arizona in 1863 and served as a scout and guide for troops at Fort Whipple. After retiring from the army, he was shown silver ore and immediately recognized having seen something similar. In company with T. M. Alexander, C.O.Bean, and William Cole, he located several claims in the Bradshaw Mountains and called the major one Peck Mine. Fish says that the first three men were prospecting while Peck hunted and he found a very heavy rock which proved out to be silver ore. In any event, by 1875 the Peck Mine was the most important in Arizona Territory and in the next three years it produced $1,200,000 in silver. A lawsuit instituted in 1878 dragged on and Peck died in poverty. From 1879 to 1910 he prospected unsuccessfully in the vicinity of the mine.[1].

"There's a spring in that lake over there in th' bend, an' that use t' b' a slough down in there below th' lake. I killed lots o' ducks over in there. There was also some water down in there. Charlie Willard drained it. Ya see th' weeds all over th' lake. Them ducks brought them in here years ago. Them darned ole weeds ruined things, but lately th' Game Department did some dredgin'. See that open water in th' middle. They dredged that.

"We're on th' ole, ole road now. Ya can see Dan Shea's ole place really good. His was one o' them thirteen farms bought b' Clark that Dad managed. 'E use t' 'ave a great big house down there in that pasture. 'E 'ad a saloon up in Jerome. That's a big, big farm. Use t' b' a wonderful farm. When Dad was workin' fer th' copper company, oh th' crops 'e raised there! Pinto beans all over where that golf course is. Use t' b' a beautiful farm! It's all pasture now. They're raisin' cattle on it. Over there's where th' Clarkdale Dairy use t' b'.

"Just look at all th' ducks an' mud hens! When I was over here a week ago with Sonny [Walter Jordan, Jr.], I 'ad them wild geese a comin' right up t' me. A-hawnk! A-hawnk! Ain't them beautiful things. They b'long t' th' man that owns this place. We turn to the right there.

"Now, ya see th' water comin' out o' Peck's Lake? Take it slow in here. Ya see them cottonwood trees an' that embankment over there?" He points to show the exact spot. "That's th' Goodwin Spring. That's where m' mother was baptized. It's a big spring dammed up there. An' that was a slough, all down b'hind. There's tules an' water in there yet. This's th' east end o' Peck's Lake.

"There's another spring 'round in th' bend over there that feeds Peck's Lake. That's water frum th' golf course there. They get water frum th' Verde. Worlds o' people come here. This's a resort an' campin' place now. What a change!

"I'll show ya where th' water comes through th' hill t' irrigate all them farms. Now here's th' gate where that guy won't let nobody go down there. 'Keep out!' th' sign says. Well, we ain't agoin' thata way anyhow!" Walt's tone of voice shows his disgust. "We'll drive right up t' th' spring.

"See that canyon? Oh, my! Water comes down through that thing. Just a flood! Course it does. Good gracious, yes! On up here I'm goin' t' show ya where I saw th' largest baptism in m' life, 'bout 20 o' them folks. That peacher'd talked t' all th' farm boys, people all over th' Upper Verde an' down as fer as Cottonwood. That was a big, big celebration!

"M' mother wanted m' Dad t' b' baptized but when th' preacher talked t' 'im about it, m' Dad didn't know why 'e needed baptism.

"'What's th' matter with me. I've raised a big family. I've provided fer 'em'

"'Mr Jordan, ya done wonderful, but ya cain't go t' heaven unless ya're born agin.'

"Dad didn't b'lieve that until 'e was near death, ('e alw'ys said 'e could take 'is bath at home!), an' then 'e told me that 'e wished 'e 'ad th' last fifty years o' 'is life t' live over.

"Now ya see right over there b' them trees under th' hill? I use' t' walk down offa th' top o' that hill t' fish.

141

It's got too many rollin' rocks. I ain't goin' t' trust it no more."

Seeing a large pile of debris he comments, "They pulled most o' this stuff out right up here. That's deep water! Stop here on this point! That's where they 'ad that big baptism. Right in there."

Continuing their drive around the lake Walt's excitement increases. "M' favorite fishin' spot's over there. Th' water's 'bout ten foot deep. I'll show ya th' stuff they dredged out o' th' lake right up here. They didn't pull it all out down there nor up above, but they got tons an' tons o' it. Just look at what they've dredged out o' there an' changed where they put th' boats in too. It'll b' good fishin' here now."

Referring to a fishing trip he and his daughter had had together many years before he states, "I don't know if ya an' I went in over here or not. I just don't remember th' exact spot where we come down th' bank an' fished.

"I'll show ya where I caught a four pound bass last March. Shorty, [a friend from Sedona], an' 'is grandson an' me stopped right here. It's awful narrow, but we did it. See them beaver huts out there. Them geese come up in there an' nest an' lay eggs. Them tules use t' b' all over this up above. Now, that's a beaver hut. Beavers are in here an' right in underneath here is where I caught a four pound bass last spring. There's that weed. They didn't git all o' it out up here. That's terrible stuff. Good fer nothin'!

"Now ya see this gap in th' hill. That's [called] a narrow. It's just a little ways over t' th' river. I walked frum th' Verde over here huntin' ducks. I'd hunt quail over b' th' river an' come over through that pass t' hunt ducks. That's th' spring I wanted t' show ya in there. A feller use t' b' able t' go out on an ole levy th' ole pioneers'd built out there. Th' spring's right out in th' middle. Now that spring was right out here somewhere. I can't tell exactly, but that's where it was. Yes, I've 'ad wonderful times!

"Th' Verde River is just over th' hill here. Makes th' bend, comes way 'round there where I went t' school an' back ag'in an' it use t' come right 'round here, maybe thousands o' years ago, but it did an' th' water come through there. Now th' golf course helps keep th' water in th' lake up. That grassy weed is terrible stuff!" Obviously Walter hates the weed which has grown over the entire lake and nearly ruined the fishing. "This use t' b' covered with tules. There's still some along th' bank. See them yonder?

"Right up there — this side o' th' clubhouse's where I got hung up with m' fishin' boat in them tules right off in this big water. That's th' time I ditched Sunday School t' go fishin'.

"The guy that helped me outta that mess o' wasps, 'e an' 'is lady, th' Powells, were livin' in that farm house there. They were pickin' watermelons up in here. I 'ad t' yell t' make 'em hear me.

"The water come through th' hill, right under th' hill, right there. [Pointing to the ditch for emphasis.] We just crost th' ditch. There's th' ditch right there t' our left. What in th' devil is that?! Well, it's right in there, comes right through th' hill underneath frum th' Verde. Ya wouldn't believe it. Ya wouldn't think when ya git up on top o' that hill, that th' Verde over there's higher than this. But it 'tis. It's gravity that brings that water over here. That ditch is right in under here, got t' b'. That ole ditch frum th' Verde's right here t' our left, an' it goes 'round. Ya see that flume crost there? Well, Shea built that. That irrigated th' farms over there. Yeah, that's it! Ya bet it is! I cin see water in there. Sure! Yeah, that's th' ditch. It comes right on through. See it? That flume's older than me. I use t' go crost that. We kids called it th' dike. We 'ad t' cross that t' git over there t' fish when I was a boy, growin' up on th' Verde. I'd come over lots o' times after school. We just lived over th' hill 'bout a mile, right through th' shortcut.

"Don't seem possible but when I was a young boy on th' ole farm, Sunset Telephone Company brought in phones t' them farms. I'll never forgit ole man Morris - Fritz Morris – comin' over t' use th' phone. 'E 'ad a little farm that use t' b' part o' Dad's place, an' 'e 'ad a lady friend in Jerome. Mr. Morris'd come down there t' use our telephone t' call ' er. 'Er name was Pearl. 'Is that you Pearl?,' in a real sweet like voice. Us kids, we'd stick our heads in th' door an' Mother'd git us out o' there, but we'd git a kick out o' it. `Is that you, Pearl?'" Walt was good at mimicking the neighbor's voice as he remembered it to be.

"That r'minds me o' Elizabeth Miller. Mother use t' board teachers. Miss Miller 'ad a boyfriend in Jerome. Oh, she 'ad quite a case on 'im, an' we were just old enough t' know it too. Sos on April Fool's day, we called 'er down in th' mornin' b' tellin' 'er she was wanted on th' phone. Oh boy, she hurried up an' got down there.

"'Hellooo. Helloooo.'

"'April Fool!'

"'Oh, I might 'ave known it!'

"She stomped th' floor an' went back upstairs. Oh, she was mad! She started apackin' up right aw'y, an' my mother lost 'er boarder.

"'Mrs. Jordan, I just cain't possibly stand it any longer.'

"She moved over t' Ev Jordan's place. Oh, boy. I'll never forgit that as long as I live. Mother didn't know we were up t' that. She spanked our tails too.

"A number o' years after that th' Oak Creek Telephone Company 'ad poles comin' up t' Jerome along that ridge on th' top o' Mescal Canyon. That was trouble, trouble, trouble. They wouldn't put a man on it an' fix it. Many a time I followed that line o' poles up t' find where th' wire was down on th' ground. That line was important t' m' business. I 'ad t' telephone all them stores in Jerome t' git m' orders twice a week when I was farmin' down here.

"Ya can see Charlie Clark's Mansion frum here." It still stands on th' edge o' Clarkdale. In the 50's or 60's, they tried to make the mansion into a restaurant. Ann and Robert (Ruthie's sister who married Lawrence Jackson's brother) and Larry and Ruthie came over for dinner one night. While there they were shown all through the mansion and how it was going to be changed. Something happened and nothing ever was done and the restaurant closed.

Although many happy memories surfaced on the Peck's Lake jaunt, there were those that brought too much sadness to purposely delve into them. When asked if he wanted to continue up the hill to visit the site of his old home his reply was adamant. "No, no. No I don't!"

After the home had been sold someone went to bed smoking a cigarette, burning the house completely, leaving only the hearth intact. This Walt didn't want to revisit.

As father and daughter resumed their trek of memories, Jerome became their destination. Walter continued his reminiscing and only the stories not previously included are related here.

"Above th' ole ranch where I went t' school Mr. Hinman drilled a artesian well in about 1905. 'E drilled it usin' horse power right up here at th' foot o' th' hill. There use t' b' lots o' badgers up in there, an' th' ole pioneers called it Badger Hill." After passing the Clarkdale water tank on the south side of the highway Walter spots another place to the north. "Th' slaughter house was up this here canyon. I hauled hay with a team an' wagons up that big canyon right there. That's th' slaughter house. It's been closed years an' years. Dad an' all th' farmers'd pull up right there on th' north side o' Badger Hill. See it down there - the old slaughter house road.

"Now ya cin see th' ole railroad up th' bank. Ole man Hinman's place was back down here underneath us about a third o' th' way up t' Jerome. That's called Bitter Creek Gulch, an' there's th' remains o' th' ole Hinman house right yonder in there. Bill Griffin, frum over in Big Park [Now Village of Oak Creek] use' t' court Addie Hinman an' 'e married 'er. 'E'd run up this hill practicin' fer th' Fourth o' July Race, down th' main street o' Jerome clear up t' that water tank. 'E'd a strong an' athletic build, an' 'e won it. Yes sir, 'e sure did.

"Lot o' that stuff out there is th' waste, th' overburden frum th' mine an' that's where th' railroad went frum th' mine t' th' smelter at Clarkdale. It hit th' mine at th' thousand foot level. That's where th' railroad went. That's th' ole railroad. See it? It looks like a dump. Well, that's it. That's where th' railroad come. This dump right up th' road here on th' right, well that's frum Jimmy Douglas' Texas shaft. It run frum way over here at th' east side at th' bottom t' tap int' 'is mine. Right over there is Dad's ole lime kiln where th' ole pioneers burned th' lime t' make lye fer soap.

"That ole road goin' acrost up there [pointing to the south again.] went 'round th' mountain t' Allen Spring [named for Bronco Jim Allen] clear on 'round t' Mingus Mountain back ont' this road where it hits th' top o' Mingus. They use that road t' maintain th' pipeline frum Allen Spring that W.A. Clark put in.

"Now we're acomin' t' th' ole town o' Jerome. I'll tell you that town is on the map!

"That big buildin' way up there's the ole hospital. Ya bet it is! That's the one where I went t' see ole Doc Carlson, when I 'ad that appendicitis. There's a road up here that goes up th' Gulch, that's what they called it — The Gulch — an' they named that ridge out there th' Hogback. Uncle Jim an' Aunt Effie Wingfield lived over there t' th' left near that ole grammar school. Speakin' 'bout Th' Gulch, the' ole road use t' come right up th' Gulch here. M' dad use t' tell 'bout Ev Jordan comin' home on th' road through here with a four horse team an' a loaded wagon. Th' road went back an' forth down th' Gulch. 'E 'ad a canvas pulled up over th' top o' 'is head t' stay dry in th' rain an' didn't hear er see th' flood a comin' down on 'im. It struck 'im right down in here somewhere. 'E made a grab fer a little bush on th' bank an' caught it. That's all that saved 'is life. They found 'is team clear down on th' Verde River. [It is about ten miles from that spot to where The Gulch joins the Verde.]

"Over there, that's th' ole Jerome Hotel an' th' other one, way around, is th' Connor Hotel. There use t' b' a little grocery store here." Walt's brother George sold fruit and produce to the owners of the little store for years. It was located at the junction where the highway split into one way up and one way down. The down hill section is extremely steep.

Looking up at the steep highway he remarks, "My that was a slick road when it got wet! M' truck tried t' change ends with m' one day on that road. It was slick with ice. I 'ad t' throw that ole truck in compound gear. I didn't want t' use m' brake, sos I come down awful slow. Now, that's steep! I was a comin' home frum Prescott. I think I stayed overnight. That was b'fore Ruth an' I was married. Charles [his nephew] still has that ole truck. When I was there farmin', I use t' use it t' cut wood.   "I got that truck when Dad an' I went over th' hill [To Prescott] an' bought it frum Samuel Hill Hardware Company in 1921 fer $750. It was an ole T-Model, ton an' a half, one drive. Comin' home acrost Lonesome Valley, I wanted t' teach Dad how t' drive. I got 'im int' th' driver's seat about half way out int' th' valley, an' I said, 'I'll show you all about this now.' Ya know drivin' scared 'im, an' 'e wouldn't learn.

"'Ah, son, I ain't got no business drivin'. There's 'nuff o' ya kids. I don't want t' drive.'

"Let's see how old 'e was at that time. 'E's born in 1859. That happened in 1921. 'E musta been about 62.

"Now I'm goin' t' show ya pretty quick where th' ole jail use t' b'. Right there. That's where Dad saw Fred Hawkins tear th' stuffin' out o' that big Austrian. Did I tell ya about it?"

Turning the corner he is distracted and begins on another subject. "That's where Charlie Ong run a kitchen. Dad would supply him with stuff. Acrost th' street th' Miller Company 'ad a hardware store. Down th' street Vic Selna run a grocery, an' right in here Kavokovich 'ad a grocery store. There's one o' them big mine wheels. [In front of the mine museum] I tell ya them's mighty big!"

Back to Fred Hawkins and the Austrian. "Well, Hawkins arrested this great big Austrian who was raisin' th' devil. 'E was agonna put 'im in jail. That big ole guy said t' Hawkins, 'Ya take that damn gun belt offa ya, an' ya won't put me in there!' Dad said Fred Hawkins dropped that gun belt an' went over that big Austrian miner just like a wildcat. 'Now ya willin' t' go in?' [Fred asked] Ya bettcha, 'e went in!

"There's th' Glory Hole, right back in there. Why, they took big chunks o' pure gold outta that thing. Oh, they took millions an' millions. Th' road use t' go way up there in th' bend t' meet that train. Gosh, Almighty! Don't seem possible.

"Oh, my goodness! Don't that bring back memories! Ya see that lime formation above? That's where th' big deposits o' ore was, right near th' lime. Acrost there's where they blasted down. I think it was 200 feet. That shaft right there went down t' th' 4400 foot level. Mercy, mercy, mercy, mercy, mercy! Ain't that terrific?

"Dad owned a fourth interest in a lot o' minin' claims over there acrost Mescal Canyon, [to the south] an' 'e woulda made a fortune if it hadn'ta been fer that darned partner that wouldn't sell."

Father and Daughter took a rest stop at the mine museum before starting the return drive to Sedona on which Walt slept most of the way. The excitement and constant talking had worn him out. The day formed another good memory for the two of them.

Walter continued a very active life with his small orchard, garden, assisting others with their "farming" attempts, and his fishing. Many times he stated, "I'm agonna wear out, not rust out!" On April 14, 1987 while digging around a water valve to repair it for irrigating his tomatoes, his often repeated wish of wanting "t' go with m' shovel er fishin' pole in m' hand," was fulfilled.

To commemorate his life, the following poem was written and read by F. Ruth as part of the eulogy at his funeral.

>A two-story house along Upper Verde
>Was the place Walter arrived in the late 1890's.
>With lands to till and hills to roam
>The great outdoors became his second home.
>
>While attending school he often was wishing
>That he was outside farming, hunting, or fishing.
>So some skunks he skinned very early one day
>And to his delight heard the teacher say,
>"Get out! You stink! Don't come in!"
>Thus the day was spent much like Huckleberry Finn.
>
>It was the sweet potato patch that he was irrigating
>When a strange noise in the river needed his investigating.
>Lo and behold, he saw Apache women
>Playing a game while in swimming.
>He threw a rock, they saw his face, and in Walt's words,
>"I 'ad t' cancel distance an' annihilate space!"
>
>He learned enormous amounts on the farm from his Dad
>And all were happy when his won ranch he had.
>Together with Ruth, they worked hard on the land
>Until he was known statewide as "the orchard man."
>His peaches and apples were delicious to eat
>Their luscious flavor impossible to beat.
>
>His hands, knarled, tough and strong
>Maintained a bowling record years long.
>They could soothe a child when ill
>Or calm a dog to remove a porcupine's quills.

Our memories will forever hold
The numerous, wonderful stories he told
While in our ears will be the ring
Of the deep bass voice when he would sing.

Tough, gentle, talented, independent, loving –
   a character – one of a kind
These are a few of Dad's attributes that remain
   in our minds.

As we say these things with love and affection
We recall his life with great admiration.

"I'm goin' t' go on m' shovel handle," he'd say,
And it is true, Daddy, you lived and died *your* way.

F. Ruth Jordan (Jackson), April, 1987

FOOTNOTES

(1) Granger, Bryd Howell, <u>Arizona Names</u>, The Falconer Publishing Co., Treasure Chest Publishers, Tucson, AZ, c.1983, page 471

Chapter Twelve
EPILOGUE

Although the two Jordan couples of Sedona were not of the era which labeled folks "pioneers," they each one truly had the pioneering spirit as all were *Following Their Westward Star* by pursuing their dreams.

Walter and George worked hard at improving their farms with Ruth and Helen always the excellent helpmates, contributing much to the success of the operations. Their efforts not only improved life for themselves, but for many of the other families of the area as well.

Walter, through the challenges of his expanding orchards and gardens, developed many unique methods of solving the problems. These ideas benefited numerous other folks as he shared them with state and county agriculturists, individuals and groups to whom he spoke. (Many tried to get him to teach classes in agriculture for University Extension programs. He always refused stating, that because he had only completed eighth grade that he didn't have enough education for anything like that. Ruth and others tried, to no avail, to convince him that all he had studied, learned and developed through experimentation was an outstanding education.) His and George's work to procure and maintain a reliable water supply not only turned a dry farm into a productive oasis, but assisted others using water from the "community" ditch. Although his major recreations of hunting, fishing, and bowling were outside the community, Walter mentored many novices interested in these activities.

In the early years, farming was George's focus and the coop he organized gave all in the area a better income. However, as the community grew, he envisioned a water system servicing the entire "town," and through his many long hours of hard work, the City of Sedona Water System was born. He gave extensively of time, talent and finances to the Sunday School, becoming a major factor in its growth into Wayside Chapel, including the donation of the land, plus involvement in the Verde Baptist Church. He greatly enjoyed providing music and fun for community events: singing and playing his wide variety of personally created musical instruments; being a "shocking spook" at the community Halloween parties; starting and continuing for several years Sedona's Fourth of July fireworks display; hosting many family and community picnics and get-togethers; and being an early member contributing to both Sedona's Westerners' Club and Photography Club.

Helen's first and foremost purpose was assisting George in whatever he needed, from packing and selling fruit and keeping the water tanks full, to singing duets and playing piano or organ accompaniments. She still found time to teach Sunday School, participate in the church music, sponsor 4-H and assist in the rearing of her nieces and nephew, including the next generation of great-nieces and great-nephews. Besides reaching a great number of people through her numerous art forms, she assisted many artists by opening her home for them to come together to paint. Her great-niece, Jacqueline Ruth Jackson, a successful artist and sculptress, received her first set of brushes and paint plus her first lessons from Helen. Jacque states, "It was her constant encouragement and assistance that enabled me to develop my talents into a career." For many she was a quiet and unassuming mentor. It seems quite fitting that the packing shed in which Helen spent many hours working and later taking art classes, is now Sedona Art Center.

For nearly sixty years Ruth and Walter gave their joint efforts to developing and maintaining their farm, starting with the setting out of the trees, continuing through the years of nurturing to the successful harvesting. Of Ruth it can be said "once a teacher, always a teacher." During WWII she returned to teach for a few years in Sedona and then one year at Red Rock School on Lower Oak Creek, about eight miles from her home. It was amazing the number of her former students who came to visit her in her retirement years and express their thanks for her helping them believe in themselves. Thus, in their minds, contributing to their success as adults. The welfare of children was a passion for her and she was always at the forefront of educational issues, often leading the way for change and improvement. A major effort was attempting, to no avail, to get the Flagstaff School District to allow students to cross the county line and attend high school in Clarkdale or Cottonwood. (It made no difference that students in Grasshopper Flat, now West Sedona, were crossing from the opposite direction to Sedona for elementary school.) For many years her diminutive figure was seen standing in the front conducting Sunday School, as well as teaching a class. As the community grew and Wayside Chapel was organized, she offered her living room every Sunday for the church nursery school. Other involvements included leading games at community parties and the summer weekly Sedona-Oak Creek night for youth at the skating rink, being an active member of Sedona Little Theater and enjoying her grandchildren. For several years she wrote articles for the Coconino Sun, a Flagstaff weekly newspaper.

In the late forties and early fifties, Ruth designed

and oversaw a large addition to and remodel of the original "cabin" and its previously added three rooms. Due to her great interest in preserving historical knowledge, she envisioned a museum, with the initial concept focusing on antique farming equipment and family history. After Walter's death she approached members of the Sedona Historical Society with her idea. Gradually excitement grew and the city officials became involved. In 1991 an agreement with these two entities was reached and the home she had "built" nearly 50 years prior became the property of the City of Sedona to be managed by the Sedona Historical Society. Her daughter Anne cared for her in the house until her health required nursing home care. Her kind, gentle and loving personality shone through until the very end. She will always be remembered for her talent as a great teacher, her quick smile, twinkling blue eyes and concern for all, especially children. She always looked for the positive in all situations and for the best in everybody. One of her descendants stated, "She never made a difference between a governor or the town drunk..."[1] In the words of Jim Eaton, a resident of Sedona, "...I went up to meet her. She got up [out of her chair] and gave me a hug... She was just an awfully nice lady. She was really remarkable. A wonderful lady."[2]

How fitting that her vision provided the vehicle for future generations to glimpse some of the major contributions made by all four Sedona Jordans. She would be doubly pleased to know that the museum has expanded to include all of the early families acknowledging the importance of each in settling and developing this fabulous scenic area of red rocks. The outstanding "army" of volunteers have donated thousands of hours and large sums of money for the creation of a great museum which houses permanent exhibits as well as numerous changing ones. A vast spectrum of special programs, designed to interest persons of all ages, continues throughout the year.

The Sedona Heritage Museum sits proudly in the center of Jordan Memorial Park located on Jordan Road in the heart of Sedona. On December 11, 2004, the extended efforts of Sedona Historical Society and president Janeen Treyvillian culminated with a celebration honoring the placement of the property on the Historical Registry as The Jordan Farmstead.

Although the curtain is closed on the stage of Central Arizona bringing to an end the drama of hearty souls who were *Following Their Westward Star,* their legacy continues to inspire and guide those who strive to follow their footsteps, while creating the legacy of the next generation.

FOOTNOTES

(1) Sedona Red Rock News Staff, Area Pioneer Ruth Woolf Jordan Dies, *Red Rock News*, Wed. Jan. 10 1996, page 2A

(2) Ibid

Submitted by Bob Wilcox Studios
George, 1960

Helen & George, 1963

Helen, 1970s

Walter & Ruth 50th Anniversary July 20th, 1980

Ruth & Walter, 1983

BIBLIOGRAPHY

"All Hail U. of R.." By William Peyton Bristow. 1922.

Arizona. Bureau of Vital Statistics, Agricultural Branch. NO. 106. Flagstaff, AZ: NAU Archives-SCA, MS 199 Box 8 Folder 85, 1914.

Arizona: the Land and the People. Ed. Tom Miller. Tucson, AZ: U. of A. P, 1986.

Ashworth, Donna. Arizona Triptych. Flagstaff, AZ: Small Mountain Books, 1999.

Barnes, Will C., and Byrd H. Granger. Arizona Place Names. Tucson, AZ: U. of A. P, 1960.

Beard, Christine D. "People and Their Environment: An Historical Overview of the Middle Verde Valley". Unpublished Thesis, 1987.

Belloc, Hilaire. "The Inn of the Mageride." Hills and the Sea. Marlboro, Vermont: The Marlboro Press, 1966.

Berry, Wendell. What Are People For?. New York, New York: North Point P, 1990. 6-7.

Bingham Press Utah. "The Smelter Smoke Fakers." Jerome Mining News 27 Apr. 1907: 2.

Bishop Jr., James. The Ancient Ones. Experience Sedona Legends & Legacies. Comp. Kate Ruland-Thorne. Sedona, AZ: Thorne Enterprises, 1989. 4.

Bourke, John G.. On the Border with Crook. Lincoln: University of Nebraska Press, 1881.

Brewer, James W., Jr. Jerome Story of Mines, Men and Money. Tucson, AZ: Southwest Parks and Monuments Association, 1993.

Bristow, Allen. Personal interview. 4 Feb. 1982.

Browne, J. Ross. Adventures in the Apache Country, A Tour Through Arizona, and Sonora, 1864. Tucson, AZ: University of Arizona Press, 1974.

Brykt, James. Forging the Copper Collar Arizona's Labor-Management War 1901-1921. Tucson, AZ: University of Arizona Press, 1982.

Chronic, Halka. Roadside Geology of Arizona. Missoula, MT: Mountain Press Publishing Co., 1983.

Corbusier. Verde to San Carlos.

Cozzens, Samuel W. Explorations and Adventures in Arizona and New Mexico. Secaucus: Castle a Division of Book Sales, Inc., 1988.

Ed. Gregory J. Lalire. Wild West Magazine Aug. 2002: n. pag.

Faulk, Odie B.. Arizona, A Short History. Norman: University of Oklahoma, 1970.

Geology and Ore Deposits of the Jerome Area Yavapai County Arizona. Comp. C.A. Anderson, and S.C. Creasey. Washington, D.C.: United States Government   Printing Office, 1958.

Granger, Bryd Howell, Arizona Names, The Falconer Publishing Co., Treasure Chest Publishers, Tucson, AZ, c.1983, p. 471.

Hasseltine, W B. "Sumner, Charles." Ed. Robert O. Zeleny. World Book. 20 vols. Chicago, Illinois: Field Enterprises Educational Corp., 1965.

Hastings, Jamres R., & Raymond Turner. The Changing Mile. Tucson, AZ: University of Arizona Press, 1952.

Henderson, Esther. Christmas Eve on a Cow Ranch at Cherry Creek in 1927. Dewey, AZ: 1999.

Henderson, Esther. Letters and Phone Interviews with F. Ruth Jordan, Dewey: 2002-2003.

Hokanson, Paula. E-mail to F. Ruth, 1 Aug. 2002.

Hokanson, Paula. Personal letter to F. Ruth, 26 July 2002.

Howard, William. Sedona Reflections, Tales of Then and Now. Sedona, AZ: The Pronto Press, 1981.

Jackson, Lawrence. Letter written to Perry and Robert Jackson, May 9, 1950.

Jerome Reporter 28 Dec. 1899.

Jerome Sun, Smelter Smoke is Ruining Valley Vegetation. 27 Nov. 1917.

Jordan, Albion M. Letter to His Wife. Jan. 1850. Museum Archives, Cape Elizabeth, Maine.

Jordan Family Records, Archives of Cape Elizabeth Museum, Cape Elizabeth, Maine, vol.5, 149.

Jordan, Helen. Unpublished diaries: 1929-1980.

Jordan, Stella M., Arizona's Beautiful Oak Creek Canyon, personal diary, circa 1920

Jordan, Stella M. Unpublished diaries: circa 1915.

Katz, Bob . General George Crook. 1996. DesertUSA.com Digital West Media Inc. 10 Nov. 2002 <http://www.desertusa.com/mag99/may/papr/crook.html>.

Lightbourn, Til and Mary Lyons. By The Banks of Beaver Creek. Nappanee: Evangel Press, 1989.

McKinnon, Shaun, Enriching the Desert: The Story of SRP, *The Arizona Republic*, Feb. 5, 2003.

Miller, Walter C. Letter to Bob. 26 Feb. 1925. Information to the Copper Co.. NAU Cline Library, Special Collections and Archives, M.S. 199, Box 32 Book 2, Flagstaff, AZ.

Mountain Men. National Park Service Saint Louis, Missouri. 14 Nov. 2002 <http://www.nps.gov/jeff/mus-mtnmen.htm>.

Muretic, John. To Heaven in The West. Sedona, AZ: Oak Creek Press, 1970.

Myhr, Margaret Goddard. Jesse Goddard, One of Arizona's Last Old-Time Cowboys. Surprise, AZ: Moore Graphics, 2001.

Newton, Charles H.. Reason Why Place Names in Arizona are so Named. Glenwood, NM: Tecolote Press Inc., 1978.

Pioneer Stories of Arizona's Verde Valley. Comp. Mrs. John Bristow, Mrs. E.W. Monroe, and Mrs. D.W. Wingfield. 2nd ed. Camp Verde, AZ: The Verde Valley Pioneers Association, 1954.

Powell, Lawrence Clark. Arizona, A History. New York, NY: W.W.Norton Co. Inc., 1976.

Ranney, Wayne N.. The Verde Valley, A Geological History, Flagstaff, AZ: The Museum of Northern Arizona Press, 1989.

Rigby, Elizabeth, Valley Native George Jordan Dies, *Verde Independent*, 1964.

Robinson III, Charles M. "General Crook and the Western Frontier." Wild West Magazine Aug. 2002.

Ruland-Thorne, Kate. Sedona Legends and Legacies, Sedona, AZ: Thorne Enterprises, 1983.

Sedona Red Rock News Staff, Area Pioneer Ruth Woolf Jordan Dies, *Red Rock News*, Wed. Jan. 10 1996, page 2A.

Sexton, Connie Cone, John J. Rhodes 1916-2003: An Effective, Humble Leader, *The Arizona Republic*, Tuesday, August 26, 2003, page A14.

Sheridan, Thomas E.. Arizona, A History. Tucson, AZ: University of Arizona Press, 1995.

Snodgrass, Richard. Ballad of Laughing Mountain. Tempe, AZ: Counterpoint Productions, 1957.

Stein, Pat. "People of the Verde Valley." Plateau Magazine Northern Arizona Museum 1981: n. pag.

Stoever, Margaret. Letter to the author. 15 Aug. 1996.

Texas and Southwestern Lore. Ed. Frank J. Dobie. Austin, TX: Texas Folk-Lore Society, 1927.

The Jordan Memorial. Comp. Tristram F. Jordan. 2nd ed. Camden, Maine: Picton P, 1995. 390.

The Random House College Dictionary, revised edition, Random House Publishers, NY, 1975.

Those Early Days. Comp. The Book Committee of Sedona Westerners. Cottonwood, AZ: Verde Independent, 1968.

Trimble, Marshall. Arizona, A Panoramic History of a Frontier State. Garden City, NY: Doubleday & Company, Inc., 1977.

Trimble, Marshall. CO BAR. Flagstaff, AZ: Northland P, 1982.

Trimble, Marshall. In Old Arizona, True Tales of the Wild Frontier. Phoenix, AZ: Golden West Publisher, 1985.

Trimble, Marshall. Roadside History of Arizona. Missoula, Montana: Montanta P Co., 1986.

United Verde Copper Co. v. Jordan et. al. and United Verde Extension Mining Co. v. Jordan et. al.. Doc. No. 4735 & 4746 14 Federal Reporter, 2d Series 299-307. Circuit Ct. of Appeals, 9th Circuit 7 Sept. 1926.

United Verde Copper Co. v. W.A. Jordan, W.E. Jordan, C.A. Jordan, et. al., etc., & United Verde Extension Mining Co. v. W.A. Jordan, W.E. Jordan, C.A. Jordan, et. al., etc.. No. 692 & 693 47 Supreme Court Reporter Memorandum Decisions 243. United States Circuit Ct. of Appeals 29 Nov. 1926.

Wahmann, Russell. Follow the Narrow Guage from Jerome to Jerome Junction. Jerome, AZ: Robert Des Granges & Russell Wahmann, 1982.

W.A. Jordan and Sons and Annie T. Jordan v. United Verde Extension Mining Company and United Verde Copper Company. N0. 7930 & 7931 NAU Cline Library, Special Collections and Archives, M.S. 199, Box 2, Folder F 3-4. Super. Ct. of the State of Arizona in and for the County of Yavapai 1926.

W.A. Jordan Place Investigation by H. Brisley, R.A. Channel & J.W. Johnson. NAU Cline Library, Special Collections and Archives, M.S. 199, Box 32, Folder 10 3. Super. Ct. of the State of Arizona, in and for the County of Yavapai 31 Aug. 1920.

W.A. Jordan Place, Property No. 29 Investigation by H. Brisley & R.A. Channel. NAU Cline Library, Special Collections and Archives, M.S. 199, Box 32, Folder 10   Super. of the State of Arizona, in and for the County of Yavapai 24 Sept. 1921.

W.A. Jordan Place, Property No. 29 Investigation by W.W. Jones. NAU Cline Library, Special Collections and Archives, M.S. 199, Box 32, Folder 10 1-2. Super. Ct. of the State of Arizona, in and for the County of Yavapai 10 April 1921.

Waldeman, Diane. Max Ernst, A Retrospective. New York, NY: Solomon R. Guggenheim Museum, 1975.

Wright, Harold B. Shepherd of the Hills. Thorndike, Maine: G. K. Hall & Company, 1907.

Wyatt, Mary. Cottonwood, AZ: 2003.

Wyllys, Rufus K., Arizona, The History of a Frontier State, Hobson and Herr, Phoenix, AZ, 1950.

Young, Herb. They Came to Jerome, the Billion Dollar Copper Camp. Jerome, AZ: Jerome Historical Society, 1972.

Zimmerman, Emily. The Stuff of Legends: The Ways of the Mountain Men. University of Virginia. 14 Nov. 2002 <http://xroads.virginia.edu/~HYPER/HNS/Mtmen/lifestyle.html>.

Following Their Westward Star
Index

Allen, H.J., 95
Allen Spring, 143
Apache Maid Mountain, 64, 71
    Apache Maid Ranch, 50
Apaches. See Indians
Arizona Power Company, 45
Arnold, Wales, 8, 16
Atascador Land Company, 42
Austin, Jim, 50

Babbitt family, 59, 60, 62
Bacon Rind Park, 107
Baptists, vii, 5, 7–10, 14, 15, 18, 30, 36–37, 45–46
    American Baptists of Arizona, 19
    baptism, 9, 46, 141, 142
    Verde Baptist Church, 71, 147
    Tempe Baptist Church, 72
Beauty, George, 29
Beaver Canyon, 50
Beaver Creek, iii, v, 2, 16, 17, 61, 64, 70, 72
    Beaver Creek Ranch, 71
    Beaver Creek School, 70, 73
Beaver Head Point, 16, 79
Bent River Ranch, 46, 140
Big Dry Wash, battle of, 26–27
Black Mountains, 85
Bloody Basin, 44, 45, 94
Boudway, Becky Tognoni, v, x
Box Canyon, 1, 52, 136
Bradshaw Mountains, 65, 141
Bridgeport
    Annie Jordan's property in, 99, 103
    Jordan home in, 7, 36, 43, 46, 51, 61, 69, 80, 104
Bristow family
    Allen, 7, 31, recollections of, 10, 16–18, 37, 38, 45, 66, 68, 86–87, 95, 102–104, 108, 136
    Annie Tabitha. See Jordan, Annie Bristow
    Calista Woods, 7, 66
    Charles Owen, 7
    Effie Burzilla. See Wingfield, Effie Bristow
    Florence Miller, 7, 140
    James Clawson, 1, 5, 7, 16, 26, 30, 33, 35, 44–45, 66, recollections of, 8–12, 14–18
    James Elwood, 10, 66, 67, 68
    John Ferris, 7, 9, 21, 22, 29, 44, 66
    Lazarus Pleasant, 7, 17, 18
    Luranda Smith, 7–11, 15, 18, 26
    Martha Ellen. See Ralston, Martha Bristow
    Mary Evangelina. See Human, Mary Bristow
    Stella Jordan, 7, 31, 38, 40, 43–44, 49, 68; photographs Indians, 29–30; recollections of, 8, 17, 18, 99
    Talitha Cumi. See Hawkins, Cumi Bristow
    William Peyton, 7, 18, 19, 22
Bristow, Pleas, 11
Bullpen Ranch, 63
Burford, Martha Priscilla, See Dickinson, Martha Burford
Burford, Preston, 8, 9, 11–13, 15, 17, 18
Buster, Charlie, 8–9

Camp Verde, 16, 17, 23–28, 35, 36
    Historical Society, 68

Canyon Kiva Arts Center, ix
Casner, Rile, 18; Mose, 60, 61, 67
    Casner Canyon, 25, 61
Catholics, 14
cattle. See ranching
cemetery, 11, 17, 18
Central Arizona Project, 130
Cherry Creek, 10, 44, 69
Chestnut, Charlie, 37
child-rearing, 17, 72
    by Annie Jordan, 38–41
    by Luranda Bristow, 26
    by Ruth Woolf Jordan, 51, 113, 117, 135
church, viii, x, 9, 18, 37– 40, 46, 72
    mission churches, 19, 30
    Old Stone Church, 68
    Mexican Methodist church, 89, 90
    Verde Baptist Church, 71, 147
Civil War, 5, 8, 34
Civilian Conservation Corps, 109, 123, 136
Clark, W.A., 95
    railroad, 37, 65, 92
    mansion, 140, 143
    mining, 43, 85–88, 90– 92, 99, 103
Clarkdale, 56, 64, 92, 95, 99, 110, 118
    Bristow homestead, 26
    Jordan homestead, 35, 37, 43, 51
    smelter, 35, 43, 90–91, 96, 99–100, 104, 134, 136, 140, 143
Clear Creek, 50, 54, 63, 66, 67
    Clear Creek School, 68
Clemenceau, 46, 88, 90
    smelter, 43, 46, 86, 88, 90, 99, 100, 104, 115, 135
Cleopatra Hill, iii, 85, 89, 96
CO Bar Ranch, 59, 63, 64, 73
Coffee Creek Ranch, 61
copper, iii, 70, 91, 92,
    Copper Chief mine, 87, 88
    "copper collar," 96, 101, 103, 104
    smelter lawsuit, 43, 87, 100–105
    United Verde Copper Company, 43, 85–86, 88, 90, 94, 96, 99–101, 103–105, 140–141
    United Verde Extension Mining Company, 46, 86, 88, 90, 99–100, 105
Copper Canyon, 29, 35, 92
Copple, B.F., 107
Cornville, 36
Cox, Cleave, 45
Crook, General, 24– 26, 29, 34

Davidson, James, 9, 14, 18
Dickinson family
    A.G. ("Dutch"), 7, 68–69
    Charles, 8
    Dora Human, 7, 17
    Martha Burford, 9, 12–13
    May, See Hawkins, May Dickinson
    Nancy Jane, 12
    Sam, 9, 12, 14, 18
DK Cattle Company, 139
Douglas, James, 86, 88– 90, 99, 103, 104, 143
Douglas, Walter, 96

drought, 2, 60, 129, 131
Drum, Lyman, 36
Dry Beaver Creek, 16, 17
Dry Creek, 24, 108, 139
Duke, Johnny, 87–88

electricity, vii, 45, 130, 132, 135
Elk's Lodge, 89
Ericson, Gus, 133
Ernst, Max, viii–ix

Farley family, 130
    Henry, 93, 132
    Jim, 111
farming, 1, 12, 35–36, 42–43, 68–69, 86, 94,
    107–112, 116–117, 120–125, 139, 141–143, 147
    alfalfa, 43, 100, 116, 117, 120, 125
    beans, 111, 116, 117, 120, 121, 125, 141
    by Indians, 2, 15, 23–25, 29
    carrots, 109, 110, 112–114, 120–122, 125
    conflict with copper mining, 99–105, 140;
    corn, 17, 18, 120–122, 125
    dry, 104, 125, 130–131, 147
    fertilizer, use of, 116, 117, 120, 121, 125
    insects, 101, 117, 122, 123, 125
    strawberries, 121–123, 125, 139
    vegetables, vii, 17, 36, 108, 111, 112, 114,
        120, 125, 130
    See also orchards, ranching
fires
    Bridgeport, 69
    grass, 117
    Jerome, 42, 90, 94–96
    mining, 88, 91, 93, 117
fishing, 54–55, 142, 147
    fish hatcheries, 49, 54
Flagstaff, vii, 49–50, 64, 108–109, 124, 136
Flannigan, Jack and Mary, 40, 60, 62
flooding, 2, 101, 108, 134, 143
    Mormon Canyon, 132, 135
    Oak Creek, vii, 50, 112, 136
    Verde River, 17, 37, 59, 67, 129, 132, 139–140
Fort Apache, 26, 27, 29
Fort Lincoln. See Camp Verde
Fort Verde. See Camp Verde
Fort Whipple, 26, 27, 29, 35, 141
Foxboro Ranch, 109

Gaddis, Mike, 9, 10, 14, 18
Gaddis, Tack, 8, 14–18, 28–29, 37
Geronimo, 23, 28, 34
Gilbert, Jack, 132, 133, 135
Gilbert, Jim and Netty, 102
Giroux, Joseph, 53, 86
Gobran, Nassan, ix, x
Goddard, Jesse, 2, 23, 26–27, 50, 63, 85
Gonzales, Sabino, 89
Goslick, Giles, 50
Gray, Alice and Bill, 40, 61–62, 81

Hackberry Mountains, 2
Halley's Comet, 30
Hance, George and John, 17
Hart family, 49, 109, 136
Hawkins family
    Bertie, 53
    Cumi Bristow, 7, 8, 15–17, 37, 96
    David Erastus, 7, 15, 17, 37
    Fred, 144
    Jim, 12, 14, 15, 94
    Lee, 54, 101
    May Dickinson, 12
    Tom, 29
Head, Justin, 29
Heath, Arthur, 66, 67
Henderson, Esther, 69
Hohokams. See Indians
Hopi. See Indians
Hopkins, C.B., 88Horseshoe Ranch, 16
hospital, 56, 88, 135, 143
hotels
    King's Ransom, 123
    Little Daisy, 89, 92
hot springs, 44–45
House Mountain, 2, 66
Houston Basin, 44, 62
Human
    Dora, See Dickinson, Dora Human
    James, 7, 10, 14, 17, 18,
    Mary Bristow, 5, 7, 8, 10, 17, 41, 42
Hunt, George W.P., 96
hunting. See wildlife
Hurst, Johnny, 66, 139

Indian Gardens, 23, 94, 107
Indians, 3, 13, 17, 37, 39, 49, 86
    Apaches, 1, 2, 19, 23–30, 33, 42, 107
    conflicts with white settlers, 10, 11, 13, 15–16, 23–30,
        33–35, 40, 59
    employed by the Jordan family, 29, 52, 67
    Hohokams, 2, 129
    Hopi, vii, 2, 7, 15
    Mohave Indians, 23, 29
    Navajos, 2, 7, 15, 30
    photographed by Stella Jordan, 29–30
    ruins, 2, 37, 71, 72
    Sinagua, iii, 1, 2
    Yavapais, 1, 19, 23, 25, 29–30, 107, 141
Iron King, 85, 87
Irrigation. See water

Jackson family
    Dorothy and Perry, 19, 30
    Larry, 7, 15, 19, 120
    Robert, 134
Jackson, Ed, 114, 115
James, Abraham and Margaret, 107
Jerome, iii, 42, 65, 73, 85–88, 90–96, 104, 114, 141, 143
    smelter, 43, 88, 91, 96
Jordan family
    Annie Bristow, 7, 26; as wife and mother, 36–46, 54,
        99; childhood in Middle Verde, 17, 18; emigration
        from Missouri, 12, 14, 15
    Charles, 46
    Chester, 30, 38, 41, 50, 53, 54, 86, 130
    Edgar, 37–38
    Everett, 33, 35, 36, 99, 143
    F. Ruth (Jackson/Van Epps), iii, x, 7, 15, 18, 31;
        memorial tributes by, xi, 144–145; youth in
        Sedona, 37, 50, 54, 118–119, 121
    George, v, vii–x, 30, 37, 38, 41–43, 102–105, 107–112,
        120, 143, 149; developed water system, 130–136,
        147
    Helen Coleman, v, vii–xi, 112, 132, 135–136, 147, 149;

examples of her work, 77–83; sales ledger of, 127, recollections of, 43, 108–109, 111, 130, 131
Ruth Woolf, v, 31, 46, 51, 55, 62, 70–73, 149; as a farm wife, 108–111, 113–119, 133–135, 147– 148, recollections of, 92
Stella. See Bristow, Stella Jordan
Sumner, 37, 38, 40
Walter, v, vii–x, 31, 80, 147, 149; as a farmer, 108–125; on his father, 33–36; on Indians, 23, 24, 26, 28–30; on the copper mines, 85–96; other stories, 49–56, 60–65, 68, 69; smelter lawsuit 99–105; water system, 130–136, 139–144; youth and marriage, 37–46, 71, 107
Will, 1, 4, 7, 8, 23, 28, 29, 33– 43, 46, 53, 64, 93– 94, 99–101, 103–105, 129; mining claim, 86–87
Jordan Farmstead, 148
Jordan Memorial Park, 148

Kinsman, Rufe, 34– 35

Lee, Johnny 61
Lee Mountain, 25, 52, 61
Lett family, 9, 12, 15, 16, 17
Loudermilk, Romaine, 70
Loudermilk, Virginia Finney (Webb), 70, 71
lumber, 42, 94, 111

malaria, 25, 35, 59, 67
Mahan Ranch, 17
Maxwell Place, 68
Mayer, 44, 45
McGuireville, 16, 17
McMillan, John, 85, 88, 90–93
meals, 39–40, 54, 55, 63, 66, 76
Miller, Duane, 139
Miller, Elizabeth, 142
Miller, Florence. See Bristow, Florence Miller
Miller, Sedona. See Schnebly, Sedona Miller
Miller, Walter, 54, 101
Miller Company, 90, 144
Miller Valley Road, 68
Mingus, Jake and Bill, 87
Mingus Mountain, 87, 91, 92, 119, 143
mining, 8, 65, 91, 96, 105
    Copper Chief mine, 87, 88
    Glory Hole, 88, 90, 144
    Iron King, 85, 87
    Little Daisy mine, 86, 88–90, 92, 99
    Peck Mine, 141
    salt mines, 85–87
    See also copper
Mogollon Rim, 1, 26, 52, 54, 62, 68
Mohave Indians. See Indians
Montezuma's Castle, iii, 2, 79
Montezuma's Well, 16
Morg's Stable, 52
Mormons, 15, 64
Mormon Canyon, 51, 132, 135, 136
Morrison, Robert, 100, 103–104
movies filmed in the area, 45, 63, 123, 136
Mulligan, Oshea, 62
Mund, Johnny, 61
    Munds Mountain, 25, 52
museums
    Douglas Mansion, 89, 104
    mining museum in Jerome, 93, 144
    Sedona Historical Museum, 110, 148

National Reclamation Act, 129
Navajos. See Indians

Oak Creek,
    fishing, 54
    flooding, vii, 50, 112, 136
    irrigation from, 93, 107, 132
Oak Creek Bar, 119
Oak Creek Canyon, 23, 49, 130, 132
Oak Creek Telephone Company, 142
Odd Fellows, 88–89
orchards, vii, ix, 43, 63, 99–101, 104, 110–112, 114-120, 122–127, 131, 136, 147
    apples, ix, 100, 112–118, 122–125
    frost, 101, 118, 124
    peaches, 100, 112–120, 122– 125, 131
    smudging, 112, 118–119, 125
    thrip, 101
outhouse, 38, 95

Page, Edgar and Jim, 139
Palakwapi, vii
Peck, Edmund George, 141
    Peck's Lake, 12, 17, 29, 39, 53, 54, 89, 91, 141–143
Pendley, Tom, 121
Phelps Dodge Corporation, 85, 86, 90, 96
prostitution, 95
Purtymun, Jesse, 130, 133–135

Quail family, 25, 37, 67
Quinn, J.R., 112, 114, 123

railroads, 37, 45, 65, 72, 87, 90– 92, 96, 104, 143
Ralston
    John Will, 7, 18, 44, 45
    Martha Bristow, 5, 7, 8, 10, 13, 14, 18, 39, 44, 66
ranches
    Apache Maid, 50
    Beaver Creek, 71
    Bent River, 46, 140
    Coffee Creek, 61
    CO Bar, 59, 63, 64, 73
    Foxboro, 109
    dude ranches, 70, 71
    Horseshoe, 16
    H Bar Y, 66
    Mahan, 17
    Soda Springs, v, 70, 71, 73, 140
    Sugar Loaf, 140
    Trigger 2 Bar, 62
    Wilbur, 17
ranching, v, 16, 18, 19, 41, 59–71, 73, 99, 101, 103, 109
    cattle, v, 1, 17–18, 29, 44–45, 50, 52, 59–71, 73, 76, 87, 100, 107, 139
    cattle rustling, 64, 65, 67
    drift fences, 69
    See also farming
Rattlesnake Hill, 28, 37, 40, 41, 43, 99

Salt Mine Road, 68
    salt mines, 85–87
Salt River Project, 52, 129
scarlet fever, 9, 95
Schnebly
    Ellsworth, 107, 108
    Pearl, 107

Sedona Miller, 61, 82, 107
T.C. (Carl), 107, 108
Schnebly Hill Road, vii, 108, 109
schooling, v, viii, xi, 7, 23, 26, 35–41, 59, 65, 70–73, 91
    Beaver Creek School, 70, 73
    Clear Creek School, 68
    Red Rock School, 147
    Squaw Peak School, 68
    Sunday school, viii, 39, 108, 147
Schroeder, Bill, 16
Secret Canyon, 62
Sedona, vii, 61
    first white settlers, 107
    Jordan property in, 104, 107, 130
    Sedona Art Center, ix, 147
    Sedona Heritage Museum, 110
    Sedona Historical Museum, 148
    Sedona Historical Society, 148
    water system, viii, x, 130, 131, 147
Shea, Dan, 141, 142
Shopper, Helen and Margaret, 66
Sieber, Al, 27, 85
Sinagua. See Indians
smelters. See copper
Smith, Ira, 62, 76
Smith, Tom, 8, 11, 14
snow, 50, 62, 68, 119, 136, 139
Soda Springs Guest Ranch, v, 70, 71, 73, 140
soldiers, 24–28
    Soldier's Wash, 24
    See also Camp Verde
Spring Creek, 108, 140
Squaw Peak, 25, 66, 67
Stoneman, General, 23, 24
    Stoneman Lake, 16, 36
Sugar Loaf Ranch, 140
Sunset Telephone Company, 142
Sycamore Basin, 139

Tanning, Dorothea, viii
telephone service, viii, 109, 115, 119, 142
Thompson family, 49, 107, 108
Tontos. See Indians, Apaches
tourism, 59, 73
Trigger 2 Bar Cattle Ranch, 62
Tuzigoot, iii, 37, 141
typhoid fever, 9, 95

United Verde Copper Company. See copper

Van Deren family, 8, 17, 69
    Earl, 62–63, 76
    Iva, 61
    Johnny Lee, 61
    Rowena, 17
Verde fault, 85, 86, 99
Verde River, 1, 33, 35, 42, 44, 49, 54, 60, 65, 130, 141
    flooding, 17, 37, 59, 67, 129, 132, 139–140
Verde Valley, 1, 2, 9, 23, 24, 59, 89
    Pioneers Association, 5, 23
    Protective Association, 100

Water
    ditches for, 18, 24, 42, 66, 123
    irrigation, vii, 93, 111, 116, 120, 125, 129–132, 136, 139, 142, 144
    pumping station, 131, 133
    rights, 130, 136, 140
    system, viii–x, 108, 130, 131, 147
    wells, vii, 37, 129–131
    wheel, vii, 130–132
Wayside Chapel, ix, x, 7, 147
Webb, Paul, 71
Wetzel, John, 51, 111, 132, 133, 139
Wickenburg, 70, 71
Wilbur Ranch, 17
wildlife, iii, 49
    antelope, 63
    badgers, 143
    bears, 49–50
    beaver, 142
    coyotes, 51
    deer, 28, 52
    ducks, 35, 53, 141, 142
    elk, 55–56
    geese, 35, 52
    hunting, iii, 4, 16, 41, 50, 53, 59
    mountain lion, 50
    quail, 52, 62, 123, 142
    rattlesnakes, 51, 72
    skunks, 41, 134
    turkeys, 49, 53–54
Willard, Charlie, 131, 141
Wilson Canyon, 49, 134
Wingfield, Effie Bristow and James, 7, 39, 90, 116, 143
    Wingfield Mesa, 67
Wobblies, 96
Woods Canyon, 68, 69, 140
Woods Ranch, 68, 130
World War I, 35, 38, 56, 96, 99, 103, 112
World War II, 59, 73, 87, 112, 147

Yavapais. See Indians.